Harrow School And Its Surroundings

15

JOHN LYON,
(from the Brass in Harrow Church)

HARROW SCHOOL

AND ITS SURROUNDINGS.

BY

PERCY M. THORNTON,

AUTHOR OF " FOREIGN SECRETARIES OF THE XIX. CENTURY.'

Armado.—Do you not educate youth at the charge house on the top of the mountain ?

Holofernes.—Or Mons, *The hill.*

Love's Labour Lost, Act v Scene 1.

LONDON:

W. H. ALLEN & CO., 13 WATERLOO PLACE,

PALL MALL, S.W.

PUBLISHERS TO THE INDIA OFFICE.

1885.

LONDON ·
PRINTED BY W H. ALLEN AND CO., 13 WATERLOO PLACE. S.W

THIS VOLUME

IS DEDICATED TO THE

Rev. Henry Montague Butler, D.D.

TO WHOSE SYMPATHETIC AID THE WRITER

IS DEEPLY INDEBTED.

JOAN LYON,
(from the Brass in Harrow Church.)

PREFACE.

Any national institution such as a public school must, of course, be affected by the vicissitudes which befall the nation; and the writer of these pages has, therefore, endeavoured to exhibit the history of Harrow by the light of contemporary events, so far as they have influenced the fortunes of the school.

It should, however, be observed that owing to the peculiar position of a poorly-endowed school, the head-master of Harrow in each particular epoch has exercised a sway far in excess of that wielded at well-endowed institutions, such as Eton and Westminster, and has not seldom stamped, in a degree proportionately marked, the impress of his individuality on the school and scholars. This feature has led to the prevalence of a biographical element in several chapters of this book. The advantage, moreover, of reference to the lately-explored school

archives proved to be greater than anyone expected, while
Mr. Edward Scott's aid in the examination and interpretation of these interesting records has been invaluable.

One result of this research remains in the fact that it
has been ascertained to the satisfaction of those best
able to judge, that a school existed at Harrow before
1571.   This opinion, originally based on the words
de novo erigere in the School Charter, has received
confirmation through documentary evidence against
which there is no appeal.   The state of things
revealed by this discovery is somewhat analogous to
that existing at Westminster before the monastic
school there was dissolved in 1540.   The educational
institution existing at Harrow before 1571, also probably ecclesiastical in origin, had doubtless fallen into
such poverty during the Reformation that John Lyon's
act of munificence practically amounted to the foundation which has always been gratefully ascribed to him.

Though the early history of Harrow was carefully
studied before the compilation of this book, yet
addenda of great importance have accidentally come
to light too late for insertion in their proper places.
Hence the Appendices claim particular attention.   But
the main fact of interest which has emerged is this—
that John Lyon was no mere yeoman, who had raised
himself a little above the peasant class, but a landowner of importance, whose family had been at Preston

since the fourteenth century. This statement is fully supported by the Lyon deeds in Appendix C.

Again, several head-masters have been recovered from oblivion; while it has been discovered how much Harrow owes to the business-like capacity of her treasurer, James Brydges, the first Duke of Chandos, who, when resident at his magnificent seat, Canons, near Stanmore, early in the eighteenth century, assisted Dr. Brian, the head-master, in raising Harrow to a considerable height of popularity. For, indeed, in the year 1721 a school of 144 boys must have justly claimed such a position in the educational world.

If all assistance were to be specially acknowledged, this preface would attain an inordinate length; but the kindness of the Dean of Ely in allowing an autobiographical record of his Harrow recollections to appear in these pages cannot pass without mention. Again, the author owes a particular expression of gratitude to the Rev. B. H. Drury. As the representative of a family which has for three generations been intimately connected with Harrow, he was able to supply materials for history such as were not elsewhere to be obtained. Thanks are also due to Mrs. Phelps for the Life and Letters of her husband, the late Archdeacon Phelps; and to the Rev. F. St. John Thackeray, Vicar of Mapledurham, for the perusal of his privately-printed family history. Mr. William Winckley, of Flambards,

Harrow, has given valuable aid on archæological points.
Nor can we forget the aid willingly rendered by the
Vicar of Harrow, or fail to appreciate Mr. A. Haygarth's
diligence in the cause of Harrow history.

Finally, we have to express our obligation to the Earl
of Bessborough for his Harrow reminiscences, and not
the least for those concerning cricket, without some
reliable account of which the youth of the dear old hill
would look askance on work undertaken in a great
measure on their behalf.

PERCY M. THORNTON.

Battersea Rise,
    October 1884.

TABLE OF CONTENTS.

ERRATA.

p. 24, l. 21, *for* Greenhill *read* Hill of Greenhill.

p. 51, l. 7, *for* fifteenth *read* fourteenth.

p. 68, note *. line 2, *for* doubtless Headstone *read* near Osterley.

p. 122, l. 4, *for* allumed *read* assumed.

p. 197, l. 16, *for* solvere *read* voluere.

p. 246, note *, l. 1, *for* Terry *read* Perry [*i.e.* Bishop Perry, late of Melbourne, a senior wrangler, and leading man in the Church Missionary Society].

p. 265, *transpose the references and both the notes.*

p. 320, l. 7, *for* 1859 *read* 1857.

p. 320, note l. 4, *for* Ye Harrow ‘boys’ *read* Adventurous boys of Harrow School.

p. 870, note l. 3, *for* first person *read* first person plural.

LIST OF HARROW MASTERS.

From the School Archives.

Masters.	*Ushers or Under Masters.*
1571–1611, Anthony Rate.*	25 Sept. 1615, Thomas Lance.
1613, Bradley.	20 May 1636, William Powder.
29 April 1615, Wm. Launce.	28 Sept. 1638, Gilbert Banford.
1621, Robert Whittle, resigned in 1628.	19 June 1665, Thomas Robinson.
28 April 1628, William Hide.	28 June 1700, John Le Hunt.
10 Oct. 1661, Thomas Johnson.	15 Oct. 1705, John Hooker.
25 Nov. 1668, Thomas Martin.	29 Jan. 172½, James Cox.
8 Sept. 1669, William Horne.	6 June 1730, Francis Saunders.
12 Oct. 1685, William Bolton.	(Mr. Saunders appears to be the first called under master, the previous ones being ushers.)
17 June 1691, Thomas Brian.	
6 June 1730, James Cox (formerly usher).	
23 June 1746, Thomas Thackeray.	20 March 173⅔, William Charles.
31 May 1760, Robert Sumner.	28 March 1743, William Saunders.
3 Oct. 1771, Benjamin Heath.	21 July 1747, William Cox.
3 May 1785, Joseph Drury.	1 June 1749, William Prior.
11 April 1805, George Butler.	Elected 1766, Richard Wadeson, resigned 1789.
21 March 1829, C. W. Longley.	11 June 1789, Mark Drury.
31 March 1836, Rev. Christopher Wordsworth.	(Benjamin Evans, mentioned as assistant master in March 1805.)
18 Oct. 1844, Rev. C. J. Vaughan.	9 Feb. 1826, Benjamin Evans, assistant master, to be under master.
16 Nov. 1859, Rev. H. M. Butler.	20 June 1833, Rev. Henry Drury, *vice* Bn. Evans.
	1841. Rev. W. Oxenham, *vice* Drury.
	Henry Reeves, writing-master in 1746, dead in 1784.
	— Reeves, writing-master in 1813.
	— Marillier, writing-master in 1826.

This list is not, of course, exhaustive as regards assistant masters.

* In the Harrow Parish Register, Dec. 26, 1611, occurs the following:—"Buried, Anthony Rate (formerly) schoolmaster at Flambards, (afterwards) elected schoolmaster for the free schole. He died on Christmas Day aboute

eight o'clock at night." Anthony Rate was evidently the first head-master of
John Lyon's Foundation, and taught the thirty poor scholars provided for
during his lifetime. The education in vogue at Harrow during the dissipating
of what was probably the old Archiepiscopal School—held originally, as some
critics think, in the chauntry, then in the church or charge-house, removed in
1745 (see Appendix B.)—was not to the liking of the Gerards. The owners of
Flambards seem to have either carried on the pristine school temporarily in
their ancient mansion, or engaged Anthony Rate to teach the younger members.
In *Twelfthnight*. Act III. Scene 2, there is mention of an individual " In yellow
stockings and cross gartered most villainously like a Pedant that keeps a school
i' the Church." Mr. Halliwell Phillips, commenting on this passage, says:—
" Pedant in those days meant Domestic Schoolmaster." This seems exactly
to describe Anthony Rate, formerly Private Tutor at Flambards, dates likewise
agreeing, *Twelfthnight* being written in 1602, while Rate paid nature's debt in
1611. It seems possible that this passage, and also that from *Love's Labour
Lost*, Act V. Scene 2, quoted on our title page, refer to the education even then
well known to be obtained at Harrow.

HARROW SCHOOL

AND ITS SURROUNDINGS.

CHAPTER I.

HARROW IN EARLY TIMES.

Where yon old church its moss-grown tower uprears,
Grey with the shadows of a thousand years.
Harrow ; a Prize Poem, by the late W. J HOPE-EDWARDS.

THE earliest records relating to Harrow date from
A.D. 825, when a suit between Archbishop Wulfred and
the Abbess Cwoenthryth, respecting certain lands in
the locality, was decided at the Council of Clovesho,
held under Beornwulf, King of Mercia.[*]

The place finds mention in *Domesday Book,* under
the name Herges, which all authorities agree is of
Saxon origin. *Herga super montem* being the ancient
Latin name, it is reasonable to conclude that the term
had reference to some church which in early Christian
times crowned the isolated eminence which we know as
Harrow Hill, and which old English records speak of
as *Hearge* and *Harewe atte Hulle.*[†]

[*] Stowe Manuscripts, in the King's Library, British Museum ;
page 1 of printed catalogue.
[†] Lysons, *Environs of London,* vol. ii. p. 559.

1

The dreary tracts of impenetrable woodland and
almost impassable morass which surrounded the agricultural oasis lying at the foot of Harrow,* might not
have prevented the occupation of a vantage-post, such
as Harewe atte Hull afforded, either by the Romans
flying (A.D. 61) before the hosts of Boadicea past Herga
hill from ruined London to Verulam, soon in its turn to
be devastated by the terrible British heroine, or by
descendants of the same Latin race who, 367 years
later, previous to their abandonment of Britain (A.D.
428), had intrenched themselves in almost every commanding position throughout the land. Nor would it
be difficult to believe that the armed bands of Egbert
might have clustered on the Harrow uplands when, in
the ninth century, engaged in keeping the Danes at
bay; neither of these probabilities, however, pointing to
permanent occupation of Herga super montem for war-
like purposes. If *Herga, Herges*, were connected with
the oblique cases of the Anglo-Saxon *heri*, "band of
warriors," it would, however, suggest that the height
had been occupied in a memorable manner by Danes,
to whom *heri* was specially applied. But, as no trace of
fortification has been discovered on Harrow Hill, we
are inclined to doubt the alleged military character
of the ancient Harrow, and, with Lysons,† accept the
explanation "church" for the word *Herges*, with a
reservation in favour of "temple" (see *Hearh*, pl.
Hearga, Bosworth-Toller, *Ang.-Sax. Dict.*).‡ Whereas
the discovery of antiquities has made it manifest that

---

* Matthew Paris, in his *History of the Abbots of St. Albans*, has
left on record the general features of the country.

† Lysons, *Environs of London*, vol. ii. p. 559.

‡ The wooded height of Harrow was peculiarly adapted for a
heathen place of worship.

the Romans frequented the less commanding but more accessible locality of Brockley Hill, in the north-east part of Stanmore, where antiquarians fix the site of the Roman City of Sulloniacæ,* preference being doubtless given to that spot owing to its contiguity to the great Roman road, Watling Street.

Thus early in Harrow history it is noteworthy that the place did not lie on the direct road between any important centres, such as the metropolis in Roman times, or St. Albans and York, leading cities of the land in mediæval days, or Oxford, when the University city and the West claimed a highway scarcely less important than that leading to Chester and the North. Throughout all changes, Harrow-on-the-Hill stood isolated; yet it was, as we shall show, destined to be rescued from obscurity by its position and conformation, in conjunction with certain health-giving advantages with which nature had endowed it.

Little or nothing being known of the history of Harrow in Roman times, we must be content to take up the thread in the reign of Egbert, the first sole monarch of England (A.D. 840); and mention the several convergent causes for the growth of Harrow indicated by the glimpses of local history which emerge through the mists of the time which elapsed between 825 and the educational conception of John Lyon's mind, which took form in 1571.

In the first place, during the sway of the early Archbishops of Canterbury, population, however rudely housed, must have gathered, more or less, on Herga's height, and eventually led to the granting of a charter to the Archbishop of a weekly market, as also of an

---

* Wright, *Celt, Roman, and Saxon*, p. 123.

annual fair on the Nativity of the Virgin.   The markets
and fairs are abolished,* while the Archbishop's rights
at Harrow only survive in traditional form, the district
being one of those termed, in ecclesiastical phrase,
" peculiar."   But the health-giving properties of Harrow
air remain, and have influenced the local fortunes most
decisively.   Secondly, the residence of the British
primates brought the locality into prominence.   How
long before the advent of William the Conqueror to
England (A.D. 1066) Harrow had pertained to the
see of Canterbury cannot be found out from any known
records ; but we learn that, in A.D. 822, Wilfred, Archbishop of Canterbury,† purchased Herges and other
lands, for the purpose of restoring them to the Church,
from which they had been taken by Kenulf, King of the
Mercians, who, by such a seizure, was certainly encroaching on the neighbouring East Saxon kingdom.
This occurred during the year 792, when Sigeric,
King of the East Saxons, was on the pilgrimage to
Rome from which he never returned.‡   Again, towards
the close of the eighth century, when monasticism
was spreading over the land, the establishment of a
magnificent abbey at St. Albans had formed a nucleus
around which smaller religious foundations sprang up.
The Church, which had alike guarded man's conscience
and conserved civilization, was destined, under the

* Lord Althorpe, writing to his father, Earl Spencer, in June
1791, speaks of a fair at Harrow.—*Memoir of Earl Spencer*, by
Sir Denis Le Marchant, Bart., p. 39.   Such a custom survived
until 18.0, the first Monday in August being the day of the
anniversary.   In 1871 the Fairs Act allowed the ancient custom
to lapse, the Justices concurring, and no owner losing *toll*.

† Lysons, *Environs of London*, vol. ii. p. 561, quoting Newcourt,
vol. i. p. 634.

‡ Kenulf, an upright and vigorous administrator, died A.D. 819,
Baxter, *Church History*, p. 142.

questionable system of unnatural seclusion, to nurture knowledge. The devotion of many hermit lives to patient study and toil at the desk in such pleasant retreats proved an unspeakable boon to literature.

In the surroundings of Harrow this tendency was specially evident, a religious house being situated near the Colne at Ruislip, while Bentley Priory nestled on the woody slopes which adorn the Stanmore uplands. Nor should we forget that the Knights of St. John had an ancient chapel in a place yclept the Cuckoo, " le Kukukes," near Tokynton (Uxendon)* and that in Harrow itself there was a perpetual chauntry, the position of which it is difficult to localise.†

It is, therefore, not surprising that after the Norman conquest in 1066, the learned Lanfranc, Archbishop of Canterbury, having renovated his cathedral, should proceed to build a church where the spire of St. Mary's now crowns Harrow Hill.

Recent research has led men to doubt whether any of Lanfranc's original work, except the west doorway, remains,‡ the architecture being generally that of the fourteenth century, during which period, and in the reign of Edward III., it was thought to have been rebuilt.§

Lanfranc, one of the most enlightened churchmen of his time, died A.D. 1089, and fortunately we are enabled, by Mr. Rule's lately published *Life and Times of St. Anselm*, to realise the scene when (A.D. 1094) the new archbishop proceeded to his first *dedicatio ecclesiæ* (vol. ii. pp. 20, 21).

* Cotton MS. Nero E. vi. f. 287b.
† *School Archives.*
‡ Edward Walford, *Greater London*, Cassell's, part vi. p. 255.
§ *Ibid.*; also Lysons, *Environs of London*, vol. ii. p. 570.

Anselm, we are there told, habited in full canonicals,
opened the ceremony with all that warm, sensuous ritual
which the Church employed on such occasions. "*Ecce
crucis signum fugiant phantasmata cuncta*" were the pass-
words which, when uttered by the Archbishop, led to
the doorway being thrown open, and the noble proportions of the interior of Lanfranc's sacred building
revealed to the assembled ecclesiastics from London
and St. Alban's, and also to the crowd of serfs who
necessarily inhabited what was at that period a purely
agricultural region.*

It is easy to conceive the excitement, the mingled
horror and surprise, which must have been felt when it
became manifest that emissaries of the Bishop of London,
as it was supposed,† had contrived to abstract the
consecration oil, and so render imperfect a ceremony
which urgent pleas and resolute protests had otherwise
failed to obstruct. We can picture to ourselves amidst
what confusion the dignified Anselm and his wrathful
ecclesiastical satellites must have wended their way back
to the archiepiscopal manor, leaving groups of priests
and peasants to discuss the strange interruption.

Harrow Manor was the occasional residence of all
the archbishops until the year 1344, when they bought
Headstone‡ from Robert de Wodehouse, and made that
place their country seat.

---

* This we know from *Domesday Book*, A.D. 1085-6.

† The Bishop of London claimed the right of officiating at
Harrow. Whether he was really responsible for the above-
mentioned outrage must remain an open question.

‡ The Archbishop of Canterbury had a manor or country house
at Harrow, to which belonged 100 hides (*i.e.* 12,000 acres) of land.
Of this property thirty hides (3,600 acres) formed what was called
the *dominium*, or demesne, surrounding the house. The traditions
and surmises as to the situation of this country seat are given

But of all these ecclesiastics, no abiding memory remains in connection with Harrow except of Thomas à Becket, who was twice a visitor in the neighbourhood. As a youth about twenty-three years old, he was taken to see Archbishop Theobald then resident on the hill. Two learned men, Archdeacon Baldwin and Master Eustace, were his conductors to the archiepiscopal presence, the visit being made when Becket was studying civil law in London (A.D. 1142)* in Master Eightpenny's office. But at the crucial moment of his life the proud prelate was destined to revisit the scene of this youthful excursion.

When recalled by Henry II. from France (A.D. 1170) the Archbishop, on his return to England, attempted something akin to a royal progress towards Worcester, then the residence of Prince Henry, who was associated with his father in the government, and was only awaiting the Archbishop's anointing to perfect his kingship. But a royal order of a peremptory character arrested Becket's advance towards Worcester, whereupon the proud churchman yielded, and turning towards his manor-house at Harrow, prepared to quarter his numerous followers in the hamlets which surrounded the archiepiscopal retreat. The demands made by a retinue designed to support Becket's dignity at a court must have been totally in excess of the resources which a spot like Harrow could

---

further on (p. 12). We know that it was surrounded with wood, and that 102 *villani*, or tenants, cultivated and ploughed plots of land between the woodlands. More than this the Rev. E. Gilliat— who has given much research to the subject—was unable to discover, either in *Domesday Book* or the Lambeth archives. Headstone stands to the right of the road as you pass from Harrow to Pinner. It presents an interesting specimen of an old moated homestead.

* Hook, *Lives of the Archbishops*, vol. ii. p 363.

afford, when at the most her people had previously been
called on to provide food and provender for the small
train which might accompany Stigand on a visitation,
attend Lanfranc when supervising the erection of St.
Mary's Church, or even support Anselm at the consecration of the holy building in Becket's time.

During this visit the notable differences which agitated
the land found an echo in Harrow. Siding with what
we must believe to be a minority of their sacred profession, Nigellus de Sackville and Robert de Broc,
respectively Rector and Vicar of Harrow, gave vent to
their jealousy and hatred of the man who had, as they
believed, both degraded his sovereign and imperilled the
kingdom. They not only treated the Archbishop with
great disrespect, but went so far as to maim the horse
which carried provisions for his table,* when, as was
doubtless true, the neighbourhood had been scoured for
such means of sustenance. Conduct this which Becket
was not slow to resent at the earliest possible opportunity, when, as Matthew Paris the historian tells us, he
fulminated forth from his Canterbury throne dire excom-
munications against the two recusant priests, and this
but a few days before his own murder. Nor is it easy
in the nineteenth century to realise what excommunica-
tion involved in those days.

To Nigellus de Sackville and Robert de Broc this
sentence must have proved overwhelming, causing them
to lose their benefices, and fall blighted under the ban of
triumphant Mother Church, when, after Becket's murder,
it became necessary for Henry II. to propitiate the ecclesiastical authorities. It is probable that the embarrassed
sovereign had no option, even if inclination prompted

---

* Lysons, *Environs of London*, vol. ii. p. 564.

him to remit penalties incurred, in some degree perhaps, in the King's cause.

During Becket's sojourn at Harrow in the year 1170, as Mr. Froude tells us in his *Short Studies on Great Subjects*,* he sent for the Abbot of St. Alban's, doubtless to confer with a potent ally who might be relied on to render every assistance in the cause of Church against State. All accounts concur in recording that on this occasion great hospitalities were exercised by the Archbishop, whose devoted followers may be supposed to have cemented the alliance between their master and the Lord Abbot by the then prevailing forms of rejoicing, which, after daily scenes of almost barbaric magnificence, culminated in the evening wassail, from which there is no reason to believe that even professed churchmen refrained.

Becket himself we may picture as engaged in discussing questions of high policy with his mitred adherent, rather than partaking in jovialities which during the latter part of his career he had foresworn. But as such a manner of life by no means implied a corresponding rule of conduct on the part of his retinue, we are free to indulge the fancy and picture to ourselves the fair Harrow pastures which surrounded the Archbishop's palace as peopled for the nonce with knight and henchman, while the stout friar on his palfrey wended his way from St. Alban's, and received the greeting which policy demanded.

In the ensuing course of our history, we meet again and again with facts that remind us of the connection between Harrow and the See of Canterbury. For instance, at the close of his primacy, in the year 1240,

* Vol. iv. p. 147.

the conscientious and self-denying St. Edmund, previous
to his retirement into a French monastery, is found
adding to the vicarial emoluments.* Again, ten years
later, A.D. 1250, when the foreign influence over
Henry III. was at its height, the Savoyard Boniface,
Primate of all England, held a visitation at Harrow:
while, A.D. 1300, Archbishop Winchelsey dates from
the Harrow Manor when conducting his controversy
with Edward I., who had resolved to appropriate half
the ecclesiastical revenues for the purpose of subduing
William Wallace and his gallant Scots.†

The archbishops do not seem to have underrated the
importance of their pleasant and healthy country retreat,
for we learn that in the year 1344 Archbishop Stratford, another bold assertor of clerical power, who carried
matters with a high hand when Edward III. refused to
summon the Archbishop of Canterbury to Parliament,
received an addition to his Harrow property at the
hands of the then Archdeacon of Richmond in Surrey
(A.D. 1344).‡

But in reference to this arrogant prelate, Stratford, it
is difficult for an Englishman to forget that had his
avowed object of subjecting Civil to Church authority
been attained, Edward III., bereft of resources necessary
for his armies, could never have fought and won the
battle of Crecy.§

The next point of interest is that Thomas Arundell,
Archbishop of Canterbury, wrote from Headstone in

* The vicarage of Harrow endowed with tithes of hay, at Headstone, A.D. 1240.
      † A.D. 1300. Archbishop Winchelsey defended the clergy from
the exactions of Edward I., but, not being duly supported by
Pope Boniface VIII., failed in his object.
      ‡ See Appendix A.
      § Battle of Crecy, August 26th, A.D. 1346.

1407,* when engaged in combating the first symptoms of popular revolt against Papal exactions (A.D. 1407), combined, as the Lollards believed, with unbiblical teaching. Afterwards, the Archbishop suffered banishment by sentence of the Parliament, and then† a survey was taken of his manor at Hayes during a general inquisition of his estates, by far the most important of which was that of Southbury, or Sudbury, in the vicinity of Harrow.

The public policy during a reign of turbulence and sedition such as that of Richard II. was specially liable to reversal, and when a son of John of Gaunt usurped the throne and was hailed Henry IV., Arundell became one of the earliest recipients of his favours and resumed his archiepiscopal office; and although the new *régime* under the succeeding king, Henry V., conferred much glory on the English name by the battle of Agincourt, in 1415, the blight of a disputed succession lay over the land.

At the death of Edward the Confessor, in 1042, the Manor of Harrow had been in the possession of Earl Lewin, who leased a portion to Geoffrey de Mandeville. Whether or not this was the property which, in the reign of Edward III., A.D. 1390, was in possession of Sir John Flambard, it is difficult to tell; but there has ever since remained a distinctive Manor of Harrow. Where, then, was the Archbishop's Manor House at Harrow, a dwelling entirely independent of the Sudbury and Headstone manors, over which they were lords paramount?

Here, unfortunately, we are thrown entirely into the

* Williams, *Concilia*, vol. iii. p. 305.
† Lysons, *Environs of London*, vol. ii. pp. 562, 590.

region of archæological speculation, because the Lambeth
registers are not old enough to let light in upon the
darkness. Tradition assigns the Grove as the site of
the archiepiscopal residence, and it is said that portions
of the small gardener's cottage, in the walled garden,
in which the new speech-room is built, was a part of
the archbishop's out-offices. Another opinion prevailing at Harrow places the archbishop's residence on the
site of what modern Harrovians well know either as
Harry Drury's, Ben Drury's, or C. F. Holmes', the
property which adjoins the school-yard on the side
towards the town,* while another suggestion points to
Sudbury as the locality in question. But the labours
of the Middlesex Archæological Society have unfortunately failed to clear up the point.

For centuries the archbishops were lords paramount,
and practically ruled Harrow outside the walls of Flambards. We have said that Archbishop Arundell dates
from there in 1407.† Later archbishops continue to
write from our Manor House at Harrow, probably from
time to time occupying Headstone as being more com-
modious.

There is a famous brass in Harrow Church to the
memory of Sir John Flambard, dated 1390, with the
following Latin inscription :—

JON ME DO MARMORE NUMINIS ORDINE FLAM TUMLAT.
BARD QUOQUE VERBERE STIGIS E FUNE HIC TUEATUR.

* In the *Harrow Gazette* for November 1861, will be found an
account of the fire at Dr. Wordsworth's in 1838. Those directing
the fire-hose upon the old woodwork of Mr. Henry Drury's
house imagined that they were protecting a portion of what was
once the archbishop's palace.
† *London and Middlesex Archæological Transactions*, in Lambeth
Library, vol. iii. p. 188.

This was somewhat freely translated by Canon John Williams (dated from Arno Court, and writing in *Notes and Queries*, Series 2, ix., p. 286) as follows :—" John Flam is now entombed within this marble by the ordinance of God: may He here by the virtue of the funeral rites, prayers, and sacrifices, defend Bard from the pains of purgatory (*verbere stigis*) "; and as this rendering stood the test of an exhaustive discussion in *Notes and Queries*, we insert it for the benefit of those interested in antiquarian research and local Harrow history.

The Manor of Flambards remained an important part of the town until the sixteenth century, when, falling into possession of the Gerards, it became connected with the fortunes of John Lyon's Free School, which had for many years on the list of governors one or more of the owners of Flambards. Ultimately, and contemporaneously with the extinction of the male line of Gerard, Flambards was sold, and became the property of the Rushouts, whose representatives, first as commoners, and then (A.D. 1797) ennobled by the barony of Northwick, have done so much to keep up Flambard traditions.

Archbishop Chichele was probably at Harrow Manor in 1443, when effecting a purchase of the contiguous Edgware property, in order that it might be settled upon his new College of All Souls at Oxford ; this lordly beneficence being doubtless stimulated by the sovereign's recent example, who under the shade of Royal Windsor, designed at Eton in 1440 a nursery for King's College, Cambridge ; and, indeed, Archbishop Chichele's above-mentioned sojourn in Middlesex occurred almost contemporaneously with the royal summons that Waynflete, Master of Winchester, received to leave his charge

at William of Wykeham's already prosperous college,
and undertake new tutorial duties, at the desire of the
pious King Henry VI.*

Within a few miles of Harrow, and in the environs of
St. Alban's, were fought two battles between the Lancastrian and Yorkist forces, the first resulting in a White
Rose triumph, and the second in a gleam of success for
the hard-pressed supporters of the Lancastrian king,
Henry VI. During these troubles, be it noted, men
generally believed the very existence of the infant college at Eton to be at stake ;† and, indeed, but for the
boldness of William Westbury, the second head-master,
pious Henry's noble foundation would have perished,
done to death by Papal pliability and Edward's jealousy of the captive kinsman whose crown he wore.
Edward IV. gave way, however, before Westbury's
importunity, and henceforth rendered a qualified tolerance of a Lancastrian foundation, which he allowed to
struggle in somewhat inconvenient poverty (see H. G.
Maxwell Lyte's *Eton*, p. 73). There is some reason
to believe that the *written promise of protection*, which
was held to be so strong a part of the Etonian case, had
been elicited from the young Duke of York, somewhere
near Hendon, for it is known that he halted before
entering London, on the road from St. Alban's, and
that he signed the above-mentioned paper when con-

---

* Winchester, established by William Long, known as William
of Wykeham, in 1383, received a charter in 1387. Eton was
founded by King Henry VI. in 1440. Bishop Wilberforce spoke
of Winchester as the beautiful Mother of Eton—a more beautiful
daughter.

† Notwithstanding that Pope Eugenius IV. had granted a bull
in 1440, and that Eton had been confirmed in its privileges by
Nicholas V., Pius II. was ready to revoke his predecessor's acts,
and allow Eton to be destroyed.

fronted with the anxious collegiate authorities, who apparently shared the views of their future neighbour, the Vicar of Bray.

It is remarkable that, up to the earlier portion of the sixteenth century, these faint traces of life in and around Harrow are almost entirely ecclesiastical. It is as an occasional residence of the Primate that we hear of the place at all, when the centre of Middlesex was almost as much unknown to the average Londoner as the wolds of Yorkshire or the borderland of Northumberland. Nor does this characteristic entirely disappear, even when time brings us within the influence of the Reformation. It is the vagary of the priest and the fall of the prelate which has to be described ; indeed, in the state of things sketched in the present chapter may be found no inadequate reason for the acquiescence of Englishmen in a revolution, the completeness of which it is almost impossible at this distance of time to realise. Before the great movement which is generally called "the Reformation," neither civil war, dynastic change, nor ominous signs of frequent, if partial, popular hostility, had yet availed much to shake the priestly fabric of ages, which was welded together by the possession of landed property all over the kingdom.

The growth of Wolsey's power under Henry VII., and its consummation early in the sixteenth century under Henry VIII., is a notable instance of this. Benefice heaped upon benefice contributed to the possession of riches, such as for the moment raised the Cardinal almost to be the rival of his sovereign, and the most powerful churchman known in England since Becket.

The history of secluded Harrow renders us flashes of

light wherewith to interpret the signs of times which, at the present day, are not generally familiar. A strange story, for instance, stands recorded in 1524, indicative of the superstition which prevailed at the epoch in question.* Bolton, the Prior of St. Bartholomew, who was also Vicar of Harrow, had listened to the story of certain soothsayers, whose predictions pointed to the swamping of London and its neighbourhood by a sudden rise of the Thames in 1524. Accordingly, he built a house of refuge on Harrow Hill, and is said to have remained two months entrenched therein. Others of the upper classes, says Dr. Mackay, in his *Memoirs of Popular Delusions*, fled to Hampstead, Highgate, and the Surrey hills, while on the day big with London's fate, crowds of less favoured people assembled to see the rising of the waters. When, however, Father Thames rolled on in his natural course, the popular indignation was straightway directed against the false prophets, who only escaped immersion by asseverating that the mistake of a single figure had caused these wise men of the West to fix the date of the expected inundation a century too soon.†

We are inclined to credit that part of the story told by Camden, even if some historical writers are silent on a matter which probably had many a counterpart in days when the credulity of mankind was encouraged rather than hindered by the powers who held sway.‡

* Camden, Tr. by E. Gibson, vol. i. col. 366 (Ed. 1722).

† For the latter part of this legend I am indebted to **Mr.** Edward Walford, *Greater London* : Cassell, part vi. p. 257.

‡ Lysons, in his *Environs of London*, when alluding to the story of Bolton's retreat to Harrow, says that he was a well-known builder, and therefore that his ordinary avocation may have been mistaken for untimely effort to secure fancied security. But, as the tradition prevailed elsewhere, we are inclined to believe that

But a more dignified figure than Bolton had been associated with Harrow as Rector in 1514, Cuthbert Tunstall, then Bishop of London, a man somewhat beyond his times, although a staunch opponent of the English Reformation in its first stages.

Wolsey is said to have been Rector* of Harrow, and there survives a very strong tradition that he lived from time to time at Headstone ; but no evidence of this is to be found in any of the authorities who searched the documents connected with the subject. The Middlesex Archæological Society distinctly rejects the prevalent story. It is prudent to distrust rumour unsupported by fact, although we are by no means prepared to throw tradition over altogether. The great minister may pos-

it has foundation in truth ; the more that the only recorded doubt is founded, as Camden tells us, on a mistaken date. We append Camden's notice of this subject :—" Gliding from hence [*i.e.* Shepparton], the *Thames* takes a view of *Harrow*, the highest hill in this County, which on the South has very fruitful fields for a long way together ; especially about the little village of *Heston*, the Wheat-flowre whereof has been particularly made choice of by our Kings for their own bread. By reason of its great height it was also chosen by *William Bolton*, the last Prior of Great St. *Bartholomew's*, in *Smithfield*, on which to build him a house to preserve him from a Deluge that was prognosticated from certain Eclipses in watery signs, and was to happen in the year 1524. With this not only the vulgar, but also learned men, were so unreasonably infatuated, that they victuall'd themselves (as both *Hall* and *Speed, Chron.* p. 1014. confidently report) and went to high grounds, for fear of being drown'd. Amongst whom was this Prior, who not only provided himself with a house here at Harrow, but carried all sorts of provisions with him thither, to serve for the space of two months. Mr. *Stow* (*Survey*, pp. 417, 419), I acknowledge, would have all this to be a fable, and that Prior *Bolton*, being also Parson of Harrow, did only repair his Parsonage-house, and build a Dove-coat, to serve him with that sort of fowl after he was spoiled of his Priory. But the date of this Deluge and the dissolution of the Priory (1539) do not agree, and therefore these Historians are not to be reconciled."—Camden, tr. by E. Gibson (ed. 1722), vol. i. col. 366.

* See, however, Appendix E.

2

sibly have sought seclusion in the Pinner meadows. But as neither Galt nor Cavendish, the Cardinal's servant, mention his residing there, we must content ourselves with the knowledge that when the fallen favourite was on his last journey north, in 1529, he rested at the Abbot of Westminster's Manor of Hendon,* having passed from Hampton Court almost under the shadow of the Harrow uplands.

It is, however, as putative Rector† of Harrow that Wolsey claims a mention here which the popular belief connecting his memory with sojourn at Headstone might not warrant; and, indeed, a volume of great interest might be written concerning the Rectors and Vicars of Harrow. We may mention John Byrkhed, A.D. 1418, whose brass is in Harrow Church. According to the inscription, nearly obliterated, but given in Latin by Weever (*Funeral Monuments*, Edition 1631) he was a good and wise man, high in the counsels of his sovereign (Henry V.). Another celebrated Rector of Harrow was Dr. Richard Cox, who was educated at Westminster, and became preceptor to King Edward VI., but had to fly to Frankfort during Queen Mary's reign. In the year 1553 he distinguished himself as leader of the English Liturgical party, as opposed to that of John Knox, which rejected prelacy *in toto*. After Queen Elizabeth had been forced into the Reformer's camp, in 1559, by the insults of Pope Paul IV., Dr. Cox was recalled to advise on ecclesiastical matters. He gave up the Rectory of Harrow-on-the-Hill in 1547, having only held the same about three years.‡ He seems to have succeeded Master Richard Leyton, LL.D.,

* Lysons, *Environs of London*, vol. iii. p. 3.
† See, however, Appendix E.
‡ *Alumni Westmonasterienses*, p. 3.

Dean of York, who held a Court as Rector of Harrow, 1543 (5).

Henceforth the course of our story runs in secular rather than in clerical lines. We pass lightly over the crash itself, when the faith so many centuries old was roughly robbed of its insignia and remoulded after immersion in the cauldron of revolutionary disturbance, which, despite the abrogation of Papal supremacy, or the doctrinal struggles which ensued during the reigns of Edward VI. and Mary Tudor, did not ensure visible improvement in the wretched condition of England's rural poor, or serve to assuage the turbulent passions of their betters.

Peers of Parliament were to be found who could neither read nor write; beds were still made of straw or rushes, which it was not thought necessary to remove so long as the couch was rendered habitable by the addition of fresh layers of the same material. Life was nothing in comparison with the gain of the monarch's end, and corresponding selfishness pervaded the various strata of society. To secure as firmly as circumstances allowed the Reformation changes, Henry VIII. had placed large tracts of land taken from abbeys and monasteries in the hands of Court favourites, who, by reason of their feudal training, might be expected to defend them by the sword, and give their children an example their interest would not unnaturally bid them follow.[*]

Yet not even lands held on such a tenure were safe from the wayward rapacity of a monarch like Henry VIII., who, relieved both from feudal checks and from clerical

[*] For these facts I am indebted to Mr. J. A. Froude's *History*, and to Draper's *Intellectual Development of Europe.*

2 *

rivalry, when Parliament lacked real power, bounded his desires alone by the impossible, and was not one whit swayed by the dictates of justice or good faith. A notable instance of this insecurity of possession occurs in the year 1543, when Archbishop Cranmer, who was in full sympathy with the Reformation, had aliened his manorial rights at Harrow, and also those in its neighbourhood, to the King in exchange for other lands, which, however, the monarch granted three years afterwards[*] to his favourite, Sir Edward North. He seems to have promptly taken possession, and by so doing brought down the royal wrath on his head. Henry, conceiving that he had some trifling cause of complaint against the lately favoured servant, summoned his subject to Court, and in anger charged the astonished Sir Edward with having cheated him of certain lands in Middlesex, to which the accused made reply by a humble negative. "How was it then," said the King: "did we give those lands to you?" "Your Majesty was pleased so to do," replied North; whose firm, if respectful, bearing prevailed, so that not only did he regain the King's favour, but, by Patent 37 Hen. VIII., was raised to the Peerage as Baron North.[†] The incident, nevertheless, demonstrates the confusion and uncertainty which accompanied a confiscatory policy, only tolerated by the nation because evils inherent to the old order of things could not then be otherwise dispersed.

A similar fate visited all the Archbishop of Canter-

[*] The Manors of Harrow, granted by Henry VIII. to Sir Edward, afterwards Lord North, 1546.—Lysons, *Environs of London*, vol. ii. p. 575.

[†] I have again followed Lysons in detailing this story, but the facts are borne out by several authorities.

bury's property near Harrow. Sudbury, Woodhall,[*] Headstone, and Hayes fell into the hands of the North family, while Kilburn, after passing to the Knights of St. John of Jerusalem, lapsed, in 1540, into the possession of the Earl of Sussex and Sir Roger Cholmeley, Chief Baron of the Exchequer.[†]

The Manor of Wymbley, or Wembley, which also pertained to Kilburn, became the property of Richard Andrewes and Leonard Chamberlayne, who conveyed it to the Page family, one of whom was chosen amongst the first governors of Harrow School.[‡]

The religious house of Bentley, near Stanmore[§] in the first throes of reformatory change was assigned to the monks of St. Gregory's Priory at Canterbury ; but ultimately, Archbishop Cranmer played into the King's hands so far as to make an exchange to the effect that Henry VIII. should dispense these lands ; since which the property constantly changed hands, and at the end of the eighteenth century fell temporarily to the Abercorn family, to the manifest advantage of Harrow School.

But these social changes followed that agricultural extension which transformed the whole face of England, more or less, during the Plantagenet reigns, and which

---

[*] Woodhall Manor was in the Pinner division.

[†] Howitt, *Northern Heights of London*, p. 42.

[‡] Lysons, *Environs of London*, vol. ii. p. 565.

[§] At the Reformation the Manor of Stanmore fell into various hands, one Peter Gambo, a Spaniard, amongst the number, who was murdered near St. Sepulchre's Church, London, in 1550, by Gavaro, a Fleming. Ultimately James I. granted Stanmore Manor to Sir Thomas Lake, whose family importance remained long a feature in the neighbourhood. The manor had belonged to the abbots of St. Albans until 1364, when the Convent of St. Bartholomew held it until the monastic dissolution.—Brewer, *Beauties of England*, vol. x. pp. 628, 629.

was most prominent when Edward III. became king. We know that this improvement in cultivation became specially prevalent on the north side of London, where the old forest of Middlesex gave way to civilisation, which the proximity of London city gradually but surely increased. These tracts Matthew Paris, in his life of the twelfth Abbot of St. Albans, described as impenetrable forest, and so infested with robbers and wild beasts, that the pilgrimage from London to St. Albans was then performed with danger. This district first became a shooting-ground for the citizens of London,* and afterwards, in presence of the increasing metropolis, was disafforested, A.D. 1218. As a consequence, we read that a partial clearance was soon effected by Londoners seeking for fuel, so that in the sixteenth century but little of the Middlesex forest remained.†

Although the pure vale of Harrow—reaching on one side to Willesden and Kingsbury, on the other to Perivale, Northolt, and Hayes—was always distinguished for its superior agriculture, it is impossible to doubt that to some extent it was early affected by the gradual approach of urban influence. Of this no more conclusive evidence can be adduced than the settlement of the Lyon family, both at Preston and Alperton. Sir John Lyon of Alperton, namesake of his more famous Preston kinsman, was chief magistrate of London in 1554, when Queen Mary came to the throne, and when the beautiful and unfortunate Lady June Grey met her tragic end. Placed amidst old families holding lay property, and seeing also new neighbours settling on the lands of expropriated ecclesiastics, the Lyon family were not

---

* Fitz-Stephens, *Survey of London between* 1170 *and* 1182.
† See Brewer, *Beauties of England--Middlesex*, vol. x. p. 628.

slow to perceive the enormous needs which such a transitional state of affairs must necessarily have created. They anticipated the day when desire for culture should advance amongst all classes, in such proportion as to produce mental improvement in unison with the great movements of their own times.

So early as A.D. 1571, the date of Harrow's birth, the bright day of Elizabethan literature was beginning to show faint streaks of dawn. Shakespeare, it is true, was then but a child of seven, and the fame of Wyatt, who composed sonnets in the style of Petrarch, or Lord Surrey, the first English writer who adopted blank verse, had scarcely become familiar to the English people. Neither had John Lyon's contemporary, Greene, made the position in the dramatic world, which has led close observers to declare him a forerunner of Shakespeare himself.

On the other hand, few Englishmen lived in 1571 who had not heard of Sir Walter Ralegh, poet, statesman, historian, and traveller ; or, by reason of his connection with public affairs, learnt to know Dorset as a lover of poesy.

Again, Sir Phillip Sidney, not having concluded his foreign travels, had not yet wielded either pen or sword ; while Edmund Spenser, the pride of English song, was a beardless lad not yet out of his teens. When, however, Harrow School was fully established, some twenty years later, English literature had blazed into the full light of sixteenth-century fame.

Previous to this period of transition, when increase of population was deprecated rather than encouraged, were enacted the Vagrancy Laws of 1531 and 1536, the latter of which provided that, when whipping at the cart-tail or ear-slitting had failed to cow a valiant beggar, a third offence was punishable by death. The original cause of such enactments was the idleness of the surplus population, who, as chroniclers able to decide* tell us, contracted lazy habits through monkish example.

However that may be settled by the modern school of scientific historians, certain as they are to sift thoroughly every formed opinion, the Harrow parish records after the Reformation certainly show little abatement of the evil in question. A main object of man seemed to be the discharging of well-thrashed beggars into other parishes.

We have carried this history to the point when the old order gave place to new. Known then no more at Harrow were the stately retinues of ecclesiastical pomp; forgotten the very site of the archbishop's ancient dwelling; while, an inventory having been rendered up of its contents, St. Mary's Church entered on a fresh phase of its hitherto chequered existence.†

A curious local relic has been discovered by Mr. Edward Scott, of the Manuscript Department, British Museum. Two brothers of the old family, yclept Greenhill, resident in the suburb of Harrow which bears their name, are joint owners of an ancient Cranmer Bible, in perfect condition, which may probably have been the local book which Henry VIII. ordered to be laid in the choir of every church, that each man who would might read the contents,‡ and which consequently belonged to

* Draper, *Intellectual Development of Europe*, vol. ii. p. 214.

† No chronicler whose pages we have consulted has been able to account for the destruction of Lanfranc's building, which necessitated its re-erection in Edward III.'s time.

‡ This Bible was printed in 1537, and Henry VIII. gave the decree in question two years before; but the most perfect edition of the Holy Scriptures attainable was doubtless placed in St. Mary's Church.

Harrow parish.   In the confusion which ensued upon
the changes of ecclesiastical policy, made when Mary
Tudor and Pole succeeded to Edward VI. and Cranmer,
the Reformation Bible may well have fallen into private
hands.

From a *Harrovian's* point of view, these opening
pages are of necessity to a great extent preliminary,
though early local history will be seen to bear upon the
question whether Harrow was or was not a place of
education under archiepiscopal or monastic auspices
before the charter of the existing foundation was
granted.   The next chapter, after a few general
remarks, will introduce the main theme of this work
—Harrow School.

CHAPTER II.

JOHN LYON'S GLIMPSE OF THE FUTURE.

From Wembley's rise and Kenton's stream,
From Preston farm and hollow,
Where Lyon dreamed, and saw in dream
His race of sons to follow.

Fairies; School Song, by E. E. BOWEN.

THE close of the sixteenth century was undoubtedly a period of intellectual awakening, as well as of religious enlightenment throughout the known world.

The sway held by barbarism in the Middle Ages had been relaxed by an ardent desire to reproduce the civilised culture of old Greece and Rome. This could hardly be marvelled at when we reflect how communication of ideas was facilitated by the invention of printing, no long time before the reaction against the dogmas of the schools and the Vatican took effect in the half-religious, half-political changes called the Reformation.

This great movement, although unavoidably tinged with the iconoclastic element, yet having princes for its nursing fathers, to a great extent escaped the stain of bloodshed which has so often disgraced merely popular revolutions. We do not forget the fires of Smithfield; but the victims of the stake were far fewer than those of the more democratic convulsions which overwhelmed the English monarch in the seventeenth century, and which amid terror and sanguinary rapine compassed the destruction of the French monarchy in the eighteenth century.

In England this desire for learning became the more prevalent, when the dissolution of the monasteries caused a blank in place of the education previously dispensed under the religious monopoly. The teaching of the Church might be defective and faulty, but the life work of many a recluse stored up in manuscript in the old monasteries and religious houses must have afforded some intellectual food for the society over which the clergy held educational sway.

But upon the dissolution of the monasteries, the libraries and their manuscript contents were also for the most part dissipated, so that it became more than ever necessary to replace the defunct educational system by the beneficence of well-to-do men, who were fortunately enabled by the advance of scientific method to supply better means of teaching than those which had vanished. But in England, during the sixteenth century, the earlier educational awakenings were, so to speak, mere vague yearnings for solid knowledge felt mainly amongst the upper classes, and even there, by no means generally.

Households, as Strype tells us in his *Life of Archbishop Parker*, were to be found wherein the ladies eagerly imbibed the classics, and spent their leisure hours in perusing the last-imported volume from the printing presses of Antwerp and Verona. But this craving after culture of a high type represented no general enlightenment of the national mind, but rather the natural impulse of the few who, by enjoyment of exceptional advantages and class privileges, had been made aware of their mission on earth, and were impressed with its dignity.

Coincidently with this more earnest striving after knowledge may be noted the influence of the Renaissance on national costume, and we may wonder at the bad taste displayed in the insular selection of a " classical " style at a period when in such matters a much purer taste prevailed both in Italy and France. Hence the strange angularities of the Elizabethan attire.

The fragmentary nature of the instruction available in Middlesex, if not throughout England, in the year 1571, becomes apparent when we reflect that it had neither root nor foundation, flourishing as an exotic, not by any means acclimatised, and out of reach of ordinary people. This lack of adequate provision for education suited to the needs of the various classes of the community resulted in the foundation of schools such as the Merchant Taylors' and Dean Colet's Foundation at St. Paul's School, institutions like the Marischal College at Aberdeen, and, more pertinent to our immediate purpose, rural grammar-schools of the type which Laurence Sheriff founded at Rugby and John Lyon at Harrow-on-the-Hill. And this is none the less true because superficial observers might have inferred from the number of royal foundations already existing in the year 1571 that mental training was duly cared for in Queen Elizabeth's dominions.

Royal Eton, proudest memory of Henry VI., took the leading position which its foundation in 1440 scarcely warranted on the score of antiquity, inasmuch as the college of William of Wykeham at Winchester had been instituted some sixty years earlier in the year 1382. But these foundations, destined as they were to influence the course of English history, were neither adapted to meet poor men's needs nor calculated to satisfy the requirements of a rising middle class.

But King Edward VI. had not concluded his short, and on the whole propitious, reign, without recognising the scholastic needs which a new religious policy had created. Hence the many local grammar-schools bearing the young monarch's name, a majority of which have remained in obscurity even if they fulfilled the local purposes for which they were originally founded. On the other hand, several institutions dating from Lyon's lifetime—Repton (1556) and Uppingham (1587) to wit —are now as household words amongst Englishmen. Again, we ought to mention that the universities in the sixteenth century were looked on rather as schools for youths in their teens than as resorts where youths of more mature age completed their preparation for life. Still the want of seminaries such as Lyon's Grammar-School at Harrow must have been at that time sorely felt.

Almost contemporaneously with the realisation of John Lyon's educational schemes there were springing up in the West of England institutions of a similar nature, taking their origin from the spirit of commercial progress which animated the land in good Queen Bess' time; it being on the coasts of Devonshire and Gloucestershire that England's great commercial celebrity was first founded. The fame of the West was greatly and deservedly enhanced when the country ports poured forth so noble a contingent to assist in coping with the Spanish Armada. Bristol and Topsham (as the late Mr. Charles Kingsley tells us), being in the sixteenth century competitors in commerce with London, became

smitten with the intellectual *awakenment* which had
passed over the Netherlands after printing and a
desire for increase of liberty had given free play to
native resources. Hence the springing up in Western
England of civic institutions for purposes of learning
in such places as Tiverton (1599), Bristol (1561), and
Henry VIII.'s cathedral school at Gloucester (1541);
while the requirements of Welsh and Salopian folk were
provided for in the historic foundation of Shrewsbury
(1549).*

But, on the whole, the schools in question seem to
have remained local, and it was inevitable that such a
result should ensue. If one fact is evolved more surely
than another from a study of parish records generally,
it is this. The feudal system left agricultural England

---

* The rise of Shrewsbury under the eminent Ashton to at least
400 scholars within twenty years of its foundation, is an entirely
unique event in public-school history. In the year 1548 the burgesses Whitaker and Edwards petitioned King Edward VI. for
the sanctioning of a free school at Shrewsbury, and in 1562
Thomas Ashton, of St. John's College, Cambridge, became head-
master, entering no less than 256 boys at the very outset, and
increasing the number within ten years to 400, amongst whose
ranks were found cadets of the noblest families in Wales, Shropshire, Cheshire, and the neighbouring counties. Whence the
majority of scholars came so promptly still remains an enigma;
but the ready commingling of class with class proves how far
nearer to one another were the different strata of society before
the civil wars of Charles I.—before "Sir Gorgeous Midas," that
creation of the eighteenth century, came on the scene, and caused
envy by ill-advised display, or demoralised society by undue
luxury. John Lyon probably hoped for a more prompt appreciation of his Foreigner clause than was actually exhibited, this
accession of prosperity being denied for many years to Harrow,
because, until some striking success drew attention to the peculiar
advantages there to be gained, the citizens of London rested content
with education provided at their very doors, at Westminster,
St. Paul's School, the Charterhouse, and also at the several city
schools, where the city merchants gave freely of their possessions
in order that knowledge might be more generally dispensed.

almost destitute of facilities for locomotion except
between great cities. It had been the object of the
owner rather to hinder than advance communication
with his neighbour, and travellers had often to traverse
districts of almost unexplored forest and heath. It was,
for instance, a far cry from the Welsh borderlands to
the then classical shades of Eton or Winchester ; and
many a squire cried "Rest and be thankful " when
enabled to avail himself at Shrewsbury of the energy
and liberality displayed by the two burgesses Edward
and Richard Whyttaker.

The student of sixteenth-century history who omits
to take notice of these sharp contrasts then subsisting
between increasing culture and crass ignorance cannot
hope to grasp the true spirit of the period during which
John Lyon lived and founded Harrow School.

That remarkable man gauged accurately the thin
veneer of civilisation covering the ignorance and savagery
which characterised the Tudor reigns, when human life
was still held cheap, and the poor received such care as
prudence bade an owner bestow on horse or ox or any
other living accessory to daily need, but was not allowed
to participate in the advantages procured by the wealth
which his toil created.

We have written evidence that with thoughtful benevolence he combined accurate judgment and business
capabilities such as have led to the formation of the
opinions expressed in this chapter ascribing to him
statesman-like forethought far beyond that which prevailed amongst country gentlemen of his own times.

Those familiar with the verdant pastures spreading
beneath Lord Northwick's park property may have
wended their way past the school bathing-place—in

Harrow language termed " Ducker "—and, smitten with the pastoral beauty of the scene, have wandered some few hundred yards into the little hamlet of Preston.

From a slight eminence may be seen the view of Harrow's famous hill, similar in its outlines to that visible from Hampstead, and yet more clearly defined as to sylvan charms, which crown the gradual ascent and complete a prospect* which it is not impossible may have helped to inspire John Lyon with his pregnant resolve. It is remarkable that owing to the boyish predilection expressed in tender song by the noble poet Lord Byron, the sad beauty of the vale seen from Harrow church-yard has eclipsed the engaging hill outline which, ever crowned with fine timber, and in season conspicuous for rich foliage, slopes gracefully down to meadows such as Milton loved, and amidst which stood John Lyon's homely dwelling.

The district however, had its imperfections. It is easy to understand why John Lyon made so great a point of road improvement between Harrow and the metropolis, when we learn that in the direction of Ux-bridge and Hayes the vale country remained a modern Bœotia even to the beginning of the nineteenth century, when it took a Harrow waggoner and his team a day to compass the thirteen miles which lay between his heavy clays and London city.†

What must have been the condition before John Lyon improved the Edgware road and the Harrow road proper, our readers may learn from Norden's graphic pen.

" It may be noted also," says Norden,‡ " how nature

---

* Perivale, near Ealing, was a part of the country in question, and its name is *said* to be derived from Pure-vale.

† E. Walford, *Greater London*, Cassell, part 6, p. 249.

‡ I. *Pars Speculi Britanniæ*, 1593, p. 11.

hath exalted *Harrow* on the hill, which seemeth to make
ostentation of it scituation in the *Pureuale*, from whence,
towardes the time of Haruest, a man may beholde the
fields round about, so sweetely to addresse themselues,
to the siccle, and sith, with such comfortable aboun-
daunce, of all kinde of graine, that the husbandman
which waiteth for the fruits of his labours, cannot but clap
his hands, for joy, to see this vale, so to laugh and sing.

" Yet doth not this so fruitefull soyle yeeld comfort,
to the way-fairing man in the wintertime, by reason of
the claiesh nature of soyle: which after it hath tasted
the autume showers, waxeth both dyrtie and deepe : But
vnto the countrie swaine it is as a sweete and pleasant
garden, in regard of his hope of future profite, for

> The deepe, and dirtie loathsome soyle,
> Yeelds golden gaine, to painefull toyle.

The industrious and painefull husbandman will refuse a
pallace, to droyle in these golden puddles."

A description this of the local characteristics such as
everyone who has lived through the year in this part of
Middlesex will appreciate.

In the heading to this chapter we have indicated an
opinion that John Lyon must have looked far ahead
when he founded the grammar-school destined to make
his name famous. This view is not impugned by the
undoubted fact that circumstances bade him give immediate heed to the wants of those around him, and grant
free educational advantages to the inhabitants of the
extensive district of which Harrow Hill was then the
centre. But in so doing, as we shall show, he distinctly
covenanted that the master should be permitted to take
for his own emolument so many scholars as could be
conveniently taught and accommodated.

3

Consequently, when the question arose in 1810 whether a narrow view should be taken of the founder's intention, or whether the school that had produced a Sir William Jones, a Dr. Parr, a Sheridan, and a Byron, should bear the form that it fortunately retains, and become national rather than parochial, the acute and learned Master of the Rolls, Sir William Grant, in a masterly ruling, pointed out that for the benefit of the inhabitants themselves it was incumbent on the governors to carry out the clearly-expressed desire of the founder. While intending to confer peculiar privileges on the immediate neighbourhood, John Lyon also desired to encourage others to resort to his school, and so, by attracting head-masters of high ability and scholars of gentle birth, to make the education in every respect first-rate. Otherwise, the people of Harrow remain no better off than their nineteenth century neighbours, one and all of whom can place their children under some educational care in the various parishes in which they live. Nor can an observer of modern Harrow life remain unimpressed with the obvious truth, practical, if not to be produced for legal purposes, that the town of Harrow owes all its consequence, not to say its present dimensions, to the presence of a great public school.

It is clear upon consideration of the subject, from other arguments than the cogent ruling of Sir William Grant, that John Lyon did look farther than Harrow parish (as men generally understand the word) when he gave his substance to the school in 1571.

It can scarcely be supposed that when the excellent man passed through the elevated church-yard, as a churchman of his character from time to time would naturally do, he could fail to observe the scene of singu-

larly fascinating beauty which lay outspread before him,
or that, seeing it, he should forget how from the confis-
cated priories of Bentley and Stanmore to the other side
of Watford lay in succession broad lands tenanted by a
new race of landlords, successors to the sleek abbots
and sturdy monks who had hitherto preserved civilisation amidst the crumbling waste of what was once
forest-land.   For the dissipation of the Church properties around the famous abbey of St. Albans had
revolutionised the neighbourhood.   John Lyon, we contend, was not the man to be ignorant of this, even if
within a few miles of his own door the broad acres of
Kilburn Priory had not fallen into the hands of King
Henry VIII.'s favourites, from whom he had himself
purchased property in the vicinity.   Neither could he
forget, in establishing a school, that his institution
would henceforth supply a need such as these men were
certain soon to feel.

Nor must we fail here to observe how great a stress
John Lyon placed in the disposition of his property*
upon the repairing of roads (one-third of his money
being assigned for this purpose) between Harrow and
London.   He might well believe future popularity would
accrue to a school favoured by easy communication with
the metropolis.

Such, we opine, was John Lyon's glimpse of the
future.

Between the hour when the idea of creating a school
which animated the Preston yeoman first took a practical
shape by the grant of the charter in the year 1571, and
his death in 1592, there elapsed some twenty eventful

---

* When the late Mr. Howard Staunton wrote his *Public Schools
of England*, in 1868, £3,500 a year went to the repair of roads,
and £1,100 to the school.

years of British history, characterised by a perpetual
rivalry between the old religion, personified by the
luckless Queen of Scots, Mary Stuart, and the Reformed
doctrines, whose living embodiment was Queen Elizabeth.   She formally accepted the settlement of the
Church of England (adopted by Archbishop Parker in
1559) in the same year that she granted the Harrow
charter.

We have spoken of the sixteenth century as a time
of contrasts, and shown that, if the reader would step
back for one instant into that epoch, he must realise
how, despite much social toleration, there yawned an
educational chasm between different classes.   He must
equally grasp the undoubted truth that, if Queen Bess'
subjects were divided into any distinct parties at all,
they would either have been classed as Queen's men, or
as rebels willing to acknowledge Mary's claim to the
English throne, and consequently to adhere to the old
religious system and the Papal supremacy.

In fact, there existed at that time no other form of
partisanship than that which men now designate as
theological ; though, to be sure, side issues such as
that of the tenure of what was lately monastic property
by lay holders, might ultimately have complicated any
open struggle between the rival schools of opinion.   But
our immediate object is to point out that, if the Harrow
founder was anything, he is conclusively shown by the
terms of his own Will to have been most emphatically a
Queen's man.

There was more in the formal heading of the charter
describing John Lyon as Queen Elizabeth's beloved
subject than under ordinary circumstances would become
apparent, though the grant of an educational charter by

the Crown in 1571 would scarcely have emanated from
men who doubted the loyalty of the testator. He was,
be it remembered, devising property for the practical
furtherance of the Queen's purposes, since the realisation of his schemes involved acknowledgment of the
above-mentioned religious settlement. Hence it came
to pass that Harrow School, although not directly
claiming Royal or Ecclesiastical origin, was nurtured
amidst Loyal and Anglican traditions, so tempered by
the politic elasticity of the foundation statutes, that
faction, either in Church or State, never permeated this
thoroughly national institution, destined to reflect
honestly, if not accurately, the needs and desires of
the English people.

Not only had echoes of controversy between the rival
Queens and opposing religions reached Harrow, at the
time when John Lyon made his Will, but political
events of dramatic interest had occurred close to his
rural retreat at Preston.

In all the range of Tudor story, there is nothing
more momentous than the unravelment of the notorious
Babington conspiracy of 1586. Anthony Babington, of
an old family, living at Dethick, in Derbyshire, was a
youth of singular beauty, possessing attainments, mental
and physical, calculated to render his natural position in
life tolerable, even if the possession of a good fortune
had not combined to place within reach the wise man's
desideratum of peace and contentment. The youth had
held the position of page in Lord Shrewsbury's household when the Queen of Scots was residing as prisoner
in that nobleman's establishment, and the fair captive
had taken some notice of the comely lad, whose appearance attracted general attention. In common with a

majority of the male sex who approached the wand of that royal enchantress, Babington became devoted to a cause, the righteousness of which he had learnt to assume through his religion, but which henceforth was enhanced in his eyes by a passion for the fair Stuart. He was of an enthusiastic nature and lively imagination. He had been, moreover, much thrown into the society of the Jesuit clergy, both near his ancestral home and in the course of his sojourn in Paris and at St. Omer. No wonder, then, that in the eyes of the young Babington the captive Mary Stuart was Queen of England, and that he should become enamoured of the idea that by his hands should the representative of his religion, and the Queen both of his country and of his heart, attain the deliverance which a majority of Christendom fondly desired. Such a conception of duty once formed, Babington lived in an ideal world of his own. Imagination pictured the achievement of his object as being practically attained, insomuch that he was positively induced to order the portraiture of himself in company with six coadjutors, attendants at Elizabeth's court, who had undertaken not only to release the Queen of Scots, but also to compass the destruction of her potent rival.

The story, had it reached us through mediæval chronicle, might have served its purpose equally well with others of like type in throwing some halo of romance over a dark deed. For, stripped of romantic verbiage, and judged even by the canons of Tudor days, when human life was held strangely cheap, Babington's plot was a foul conspiracy to murder a woman. This remains the fact, though it may be plausibly urged on behalf of the Catholic and Anti-English party—for it derived its chief strength from foreign intrigue and the

assent of declining Spain—that, the conflict between
Elizabeth Tudor and Mary Stuart being *to the death,*
the Scottish Queen's deliverance from mere captivity
could bring little permanent change in her affairs,
unless accompanied by the removal of the rival who
was waiting for an opportunity to strike her prisoner
down. Anyhow, Babington's implication in a design of
seditious murder is undoubtedly clear, and appeared to
involve the guilt of the fair and unfortunate lady, whose
beauty and misfortune has since turned wiser heads and
captivated the imagination of better men.

Betrayed by a recreant conspirator, one Gilbert Gifford,
a Jesuit, and—unkindest cut of all—by a trusted friend,*
Babington fell into the skilful toils prepared for him by
the astute Walsingham, whom the unfortunate youth
believed that he was himself misleading. Through a
Jesuit agency previously established, utterly compro-
mising admissions were obtained from Mary Stuart
herself, who believed that her letters would be seen

* " We have vowed and we will performe or dye."—Babington
to his friend Tichbourne. The following letter will show how
Babington's conduct was influenced by religious fanaticism. It
is difficult not to feel some antipathy to the informer and conspirator, Pooley. Babington writes as follows to Pooley :—
"Robyn, Sollicitæ non possunt curæ mutare rati stamina fusi—I
am ready to endure whatsoe^r shall be inflicted. Et facere, et
pati Romanum est. What my course hath been towards Mr.
Secretary you can wyttnes, what my love towards yo^u yor self
can best tell. Proceedings at my lodgings have been very
strange. I am the same allwayes pretended. I pray God yo^w be,
and ever so remayne towards me. Take hede to yor own p^{te}
least of these my mysfortunes yo^u beare the blame. Est exilium
inter malos vivere. Farewell, swete Robyn, if, as I take the true
to me. If not, Adieu, omnium bipedium inquissimus. Retorne
me thyne answere for my satisfaction and my dyamond and what
else thou wilt. The furnace is prepared, wherein our fayth must
be tryed. Farewell till we mete, wch God knowes when. Thyne
ho^w farr tho^u knowest, ANTHONY BABINGTON."—Lingard, *History
of England,* 5th ed. vol. vi. pp. 695, 696.

by Babington only.   She concurred in the plot of
which Babington was the nominal leader, and approved
of her royal cousin's destruction.   The vain and foolish
young traitor, who for a time had been lulled into false
security by the plausible wiles of Walsingham and his
agents, suddenly found himself watched and followed.
The cause for which he had lived was clearly lost, and
yet life remained sweet.   He would fly.   But whither ?

The emissaries of Government were watching every
outlet of escape leading to the south coast, whence it
might be possible to join Catholic sympathisers, waiting
on French territory for the result of their thus early
exploded machinations ; moreover, public excitement
blazed out, and the flame was fanned by Government.
To reach Dover, or make way to the west, was clearly
impossible in the presence of a general hue and cry.
Neither direction afforded any safe path for marked-
down men, and there remained but a hasty plunge into
the almost pathless St. John's Wood, then on the
confines of forest land.

To the left of the old Roman road of Watling Street,
and at a distance of seven miles from Westminster,
wild and open country stretched past the former priory
of Kilburn, and reached, almost unbroken by human
dwellings, up to the farm-house of Uxendon, and further
across the Brent to Preston.   Into this secluded region
wandered the unfortunate Babington and his hunted
associates.   We read that, after vain attempts to
procure horses, they were reduced to making cautious
progress on foot.   Staining their features with walnut-
juice, they begged from door to door for the space of
ten days, until, tracked by the officers of justice, the
wretched fugitives were discovered hidden behind a

wood-stack on the farm of one Belamy, at Uxendon, within a mile of John Lyon's home at Preston. Appalled at the evident approach of a painful and degrading end, Babington quailed before the fate which his detection had rendered inevitable.   He is said to have asked Elizabeth for pardon, and to have scarcely borne himself as one who had, in the great Marquis Montrose's words, "Put it to the touch to win or lose it all."   But it is reasonable to believe that the hideous character of the penalty incurred had overcome the frail nature of a mentally-tortured and half-starved man.   Babington suffered semi-strangulation at Tyburn, the still quivering frame being, at Elizabeth's instance, thrown to the ground and slowly hacked to pieces, so that a maximum of suffering might be undergone by the subject guilty of high treason with murderous intent against the Tudor Queen.*

We have told the story at length in this place, in order that our readers may at once realise the extent of savagery which still animated all parties alike, even in these Reformation days, and to point out how the need for instruction being given to each class must have been forced on John Lyon's watchful and able intelligence, as he meditated on perfecting his scholastic designs by the rude fireside at Preston.

One is likewise led to wonder whether the wretched Babington and his companions in disaster asked alms, during their wanderings, at the sage Preston yeoman's gate, and also to ask why the farmer Belamy of

---

* Queen Elizabeth only concurred in the ordinary mode of execution being observed, provided, as she phrased it, the deaths were "protracted to the extremitie of payne."—Lingard, 5th ed. vol. vi. p. 418. For the general account of Babington's conspiracy, Hume, Lingard, and Froude have been consulted.

Uxendon was condemned to the scaffold without any evidence of previous complicity in treasonable practices?

For even Mr. Froude, holding a brief against the Catholic party, could find no adequate cause for the punishment which Belamy underwent on Tyburn tree, his brother only escaping a felon's end because he met a natural death in prison; while Mrs. Belamy, the staunchest Catholic of the Uxendon household, escaped conviction on a technical point of law, having been styled Elizabeth in the indictment instead of Catherine,[*] demonstrating, at any rate, that the legal rights of the subject were not placed in total abeyance, even when claimed by a family marked down as friendly to the Catholic cause, and who had secreted traitors such as Babington and Tichbourne.

The papist Belamy seems to have been on friendly terms with the loyal John Lyon. Their homesteads were only divided by the river Brent, and the two families had evidently been for some time in intimate relation one to the other. On the 3rd of July, A.D. 1568, there is record amongst the Lyon papers in the Harrow School muniments of a transaction between these neighbours. Belamy had lent Lyon a sum of money, but having lost all documentary evidence of the debt, gave a quittance in full to the Preston squire, when he received back the loan in full. But at the foot of the paper in question, and after the parties had signed, Belamy (for the handwriting is his) added the words Jack Straw and Wat Tyler.

Now, as Jack Straw was a coadjutor of Wat Tyler in his rebellion against the Government of Richard II.

[*] Lingard, 5th ed. vol. vi. p. 418.

in 1380, an unfriendly critic might suggest that, as this
agreement between Lyon and Belamy was of a private
nature, so did its concluding words reveal the contemporary sentiments of the contracting parties as
regards the rule of Queen Elizabeth. But we can
adopt no such theory here, furnished as we are with
the knowledge that, had John Lyon been otherwise
than a staunch supporter of Queen Elizabeth, he would
never have been permitted by Walsingham and Cecil to
receive a charter for his school in 1571, three years
after the signature of this strange legal instrument.
Therefore it is that we believe Belamy to have been
joking when he wrote Jack Straw and Wat Tyler at the
foot of the deed in question.

It is worthy of passing mention that Uxendon, the
residence of Belamy, is a spot of antiquarian as well as
historic interest. It is spoken of as Tokyngton in older
documents, while the Knights Hospitallers of St. John
of Jerusalem formerly had a chapel at the place called
" the Cuckoo " there. Together with Preston, Canons,
Bentley, and other Harrow suburbs, it should be visited
by those interesting themselves in this history.

But to return to our subject. We have shown how
improbable it was that one of John Lyon's sapient
intelligence and reflective habit—for his school regulations prove him to have been so constituted—should have
given his whole substance for merely local objects in
the narrower sense, or have remained unmoved by the
lesson which passing events enjoined on a thoughtful
mind ; and to those conversant with the writings of the
Elizabethan age it will not seem strange that, while
evincing the forethought peculiar to the higher cast of
mind in all ages, John Lyon should have leavened his

scheme with a characteristic foible of the sixteenth
century, an epoch when men of culture believed classical teaching to be the universal panacea for ignorance,
no matter in what class of life encountered. Hence
the foundation of a *grammar-school*, wherein the dead
languages were to be placed in the forefront of the
educational battle, and this whether the peasant's
son from Pinner or Northolt was the pupil, or the
rich merchant's child from London city was to be
found repeating his *Propria quæ maribus* in company
with the offspring of that new aristocracy which inhabited the dispossessed church lands of St. Albans or
Bentley.

Letters patent and a royal charter had been obtained
from Queen Elizabeth, as early as the year 1571, for
foundation at Harrow of a free grammar-school for boys,
to the special exclusion of the female sex. John Lyon
during his lifetime was "used to give twenty marks of
lawfull money of England" annually for the teaching
of thirty poor children of the town of Harrow, reserving
his larger designs until one of the most remarkable
documents had been formulated which ever expressed
clearly and concisely a founder's intentions.

The Harrow School orders, statutes, and rules are
full of historical interest, besides pourtraying beyond
all cavil the character of his hopes. It is just as
improbable that if this foundation had remained a
parochial day-school, masters such as Sumner or
Vaughan (masters in 1770 and 1850) could, in their
respective centuries, have been attracted to Harrow,
as it clearly is impossible that the founder desired such
a paltry outcome of his life-work.

Amidst the statutes of Harrow School will be found

the following significant and, to the acute mind of Sir
William Grant, all-sufficing phrases :—

" The Schoolmaster may receive over and above the
youth of the inhabitants within this parish so many
Foreigners as the whole may be well taught and applied
and the place can conveniently contain, and of these
Foreigners he may take such stipend and wages as he
can get."

And, indeed, it is difficult to conceive how the politic
designer of an institution which must necessarily take
root before rising to maturity could express his initial
conception with greater distinctness.   Nor is it easy to
believe, as some would have us do, that if John Lyon
limited his educational sympathy for the bettering of a
few peasants and shop-keepers to the absolute exclusion
of others, he should yet have enforced on parents the
purchase of *articles de luxe* (as they certainly were in
the sixteenth century, when regarded from the point
of view of a Roxeth or Pinner cottier) ; articles, for
instance, such as sufficient paper, ink, pens, books,
candles for winter, and all other things requisite for
study, together with a bow, three shafts, bow-strings,
and a bracer, to exercise shooting —requisites, to obtain
which for one young hopeful, to say nothing of more,
would necessitate, at the time we write, resources considerably in excess of those resulting from the most
prosperous husbandry, whether calculated on average
profits of such industry in the year of grace 1590 or
1883.   And this, although by the terms of Queen
Elizabeth's charter it is most clearly expressed that
the local advantages, educational and otherwise, which
have accrued to the town—for, thanks to the great
school, it is no more a village—were to be participated

in by residents in the locality, whereby, be it noted, Harrow claims the learned Parr as one of her alumni.

But to proceed with Lyon's directions :—" Six discreet and honest men which shall bee, and be called the Governors of the Possessions, Revenues, and Goods of the said Schoole," were given control over the studies and discipline. " Meete and convenient roomes " were to be built for the master, together with a large and convenient school-house.

Religious training was carefully provided for.* All the scholars were to attend CHURCH and there hear Divine Service and the Scripture read ; while as regarded rules of conduct, John Lyon provided against scholars coming to receive instruction " uncombed, unwashed, ragged or sloven-like ; but, before all things, the master was enjoined to punish severely *swearing, lying, picking, stealing, fighting, filthiness, or wantonness of speech.*" Vices, these latter, which a contemplative survey of the world's story in 1590 will show to have then required correction almost as much in the ruling class as amongst their inferiors.

Amongst the amusements specified by John Lyon, that of archery stands out prominently ; and the picturesque exhibitions at the historic shooting-butts will ever remain famous in Harrow story, even if, in company with the Eton " montem," such celebrations have been relegated to the past. Of John Lyon himself it is not possible to know much more at this distance of time than may be learned by deciphering carefully the school statutes.

Considering how little the world really knows of

* Thirty good, learned, and godly sermons were to be preached yearly for ever in the parish church of Harrow ; two scholarships at Oxford and two at Cambridge being likewise instituted.

Shakespeare (who in 1590 was a young man) personally, notwithstanding all the research expended at Stratford-on-Avon and elsewhere, we must rest content that our more prosaic hero, John Lyon, should receive the respect afforded to scholarly forethought throughout the world, and with it the thankful regard of Harrovians in all time.

No all-powerful prince made Harrow School. No successful churchman robed the new institution with the trappings of ecclesiastical supremacy, and so rendered its constitutional reform difficult, if not impossible. It was left to a country gentleman to design a school where, though religion is treated as of primary importance, yet the rocks of ecclesiastical controversy have ever been avoided by faithful adherence to that spirit of compromise resolved on by the wisest of England's rulers who flourished in John Lyon's time.

Similar breadth of politic tolerance has likewise enabled Harrow, despite a Whig flirtation between 1745–1771, to acknowledge no peculiar politics, and so consistently to hold aloof from the Babel of party difference when other schools stooped to catch the breath of popular, if not party, approval. The Harrow authorities were thus prepared to assimilate any new elements of better instruction which experience recommended, whatever their source, not even rejecting those of foreign origin, provided that they were compatible with loyalty to the Throne and the English Church.

Tolerance in accordance with rational law and her founder's intention is, and has ever been, the key-note of Harrow government. The chief cause why she attained such excellence is so well expressed in the closing stanza of one of Mr. Howson's last songs

written for the school, that, in some sense risking
chronological anticipation, we shall leave the minstrel
to speak, and so conclude this chapter.

> And if they ask what made her great,
>   Harrow-upon-the-Hill,
> Was it her riches, pride, or fate?
>   Harrow-upon-the-Hill.
> Say that she rose because she would,
> Because her sons were wise and good,
> And bound in closest brotherhood,
>   Harrow-upon-the-Hill.

CHAPTER III.

FOUNDER'S KIN.

Who this, with stalwart mien and frosty beard?
John Lyon. He who this our school upreared.
Tercentenary Prize Poem, by H. W. E. SICHEL.

THE resuscitation of education in Harrow town must
have formed the subject of many an anxious conclave
between neighbouring magnates, aghast at the outlook
which an era of neglect presented. The cessation of
those influences which a former connection with the See
of Canterbury afforded had left the training of youth to
voluntary agencies, which from their nature could not
prove abiding.

When the archbishops surrendered their residence at
Headstone, and lost their manorial rights at Harrow,
they were no longer called upon to find the means of
instructing the neighbouring youth, possibly in that old
house which the school archives tell us was used for that
purpose.

We may conclude that, for some years before John
Lyon took the matter in hand, funds were raised in
support of the local school from those resident in and
around the pure vale of Harrow. Chief amongst these
were the Gerards of Flambards; Sir Gilbert Gerard,
Queen Elizabeth's future Attorney-General, being, from
what we know of him, unlikely to overlook such respon-

4

sibilities. Nor can we believe that Dr. Caius of Ruislip, rendered famous by Shakespeare in *The Merry Wives of Windsor*, was absent from any local educational council when designing the college on the banks of the Cam, which to this day not only bears its founder's name but retains the original connection with Harrow School, which was doubtless the outcome of a neighbourly friendship with John Lyon.

But, at Harrow, it must have been felt that friendly liberality and abundant good-will could not alone secure the town and its surroundings from comparative ignorance in a time when enlightenment was manifestly spreading abroad in the land. Funds were needed for endowment, however small, so that if the neighbouring clergy, gentry, and yeomen, Wildbluds, Norths, or Pages, cared to bestow their bounty to improve the prospects of those amidst whom they lived, their liberality might find a worthy object ready to hand—an *institution* with an assured future to support. This need we know to have been satisfied by John Lyon of Preston, who, hitherto looked upon as a struggling peasant, we now learn was a leading landowner in Middlesex. For it needs no very recondite knowledge of fourteenth-century English history to know that any possessor of lands in Preston, Kingsbury, Harrow, Ruislip,* and

---

* "This Indenture, made the Second Day of January, in the Twentifirst year of the Reign of our Soveraigne Ladie Elizabeth, by the Grace of God Queene of England, France, and Ireland, Defender of the ffaith, &c., Between Roger Goad, Doctor of Divinity, Provost of the King's College of our Blessed Lady of St. Nicholas in Cambridge, and the Scholars of the same College, being the Lawfull owners of the inheritance of the Manor of Ruyslippe, in the County of Middx., of the one partie, and John Newell Esquire." [Here follow names of the copyhold tenants of the Manor, among them John Lyon.] The deed is too long to insert. The principal effect of it is that the tenants are to enjoy

Roxeth in 1370 received feudal service which entailed responsibilities, such, for instance, as providing men to assist the lord of the soil when collecting forces to protect the realm.

When, therefore, we read of a John Lyon being admitted to lands at Kingsbury, in a court held at Edgware in 1370, and know that before the fifteenth century closed property at Preston had also been acquired,* it becomes clear that the founder of Harrow School was more than a yeoman. The title of Lord of the Manor would better apply to the owner of broad lands, which in all periods of English history has conferred local importance.

It was to shatter such homage to position, and render it a thing of the past, that Wat Tyler induced a vast multitude to believe in that serious agitation for equality which, after the Parliamentary Session of 1380, threatened Richard II.'s throne, which, together with the dignity of future kingship, was only saved by timely assertion of power and authority. Probably the King's army of 40,000 loyal retainers received a quota from Kingsbury, where dwelt the John Lyon of those days, ancestor of the man whom Harrow delights to honour.†

all their ancient rights, and to be subject in future to fines not exceeding one year's quit rent of their several holdings, on their agreeing to pay an annual composition, of the same amount as the quit rents, to the Lords. Mr. Deane, J.P., of Uxbridge, extracted this evidence from a deed in his possession. We are indebted for its appearance here to William Winckley, Esq., of Flambards, Harrow.

* For the title deeds to support these facts, see Appendix C.

† In Lord Berners' *Translation of Froissart* we read, in the account of Wat Tyler's insurrection, "they slewe in the cytie a riche marchaunt called Richarde Lyon, to whom before that tyme Watte Tyler had done seruyce in Fraunce; and one tyme this Rycharde Lyon had beaten hym whyle he was his varlet, the whiche Watte Tyler then remembered."

4 *

Throughout the fifteenth century, and when England
was in the throes of internal quarrel, the Lyon family
seem to have bent their energies upon consolidating
their Middlesex properties.   They acquired part of the
land formerly held by the Redyng family, afterwards
employed by the Harrow founder in the Free School
Government.   We do not always hear of a John Lyon
at the head of the family.   Sometimes William and
occasionally Andrew breaks the monotony of the roll
which mostly claims the familiar Johannes as a Christian
name.   In 1534, a roll of a Court held at Harrow
speaks of John Lyon becoming owner of his father's
two and a half hides,* property certainly situated in
Harrow parish, and probably that around the home of
the Lyons at Preston.   This is manifest because the
Kingsbury estate had its business matters transacted at
Edgware, not at Harrow, a fact that may be verified by
reference to John Lyon's title deeds. |

In the year 1549, when Protestant Edward VI. was
on the throne, the founder of Harrow School inherited
his father's property at Preston ; while in 1571, the year
from which the school dates its real life, we find that
John and Joan Lyon made a purchase of land in Harrow
of the Gerard family and Mr. Hill of Southwark.   Is
it too much to suppose that this transaction may have
referred to the actual site of the school buildings and
its precincts ?   The Lyon holding in and around the
hill seems gradually to have increased up to 1580, when
in the family deeds a first mention is made of the
keepers and governors of the school ; while not the least
remarkable revelation contained in the school archives

* 300 acres.   † See Appendix C.

is that which proves the Harrow founder to have held a definite office. He was *Collector secundæ solucionis cujus-dam subsidii,* or Collector of local subsidies, those, to wit, which complications in the Low Countries and threatened conflict with Spain rendered general over England during 1567. This office, in so extensive and fertile a district as that of Harrow, was necessarily entrusted to one above the mere yeoman class, and was doubtless given to a leading inhabitant of the vale which spread beneath Harrow Hill.

The Lyons of Perivale, who were, we have assumed, a collateral branch of our Lyon family, gained some noto-riety during the reign of Philip and Mary. Thomas Lyon of Perivale, or Peryfare (as it was sometimes called), a member of the Grocers' Company, was Sheriff of the City of London in the year 1550, in which year he died and was buried in St. Syth's Church, Bucklers-bury, which building is said to have touched the south side of his dwelling. This notable grocer was very wealthy, and had availed himself of the trade revival between England and those marts of the world, Antwerp and other ports of the Low Countries. The mansion of the Lyons, together with St. Syth's Church, seems to have perished in the great fire of London, but the family arms have been preserved.

They were as follows :—

Azure on a fess engrailed between three plates, each charged with an eagle's head erased. Sable a lion passant between two cinquefoils gules.

The son of this excellent citizen was named John, and, as we have already stated, gained the coveted dis-tinction of Lord Mayor in the year 1554, when Queen Mary and her Spanish consort entered the capital.

Knighthood was then conferred on the chief officers of
London; so that history knows him as Sir John
Lyon, Kt.

From the diary of Henry Machin, a citizen resident
in London at this period, we are enabled to reproduce several picturesque details of Sir John Lyon's
mayoralty.*

"The xxix day of Oct^r [1554] the nuw Lo[rd]
Mayre of London, M lyons, Groser, toke ys h[othe] at
Westmynster, & alle ye craftes off London [in] ther
barges, & w^t stremars, & ther was a g[rett] penoys
decked w^t ij topes, & stremars & m[anye] gones & drumes
& trumpetes, rohynge to Westm[ynster] vp & don, &
when thay cam hom they landed at [Sant] Powlles warff
(*id est*, Paul's wharf), & ther mett the Mayre LX in
[ther] rosett gownes & w^t targettes & gryffelyns & blu[e]
hattes, & then a goodly pagant, a gryffon w^t a chy[ld]
lyung in harnes & Sant John Baptyst w^t a lyo[n] & ij
vodys & a dulle w^t squybes bornyng, & trumppettes
blohyng & drum & flute, & then ye bachelers w^t creme-
sun damaske hodes, & then trumpeters, & ye wettes of
ye cete & so to yeld Hall to dener, for ther dynyd my
lord Chanseler & all ye nobuls & y^o spaneards & y^e
Juges and lernyd men."

The public taste for civic revelry was apparently
much the same in 1554 as it remains in 1884. But
of the lyons we may learn yet more from these quaint
records.

"The x day of September [1555] was ber[yed my]
Lade lyons, ye Mares of London, w^t a goodly [herse]

---

* Cotton MS., Vitellius F. v. f. 37b. [Printed for the Camden
Society in 1848, *Diary of Henry Machin, Citizen of London*, 1550-63,
pp. 72, 73.]

mad in sant benet sherog parryche w^t ij [   ]
branchys & xxiiij gownes of blake for [pore] men, and
thay had xxiiij torchys & w^t v [baners], one of armes &
iiij of emages & vj dos[en of] penselles & vij dosen of
skochyons & ij ha[raldes] of armes, & a C mornars in
blake & [the] althermen ffolohyng ye corsse, & after y^e
co[urt of] ye grosers, & ye morow ye masse, and M
H[   ] dyd pryche, & after a grett dener.*

The account of a welcome given by the Grocers' Company in 1561 to their distinguished alumnus, the former
Lord Mayor, presents a picture worthy of the brush
wielded by some future E. M. Ward or Marks.

[The] xvj day of June was ye Masters ye Grossers
[feast the]r dynyd my lord mare ser roger Chamley,
ser John ly[ons, ser] marten bowsse, ser wylliam
Huett, & Ser wyllam garrett, [w^t M] Loge, M John
Whytt, M Cryster, draper, M rowe, & M ch[M]
Marten, M baskerfeld, & M chamburlayn of london,
[w^t mon]y worshephull men & mony lades & gentyll-
women, [& w^t] grett chere boyth ye whettes and clarkes
syngyng & a no[mbur of] vyolles playhyng & syngyng,
& they had xxx bokes [&   ] stages.†

The Lyon family does not seem to have been by any
means long lived. As John Lyon of Preston was
destined to lose his son Zachary(?) prematurely, so had
the worthy knight to lament the loss of his heir in 1557,
when the youth was laid with his family in St. Syth's
churchyard.‡

Sir John left the bulk of his property to a nephew,

* Cotton MS. Vitellius F. v. f. 49.
† Ibid., f. 137b.
‡ [Printed for the Camden Society in 1848] Diary of Henry
Machin, Citizen of London, 1550–63, p. 218. Lyon's son was born
after or died before 1579.

Richard, son of his brother Henry Lyon, while in devising a sum of money to his great niece, Dorothy Lyon, he charged the same with "repairs of the highway from Harrow-on-the-Hill towards the Uxbridge road from the hanging wood."*

That eminent antiquary the late Mr. C. E. Long, held that the similarity of their bequests for the purpose of opening out the neighbourhood through the agency of good roads argued collusion between the two kinsmen, Lyon of Preston and Sir John Lyon of Perivale. For kinsmen Mr. Long deliberately believed them to be, giving it as his opinion that the man who founded Harrow was a nephew of Thomas Lyon, formerly resident at Perivale, or Peryfare, and therefore either first cousin or first cousin once removed to the Lord Mayor.†

This conclusion was in some degree seconded by the result of certain researches emanating from the Rolls Office, which extracted from public records particulars regarding the Lyon family and showed the men in question to have been *first cousins*. But as the discovery was hastily made while vainly endeavouring to connect an American gentleman's family with that of the founder, we are still left without certain ground for this opinion.‡

We agree with the late Mr. Long that the probabilities are very strongly in favour of the correctness of his theory; but, on the other hand, it is impossible, as the Rolls Office genealogist would have us believe, that Sir John Lyon was son of an elder brother. That the Preston Lyons represented the main stem of the family

* Extract from Will of Sir John Lyon, at Somerset House.
† Letter of the late C. E. Long.—*Harrow Gazette*, March 1856. For *résumé* of Mr. Long's research, see Appendix D.
‡ *Harrow Gazette*, February 8th, 1873.

tree no manner of doubt can now exist when we scan the records of a land roll such as might have pertained to an abbey, or have satisfied the cravings of most contemporary barons.*

But whatever the relationship, the connection can scarcely be doubtful, when neighbours of like name and identical objects in life had mutual friends whom they trusted on crucial occasions. Thus, when Lady Lyon died, Thomas Page was left her executor in the will which was proved in 1569, while when John Lyon founded Harrow, he appointed Thomas Page,† of Sudbury Court, to be one of the governors.‡

Again, Sir John Lyon's house adjoining Alperton, viz. Twyford Abbey, is only about three miles from Preston, and close to the parishes of Perivale and Willesden. These coincidences are too manifest to escape observation.§

John Lyon and his wife Joan, in their little fourteenth-century dwelling—the older parts of which are wind and water tight to this day—had, as we have said, a son

---

* See Appendix C.

† It is possible that the Pages of Wembley and Sudbury Court were connected with the Pages of Blackburn, where Archbishop Cranmer took land from Henry VIII. in exchange for land at Harrow; for among the first governors of Blackburn Grammar-School were Gilbert Gerard, Esq., Attorney-General, a Harrow governor, and Richard and William Page, of Blackburn.

‡ Letter of Mr. C. E. Long, in *Harrow Gazette*, March 1861.

§ The subjoined pedigree, in Appendix D., was drawn up by Mr. Sims of the British Museum, in conjunction with Mr. Edward Scott. Great experience has enabled them to construct out of the Lyon deeds a family tree, which conveys knowledge of the founder's family far in advance of anything previously discovered. The connection between the Preston and Twyford branches being derived from other sources less direct than those given in the text, the names of Thomas Lyon of Perivale, Sir John Lyon, and his immediate descendants have been placed in a different quarter of the document.

and heir, Zachary(?), whose patrimony consisted of such
portions of John Lyon's land as was not expressly
mentioned in the famous Will, the original of which has
so mysteriously disappeared.*

If Lyon's infant had lived until manhood, Harrow
School would not have been as well-to-do financially as
it is, and this is not saying much.   But it was ordered
otherwise.

In the Harrow parish register occurs this extract :—
" Anno 1583, the xith day of May, [buried] Zachary
Lion."   Another entry, dated nine years afterwards,
reads, " [Buried] the iiiith day, John Lion," in a different hand, " of Preston."   The following note is written
underneath, apparently of a later date, " John Lyon, the
founder of the school, deceased 3d October 1592; see
the brass plate in the church."   The month October
is omitted in the register, but September occurs to
another entry just above.   Lastly, on August 30th,
1608, " was buryed wydowe Lion of Preston," leaving
the lands and hereditaments in Middlesex and Bedfordshire free to be devoted for the newly-designed school.

That the subsequent erection of the red brick building
was not by any means the outcome of an ill-digested
design, is shown by the fact that amongst the school
papers there has lately been found a complete plan,
a tracing of which will be found at the commencement
of this chapter, differing in some degree from the present structure as regards proportion, but still the work
of one who had something *very* like the fourth-form
room in his mind's eye.

* Sections 11 and 12 of John Lyon's Will show that he provided for the possibility of leaving issue, and yet protected his
scholastic design.   Lyon undoubtedly had a son, though the name
is doubtful.

Claimants to the position of founder's kin are legion.
Holland and America send their quota, while Scotland
has her representative. In England they abound, while
an Hibernian flavour clings to the Christian name of
at least one applicant who desires to be considered as
a member of a family whose crown of honour consists
in relationship to the Harrow founder. Of these the
Smiths of Eastboro, near Watford, boast the strongest
traditional claim, the family belief being that through
a marriage with Anne Lyon, of the Ruislip branch,
they are of the founder's kin; and although divers
attempts to unravel this genealogical knot have proved
unfruitful, we must lend an ear to such a strongly-
rooted tradition.*

* Several families in the neighbourhood of Harrow assert that
they are of Founder's kin, particularly those descended from the
Smiths, formerly of Eastboro, Herts, near Watford and Pinner.
The following singular and amusing Statement of one of these
claimants is here inserted:

Statement of Martha Claxton with regard to her being of Kin to
     John Lyon, Founder of Harrow School, &c. &c.

I am the widow of Henry Claxton, to whom I was married at
Harrow; am the daughter of John and Sarah Smith, formerly
Aldwin; was born at Eastboro near Watford, baptized at home,
and registered either at Watford, Rickmansworth, Ruislip, or
Bushey. My father was the son of William and Ann (or Mary)
Smith who was the daughter of one John Lyon, who I suppose
lived near Aldbury, as my grandmother came up from that part
about the time of her marriage to my grandfather. She had
brothers named John, William, and James, and a sister Jane, or
at any rate I was always given to understand they were my great
uncles and great aunt. I remember my great uncles John and
James; they resided in the parish of Ruislip, and were small
farmers. I also remember my great aunt Jane. I remember my
grandfather Smith used to say to my father " Why don't you send
your sons to Harrow School which is their birthright? " I have
always been given to understand as long as I can remember that
we were of the same family as the Founder of Harrow School.
About the year 1806 or 1808 I came over to Harrow on business;

It would be vain to pretend that research has enabled
one to form any very definite idea of the personality of
the ·man who, despite its proved pre-existence, really
founded Harrow School. With respect to his pedigree
more solid results have been obtained. Mr. Edward

a Miss Hill came with me, and on passing the School I made the
remark " See how my old uncle shakes ;" it was a very windy day,
and I was alluding to the Lion which supported the weather-cock.
Some time after this the parish went to law with the Governors of
the School ; one of the most active persons on behalf of the parish
was one of the Churchwardens, Mr. John Foster, to whom, somewhere about this time, the above Miss Hill was married, and she
mentioned to him the circumstance of my making the remark
respecting the weather-cock, which excited his curiosity that he
came to me to learn more particulars, and he was so satisfied with
my statement, that he requested me without delay to procure all
the requisites that could be obtained, or anything else that might
throw some light upon the matter. In accordance with his request,
and through the hopes held out of the advantages that would
accrue to my family should we be fortunate enough to prove a
relationship to the Founder, I and my sister Sally Dean, went to
a great expense in searching the registers of Ruislip, Aldbury,
Tring, Harefield, &c. ; but not being accustomed to make searches,
and the expenses in consequence being so great, we were obliged to
give up the pursuit. *We however had the satisfaction of tracing
back our pedigree for a period of one hundred and seventy years,
within Forty-four years of the Founder's death.* A Powter Plate
which belonged to my cousin Mary Smith, (which with many
others had been in my family a great number of years,) was taken
with the registers found by the said Mr. Foster, to the Herald's
College, where he was told that there was no doubt but that we
were of the same family as the Founder, from the Arms engraven
upon the plate, but that as the Arms had not been paid for,
renewed, or something to that effect, for a period of Two Hundred
years, they were lost. The plate was returned, but I rather think
the registers were left at the College. My Grandfather and Grandmother Smith (whose maiden name was Lyon) lived at Eastboro,
between Pinner and Watford, and I remember hearing it said that
the Royal Family lunched at their house on the first day of
hunting. One of my relations has a plate with " W. L." upon it, but
all the plates that had the Arms or Crest upon them I am afraid
have long been melted down, in consequence of the high price at
one time given for that metal, and the low circumstances of those
into whose hands they came. My age is from 77 to 80 years.
My Father and Mother I believe were married at Ruislip. I have

Scott, by reading and arranging the various muniments
in chronological order, has discovered more about this
good man's ancestry than the most hopeful student
could have hitherto deemed feasible, and he has pieced
together a pedigree up to 1580, which, if it cannot
claim to be complete, is at least trustworthy so far as
it goes.

We only wish that the brass in Harrow Church had
been dealt with by someone of Mr. Scott's antiquarian
talents and kindred enthusiasm. In the year 1847 the
brass was absolutely taken up from the floor, where it
marked the actual spot under which lay John, (?)Zachary,
and Joan Lyon, and placed on a mural tablet by Flaxman, whereon the great Dr. Parr wrote one of his
famous Latin inscriptions. But the mistaken if doubtless well-meaning actors in this most deplorable scene
contrived to tear away part of the founder's left foot,
both feet of his wife Joan, and the whole of the child's
(Zachary's ?) figure, whilst, piling horror on horror, they
actually left only a seat and a flue to mark the place
where John Lyon's remains really do lie.

Now, surely, if the adage be true that it is never too
late to mend, a simple but durable plate should

always been told that my Grandmother's family in every generation endeavoured to keep up the name of "John."

The foregoing Statement is true and correct, to the best of my
belief, it having been carefully read over to me.

As witness my hand this thirteenth day of February in the year
of our Lord One thousand Eight Hundred and Forty-five.

MARTHA CLAXTON.

Witness, JAMES CLOWES, Harrow.

Handbook to Harrow-on-the-Hill (1850), pp. 48–50.

Mr. C. E. Long, *Harrow Gazette*, March, 1861, writes telling
how Lady Lyon, widow of Sir John, left a profusion of plate
with Lion (*sic*) covers. In Appendix D. the Lyon Pedigree will
be found, together with notes based on the latest researches.

straightway be placed on the afore-named spot, bearing
the names of John, (?)Zachary, and Joan Lyon. It
would tell its own tale to those who love Harrow history.

But we must fain rest content with small mercies,
after ages of forgetfulness, threatening soon to merge
into perpetual ignorance. For had not Dr. H. M.
Butler, during the year 1883, bethought him of Mr.
Edward Scott's readily-afforded skill, the School
Charter and the accompanying deeds and seals would
have remained still exposed to the danger of the imminent destruction which confinement in the venerable
school-chest necessarily entailed. They were nearly
obliterated by damp, and lay in peril of total annihila-
tion ; indeed, in the opinion of those experts at the
British Museum who, with reverent and admiring appreciation, have scanned this remarkable collection of
historic muniments, the succour rendered by Mr.
Edward Scott came none too soon. Had another generation been allowed to elapse, all hope of learning the
truth concerning the founder's origin and family would,
the British Museum authorities believe, have passed
away for ever.

It will be remembered of Dr. H. M. Butler's head-
mastership, amongst other distinctions, that through
his initiation the charter and its attendant manuscripts
were brought to light, and the form of John Lyon
made to stand out less indistinctly through the mists
of time.

There is now reason to hope that all the deeds will
be duly catalogued, and that Harrovians past and
present will have such access to these scholastic
treasures as due care for their safety shall warrant.

We are fully aware that the governors owe it as a

duty to posterity to take effectual measures to prevent the Harrow archives from being for one instant in danger from fire, theft, or any other means of permanent destruction or dispersion ; but, fortunately the photographic art is available for the preservation of the form and tenor of these records, and we believe that it will be fully utilised in this worthy cause.[*]

There is no need to despair of something more definite being yet learnt as to the personality and later lineage of the founder. We had cherished a secret hope that the report current amongst local Harrow antiquaries was not ill-founded, and that amongst Lord Northwick's muniments would be found such information as the lords of Flambards might not unnaturally have amassed. The present Baron promptly responded to the request made to him, and after due research produced a copy of the well-known rules and regulations; also a rough presentment of the charter, both of the originals being found amidst the lately deciphered archives. Where, then, let us ask, is our founder's will ? No will or administration of his effects has been found either in the Prerogative Court of Canterbury or in the Bishop of London's office.

We would gladly have closed this chapter by adducing proof of converse between the founder and thinking men who lived near Harrow, such as Dr. Caius,[†] Sir

---

[*] The order has been given to preserve the muniments.

[†] The tradition of Dr. Caius' friendship with John Lyon has been confirmed by the evidence afforded of the Founder's connection with Ruislip, in which parish Dr. Caius resided.

Mr. F. H. Deane, J.P., of East View, Uxbridge, contributes the following, in addition to producing evidence previously mentioned that John Lyon was a Copyholder at Ruislip :—

" In a paper dated 1649, and entitled *The Valuation of Ruislippe*,

John Lyon, Sir Gilbert Gerard, Henry Lyon of Ruislip, and Sir Nicholas Bacon at Gorhambury.* Strong as is the presumption that the subject of local education occupied their attention, we have no references to give which can settle the matter with any surety. In the absence of evidence, we may claim indulgence for avowedly giving rein to fancy and assuming that our founder enjoyed the advantages of such society.

This we do know for certain. John Lyon provided the funds which established Harrow School, thereby justifying the respect which many who read these pages feel for his name, and in their eyes at least conferring some interest on the most imperfect details connected with the founder's kin.

containing the number of acres and the valew of them by the yeare, occurs the following :—

	Acres.	Roods.	£	s.	d.
" ' House John Lyon	27	000	17	12	6 '

"Again, in a *Booke of Entreys* of all surrenders and licenses that passed between the manor of Ruislip and King's College, Cambridge (The Kings Colledge of our Blessed Lady and St. Nicholas in Cambridge) there occurs the following amongst other entries—

" ' At a Court Barron held for the Manor of Ruislip the 29th day of April 1687.

" ' John Lyung surrᵉ a cottadge in part lying neere ye town to Samuel Coch and his heirs,

2 with rent	. .	0 4
2 comp rent	. .	0 4 ' "

It is not inconceivable that Shakespeare himself may have occasionally joined their circle, as *The Merry Wives of Windsor* indicates his intimacy with Dr. Caius, as well as with places bordering on the Ruislip neighbourhood.

* As Sir N. Bacon and Sir G. Gerard were joint treasurers of Gray's Inn, and as, moreover, the regulations of Sir N. Bacon's foundation at St. Alban's are in many respects similar to the Harrow regulations, we may infer that Lyon communicated directly or indirectly with Bacon. But we may hold a pious opinion that Lyon, having more leisure than the knight, was the chief author of the said regulations.

CHAPTER IV.

THE DARK AGES OF HARROW SCHOOL.

Gleamed the star of hope before us.

Constant; School Song, by ARCHDEACON FARRAR.

It is worthy of remark that the Reformation which
threatened to destroy Eton* may be said to have created
Harrow, but the younger foundation was not without its
own difficulties and dangers arising out of legal disputes
about the interpretation of John Lyon's will. This
worthy had provided that a school-house should be
erected immediately after his widow's death, and had set
aside a sum for that purpose, but had not covenanted
for any diminution in the expenditure upon the several
highways between Harrow and London to be defrayed
out of his estate.

John Lyon died in October 1592, and when in 1608
his relict, Johan Lyon, was laid by his side in Harrow
Church, the governors began the building operations
distinctly enjoined upon them by the founder. But in
carrying out this part of the founder's plan, the keepers

---

* That Henry VIII. did contemplate the extinction of Eton
will be seen by reference to Creasy, *Eminent Etonians*. p. 74;
also to Maxwell Lyte, *History of Eton*, p. 121.

of the school overstepped the mark to the extent of
£300, for which amount attempts were made to hold
them personally liable.

Hence the exhibition of an information in Chancery
against the governors dated 1610 for alleged misapplica-
tion of the founder's money.* The case came before
Lord Ellesmere, a famous judge of that time, who, while
carefully guarding the future roadways between Harrow
and London, still freed the school government from
personal responsibility.†

John Lyon seems to have been judicious in his choice
of the first governors of his free school. John Page
represented a family destined to remain in his manor of
Wembley for over two hundred years, while Thomas
Page, a cadet of the same stock, rented land at Sudbury
of the Norths. Again, Thomas Redyng represented a
family located at Headstone in 1451,‡ while Edlyn of
Woodhall was also a tenant of the Archbishop's.

But the connection most useful to Harrow was undoubtedly that of Gerard; although Queen Elizabeth's
eminent Attorney-General never lived to see the school
built. Our readers may be reminded that Sir Gilbert
Gerard defended the Princess Elizabeth in Queen
Mary's time with conspicuous ability and consequent
success. Moreover, a chronicler of *res Harrovianæ*
must not forget that Sir Gilbert Gerard's grandmother
was a Byron of Newstead,§ the family to which Harrow

* *Additional Manuscript*, No. 29,254, British Museum, contain-
ing a description of Harrow generally, by Taylor Combe, an old
Harrovian.
† *Ibid.*
‡ *London and Middlesex Archæological Society*, vol. iii. p. 188.
§ William Gerard, of Ince, in Lancashire, married a daughter
of Sir John Byron, of Newstead. His son William was the father

stands indebted for one of her chief ornaments. Into
the hands of the Gerard family fell the property of
Flambards (a name preserved in the High Street of
Harrow to this day), owned by a Sir John Flambard
in the reign of Edward III. But not until 1609 did
William Gerard, one of the first chosen governors
of Harrow, and brother to the Attorney-General,
die—the first of his name seised of this estate, which
remained in his family for several generations.

It is remarkable that at the period of Lord Ellesmere's
above-mentioned decision (1610), Harrow is spoken of
as a populous place; * and indeed there is reason to
believe that it might be so described according to the
then prevalent notion of a country village. A contemporary author, Norden (perhaps personally acquainted
with the locality, for he lived at Hendon), writes of
the school, possibly during John Lyon's lifetime, in
the following terms :—" There is a schoole at Harrow,
as yet no free schoole, but intended, whereunto one
John Lyon hath given to be employde after his decease
£300,† and £30 per annum for a master and £10 for
an usher. It is a good president, *but I fear too good
to be often followed.*" This expression of opinion proves
Norden's knowledge about schools to have been limited
to his own locality, as instances of such benefactions
are numerous during the sixteenth century.

At this period the best corn near London was procured at Harrow, so that the Tudor sovereigns were

of that Sir Gilbert Gerard who, when Attorney-General, figured
so conspicuously as an original governor of Harrow School.—
Burke, *Extinct Peerages*, p. 217.

* *Harleian Manuscript*, 2211.

† The £300 was the limit for building purposes which the first
governors overstepped.

wont to replenish their own tables therefrom.* Thus
we read :—

As Coln came on along, and chanc'd to cast her eye
Upon that neighbouring hill where Harrow stands so high,
She Perivale perceived, pranked up with wreaths of wheat,
And with exulting terms thus glorying in her seat :
" Why should not I be coy, and of my beauties nice,
Since this my goodly grain is held of greatest price.
No manchet can so well the courtly palate please
As that made of the meal fetched from my fertile leayes."
Drayton, Poly-olbion, Song 16, written in the reign of
James I., about 1620.†

This condition of things has given place to the production of hay that meets no superior in the London
market, so that there is manifestly no decline in the
fertility of the district.

About twenty years after Norden's previously-quoted
mention of John Lyon's bequest, viz. 1614, Ben Jonson,
himself an old Westminster, relates in his comedy—
*Bartholomew Fair ; the Adventures of one Bartholomew
Cokes, a tall young Squire of Harrow-on-the-Hill*—how,
after various revels at the fair, such as scrambling for
pears from a stall which has been upset, a bystander
remarks of Cokes, " a delicate great boy ; methinks

---

* Harrow Hill is the highest in this county, under which lies
fruitful fields, especially about Heston [doubtless Headstone],
which yields such fine flour that the King's bread was formerly
made thereof, and Queen Elizabeth received no money from
these villages, but took her wheat in kind for her own use.—
Burton, *Admirable Curiosities,* p. 85.

† In the time of Richard II., the lord of Harrow manor had a
custom that by summons of his bailiff upon a general *reap day,*
then called *Magna Precaria,* the tenants should do a certain quan-
tity of work for him free, every tenant owning a chimney-pot
being obliged to find a man.—W. C. Hazlitt, *Tenures of Land,*
p. 146.

he out-scrambles them all. I cannot persuade myself but that he goes to grammar-school yet, and plays the truant to-day."* This is certainly one of the earliest contemporary allusions to Harrow as a place of learning.

It is difficult to keep clear of the region of tradition when taking a last glance at the career of John Lyon. We know so little for certain that the imagination is inclined to elevate mere rumour to the level of sober fact. For instance, it is stated in *The Harrovian* (Feb. 1870) that John Lyon may probably have been an old Westminster, because, when introducing the monitorial system into Harrow, he evinced acquaintance with the customs of St. Peter's College, Westminster. Again, the legend is repeated which attributes the Harrow founder's broad acres to the rumoured gifts bestowed by pilgrims in search of health, as payment for the salubrious draughts from certain medicinal springs near Preston. This story would doubtless have held its own but for the proof furnished by the Harrow muniments that Lyon was living in 1571 upon land which had belonged to those of his name from the reign of Edward III.

Each British Museum or Rolls Office document which mentions the Harrow founder bears witness to his local importance. For instance, in 1562, he heads the rental list of Harrow Hill, where his name stands recorded in company with those of Page, Belamy, and Grenhill— names not unfamiliar to our readers. Again, in 1580, he figures in a Harrow lease as Bailiff and Parish Officer†

---

* Ben Jonson, *Bartholomew Fair*, act iv. sc. 1, quoted in *The Harrovian*, Feb. 26, 1870.

† *School Archives.*

(Prepositus et Bedellus), and we have previously shown
him to have been Collector subsidii ; while, most important fact of all, the Clerk of the Signet responsible for
Harrow district in 1579 looked upon John Lyon as the
man best able therein to make a (forced) loan of £50
(equal to about £600 of our money) for State needs.
Sir Gilbert Gerard, demurring to this, writes to the said
Clerk, one Johns, saying that Lyon should not be
pressed for such a sum, his means of procuring ready
money being not in accordance with the extent of his
landed property, which, as the astute lawyer adds, had
been increased by purchase and assigned to the erection
of a school at Harrow. The letter* is very curious,
and offers evidence of John Lyon's self-denial in
straining his means for the purpose of founding Harrow
School.

* A paper has turned up in the Rolls Office which is a holograph
letter from Sir Gilbert Gerard, the Attorney-General, in 1579,
to Mr. Johns, who desired to borrow £50 from John Lyon.
Gerard begs him not to make the demand, and so put pressure on
Lyon to make him sell lands which he (Gerard) knew were
intended to endow the School at Harrow. The letter tells us that
John Lyon was childless A.D. 1579, so that his son (? Zachary,
buried in the year 1583) died in infancy, or else before 1579.
Gerard's anxiety about the loan suggests that Lyon's munificence
taxed his resources severely. We give the original letter (the
words in parentheses are crossed out in the manuscript) :—

" Mr. Johns, I perceyve by my neighbore John Lyon that he ys
yet called on for the lone of l^u, and ȳf I shuld say what I knowe
of hym, surely I thynke that he hayth not somoche redy money
nor ys not alyke to make so much presently of hys goodes, for in
dede he hayth lately bought summe land and for the same dyd
disburse all he was well abyll to make, and restyth yet indettyd
for summe part thereof, and to dryve hym to sell any of yt were
pety, for I knowe hys meaneyng ys to bestowe hys laudes vppon
the erreccion of a scoole in the paryshe of Harrowe, becawse he
hayth noe chylderen (there be summe of hys neighbores spared
wyche he thynketh appere moche better abyll then he is butt)

John Lyon's brass tablet in Harrow Church contains a rough portrait of him, which tells of the times, although unfortunately it leaves no very clear impression of what the subject's living features may have been. Yet much antiquarian interest undoubtedly clings to this relic of the glorious days of good Queen Bess.

Below John Lyon's effigy on the famous brass are the following words :—

HEARE LYETH BVRYED THEE BODY OF IOHN LYON LATE OF PRESTON IN THIS PARISH YEOMAN DECEASED THE . IIITH . DAYE OF OCTOBER IN THE YEARE OF OVR LORD . 1592 . WHO HATH FOVNDED A FREE GRAMMER SCHOOLE IN THIS PARISH TO HAVE CONTINVANCE FOR EVER AND FOR MAINTENAVNCE THEREOF AND FOR RELEYFE OF THE POORE AND OF SOME POORE SCHOLLERS IN THE VNIVER-SITYES REPAYRINGE OF HIGH WAYES, AND OTHER GOOD AND CHARITABLE VSES HATH MADE CONVAYAVNCE OF LANDS OF GOOD VALVE TO A CORPORACION GRAVNTED FOR THAT PVRPOSE PRAYSE BE TO THE AVTHOR OF AL GOODNES WHO MAKE VS MYNDEFVLL TO FOLLOWE HIS GOOD EXAMPLE.

Harrovians will doubtless hail with satisfaction the scantiest illustrative details which research has given them concerning their prescient founder. His views on

becawse he hayth noe charge of chylderen, therefore summe doe preferre hym to thys charge to spare theyme selffes. And thys ys all I cane say of hym, and soe I byde yow hertely farewell and pray yow helpe hym as you may.

        " From Sydbery thys xijth of August 1579,
                " Yours, assurydly,

                        " G. GERRARD."

(On the back)

        " To hys very frende Mr. Johns, one of the Clerks of the Signet."

    Rolls Office, *State Papers, Domestic Series*, 1579, vol. xxvi.

education must be studied somewhat in detail, as the mere mention of the statutes which direct the course of young life in his free grammar-school gives little adequate idea of their scope and meaning.

School was to begin at *six* in the morning or *as early as boys could assemble, taking into consideration the season of the year and the distance of their homes.* Prayers were to be read the first thing in the morning and the last thing at night, while a programme of almost uninterrupted work made a whole school-day such as might delight the most rapacious educational glutton of our own times. Latin and Greek formed, as we have previously stated, the staple of Harrow learning. Just before breaking up for the night, the master was to give the interpretation of three Latin words, and the scholars were called upon to repeat them at school on the ensuing morning.

Youths who were specially backward were placed in a class by themselves, and called the Peties. The rest were divided into five Forms, a list of which, with the books used in each, we subjoin.*

The First Form.—Principles of grammar, *Qui mihi Discipulus, &c.*; select epistles of Cicero and Cato's *Disticha.*

The Second Form.—Grammar (more advanced); Æsop's Fables; Cato, *Dialogi Erasmi, Mancini Carmina de iiii Virtutibus.*

The Third Form.—The rest of the grammar; Terence, Cicero *Ad familiares*, Ovid's *Tristia*, and the art of writing epistles.

The Fourth Form.—Cicero, *De Amicitia, de Senectute,*

---

* This dissection of John Lyon's statutes we owe to *The Harrovian* for February 1870, p. 85.

and *de Finibus*, Virgil's *Bucolics* and *Georgics*, Horace, Prose and Verse exercises, and Greek Grammar.

The Fifth Form.—Virgil's *Æneid*, Cæsar's *Commentaries*, Cicero *De Naturâ Deorum*, Livy, Demosthenes, Isocrates, Hesiod, Heliodorus, Dionysius Halicarnassius; Verses and Themes.

The absence of Greek poets from John Lyon's list of studies will be especially remarked by the classical scholar, while others will deplore the omission of any notices of the English tongue, of history, and of general literature.

No doubt the curriculum was an excellent introduction to the pursuit of the learned professions, but what we now understand by a general education was singularly defective, by comparison with the present standard of most schools.

We cannot believe that exclusive classical teaching could do more than sharpen the ordinary scholar's memory, furnish him with a stock of general maxims, and possibly elevate his taste, but scarcely store his mind in the manner that was requisite, even so early in the seventeenth century, for effective participation in the struggle of life.* We can scarcely read the story of those troublous days so soon to ensue after James I.'s demise in 1625 without regretting the apparently almost universal ignorance of the British people concerning monarchical prerogatives and their own constitutional rights, matters unfortunately and more or less necessarily

---

* We gain little by familiarising ourselves with Greek or Latin speech unless we enter by sympathy and imagination into the innermost existence of antiquity.—(Howard Staunton, *Great Schools*, Introduction, p. 22). This thought is also clearly expressed in Mr. G. O. Trevelyan's address to the students of Dublin University in October 1883.

relegated to the attention of professional experts, little careful of the divers interests needing guardianship when poor people had lost feudal protection, and exchanged it for theoretical, but, alas! not recognised liberty. But we must not ascribe to these statutes, whether originated by Sir Nicholas Bacon or John Lyon, faults of omission which were peculiar to the days during which the authors lived, when the desire to imbibe ancient lore seems to have been the necessary concomitant of the artistic revival in painting, sculpture, and architecture, which thus early had, in a rude form, reached England.

No *Sixth Form*, be it observed, appears in John Lyon's original Harrow scheme, and, indeed, we learn that it was not until the eighteenth century (1775) that the now famous institution gained its footing.[*] At the head of his school, John Lyon appointed three monitors, two of whom had it as an especial duty to report every Friday to the master any offences committed; while, to press the monitorial system to its logical conclusion, a third monitor had in turn to watch over the demeanour of his fellows, and to keep the master informed thereof. Punishment, which it is interesting to mark, was *not to be inflicted by the monitors themselves,*[†] consisted of MODERATE chastisement with rod, also ferule on the hand for *slight offences* : conclusive evidence, we take it, that the founder desired the afore-named rod to be kept

---

[*] *Harrow School List for* 1775, in collection by Dr. George Butler.

[†] At the risk of anticipating, we may here state that the monitorial privilege of whopping or caning, under restrictions, did not gain footing at Harrow until late in the 18th century. Dr. Parr, who left in 1771 for Stanmore, assured the late Dr. George Butler that no such custom was in vogue during his Harrow days, and that, therefore, the use in question must have crept in gradually when Harrow was under Heath and Drury.

in terrorem, and reserved for the graver faults which public opinion holds it should correct. Any severe chastisement in sympathy with the brutal instincts of the times, we happily find distinctly forbidden.

Considering the length of time marked out for close study in the original Harrow programme, it is a relief to read of the prescribed amusements, which were practically those in vogue amongst the youth of the sixteenth century. An Harrovian might drive a top, toss a hand-ball, run, and, above all, indulge in archery, which at that period was the national sport. An old illustration, made within a year or two of the school foundation, testifies that shooting with bow and arrow was *facile princeps* among the games of London citizens, who may be seen crowding around the ground much as, on a larger scale more in accordance with the increased population, anxious Londoners throng Lord's or Kennington Oval on a great match day. The most popular amusement then in vogue was consequently chosen by John Lyon when he established archery at Harrow.

To this choice the school owes one of the most engaging and picturesque phases of its varied career, viz. the annual shooting for the silver arrow at butts, situated near Mr. Stogdon's present house, to the west of the London Road, a ceremony uninterruptedly held for at least 170 years. We may, however, venture to try to comfort those who, in sympathy with Mr. Howard Staunton, in his *Great Schools of England*,* lament the continued disuse of a graceful, and by no means defunct, recreation, by expressing a strong opinion that pursuit of the national game *par excellence*, which cricket is now allowed to be, quite fulfils in spirit the intention of

* P. 272.

John Lyon, who clearly desired that Harrow boys
should hold their own in the world's strife, be it
intellectual or physical. The abolition of the time-
honoured archery at butts will be recorded in its proper
place in this history.

No doubt it is open to any future band of Harrovians,
jealous of their founder's intention, to fulfil to the letter
his behest concerning an exercise which, as Mr. Staunton
phrases it, is both graceful and invigorating. Thus we
see at the outset of his scheme the sage Lyon providing
for the bodily wants, without which the *mens sana in cor-
pore sano* cannot long be preserved; but we nevertheless
wonder that he should have seen fit to clog natural
enjoyment in the playground by enjoining on his monitors to encourage a continued flow of Latin from
youthful tongues when their elders were scarcely able to
mouth their own language. For the phraseology of
Stowe or Norden, if quaint and characteristic of their
surroundings, needs the Shakespearian genius to elevate
its rhythm, and does not under ordinary circumstances
flow with the ease and grace of our modern speech
as illustrated by Macaulay or Froude.

Lastly, and most important of all, John Lyon
enjoined a strict attendance to the principles of religion,
directing, as we have previously averred, the daily reading of prayers both morning and evening. All the
school were to be taught the Lord's Prayer, the articles
of religion, and the Church Catechism, while they were
to go to Church regularly on Sunday, and the master
was to speak to them afterwards on matters of religion.
It is, therefore, no infringement of the wholesome
national, and in a non-party sense liberal policy, which
was from the very outset prevalent at Harrow, to declare

that the school *as a body* must receive the religious
education enjoined by the Church of England, so that
whatever exceptions the governors may legally make—
and their power is alike wholesome and unquestioned—
still a belief in Christianity is the very ground-work of
the education provided at Harrow ; nor can a different
policy ever there obtain, without a gross contempt of
the good founder's intention. After commanding cleanli-
ness, tidiness, and punctuality, John Lyon winds up
with a wise proviso that, under differing circumstances
and in default of a clear understanding concerning any
of the matters touched on, the governors and master
were empowered to make such alterations in the management and regulation of the school as they should think
necessary. And the writer in *The Harrovian* argues
wisely and with truth when he declares that in so acting
the Harrow founder proved that he entertained a proper
appreciation of the requisites of real advancement.[*]

Whether or not John Lyon had been at Westminster
must, we fear, remain an unsolved question to the end
of time, but in sympathy, as we have stated, he clearly
accorded with the system in vogue there, while he likewise probably studied William of Wykeham's famous
Winchester statutes, and for the historic *Disce* and
Discede, together with its disagreeable alternative, the
rod, substituted a year's probation for the idle and in-
competent, after which period the master was to remove
the incorrigible from Harrow.

When Queen Elizabeth confirmed the charter of St.
Albans Grammar-School, which, dating from 1145, had
been re-established by Edward VI. in 1543, and approved by Mary in 1559, Sir Nicholas Bacon, then

[*] *Harrovian*, Feb. 12, 1870, p. 85.

resident at Gorhambury, composed certain rules and
regulations which, as has already been stated, bear a
strong affinity to those drawn up by John Lyon for
Harrow.*

The instructions concerning the finding of paper,
ink, pens, lights, and books, together with the materials
for archery, were common to Harrow and St. Albans.†
It is not, therefore, improbable that Sir Nicholas
Bacon may have been one of Lyon's friends and a
collaborator in his scheme.

We shall not here pause to consider the obvious
wisdom of the well-known Foreigner clause, justified
as John Lyon's forethought has been proved to be by
a splendid success, consecrated as regards its lawful
stability by legal acumen in succeeding ages.   Probably
knowledge of the collapse which has befallen scores of
sixteenth-century grammar-schools better endowed than
Harrow, but limited to their several localities, would have
opened the eyes of the Harrow townspeople, and prevented their several attempts first to narrow Harrow
influence and then erase its fame.

We are fortunately not destitute of material wherewith
to form a picture of Harrow when the thirty poor
scholars were profiting from the charity of John Lyon,
who in his lifetime devoted twenty marks a year to the
education of young children ; this bounty being perhaps
designed to keep alive the embers of a former educational institution.   Passages in the school minutes go
to show that from the earliest times of which record is
kept, dames were appointed at Sudbury, the Weald,

* *Public Schools*, by author of *Etoniana*, p. 260.
† Carlisle, *Endowed Grammar Schools*, vol. i. pp. 508–9, and
517–18.

and other outlying hamlets, whose duties were to teach
reading and the elements of Christianity.*

This entrusting of those of tender age to female care
has been by some believed to have originated more
particularly at Eton, where the system has doubtless
been found of the greatest advantage when mere children
have been thrown into the world of public-school life.
But the lately-explored archives show that this custom
also pertained to old Harrow life, where it was a recognised feature from the very beginning.   Anyhow, we
also have direct mention of some place of gathering
extant before 1610, when the school accounts were first
carefully kept, inasmuch as we there read of payment
for work done on the *old house*,† and this when Harrow
was alive with the bustle and excitement of erecting the
Fourth Form room and the left wing of the school-
house with which Harrovians of all ages are so familiar.

In 1580, during Lyon's lifetime, license was granted
to John Lyon, Joan his wife, and the keepers or governors of possessions, revenues, and goods of the Free
Grammar-School of John Lyon at Harrow-on-the-Hill
in Middlesex, to lease for forty-one years lands at
Harrow Hill.

Surviving her husband some sixteen years,‡ Joan
Lyon died in 1608, and the family funds became then
applicable to such fulfilment of the founder's design as
circumstances allowed.§   Nor did the governors enume-

---

* *School Archives.*
† *School Account Book*, 1610.
‡ John Lyon died in 1592.
§ It is worthy of remark that the early Governors seem to have
so far yielded to the dictates of human nature as to have consulted
the interests of their kinsmen when contracting for the school
building. Hence, in 1610, we read of £125 11s. 6d. owing to Mr.
Felix Gerard for bricks.

rated in Appendix A., who took up the trust in 1610 leave a stone unturned to make a reality of the Free Grammar-School. *The Harrovian* for February 12th, 1870, contains the following well-considered remarks in a chapter on early school history :—" We have now to inquire when the school was actually built. Six governors were appointed . . . and were enjoined if, on the death of John Lyon and Johan his wife, the school had not been yet built, to take for three years £300 of the rent which had been set aside for the repairing of highways and apply them to the erection of the school."

Now, as Johan Lyon did not die until 1608, it is, as *The Harrovian* points out, impossible that the school could have been finished, as some writers have it, in 1595. Indeed, the archives show that 1615 was the date ; and some time after that we read of items only lately accounted for which had to do with the left wing of the old schools. Hence the interest appertaining to the fact that school had hitherto been held in what was then designated the " Old House."

The Harrow account-books relating to this time are very curious. We read of a Mr. Thomas Page, of Roxey, being chosen as builder, to whom was paid £306 16s. 6d. straight away, while consignments of oaken boards,* glass,† and wood for flooring, alternate with records telling of the erection of a school-gate, together with the cost of the very iron chest in which these archives were preserved up to their temporary removal to the British Museum in November 1883, and also an estimated cost of the same

* 1,000 of oaken boards, £4 10s.
† 290 feet of glass, £7 5s.

account-books out of which we have culled these memoranda.*

But it is to the earlier records of the school itself that our readers will turn with the greater interest, where we learn that in 1615 the governors met and were able to resolve that the number of free scholars should not exceed forty at first (an advance on the original number), which injunction, frequently repeated, proves that thus early in her history the benevolent intentions of the Harrow founder were so appreciated by the neighbourhood that the demand for education exceeded the supply for which he had provided. Moreover, it was resolved to purchase the following literature; *viz.*, a Rider's Dictionary, a Calepin Dictionary, Cooper's Dictionary, Ovid with a Commentary, Virgil with Servius' Commentary, Demosthenes and Æschines, Scapula's Lexicon, whilst last, not least, is found an English Bible. The governors then agreed that they "by the grace of God doe yeerely meete att two several times from henceforward, namely, on the Munday before Michaelmas and the Munday before Easter."†

The first head-master mentioned in the school archives was by name Bradley. He held the post for scarcely two years, viz. 1613 to 29th April 1615, when the Rev. William Launce succeeded, his brother Thomas, also a clergyman, being elected usher in September of the same year. They seem to have aided Mr. Wildblud the Vicar in preaching John Lyon's sermons.—(*School Archives*).

* The ironwork for the chest cost £5, and *this paper book*, with seven volumes more, led to an expenditure of £7 3s. 6d. Rather expensive stationery, according to modern ideas, especially when the value of money is considered.

† The exact words and mode of spelling are reproduced from the Governors' minute-book.

The first recorded Harrovian is one Macharie Wildblud, son of the same Vicar Humphry Wildblud, whose
entry is recorded in 1615. This Vicar, Mr. Wildblud,
may, though we have no evidence on the point, have
aroused or given shape to the benevolent designs of
John Lyon.

No governors' meeting between 1615 and 1621 has
been recorded, so that we can hardly think that the
minutes were then as carefully kept as the otherwise
exact nature of the entries, both in the governors'
minute-book and rent account books, might lead one to
expect ; and some meeting of the governors must
clearly have occurred in 1621, when the Rev. Mr.
Whittle attained the position of Free School master,
and one Joseph Greenhill attained the honour of being
elected the first University scholar.

The minutes of the earlier governors' meetings contain much necessary correspondence about the letting
of farms and outlying hamlets, and other records of dry
business transactions in Harrow itself. Thus we learn
that as early as 1621 a house was in Harrow hired of
the Reeve for school purposes ; while before the next
recorded governors' meeting, in 1634, a new head-
master had been found to replace Mr. Whittle.

The individual in question was one William Hide,
who, according to the school account book, was elected
28th April 1628, and who held the office until his death
in 1661. It was his lot to hold his office during times
when political differences were destined to drift into
civil discord, such as forbad that healthy intercourse
between different parts of England which alone could
lift Harrow out of obscurity. The temporary isolation
which resulted, if it contributed to render her small

income safe from seizure, yet retarded the growth
which exceptional advantages were certain to develop.
And how could any educational life be possible in
hours of public agony, when the father was liable to
draw sword on his child, while outside the metropolis
no family was secure from the calamity of seeing the
homestead made a battle-field, whereon should be
decided the fate of a dynasty; while at best the household might be called upon to find food and shelter
for the stolid soldiers of Fairfax, or to surrender all to
the wild cavalier troopers who followed Prince Rupert.
We have no record which tells us that Harrow was
occupied in a military sense by either of the rival
factions; and, indeed, there is a significant blank in
the governors' minutes between 1634 and 1648, when
necessary business connected with the giving of leases
is briefly recorded.   During that terrible fourteen years
men like Sir Gilbert Gerard, the Baronet and M.P. for
Middlesex, had other duties more pressing than any
connected with schooling youth, and, indeed, it is
recorded that he embraced the popular cause with
ardent zeal.*

Few subjects exist more worthy the historian's pen or
the artist's brush than that afforded by King Charles I.
resting at Harrow on April 27th, 1646, when, after a

---

* A curious indenture, dated A.D. 1639 (the year of Bucking-
ham's murder), exists in the British Museum.   It contains a
proposal that Sir Gilbert Gerard should let an outlying piece
of his property near Hanwell to a certain inhabitant of that
place named Millett.   Sir Gilbert gives evidence of his political
leanings by twice striking out the word "Kingdom."   Probably
his indignation at being called on to pay taxes for the maintenance of an army in France and another on the Scotch frontier,
and to do so for "defence of the King," led him to alter the
document, which was drawn up before civil war broke out in
England.—British Museum, Additional MS. 6840, folio 107.

6 ˘

flight from Oxford with Hudson a cleric and Ashburn-
ham an officer, he rested on the brow of the famous
Middlesex hill, and looked thoughtfully over that great
city which had tolerated, if not freely accepted, revolt
against his kingly authority.*

* There are discrepancies in the several accounts of Charles's
flight from Oxford, but the king clearly came to Harrow. When
Hudson was first examined by Parliament, he is said to have
mentioned Dorchester (Oxfordshire), Henley, and Maidenhead, as
places which the fugitives passed when on the road to Wheat-
hampstead and St. Alban's (Peck's *Desiderata Curiosa*, ii. p. 350) ;
but as His Majesty had commanded Hudson not to divulge his
resting-place on the Monday night, this examination was supplemented by a similar ordeal undergone before Parliament. During
the second inquiry Hudson swore that the King's party passed by
Harrow at 4 o'clock on Monday afternoon, April 27th (Peck's
Desiderata Curiosa, ii. p. 360). Rushworth was of the opinion
that Charles and his companions *stayed some time* at Harrow (see
his *Historical Collections*, vol. vi. p. 267) ; likewise relating how,
when the King was on the road between Harrow and St. Albans,
he "was overtaken by a drunken man, well horsed, and riding
violently, which put his party to some apprehension." This latter
incident was taken from Hudson's printed examination. Heath,
in his *Chronicle of Civil Wars in England, Scotland, and Ireland*,
p. 167, gives as a reason for the Royal hesitation before London,
that, "when expected to come to Hyde Park by his adherents,
there was a general training of the city forces in progress, General
Essex being in command. His Majesty, the author tells us, was
almost persuaded to venture himself into their hands, but, other
counsels prevailing, went to St. Alban's. It is remarkable that
both Heath and Rushworth speak of the King as having gone to
Brentford, a town which he naturally would have passed through
when journeying from Hillingdon to London. Whether the party
slept the *Monday* night at Brentford or Harrow has never been
decided ; but the careful Guizot, in his *English Revolution*, ii.
p. 153, was doubtless justified in stating that the King stopped
and gazed upon his capital when he arrived at Harrow-on-the-
Hill, looking down upon the city with a heart full of anxiety ;
Harrow, from its altitude, being the only vantage post from
whence London could be contemplated. Guizot, moreover, supple-
ments this statement by saying that Charles, *after a few hours'
hesitation*, went to the north, though slowly, and as if by chance,
like one who is yet undetermined. Rapin and Whitelocke both
give their countenance to the fact of the fugitive monarch passing
by Harrow, while the elder Disraeli, in his *Life of Charles I.*,

Should he throw all on one cast of the die, and cast himself on his people's generosity ? What passed in the monarch's mind at that moment will never be known, and without charging him with irresolution, as does Guizot, we are yet free to believe that, although the King of England would have been in his proper place amongst his subjects, he could have hoped but for little from a fanatic military caste, who held London in a vice, and at the moment in question were drunk with the successes achieved on Marston Moor and Naseby field.* Such, however, was the first royal visit that the Harrow historian can narrate, and its traditions linger around the local well, called after the luckless Charles.

We have seen that Mr. Hide's Harrow scholars were not directly called on to take sides in the civil war, as were many of their Etonian compeers at this period ;† but immediately upon the Commonwealth coming into power do we find that attacks were made on the Lyon funds in order that a friendly sentiment might induce the Court to solve the roads question in a manner

speaks of Hillingdon and St. Albans as being in the course of the monarch's wanderings. Whitelocke adds his authority to that of Rushworth and Heath in regard to the alleged sojourn at Brentford. On either hypothesis, a knowlege of the country will show that the wanderers must have passed through Harrow, or they could not have reached the neighbourhood of St. Albans, whether Hillingdon or Brentford was the place of departure. It is unfortunate that neither Guizot nor Disraeli gave references for their respective statements.

* Later researches collected by the Camden Society have made known the fact that the British Presbyterians in London had opened negotiations with their monarch.

† But nine scholars were admitted to King's House, Eton, between 1642 and 1644, while many scholars, being the sons of Cavaliers, laid aside their books and took up arms.—Maxwell Lyte, *Eton College*, p. 238-9.

favourable to popular instinct, and adverse to the school. The petition of one Leonard Stockdale, of Kingsbury, in 1655, is a case in point, the petitioner praying that the governors might be called to account as to their administration. Beyond a confirmation by Lord Chancellor Ellesmere of the rights claimed on behalf of the Harrow and London highways, nothing seems to have resulted from this application, while the infant Harrow community, at least, escaped the fate of Eton, whose Provost, Rous, was made Speaker of the Barebones Parliament.* Nor were loyal Harrovians called upon to attest their fidelity to the Crown in the manner which befel the Westminster scholars, when, at the famous Dr. Busby's instance, they publicly prayed, with their master kneeling amongst them, for the anointed sovereign of England, before his life was taken by insatiable enemies, January 30th, 1649. With regard to Mr. Hide, it is not impossible that he was of founder's kin, as an intermarriage took place between the families of Lyon and Hide of Berkshire. The name, moreover, is found amongst the Harrow School tenants for some time after William Hide died.

The Rev. Thomas Johnson was elected head-master, October 10th, A.D. 1661. What his title to preside over Harrow School may have been we know not, and probably the selection was made, at Mr. William Hide's death, without reference to any political bias ; although the absence from governors' meetings of the Roundhead partisan, Sir Gilbert Gerard, from 1660 (the Restoration year), is very remarkable. Indeed, the name of this active promoter of Harrow's welfare does not again appear in connection with the school history, while, in

* Lyte, *Eton College*, p. 246.

the Parish Register for January 20th, 1669, we read of
his burial.

In *Nonconformity in Herts*, by the Rev. William
Urwick, Pastor of the Congregational Church, St.
Albans, p. 751, we read that Thomas Pakeman, M.A.,
was M.A. of Clare Hall, Cambridge, and was first
minister at Hadham, whence he was ejected in 1660,
with ten children (and afterwards from Harrow in
Middlesex in 1662).

At Harrow he was in great esteem with Sir Gilbert
Gerard, and soon had the instruction and boarding of
several children of persons of quality, and preached as
he had opportunity. Mr. Urwick is quoting from
Calamy.

As Sir Gilbert Gerard was an active governor of the
school, it might be supposed that Mr. Pakeman's pupils
were enjoying the benefit of John Lyon's foreigner
clause. But, on the other hand, it is noteworthy that
the commencement of Pakeman's short Harrow career
was coincident with Sir Gilbert's abstention from
governors' meetings.

Some may wonder that, after accepting a baronetcy
from James I., Gerard should have joined the Parliament
in the next reign ; but, whatever may be thought of his
political conduct, he no doubt exercised a remarkable
and beneficent influence on early Harrow history; for
it is impossible to scan carefully the accounts and
registers of this period without seeing how much credit
is due to the men of business, who, serving at a
nominal remuneration, spared no trouble in management of the estates entrusted to their care.

In the year 1667 a list of the school library was
taken, and, amongst other volumes of a more classical

type, we learn that twelve volumes of Calvin adorned the shelves,* an indication, one would suppose, that the Puritanical *régime* had not passed by without, in some degree, leaving traces behind it, even at Harrow. The parish registers do not show signs of any immediate social relief having been brought to Harrow parish by the generally welcomed Restoration. The barbarity of whipping an old man of eighty, called Dyton, as a vagrant rogue, was perpetrated on June 14th, 1665, while less than a month after that event one Peter Owle, sixty years of age, suffered a similar fate, and probably aged paupers avoided Harrow Hill for the future.

Progress about the country was not by any means cheap at this period, for we learn from the record† that the usher, Mr. Robinson, spent £2 10s. 6d. on his journey from Oxford during 1665—no mean amount when the value of money is considered. And with these faint traces of a time which still remains one of darkness, so far as Harrow is concerned, must we take leave of Mr. Johnson and his scholars (1668), so soon to be reinforced from various parts of the kingdom.

On the 2nd of November 1668, Johnson announced his intention of resigning and going to Lincoln, and on the 25th of the same month Thomas Martin, of Christchurch, Oxford, was chosen master, with full intention of developing the free-school system by means of enticing gentlemen's sons from the neighbourhood and from London. But nine months' trial convinced the governors that their latest choice lacked the requisite stability,

---

* *School Archives.*
† *School Account Book,* 1665.

such as allowed them to declare him a godly, learned, discreet, diligent, sober man, according to John Lyon's desire, and, accordingly, they declared his removal by a written declaration of June 14th, 1669, which remains on the minutes, and is signed by Francis Gerard, Daniel Waldo, Edward Waldo, E. Fenn.

The scanty income provided for a head-master, according to Lyon's will, was not sufficient to attract first-class men to the free school, even when the foreigner clause was in operation, while the blight of enforced celibacy hung over the hill. A relic of monkish prejudice, this restriction was left standing in the founder's directions, but was fortunately subject to the ruling of the governing body, who, as they phrased it on October 21st, 1669, " Having by long experience proved the rule to be very inconvenient, abolished it in the case of the Master," the resolution being attested in due form by the new master, William Horne, receiving, moreover, an after-confirmation thirty years later, when a fair trial had proved that men of culture were more likely to endure genteel poverty in a country village, when accompanied by the partner whose sympathy and aid is more particularly needed by those responsible for the health and morals of youth. This we state, though quite conscious that modern school life has introduced us to very excellent bachelor masters, when, with the appliances of advancing civilisation to hand, an efficient matronly aid is secured by purses longer than those of grammar-school teachers in the seventeenth century.

All these occurrences are related in detail, because, to realise at all through what apparently relentless barriers Harrow forced its way to the front, it is necessary that the reader should learn how inadequate means placed the school at a disadvantage with nearly every other rival community. Indeed, but for honest faith in the Harrow future, entertained by the gentlemen who so faithfully represented Lyon's views, and carried out his wishes in spirit, if not always to the letter, there could have been no continued struggle against discouragement, and the period of success and fame would never have been reached.

CHAPTER V.

LIGHT IN THE DARKNESS. 1669–1746.

A fuller tide
Hath borne me forth upon a broader sea.
The Tyro, p. 237.

AT last we emerge from that portion of our story which, with all its charm in Harrow eyes, yet, perhaps, needs antiquarian taste in a disinterested reader to redeem the narration from sterility. Only in regard of certain scraps of history which the early story of Harrow School reveals have we, hitherto, hoped to awaken general interest. But the case stands otherwise when, ninety-nine years after the granting of the school charter, William Horne* came from Eton in September 1669,

* William Horne, born at Leicester, one MSS. says Tunbridge in Kent, son of Thomas Horne, then schoolmaster there (*see* Thomas Horne of the year 1658, who, and Hezekias Horne, A.D. 1666, were younger brothers to this our William Horne), came in the place of John Cook of the year 1652 Fellow, and when B.A. he went Usher to Eton School, 1662; after that M.A., married daughter of Matthew Day of the year 1629. Resigned his Ushership, 1670. Then head-master of the Free School at Harrow-on-the-Hill in the county of Middlesex. He also resigned his fellowship here, 1670. William Horne's father, Thomas, succeeded Dr. Nicholas Gray as head-master of Eton, died August 22, 1654. William Horne's younger brother Thomas was Fellow of King's, Chaplain to Charles II., and Vice-Provost of Eton.—Anthony Allen's Catalogue, made in 1750.

and introduced the method pursued at the great public
school, where his father and namesake had governed
in capacity of head-master between 1648 and 1654,
when the once royal and aristocratic foundation was
most completely leavened with Puritanism, and, despite
much personal sacrifice, had bowed to the Image which
Protector Cromwell set up.*

Nevertheless, young William Horne, whom we read
of as a good scholar, was probably not distinguished
for Puritanical leanings ; for such a reputation could
scarcely have furthered his career during the Restoration epoch, when he was charged with the task of
rendering Harrow education attractive to English
gentlemen.

Modern writers, who have not been furnished with
more recently disclosed information, have assumed that
the Foreigner clause was not put into practice so early
as William Horne's mastership.† But if so, how could
William Baxter, the philologist and antiquary, who was
born at Llanlugen in Shropshire A.D. 1650, have enjoyed
the Harrow education to which he owed so much, and
have learnt under Johnson's head-mastership at Harrow
not only to become a classical scholar, but to master the
English tongue, of which, being brought up amongst
the Welsh, he knew not a word before the year 1668.‡

---

* Lyte, *Eton College*, pp. 246-249.
† Pitcairn, *Harrow School*, Provost and Co.. 1870, p. 11.
‡ See *The Great Schools of England*, Howard Staunton, p. 276.—
William Baxter edited several editions of the classics, his most
celebrated philological work appearing in 1719. He speaks as
follows of his Harrow education in a note on Horace, Epp. I.,
xvi. 3 :—"Rusticus quidam cognomento Plumburius, in vico agit
vernacule appellato Harrow-on-the-Hill, quod est Herga sive Castra
super Colle, qui quidem vicus satis notus est in Medio Saxonum
nostrorum pago ; præsertim vero nobis qui in sacio isto Monte
Musas primum adivimus." "A countryman, surnamed Plumbury,

Indeed, it is clear that, profiting by what was probably Johnson's experiment, the governors intended to let Horne develop a portion of the founder's policy, which a disturbed condition of the kingdom had rendered null and void for nearly a century. Thus we find Horne's allowance increased in 1671 and 1672,* a privilege which could be granted for no other object than that of allowing him to increase the Foreign connection which his predecessor had created.

Probably the scholars thus attracted were at first very few, and we have indications in the school records which go to show that the original number of natives who received free education remained at the forty declared desirable in 1615.† On the other hand, we know, by reference to a letter written in 1691, by Charles Roderick, Provost of King's,‡ in support of Brian's candidature, that Harrow School had within his memory flourished under a master of Eton education, who could have been none other than Horne, whose connection with the Royal Foundation of Henry VI. was so notorious, and of whom we find it

lives in the town commonly called 'Harrow-on-the-Hill,' that is, *Herga* (=the camp) *super collem*. This town is very well known in the county of Middlesex, particularly to me, who on that hallowed height received my early education in the classics (*lit.* first listened to the Muses)." William Baxter was elected master of the Free School at Tottenham after leaving Harrow, and subsequently ruled over the education provided by the Mercers' Company. He was nephew to the celebrated Nonconformist divine, Richard Baxter, author of the *Saints' Rest* (*Beauties of England*, part v., vol. x. p. 703). John Dennis, dramatist and critic, who was born in London in 1657, must probably also have been at Harrow under Johnson some time between 1663 and 1668, when Mr. Martin was elected head-master.

* Harrow School Governors' Minutes.
+ *School Archives*, 1678–80.
‡ *School Archives*, 1691.

recorded on his monument in Harrow Church chancel that he was *Preceptor Strenuus.*

The position of Harrow at this period cannot be thoroughly comprehended without a glance at the contemporary condition of other school communities.

At Eton, in the year 1678, was published the first school list, which showed that there were then seventy-eight collegers and 124 other scholars being educated beside Father Thames, and that amongst these was an aristocratic connection, which, if it included only one peer's son, yet numbered five youthful baronets in its ranks.*

Busby, it must be remembered, was still in the majesty of office at Westminster, so that the upper classes of the metropolis had an educational resort close to their own doors, such as then partook somewhat of the surburban character which pertains to Harrow in the present day. In the year 1678 Rugby had not yet entered into competition with the great schools of England, although Robert Ashbridge, then head-master, had commenced the Rugby register, that precursor of coming fame, to be attained A.D. 1687, under Holyoak, who not only taught Laurence Sheriffe's foundationers, but also attracted children of the Midland aristocracy, even if in mere numbers the school remained insignificant.†

William Harris was also at this period about to enter on his mastership at Winchester, which, though an epoch of high scholastic reputation, did not increase the numbers of England's most venerable college ;‡

---

* Lyte, *Eton College*, p. 272.
† *Public Schools*, by author of *Etoniana*, p. 339.
‡ *Wykehamica*, p. 97-99.—Winchester then appears to have averaged about fifty commoners in addition to the collegers.

and, if Westminster was ever present to supply the
needs of high-born London, was there not the Charterhouse, where Addison and Steele actually were scholars,
together with St. Paul's and Merchant Taylors' Schools,
where inhabitants of the City and its surroundings
(including the approximate portions of Kent and
Surrey) could satisfy such educational cravings as
might be felt by well-to-do merchants, or ordinary
gentlefolk, when the political out-look by no means
promised peace and contentment. Under these circumstances, and having regard to the contemporary
advance of local institutions, such as Shrewsbury
remained at that time, we cannot fail to appreciate
Horne's endeavours at Harrow-on-the-Hill.

It will be seen from these contemporary jottings that
neither were public schools the general resorts of those
claiming high lineage that they became in the next
century, nor were their limited numbers necessarily
indicative of inefficiency, when needs were limited by
the slow growth of population.

Moreover, the Restoration was never really a time
of healthy settlement, during which men sought to
allay evil passions by exercising and training the intelligence. Drunk with joy at escape from civil war, the
English people betook themselves to savage and un-
reasoning jealousy of their Roman Catholic fellow-
subjects, which alternated with a revival of intolerance
towards Dissenters, combined with tolerance of loose
morals, and a savage lack of sympathy as regards
mankind generally.

Not one whit better off were the wretched tramps
who passed through Harrow parish at the close of the
reign of King Charles II. than we have shown them to

be twenty years before. The public whippings for
vagrancy continue to be recorded, two brothers, Richard
and Peter Halles, suffering thus on May 8th, 1674,
while the churchwardens seem to have been absorbed
in delivering passports into other parts of the kingdom,
amongst the latter being a pass for a blind man into
Kent, and a poor boy into Surrey. Amidst these
indications of parochial life we come, in June 1676,
upon an evidence of charitable thought for others
amongst Harrow townspeople, in the shape of a receipt
for £10 12s. 11d., collected for " ye fire of Northampton," a document which assumes a somewhat
ludicrous form when signed by " John Street, hi (*sic*)
Constable."*

Almost contemporaneously with the accession of
the Rev. William Bolton, second master of Charterhouse, to the head-mastership of Harrow in 1685 died
Charles II., whose *bon mot* concerning Harrow Church
is well known. Certain divines, disputing as to the
Visible Church, were told by the royal wit that it was
to be found on Harrow Hill. This is a good companion story, by the way, to the same monarch's
indictment of Isaac Barrow, that he was the most
unfair preacher ever heard, because nothing was left
for anyone else to say.

Despite the temporary fame of Horne at Harrow,
there was that in national affairs which rendered any
abiding success in developing the Foreigner clause
improbable. Men did not seek to instruct youth
through fresh channels of education when life and
property were threatened by internal quarrel.

* *Harrow Parish Register.*—Throwing at cocks prevailed at
Harrow until 1680, and is mentioned in the registers.

At Horne's death, A.D. 1685, William Bolton was elected to the vacant head-mastership.* It is a remarkable fact that, until the late Mr. Charles Edward Long discovered, in the year 1856, a Latin poem composed by Bolton, it was not known that he had ruled over Harrow.† The lyric in question, entitled *A Poem upon a Laurel Leaf*, was purchased at Mr. Russell Smith's shop in Soho Square, and presented to the Harrow School Library. Mr. Bolton styled himself *Archididasculus* of the public school, and dedicated the poem to the then governors, Sir Charles Gerard, Bart., Sir Edward Waldo, Kt., Cheek Gerard, Daniel Waldo, William Fenn, and Edward Waldo, Esquires. It was printed by W. Cooke, at the sign of the Green Dragon, without Temple Bar, in 1690.

A rheumatic affection oppressing the head-master, Lady Gerard had prevailed on him to try the cure of a laurel leaf, which the following extract from his poem will show was in the first instance efficacious.

> Now, O Physicians, torture whom you please
> With nauseous Potions, worse than the Disease.
> Who 'll now esteem those medicines you impart,
> When our poor Leaf can baffle all your art.
> Mock as ye will, ye have my leave to grin,
> I 'll trust the Proverb, *Let them laugh that win*,
> And with that safer Physick still pursue
> Which gives me Health, and saves my money too.

* The following remarkable baptism took place at the Parish Church of St. Mary in August 1686:—" The 4th day was baptised Thomas ye son of Mr. Thomas Nicoll of ye Hermitage; Mr. Thomas Nicoll and Mr. Thomas Smyth, his two great-grandfathers, being godfathers (a third great-grandfather being alive, viz. Mr. Gee of Isleworth); Mrs. Nicoll, the grandmother, being god-mother."—*Harrow Parish Registers.*

† *Harrow Gazette* for May 1856.

But unfortunately the good effects were not abiding. The Latin poem, with translation, is in the Vaughan Library at Harrow.

Of Mr. Bolton's previous career we have also some records. He was elected a scholar on the Foundation of the Charterhouse in 1656. Thence he removed to St. John's College, Oxford, where he graduated B.A. in 1671. In 1679 he was chosen one of the Charterhouse. In 1685-6 he was presented to the rectory of Dunsby, in Lincolnshire, a Charter-house living, and in 1690 he was incorporated at King's College, Cambridge, B.A. at that university.*

As regards Mr. Bolton's career at Harrow, there is no contemporary trace of any remarkable rise in numbers, although an extra £10 was granted for the purpose of enlarging the master's house, while a tenant named Hyde received notice to quit. But the free scholars remained at their normal number, viz. forty, while the dames continued to be entrusted with the nurture of younger children.

In the year 1691 the Rev. W. Bolton died, and gave place to Mr. Brian, Fellow of King's College, Cambridge, who, as head-master, beheld the first genuine movement which tended to make Harrow widely known, and so laid the foundation of future progress.

Dr. Roderick, the Provost of King's, writing to a Harrow governor, said, Mr. Brian "has for many years taught the school in the said College with diligence and good success, and I believe is very well qualified for the care of a greater school. I am bold therefore . . . . to recommend him to your favour. And if you and the other . . . Governors . . . make

* *Harrow Gazette*, February 1856.

a choice of him . . . I am persuaded you 'l provide well for the credit of the school which has once already in my memory flourished under a master of Eton education."*

Brian probably shared the lot of his immediate predecessors during the first few years of his life ; for, although William and Mary held the throne *de facto*, men had reason to dread a recurrence of civil war, or at least the condition of things which had prevailed in Bolton's time, when James II. was threatening both the religion and the liberties of his people.

But the general satisfaction and contentment induced by the constitutional settlement of 1688 soon had its effect even at Harrow, where at last, in 1698, Thomas Brian's skilful teaching attracted foreigners in considerable numbers. Indeed, the governors were apprised at this period that a controversy was in progress between the master and his usher concerning the proportionate division of the increased income derived from new arrivals ; and, although when the matter came up for adjudication on March 6th, 1699,† they fully endorsed Dr. Brian's policy, the matter cropped up again in a few years' time, and was then, as we shall show, completely settled. The year 1699 will thus be henceforth considered a crucial epoch in our story.

Harrow, during the seventeenth century, presents

* Letter of Charles Roderick to Governors, 1691 ; also Brian's testimonials from King's College.—*School Archives.*

† The Governors present were :—Charles Gerard, Richard Page, William Fenn, Edward Waldo, Cheek Gerard. It must have edified the youths who had just entered Harrow to witness the following spectacle, March 2nd, 1698 : — "Isabel Smyth, *alias* Pierson, aged 20, was whipt for a vagrant and passed away to Greenford."—*Harrow Parish Registers,* 1698.

7 *

several points of antiquarian interest. During the Great Plague of London many persons of quality took refuge on the breezy Middlesex hill-residence there between 1664-66, several of whom were buried in the churchyard.

Archery at the butts is so thoroughly a part of this history, that its constant mention in the school archives has an antiquarian interest ; but we cannot refrain from narrating how constant are entries in the Harrow accounts of the ringing of John Lyon's so-called knell at the school expense. This annual custom has lapsed altogether at the present time.

The politics of the reign of James II., and the foreign needs of William and Mary, are exemplified by constant mention of certain local taxation, which we find to have been levied some years after it was originally instituted. Thus, the governors of Harrow School were called on to find men to serve in the Militia, and be responsible for their accoutrements; while an allowance for Trophy money* is mentioned continually à propos of the school tenants who had been called on to contribute since the year 1685 towards this impost. Troops originally en-gaged in the suppression of Monmouth's rebellion were retained by William III. for the protection of England, when her regular troops were on the Continent. This device, to avoid the undue increase of a public debt, may have served the passing purpose ; but, after 1688, the House of Commons restrained the levying of armed men.

To present Harrovians, perhaps, the most interesting

---

* Money formerly collected and raised in London and the southern counties, providing maintenance for the militia.— Wharton's *Law Lexicon*, p. 737.

event of all is the levelling up of the school-yard, which, according to the archives, was accomplished A.D. 1682. This achievement all young Harrovians will appreciate when they realise that the original yard was on the side of the hill.

The well-abused eighteenth century was entered upon amidst prosperity which promised to develop speedily and render Harrow at last what John Lyon had desired;* but an unexpected bar to progress, such as we associate with the school's name, was disclosed in the year 1709, when Mr. Brian's energies were partially paralysed by a lack of money to support his schemes to the full. What with constant payments to the highways, and poverty on the part of tenants, the scanty funds of John Lyon did not suffice to supply the increasing monetary needs of the school, when, at the end of Queen Anne's reign, the country gentlemen perceived the advantages which Lyon's foreigner clause offered for their children.

We find evidence, dated May 30th, 1709, that it had been found necessary to spend £581 15s. 0d. on the founder's Preston farm. The tenant was described to the governors as almost penniless and quite unable to fulfil his duties in this respect; while the school exchequer had drifted to such a low ebb, that, after it had been drained to the uttermost,† not only was it found necessary to borrow £260, but also to dismiss the dames, who, for a small annual payment, instructed the free scholars in their various districts in reading and

---

* The first name carved in the Fourth Form room is that of T. Basil, 1701. A chance observer would imagine that many of the eighteenth century records belonged to the seventeenth century. It is not so, and only one sixteenth century date appears, bereft, unfortunately, of any accompanying name.
† Governors' Minutes, 1709.

grounded them in religion. A policy, this, which necessity alone could excuse. We find, also, from the minutes, that as the foreigners increased in number so did the Harrow peasantry shrink from contact with social superiors in the matter of their children's education.

It remains a notable fact that at the very first blush of returning financial prosperity the governors restored the dame system, which they had been led temporarily to withdraw.* Nor did the institution of dames, as presenting the form of early education most acceptable to parents, cease to form an important feature in Harrow life until late in Dr. George Butler's time. For, when John Lyon's forty poor scholars became merged in what in modern parlance we know as home boarders, dames were not eliminated from the renovated system, since it was no doubt felt that by their care very youthful Harrovians might be gradually weaned from the home life they had somewhat prematurely† exchanged for school discipline. It is difficult to suggest any alternative process of equal utility, whereby those least furnished with the good things of this life should, by education with the sons of the wealthy, attain the benefits which residence in an ordinary gentleman's household might be otherwise supposed to confer; albeit the slightest knowledge of history goes to show that good home-training in the tender hours of childhood was not of necessity the heritage of wealth or position while Queen Anne reigned, or even when George I. accepted the throne which descent from James I. placed

* Governors' Minutes, 1718.
† It was the fashion early in the present century to enter Harrow at eight years old.

in hesitating bands. Hence the female tutelage, originating as we have described, became an incorporated part of Harrow life and lingered on far into the nineteenth century.

Without dwelling further on the minutiæ of a school life which had no extensive influence in the moulding of national character during the first decade of the eighteenth century, we are in due course bound to narrate events which to some will appear a mere digression, but the details of which rise into importance, since their outcome was the foundation of a name which has vied with royal Eton itself, and struggled successfully to maintain its prestige even in face of the competition of ancient Winchester, aristocratic Westminster, or popular Rugby, furnished, as these institutions were, with all the advantage that superior wealth affords.

In the year 1707 James Brydges, late Paymaster of Queen Anne's forces, began to build a magnificent dwelling on the more northerly quarter of Stanmore, which, stretching to the left of the road between London and St. Alban's, afforded a site unsurpassed for beauty or salubrity. The princely residence erected at Stanmore, on the property of Canons, became the theme of poets and the source of a controversy familiar to those who have studied the history of Middlesex as recorded by Lysons, or scanned, however cursorily, the social literature of the time.

The owner of Canons had gained his interest in this ancient property by reason of a marriage with a daughter of the Lake family; and, with evident judgment in choice of position, commenced an undertaking not destined to close without manifesting a leaning towards

extravagant display which, if traceable to the manners
then in vogue, seems to have in some degree discarded
the truer artistic instinct, even if it did not absolutely
outrage pure taste. And yet there was much at Canons
to charm ordinary eyes.

For instance, we are told that the angles of the house
were so arranged that a spectator, peering up the several
leafy avenues, might embrace in his view a width of
apparent front such as on closer inspection proved to
pertain to two, if not more, sides of the mansion. And
here James Brydges lavished all the wealth which he
had gained through holding the paymastership of the
forces during Queen Anne's wars, when Marlborough
and Blenheim saved Europe from the domination of
France and Spain.

In the conduct of his official duties Brydges had
amassed one of those immense fortunes, the gaining of
which out of public perquisites it should be one of the
first duties of a well-governed State to discourage. And
yet the direst invective can scarcely avail to injure the
memories of men who acted as the custom of their days
directed, and have the right to be judged according to
the canons of a morality universally recognised in
Queen Anne's time. We must be thankful, if a more
wholesome tone animates the majority of officials now,
that the limits of advancement through the public
service are more defined, without being too severe in
our criticism of past laxity.*

James Brydges, when he contemplated this palace at
Stanmore, fixed Cavendish Square as the situation of

* Few of our readers can fail to recognise the difference which
the twenty-five years just passed have made in this particular.
Interest is now nearly useless at the *outset* of an official career.

a London residence of kindred pretensions; but the
latter design was never carried out, and all available
wealth and energy were concentrated on Canons.
Three architects were engaged on the building. The
marble employed was massive and of great beauty,
each step of the grand staircase being of one piece
twenty-two feet in length.*

The whole expense reached the then almost incredible
sum of £250,000. The owner, it is said, affected a
grandeur which approached that of a sovereign prince
—dined in public in the French royal style, each
change of dishes being hailed by flourishes of trumpets.
Moreover, in his very passage to chapel he was attended
by a military guard of eight Chelsea pensioners, whose
numbers were exaggerated by general rumour.

On reading of this 176 years after the events took
place, it is impossible not to regret that so clever and
methodical a man as the Duke of Chandos (for he
reached this dignity under George I.) should have
encouraged extravagant display, such as no thinking
man ever valued for itself. On the other hand, it is,
we believe, vain to deny that by fostering music, and,
above all, patronising Handel (who composed twenty
of his anthems for the use of this chapel), art owes a
deep debt to the magnificent Duke.†

Not so, however, ruled Pope, whom men believed to

* *Beauties of England and Wales*, part v., vol. x. p. 636. On
the north side of Cavendish Square may be seen a façade of the
Duke's London residence, built in the style of Canons, of which
no complete picture is to be found in the British Museum. In
the library at Lincoln's Inn, however, the curious reader may
feast his eyes on the work of the three architects, Gibbs, James,
and Sheppard, who designed the Duke of Chandos's magnificent
dwelling.

† Hawkins, *History of Music*, vol. v. p. 198 ff.

have devoted a page or more of his Poem on False
Taste to sarcastic comments upon life at Stanmore,
such as not only stung the lately ennobled owner of
Canons to the quick, but became a matter of general
interest.*

* We subjoin such portion of Pope's poem as was supposed to
speak of Canons and its owner, satirised under the name of
Timon :—

> " At Timon's Villa let us pass a day,
> Where all cry out, ' What sums are thrown away ! '
> So proud, so grand ; of that stupendous air,
> Soft and Agreeable come never there
> Greatness, with Timon, dwells in such a draught,
> As brings all Brobdignag before your thought.
> To compass this, his Building is a Town,
> His pond an Ocean, his parterre a Down :
> Who but must laugh, the Master when he sees,
> A puny insect shiv'ring at a breeze !
> Lo, what huge heaps of littleness around
> The whole, a laboured Quarry above ground.
> Two cupids squint before : a lake behind
> Improves the keenness of the Northern wind.
> His Gardens next your admiration call,
> On every side you look behold the wall !
> No pleasing Intricacies intervene,
> No artful wildness to perplex the scene.
> Grove nods at grove, each Alley has a brother,
> And half the platform just reflects the other.
> The suffering eye inverted Nature sees
> Trees cut to statues, statues thick as trees."

Pope was supposed to have received pecuniary assistance from
the Duke, and was certainly on friendly terms with that reputed
sybarite ; and, therefore, much feeling was evoked on the part of
many friends, who resented the attacks on noble Dives. After
sneering at the ducal taste in books which, according to Pope,
lavished care rather on the ornamental covers than on the contents,
the satire is resumed :—

> " His study ! with what authors is it stored ?
> In Books, not Authors, curious is my Lord ;
> To all their dated backs he turns you round ;
> These Aldus printed, those De Sueil has bound.
> Lo some are Vellum, and the rest as good ;
> For all his Lordship knows, but they are Wood.
> For Locke or Milton, 'tis in vain to look,
> These shelves admit not any modern book."

We are here concerned to show how potent was the
aid that unsurpassed business capacity and great influence brought to the task of building up Harrow School,
strengthening its financial stability, and, by sympathetic
support, adding to its numbers.   When the whilom
Paymaster-General came to his wife's property at
Stanmore in 1707, it was impossible to glance over
the extensive prospects which a stroll in the surrounding country afforded, without beholding from more
than one vantage post those bewitching uplands, their
wooded crest crowned by the ancient church of St.
Mary.   And we know that but a short time elapsed

The Brydges' library at Canons consisted, doubtless, more of
curious than useful volumes, but contained, nevertheless, historical
documents of great value referring to Irish affairs, and which had
belonged to Lord Clarendon when Lord Lieutenant of Ireland,
and which Dean Swift wished placed in the Public Library at
Dublin.   Pope proceeds:—

> "And now the Chapel's silver bell you hear,
> That summons you to all the Pride of Prayer:
> Light quirles of music, broken and uneven
>   (almost exclusively compositions of Handel),
> Make the soul dance upon a jig to Heav'n.
> On painted ceilings you devoutly stare,
> Where sprawl the saints of Verrio or Laguerre,
> Or gilded clouds in fair expansion lie
> And bring all Paradise before your eye.
> To rest, the Cushion and soft Dean invite
> Who never mentions Hell to ears polite."

Probably the lines regarding sprawling saints referred to a blot
on the *ménage* at Canons, due rather to the graceless striving for
artistic ornament prevailing at the time than to any shortcoming
of the Duke's design.   Architectural and pictorial copies of
Versailles were not always famous for grace or taste in the
eighteenth century.

Pope denied that he intended to hold the Duke of Chandos
up to ridicule as Timon ; but Dr. Johnson, in his life of Pope,
states that the Earl of Burlington, to whom the poet addressed
the lines in question, had privately allowed that the satire was
meant for that nobleman.—See *Beauties of England*, part v., vol. x.
p. 642.

before he, like other English gentlemen who inhabited
the neighbourhood (in accordance with John Lyon's
expectation), fell under the spell of fascinating interest
which familiarity with those pleasing shades is wont to
create.

As early as June 2nd, 1713, we find James Brydges
serving in the capacity of a school governor, and
henceforth, as Marquess of Carnarvon, and more
particularly as Duke of Chandos, throwing all his
energies into furtherance of John Lyon's aims, and
this at a crisis of Harrow history.* It is interesting,
at this distance of time, to mark the effect which pure
business capacity exercised alike on the accounts proper
as on the mode of keeping minutes ; and, indeed, the
spirit of this remarkable new-comer seems present even
now, as one glances over dusty pages dull with the
dust of a hundred and sixty years.

While James Brydges, Duke of Chandos, was
destined to become the *Deus ex machina*, whereby the
business matters of John Lyon's foundation were placed
upon the best possible basis, there were likewise other
events working towards the recognition of Harrow as
one of the great public schools.

In November 1718, as we learn from the minutes of
the governing body, reviving financial prosperity allowed
of the re-establishment of the six school-dames, and
also that £30 should be bestowed on some charity of
the character that John Lyon designed to assist.
Agricultural depression had clearly been succeeded in
some degree by a period when tenants were enabled

* The Governors' Minutes tell us that upon the death of
Warwick Lake, the Honourable James Brydges was elected
governor on June 2nd, 1713. He signs an important minute as
" Carnarvon," on January 29th, 1715.

to pay their rents to the day, so that, while indicating
the timely assistance of the Duke of Chandos, it is yet
necessary to ascribe the ups and downs of Harrow in
some degree to the ever-changing conditions consequent
on a variable climate, when the school income depended
mainly on the fruits of the soil. For, however prudent
the external government, or the internal administration
of a scantily-endowed school struggling to assert its
position, the partial withdrawal of pecuniary resources
might well prove fatal to the maintenance of a good
position gained by toil and skill. It was, indeed,
specially fortunate that no such calamity afflicted Harrow
in the year 1718.

Although the accession of George I. had not met with
any open hostility, all accounts agree as to the prevalence of a sentiment for the princes at St. Germains,
which, by no means confined to the Jacobites proper,
had its source in instincts characteristically Anglican.
When, as Lord Stanhope tells us, the Electress Sophia
of Hanover herself, grand-daughter of James I., chosen
to represent the royal race of England, and perpetuate
a Protestant succession to the British throne, straightway displayed undisguised sympathy for her cousin, the
Chevalier St. George, who, she thought, might easily be
brought up to accept the duties and responsibilities of
his rightful position, we can scarcely marvel that there
was a popular sentiment of a like description rampant
in England, the more that the excellent Sophia's
progeny were German in feeling, and loved not their
adopted land.

This legitimist sentiment found very frequent expression amongst certain of the clergy—probably a majority
—who, though they had tolerated a distorted succession

when Queen Anne was on the throne, and her child, the youthful Duke of Gloucester, stood as heir apparent; yet broke out into intellectual rebellion when the choice fell upon a Hanoverian prince. If they were to do homage to a foreigner, why was the legitimate heir at St. Germains to give place to his German kinsman at Herrenhausen? The divine right of kings was then part of the churchman's creed, a doctrine which led men like Bishop Atterbury to be ready (as in an unguarded moment that Prelate avowed) to proclaim the Pretender in full canonicals.

In such sentiments Dr. Andrew Snape, head-master of Eton in 1717, participated. He therefore took an active part in what was then called the Bangorian Controversy. Dr. Hoadley, Bishop of Bangor, preached a sermon before the Lord Mayor, and gave vent to his Latitudinarian proclivities, putting forward doctrines which his opponents assumed were incompatible with orthodoxy. Anyhow, the battle waxed fierce, and became the talk of coffee-houses and of ladies' tea-tables.*

It was generally assumed that, while the friends of Divine Right and unbending Legitimacy espoused the anti-Hoadleian cause, so did those well-affected towards the dynasty chosen by the nation elect to be considered partisans of the Bishop of Bangor.

A conspicuous champion then of the High Church party was the afore-mentioned Dr. Andrew Snape. He had governed Eton with remarkable success, running the numbers up to 400,† at the very moment when this unfortunate controversy broke out.

* Maxwell Lyte, *History of Eton College*, p. 285.
† It is rumoured that he induced a townsboy to join the school and so make up his fourth century.—Maxwell Lyte, *Eton College*, p. 287.

Whatever may be thought of the various pamphlets which then followed one another with such quick succession, there can be no question that Dr. Snape's activity in the matter did for the nonce lead the Whig party to regard Eton with distrust, as being a veritable nursery of Jacobite opinions, and this notwithstanding that Mr. Thomas Thackeray, the second master, resigned his office after abjuring Dr. Snape's opinions, speaking, moreover, as the mouthpiece of an intelligent minority. Although numerically small, these dissentient voices were after all representative of the national feeling as expressed in Parliament; and because they were deemed specially faithful to the Hanoverian dynasty, men like Mr. Thackeray were in sympathy with the powers that ruled Great Britain.

Eton fell slightly in numbers within a year, and when Dr. Bland succeeded the polemical Dr. Snape in 1718, 353 boys were found, where a few months before the numbers were up to 400. The decline was neither large nor permanent, and yet the fact possesses a special bearing on the subject-matter of our story.

We have seen how Mr. Brian's laborious efforts at Harrow had been seconded by the patronage of the Duke of Chandos, whose fidelity to the family of George I. was so notorious. Stanmore became, as we may well believe, a nucleus for the Government men, who dreaded the Pretender as the possible restorer of Roman Catholicism, or were by principle or interest otherwise induced to remain loyal to George I. It can, then, scarcely be doubted that the Duke's position as Governor of Harrow School led many a parent to choose John Lyon's foundation as a place for educating their sons,* when the recent ebullition at Eton had disclosed the Jacobite spirit prevailing in high places, and led to that most injurious episode in school existence—a public controversy. No matter that the Latitudinarian, Dr. Bland, did succeed Dr. Snape; still the embers of the quarrel were scarcely quenched, when the suppression of Convocation stood as evidence of the importance which Government attributed to the still smouldering bickerings which had agitated the land, and affected Eton in particular.

Anyhow, the increase in numbers at Harrow from this juncture was steady, and they reached 144† ; a notable crisis occurring when Mr. Brian, the head-master, appealed for further assistance, urging that with such an access of numbers, it was not reasonable to suppose that all the children could be regularly taught and cared for.

This occurred in the year 1721, and was contemporaneous with a renewed dispute between Mr. Brian and the usher concerning the proportion of entrance-money received from the foreigners who inhabited the head-master's house. The adjudication of the governors on each of these points was prompt, and bore markedly on the school future. They unhesitatingly apportioned *all* the entrance-money to the head-master, and also three-fourths of any other money derived from teaching these said foreigners, thus making it once for all clear that the chosen chief at Harrow was to reign supreme, and

* We know that the Duke sent to Harrow his ward George Brydges Rodney, afterwards the famous admiral.
† The *School Archives* say 104 foreigners and 40 free scholars. 38 foreigners were under the head-master's direct tuition, and 66 under Mr. Hooker, the second master, who founded a grievance on these figures.

Chandos

Faithfull Servant

Tho. Brian Schole=master.

a. Last. 1693.

receive an income which depended for its expansion on the popularity of the school over which he ruled.

Subsequent events have proved that this decision has shaped the high destiny of Harrow by tempting men of scholarly repute to devote their lives to duties which preclude nearly all recreation, literary and domestic, while subsequent rest is not always accompanied by such preferment as the character of the duties performed seems to deserve.

With regard to the request for more school assistance, the governors responded by granting Mr. Brian a coadjutor, to wit the Rev. James Cox of Merton College, Oxford, who, as they phrased it, without power of the rod, should act as second master, while the writing-master, Mr. Robinson, still held his position.

These three preceptors, in conjunction with their female coadjutors the six dames, made up the staff whose duties extended to the teaching and overlooking of some 140 youths, a number which, although large in 1721, is equalled at the present moment by some private seminaries in the kingdom.

It is clear from study of the Harrow archives that, though the numbers may have fallen on account of causes purely ephemeral, the school never permanently retrograded from the position into which good Dr. Brian and the Duke of Chandos had lifted it in 1721. But as the increased reputation brought an access of the so-called foreign element, so do we find that the free scholars became fewer in number.*

Henceforth we must regard Harrow in the light rather of a resort for children of the upper classes,

* In 1738 they were reported to the Governors as standing at 19. In 1739 they numbered only 14.

attracted by the charms of a healthy and beautiful locality, than as the sixteenth-century grammar-school where poor neighbours allowed their progeny to profit by teaching such as by no other means could they have hoped to enjoy.

When the education became more refined and scientific even than that of Horne, Bolton, or Brian, the poor scholar was disposed to hold aloof and his friends to clamour, not without some show of reason, for an equivalent such as never really seemed within reach until, through Dr. H. M. Butler's agency, the stipulated education was conferred, as John Lyon desired, upon poor children of Harrow ; and this while their fathers were likewise profiting by the noble school raised by the faithful fulfilment of the founder's proviso in favour of so-called foreigners.*

During the last ten years of Thomas Brian's mastership the Duke of Chandos was surveyor and acting trustee for the school affairs ; and when in 1731 the veteran head-master, after forty years' service, was buried in Harrow churchyard, not the least important epoch of Herga's long history remained indelibly connected with their joint names.†

* Upon the higher part of the school cricket ground, overlooking the present Pavilion, may be seen the edifice where John Lyons scholars are taught. It is unfortunate that circumstances should have prevented the Public School Commissioners in 1868 from conferring on these youths the prestige which the Harrow name possesses.

† Thomas Brian, born at London, admitted June 23rd, 1678, Fellow of King's, Schoolmaster of King's College School, Master of Harrow, 1691, Senior Fellow and Vicar of Prescot, in Lancashire. Resigned vicarage 1699. Died, very old, at Harrow, " having been schoolmaster there with great reputation forty odd years, and raising that school to about 150 scholars. Was much of a gentleman. Void of all pedantry so often met with among pedagogues." His son, Thomas Brian, won a prize of £10,000

The governors proceded in April 1731 to elect the second master, the Rev. James Cox,* to fill a place which his faculty for teaching and proved good conduct seemed to fit him to hold. Mr. Cox, moreover, became the husband of a lady celebrated alike for her beauty and longevity, viz. the eldest daughter of Mr. Brian. Would that our record could there close without in the interests of historical truth, being called on to tell how, after years of success as a tutor, and after educating such men as James Bruce, the celebrated Abyssinian traveller, and Robert Orme, the historian of Hindustan and Member of the Madras Council, Mr. Cox fell into such irregular habits as led to his absenting himself from his duties, so that he was at last called on to resign on April 26th, 1746.

The record of this disgraceful affair we leave to the Governors' Minute of that date, which runs thus :—

" Whereas the Revd. Dr. James Cox, Master of the Free Grammar Schoole, has for a great while last past lived a disorderly, drunken, idle life, and neglected the care of the Schoole, by which means it is very much decreased, did on or about Easter Week abscond upon

in a State lottery. Had a considerable post in the Custom House. After 1741, Solicitor of the Customs, and counted a rich man and a very able officer ; but, falling under the displeasure of Sir J(ohn) R(ushout), who had been his good friend, because he would not sell the Baronet a small estate he had near Harrow-on-the-Hill, which Sir J. R. coveted, he was thrust out of his office. Preferred in Ireland. Whose books and curiosities were publicly sold in 1752. Died of fever in Gerrard Street, March 1748.— From Anthony Allen's *Catalogue of King's College Scholars.*

* A trace of Harrow in Dr. Cox's time is to be found in the *Gentleman's Magazine*, vol. i. Thursday, 5th August, 1731. According to an ancient custom, a silver arrow, value £3, was shot for at the Butts, at Harrow-on-the-Hill, by six youths of that free school, in archery habits, and won by Master Brown, son of Captain Brown, Commander of an East Indiaman.

8 *

account of his great extravagancies, and running into
debt more than he is able to pay ; therefore, for these
his misdoings we are of opinion that he shall be dis-
placed from being schoolmaster, and declare the place
to be void.

"DANIEL GRAHAM.
"CHANDOS.*
"J. RUSHOUT.
"J. BUCKNALL."

It may interest the readers of this book to know that
a tradition exists, to the effect that Dr. Cox was once
seen amongst his scholars in the school-yard, reclining
in a chair, and regaling himself with the proverbial
pint-pot and its accompanying pipe, then just coming
into fashion.

A temporary decline in the numerical strength of the
school naturally resulted from conduct totally antagonistic
to the previous career of one held in high honour and
trusted faithfully by those who had led Harrow from
ranking as a primitive grammar-school to achieve
the prestige of becoming a nursery for children of
English gentlemen ; and as such destined ever to preserve a place on the roll of fame.   And after recording
this most untoward event, we may close the account of
the period during which the public first perceived those
advantages which John Lyon's foundation afforded to
the British youth generally, with a parting glance at
one who contributed powerfully towards this access of
popularity—we mean the Duke of Chandos.

In the year 1740 the most timely and potent friend
that Harrow possessed since the days of John Lyon and

* Not the magnificent Duke, but his son.

Sir Gilbert Gerard was brought to sever his connection with the school which he had served so well, and in his own words let him tell the reasons which urged him to such a decision, and which stand recorded in the Governors' Minutes.

Canons, March 31st, 1740.

I have been under much uneasiness whenever I have reflected how little assistance I have for some time past been able to give to the gentlemen I have the honour to be joined with in the trust for Harrow Schole, and what adds greatly to this mortification is that I find by last winter's experience the infirmity of age grows so fast upon me as to leave no room to expect I can by my future application to the discharge thereof become more useful to them. Under these circumstances it would, I think, be greatly misbecoming me to continue longer in it, where I do so little good myself, and yet at the same time deprive your society of the benefit of some other gentleman in my room more capable of promoting the laudable intentions of our founder.

I must therefore entreat the favour of you to represent what I have troubled you with in such a light to the gentlemen of the Trust as may induce them to excuse the resignation I make of my trusteeship, and that you will have the goodness to acquaint them.

I retain my most humble thanks for the many instances I have received of their favour and civility during the time I had the pleasure of continuing one of their body.

That I shall ever preserve grateful remembrance of them, and on all occasions show that I am, with the utmost truth and esteem,

Yours and their most
Humble Servant,
CHANDOS.

Readers of this letter will possibly reflect how misleading are arbitrary distinctions between the sixteenth and seventeenth centuries, when a prominent subject of George II. could thus phrase sentences Elizabethan in their ponderous lack of finish.

A few years after the Duke severed his connection
with Harrow, the magnificence of Canons was also
destined to disperse like a fairy vision, leaving but a
name behind ; so that the visitor to Stanmore in 1883
finds it as difficult to realise the former presence of the
gorgeous company that lounged about there in the first
part of the last century as to re-people the neighbouring
Brockley Hill with the Romans who inhabited the
ancient Sulloniacæ with which that spot is identified.

In Pope's satire, but for which John Brydges' life at
Canons might have sunk into oblivion, we read the
following lines :—

> Another age shall see the golden ear
> Imbrown the slope, and nod on the parterre.
> Deep harvest bury all his pride has plann'd,
> And laughing Ceres reassume the land.

A fulfilled prophecy this which strikes a beholder who
contemplates the site of this once princely domain ;
while those curious as to the Brydges family may pass
into Little Stanmore Church and contemplate the marble
monuments which commemorate a phase of local history,
claiming interest, nevertheless, of a wider scope. It
had been rumoured that the Duke's great fortune suffered in the South Sea Scheme during that financially
black year 1720.* If so, never could be instanced fitter
illustration of the Scripture adage that riches take to
themselves wings, inasmuch as if ever business capacity
was evinced, the Duke of Chandos stands in history as
the man who of all others in Queen Anne's reign and that
of George I. displayed this quality most strikingly, both
in the acquisition of wealth and management of property.

* *Beauties of England and Wales: Middlesex*, vol. x. part 5,
p. 642.

His talents in these departments were not alone, as we have shown, demonstrated when most needed, as in the case of Harrow School, but also took effect in the household arrangements at Canons, where, however extreme the profusion, expenditure was so arranged as to have due regard for economy. James Brydges there, at least, got his money's worth.* But with regard to the South Sea Scheme, if that notorious swindle had only duped the fools and left wise men unstricken, ruin would scarcely have been recorded on the scale we now contemplate.

So general was the distress amongst well-to-do people, that Mr. Maxwell Lyte, in his history of Eton College, observes how palpable was the decline of numbers at Eton just about that period ; and this, strange to say, just before Dr. Brian at Harrow made his historic appeal of 1721, wherein the governors were besought to give him assistance in order that he might cope more satisfactorily with duties which the *large increase* of the school had entailed.

We have elsewhere attributed this in part to the echoes of Dr. Snape's polemics when engaged in the Bangorian controversy as Eton head-master, and also in no small degree to the Duke of Chandos' patronage. We would now suggest that possibly the prospect of cheaper education in good company may have also tempted a portion of the Etonian connection who had not escaped unscathed from the South Sea Bubble, to choose John Lyon's foundation in temporary preference for that of Henry VI.'s more courtly academic shades,

* One of the most able accountants in England was employed to keep expenses within certain limits defined clearly both for months, weeks, and days.—Hawkins, *History of Music*, vol. v. p. 198.

or even prefer Herga's slopes to the aristocratic purlieus of St. Peter's College, Westminster. Be that as it may, we have traced the Harrow School history to a point whence a still greater advance was *certain* whenever teaching scientific and judicious could be secured.

How the man was found,* capable of conferring these advantages on Harrow, we must describe in a future chapter.

* Public School education seems to have been coming into vogue at this period. After 1724 Winchester made a step forward under Dr. Burton. The numbers at Westminster in 1727 were 434.

CHAPTER VI.

ARCHDEACON THACKERAY AT HARROW, 1746 TO 1760.

Thou, too, wert worthy of our famous isle.
Tercentenary Prize Poem, by W. S. SICHEL.

THE career of Brian as head-master had proved beyond all cavil that Harrow School possessed the elements of success. The decline to almost normal numbers* coincident with Dr. Cox's unfortunate neglect of his duties was so plainly exceptional in its nature, that the governors were ready to grasp at the opportunity when a really first-class scholar was found to sit in the chair of Horne and Brian.

Previous circumstances undoubtedly conspired to render that auspicious advent an immediate advantage to John Lyon's foundation, inasmuch as, by reason of faithful adherence to his opinions, Dr. Thackeray,†

---

* In the records of Archdeacon Thackeray's family the number given is forty.

† "In May 1746, he, T. Thackeray, was unanimously chosen by the trustees for the school at Harrow-on-the-Hill in Middlesex, master of the same school in the room of the Rev. Dr. Cox, who resigned the same. And N.B. it is assured the said trustees at the same time, with the same unanimity, directed that the scholars of the said school should be educated in every respect in the same manner as is observed in Eton School. And indeed that way of education has for so many years so far received the publick approbation and preference, that you find those gentlemen that have been educated at Eton School have been sought out to

when a master at Eton, had incurred the displeasure
of those with whom he lived by combating the extreme
doctrines put forward by theological assailants of
Bishop Hoadley, with the allumed Latitudinarianism
of whose views the future head-master of Harrow,
judging from the record of his life, can have felt little
sympathy.· But there existed just this much affinity
between the Bishop of Bangor and the high-minded
gentleman who braved so much on that Prelate's
behalf, viz. they were both loyal to the Brunswick
dynasty, whereas the majority in convocation, together
with most of Dr. Snape's adherents in Eton, were at
heart Jacobites. And Thackeray's conduct in resisting
doctrines subversive of the principles upon which
George I. came to the throne, appears the more
disinterested when we learn that he was known to be
the friend of Frederic, Prince of Wales, a fact by no
means likely to advance Thackeray's cause with the
royal father, whose aversion to his son and heir remains
to this hour an inexplicable fact in history. Therefore,
it is, we think, much to the credit of the amiable but
(as a majority of churchmen believed) *unsound* Hoadley
that, disregarding the minutiæ of theological dis-
putation, he perceived the broad ground upon which
Mr. Thomas Thackeray's opinions and his own were

be set out of other schools. . . . And Dr. Coxe himself was so
sensible of the influence an advertisement to that purpose, July
23, 1746, was likely to make, that he likewise published to the
world that he continued the same method of teaching at West-
born Green that he did at Harrow-on-the-Hill, which method was
above fifty years ago introduced into that school by Dr. Coxe's
immediate predecessor, the Rev. Mr. Bryan, also Fellow of
King's."—From Anthony Allen's *Catalogue of King's College
Scholars.* We may add that a careful search through the peri-
odicals of that day has failed to bring to light Dr. Cox's advertisement.

found in unison, and, although personally unknown, approached the loyal but liberal-minded clergyman for the purpose of rewarding bold integrity by such means as were within the Bishop of Bangor's power.

It is curious that, as Harrow had in 1721 profited by the doubts of parents who were careful to avoid for their children the polemical atmosphere which was prevalent under Dr. Snape, so was the school destined to gain prestige, aye, and attain numerical strength hitherto unprecedented, through the agency of one who conspicuously defended the King's cause when assailed under the guise of Church Defence at Eton.

But these events—commencing as early as the year 1717, ten years before George I. paid the debt of nature, form, so to speak, the prologue of a drama enacted during the greatest dynastic crisis through which the House of Hanover passed, a crisis which, from its external aspect, became threatening when England came into collision with the power and influence both of France and Spain—nevertheless have a domestic aspect such as shed its influence on the lives of young and old, no matter how confined the sphere in which they were destined to move.

It was on June 23rd, 1746, that Thomas Thackeray was elected master of Harrow School. But a few weeks previously the army of Charles Edward Stuart had been wrecked at Culloden,† and the hopes of disloyal Churchmen, both at Eton and Cambridge, were at least temporarily destined to be shrouded in politic silence, or changed for unwilling acquiescence in the inexorable course of events.

* Culloden, April 16, 1746.

On January 15th, 1747,* was born at Harrow-on-
the-Hill the greatest home boarder† that the school of
John Lyon ever nurtured ; we mean Samuel Parr,
whose future, despite sundry peculiarities, and a somewhat premature severance from the scenes of his youth,
was nevertheless destined to leave an impress on the
character, not alone of contemporary actors in the world
of school life, but rendered the Middlesex hill famous
as the source of profound scholarship, and the home of
literary effort.   And if all this intellectual advance was
not made by Parr himself, but in the company of his
schoolfellows, Sir William Jones and Dr. Bennet, the
erudite Bishop of Cloyne, yet the moulding of Parr's
Whig opinions exercised such a potent influence over
those around him that, despite an apparent chronological digression, we must tell the story of the future
pedagogue's origin.

Young Parr's father, likewise named Samuel, was the
child of the Vicar of Hinchley and Stoke in Leicester-
shire.   He is said to have boasted ancient, if not royal,
lineage,‡ and hence this Midland branch of the family
developed their attachment to the throne, and faithful
adherence to principles of *divine right*, both as regards
Church and State, the consequences of which were
destined to fall heavily upon the most notable cadet

---

* Several writers have stated January 26, 1746, as the date of
Parr's birth ; the fact being that the Harrow registers began
according to the ecclesiastical reckoning, the 25th of March, under
which computation a birth in January 1747 would be included in
the year 1746, not destined to close until the March winds had
spent their force.—For this discrepancy, see *Parr's Works*, by
John Johnstone, vol. i. p. 9.

† *I.e.* day-scholar.

‡ The Parr family were descended from Sir Thomas Parr, father
of Queen Catherine Parr, sixth wife of Henry VIII.—Field, *Life
of Dr. Samuel Parr*, p. 2.

of their honourable race. The Harrow scholar's great-grandfather seems to have been a determined non-juror, while of his great-uncle, a notable scholar, it is pithily recorded* "that he loved not money, but the Greek Fathers, the Pretender, and the Church."

As for the future Harrovian's father, then a medical man in the village of Harrow-on-the-Hill, not only did he hold firmly to the family faith, but gave nearly all his possessions to the agents of the Young Pretender,† who, it is worthy of note, must have then spread their nets under the shadow of Harrow Hill. Such intrigues occurred during the closing hours of Dr. Cox's unfortunate mastership, and the temporary relapse in the condition of John Lyon's foundation.

Mr. Parr lost £800, sunk in providing means for the ill-fated campaigns of 1745–6, and the family fortunes were found at a proportionally low ebb when, in 1747, the future scholar was born. Hence, as Mr. Field points out in his biography of Dr. Parr, the Harrow boy was led to contrast principles of civil and religious liberty, as set forth by the historian Rapin, with those of highest Toryism in Church and State, adherence to which had almost ruined his father ; the natural result being that he was at the outset inclined towards Whig principles, like others of those earlier scholars whom Dr. Thackeray reared, giving a tone to the contemporary Harrow opinions ; and, indeed, previous to Dr. Thackeray's time, no school of thought was known to have originated at Harrow, nor were many distinguished men found who owed their early training thereto. We read, it is true, of two great sailors, Lords Rodney and

* Field, *Life of Dr. Samuel Parr*, p. 2.
† *Ibid.* p. 4.

Hood, passing a portion of their childhood under Brian
at Harrow, and can find trace of timely assistance given
to the school by the Ducal house of Chandos, but
cannot discover any peculiar genius destined to influence society at large.   Hence it is that Archdeacon
Thackeray's mastership is so famous in Harrow story,
and that the Preceptor himself merits the title which
Dr. H. M. Butler is said to have assigned to him, viz.
" that of *second founder of Harrow School.*"

The School Archives help us to understand why a man
of such eminence was induced to venture his reputation
and risk his hopes of advancement in a place which
lack of information formerly led men to believe was only
an ordinary local parish school.   That a most crucial
enlivenment of Harrow life, intellectual and physical,
aye, and one abiding in character, took place in Archdeacon Thackeray's time, we believe no reader will
deny, after perusing this chapter.   We shall endeavour,
as it were, to photograph the archdeacon's appearance
and character upon the pages of this chapter by faithful
reference to a privately-printed work of much biographical interest, and, we venture to say, worthy of
the high literary reputation of the family.*   We are
indebted to the Rev. St. John Thackeray, Vicar of
Maple Durham, for access to these valuable memorials.

" Thomas Thackeray was born at Hampsthwaite,
York, in the reign of William and Mary, December
8th, 1693; was educated at Eton, and became a
scholar of King's College, Cambridge, in 1712, and a
fellow in 1715.   He took his B.A. degree in the same
year, and his M.A. in 1719.   Shortly after he became

* *Memorials of the Thackeray Family*, by Jane Townley Pryme
and Alicia Bayne, privately printed, pp. 13–19.

a Fellow of his College, Mr. Thackeray was appointed
to be an assistant master at Eton. In 1728 he was
presented by Sir Peter Soame, Bt., to the rectories of
Haydon (now spelt with an *e*) and Chishall Parva, in
the next parish. Their united populations, even in
1879, only amounted to 375 ; their value to £681 per
annum.

"Mr. Thackeray took his degree of Bachelor in
Divinity on the occasion of a royal commencement at
Cambridge, in July of the same year. It may probably
have been at this time that he preached in Great St.
Mary's (the University Church). It is said that on
some occasion when he did so it was crowded to excess,
for there was as much to see in him as to hear.

"He is mentioned in Cole's MSS., in the British
Museum, as a man of a very graceful and portly stature,
of a most humane and candid disposition, and generally
beloved by all his acquaintance. At the age of thirty-
five he was married, on July 26, 1729, at St. Bartholomew's the Great, London, to Ann, daughter of
John Woodward, Esq., of Butler's Marston, Warwick.
She was a beautiful woman, not more than twenty years
of age, and they were then considered to be the hand-
somest pair that were ever seen. The only trace left
of their wooing consists in two lines, which were traditional in the Thackeray family as being composed by
the archdeacon, and were probably repeated by him :

"A part of a grove, and the place for a key,
Is the name of the fair one who best pleases me."

In January, 1743, occurred a memorable contest for
the Provostship of King's College, Cambridge, wherein
Dr. Thackeray came out but second best, having been
defeated in consequence of Sir Robert Walpole's pre-

dilection for another of the candidates, *viz.* Dr. George,
master of Eton, who therefore received many of
Thackeray's votes, and so won the day. Both in Mr.
Lyte's *Eton College*, and in the memorials of the
Thackeray family, are amusing accounts of the election
in question, on the occasion of which the King's Fellows
passed their night in the chapel, warming themselves by
charcoal fires. The weather was frosty, and a letter
from Cambridge expresses wonder that the cold had
not killed any of these strange disturbers of the night.
It was held that during the forty-eight hours allotted
for election no adjournment could be made, so that,
despite the sacred character of the place, we read that
the Fellows continued scrutinizing, walking about,
eating, sleeping, some of them smoking, until, having
remained in the sacred edifice from a Monday before
noon until the time of election had expired, they were
released from their unwonted duties. A looker-on thus
describes the scene as he beheld it at two o'clock in
the morning :

" Some wrapped in blankets, erect in their stalls
like mummies ; others asleep on cushions like so many
Gothic tombs. Here a red cap over a wig ; there a face
lost in the cape of a rug ; one blowing a chafing-dish
with a surplice sleeve ; another warming a little negus,
or sipping Coke upon Littleton, *i.e.* tent and brandy."†

Strange, not to say marvellous, irreverence ! They
scarcely at this moment, one would opine, needed the
Hoadleian doctrines to dissipate undue veneration for all
that the wisest and best of mankind had hitherto
deemed inviolable. But the good Dr. Thackeray cannot
be held responsible for the shortcomings of the times in

---

* Maxwell Lyte, *History of Eton College*, p. 307.

which he lived ; while this failure to secure the King's
Provostship, January 1743, led to his acceptance,
in May 1746, of the mastership vacant at Harrow
School.

The Thackeray family records tell us that his very
large family induced him to undertake this responsibility, which, with all its elements of hope and promise,
involved an effort such as could alone be successfully
sustained by a man of great ability and energy.   Dr.
Thackeray, being a friend of Frederic, Prince of Wales,
and being further known as a man who, under great
discouragement, had scorned advancement at the cost
of principle—no common thing at the best of times
—might be expected to receive preferment at the hands
of the Prince's party.   But if, as men thought, marked
out for a bishopric and its accompanying worldly
benefits, any such prospect of power and wealth was, at
the best, uncertain and remote, as the realisation would
probably have been deferred until Frederic I. had
succeeded to the throne of England.   Hence it came to
pass that, fired with the well-founded belief that Harrow School was endowed with capacities for greatness
which his talents and ardour were likely to develop,
Thomas Thackeray entered upon his hard though
hopeful task.   In his own immediate exertions lay a
surer and more honourable road to distinction than in
the precarious chances of the favour of the Heir
Apparent.

At Harrow itself, judging from the Governors'
Minutes, something akin to *carte blanche* was given to
Dr. Thackeray, who seems to have been regarded as
master of the situation, chosen to bring with him from
Eton the latest culture and the most approved customs.

9

For instance, he soon altered the holidays,* and is responsible for the tripartite arrangement of the year at Harrow so puzzling to parents, who fail to understand how a year can contain but three quarters.

The striking feature of Harrovian life was at this period the practice of archery, the annual shooting for the Silver Arrow being a famous local function, which, we fear, attracted the swell mobsman of the period from London—aye, and probably from royal Windsor also; so that it became necessary for Dr. Heath to suppress the most characteristic of all Herga's customs, one, moreover, which might have co-existed with modern cricket and rifle-shooting, and youth generally have still been the gainer. The story of this suppression will be told in its proper place; but it may be mentioned here that, when Archdeacon Thackeray chose arms for his family during his Harrow sojourn, the silver arrow was a prominent object therein,† leading, not unnaturally, to the supposition that the arms of the school were likewise adorned with this patriotic trophy by the same benefactor to Harrow. We are inclined to believe that here is the only possible solution of a difficulty which has perplexed Harrovian antiquaries, when they found that the original device as deposited with the school lawyer is not crossed with the familiar arrows, but consisted

* The original Harrow holidays had been a month at Christmas, a fortnight at Easter, and a fortnight at Whitsuntide, an arrangement which Dr. Brian induced the governors to modify by abolishing Easter holidays and adding a fortnight to the Whitsuntide vacation. This was in 1728. Now in 1759 Dr. Thackeray ordered that there should be four weeks at Christmas, two at Easter, and four at Bartholomew-tide, the latter corresponding to the modern Midsummer holidays (*School Archives*).

† *Memorials of the Thackeray Family.*

simply of the lion rampant, and the accompanying
motto, *Donorum Dei Dispensatio Fidelis.*

It was in the year 1753 that Bishop Hoadley, who
had never seen Dr. Thackeray in his life, presented him
with the Archdeaconry of Surrey. We cannot believe
that the head-master of Harrow ever held Latitudinarian opinions, such as those which animate the
disputations of that strangely-constituted Prelate, who,
as Mr. Maxwell Lyte tells us, never visited his diocese
of Bangor at all,* and now considered the Archdeaconry
of Surrey as an appendage to his see at Winchester,
and one the duties of which might be adequately discharged in the leisure of a Harrow head-master's
Easter holiday. We know that Dr. Thackeray was
the man to give all time, not already, so to speak,
mortgaged elsewhere, to an office originating in the
third century, and involving attendance on the Bishop,
whom he aided in the management and disbursement
of the revenues of the see, together with other duties
such as Archdeacon Thackeray was not the person to
neglect, and which, in conjunction with overwhelming
school responsibilities at Harrow, probably sent the
good man to a somewhat premature grave.

We know with what vigour and effect Dr. Thackeray
addressed himself to his Harrow duties, not, we fear,
rendered lighter by the additional cares which a large
family was gradually heaping up. To a man with
sixteen children, nine of them daughters, one can
scarcely wonder that an addition of income, such as
the Surrey Archdeaconry brought,† was cheerfully

---

* Maxwell Lyte, *Eton College*, p. 286.
† The Thackeray *Memorials* say £130, with dependencies that
may bring in a deal of money.

accepted, and the onerous duties connected therewith
faithfully discharged. However this may be, Dr.
Thackeray did not forget to cultivate at Harrow the
aristocratic connection which his Whig principles,
despite their popular origin, recognised as a power
in human affairs. So it is that we read in the
Thackeray *Memorials* that the Scotch nobility whose
children were under his care persuaded the archdeacon to accept a degree in Divinity from one of the
universities north of the Tweed.

At Harrow in 1752 were the Duke of Gordon, Lord
Downe, Sir John Rushout, and the Honourable George
Forbes, Lord Granard's son. Thus early do we find
evidence of the establishment of the noble connection
which constituted an indispensable element of any
striking school success in the eighteenth century. For
it is one of Dr. Arnold's proud titles to fame that he
may be said to have substituted an aristocracy of intellect for one of mere birth, as the basis of the high
reputation attained by Rugby. But in 1746 popular
principles had need of the support which patrician
connection supplies; while what unfortunately was at
stake, not only at Harrow in the eighteenth century,
but all over Europe, was the right of a poor man to
spend his shilling as the rich man his pound, as contended for by Charles Fox in eloquent language, which
averred such advantage to be an inherent privilege in
any free community. It was a red-letter day for Harrow
when nobility was first attracted thither.

Although in Dr. Thackeray's time the numbers never
reached the 140 which they had attained in 1721
under Dr. Brian, they approached to within ten of that
figure. Yet neither this numerical success nor the accom-

panying social advancement seems to have been attained
without some questionable sacrifices. For otherwise we
should not read of one Dr. Glasse setting up a private
boarding-house wherein youths of gentle blood might, if
they desired, enjoy foundation privileges and yet hold
limited converse with the home boarders pure and
simple ; nor, again, could the story of Tate Wilkinson's
Harrow career ever have been placed on record.

Tate Wilkinson, a handsome and taking youth, was a
son of the then minister of Savoy Chapel in the Strand,
who, on going to Harrow School in November 1752 at
the age of thirteen, became the *fidus Achates* of young
George Forbes, son of Lord Granard. But the London
boy had conceived a liking for play-acting, which led
him to shrink from the rough school life at Harrow, and,
relying on parental susceptibilities, he made his escape
on foot, reaching the Savoy just as his father was
engaged in clerical duties on Sunday evening. But when
the reverend gentleman, returning home after Church,
realised the situation, he displayed a heart which to his
imploring child seemed as hard as adamant, neither
Tate's tears nor expostulations availing anything to prevent his speedy return to Harrow Hill in a post-chaise
hired for that purpose. On arrival at the foot of the
familiar ascent he found a rough greeting from his associates, who seem to have gloated over the trouble in
store for this youthful *devoté* at the shrine of Melpo-
mene. It appears, however, that Mr. Reeves, the
writing-master, in whose house both Tate Wilkinson
and Mr. George Forbes were located, had certain
womankind about him who both loved acting and had
been captivated by the little Tate Wilkinson's personal
attractions. Anyhow, they joined with George Forbes

in inducing Mr. Reeves to shield the erring youth from
chastisement, and refrain from speaking the word to the
head-master which must have sealed the culprit's fate.

All appeared likely to go merrily as a marriage-bell,
and the last scene of the comedy to be such as delights
the actor's sense of propriety, when, lo and behold,
George Forbes's guardian and uncle, Admiral Forbes,*
appeared on the scene, and, urging the danger to his
nephew of such an example being allowed to pass by
without punishment, called on Dr. Thackeray to exact the
penalty, and, strange to state, urged his cause with success. Although, as Tate Wilkinson tells us, the benign
and humane head-master demurred, and probably in his
own heart felt the shame of for one instant tolerating such
external dictation, he gave way so far as to render Tate
Wilkinson's person up to the tender mercies of the Rev.
Mr. Prior, the second master, whose power of the rod
seems clearly unconstitutional, whether considered from
the aspect of the first institution of the second master's
post in 1721† or judged by the canons of Harrow un-
written law which obtain at the present moment.

A flogging at Harrow in 1752 or 1753 was probably
a sterner affair than delinquents are familiar with in the
year of grace 1884. To begin with, Tate Wilkinson
suffered publicly in the Fourth Form room, the sensations

* This Admiral Forbes was the only officer who protested
against Admiral Byng's execution, doing so on technical grounds,
founded on the nature of the ruling whereon the severe sentence
was based. Admiral Forbes was also the historian of the House
of Granard. See the *Earls of Granard*, by Admiral Forbes (Long-
mans), Preface.

† The School Minute that provided Mr. Brian with an assistant
specially *precluded* his having power of the rod. For account of
Tate Wilkinson's Harrow experiences, see *Tate Wilkinson's
Memoirs*, pp. 39–52.

which the unlucky victim experienced being described
by Tate Wilkinson himself in somewhat bald rhyme.
Let us, however, on this occasion draw a veil over the
scene that ensued, and only remark in passing how, as
Tate Wilkinson relates, he saw exultation on every
youthful face but that of George Forbes while the dire
preparations were in progress. Truly the misfortunes of
our friends are not always displeasing. The boy seems
to have afterwards learned to love Harrow, and to have
actually prevailed with the good Dr. Thackeray to
tolerate theatricals, and to patronise *Romeo*[*] and the
Provoked Husband, in which Tate Wilkinson was Lady
Townley, the archdeacon soon, however, withdrawing
his sanction in deference to public opinion, which, in
a vague form, even then reached Harrow-on-the-Hill.
We know also that the head-master withdrew his
embargo on Harrow theatricals in a few years' time,
when under the ægis of Sir William Jones they assumed
a more classical type.[†]

Having illustrated by Tate Wilkinson's story[‡] evidence of the peculiar social influences dominant in still
struggling Harrow, we may touch upon the more purely
educational aspect of the school. The names of such
noted scholars as Sir W. Jones, Samuel Parr, and
Bennet, the future Bishop of Cloyne, have rescued
Archdeacon Thackeray's *régime* from the stigma of alone

---

[*] Wilkinson played *Romeo,* and the young Sir J. Rushout
Juliet.

[†] *Apropos* of school theatricals, we may remind our readers
that the earliest extant English comedy, *Ralph Royster Doyster*
was composed by Udall, head-master of Eton, for performance
by the Eton boys.

[‡] Tate Wilkinson became a well-known playwright and comic
actor, and his *Memorials* deal with the most striking incidents
connected with the drama in the middle of the last century.

nurturing sundry high-bred youths, of whom it may in
the main be recorded that they lived and died without
placing themselves on the roll of fame, and were better
known in their own times than in 1884. And we must
remember that although the halcyon days of Harrow
scholarship in its more mature phase are associated in
men's minds with the times of Sumner, yet the foundation of this remarkable culture was laid when Thackeray
instructed Parr, Jones, Bennet, and Archdale.

Parr, we are told, was always a serious child, and
was wont to sit still in the meditative mood while his
school-fellows were playing about.* Jones and Bennet,
on the other hand, we read of as entering naturally into
the amusements and occupations of other boys. And in
a juvenile literary work of Bennet's called *Pugna maxima*,
we find allusion to a house battle fought in December
1757 between Hawkins' and Thackeray's houses. The
rivalry which then culminated in hostilities is perpetuated, as most Harrovians know, in traditions of
more recent date. On the occasion in question the
Thackerites had attacked the Hawkinsites to get some
fireworks, and in the battle which ensued one Murray
stands as the hero, while the Duke of Gordon, Middleton, Thwaites, Rawlinson, Bennet, Jones, Tuffnel, West,
Earl, Norton, Wilmot, Rosse, Cranston, Lord William
Gordon, Brudenell, Cotton, and the Earl of Barrymore
are amongst the names of those who entered *con amore*
into this most charming *melée*.

Bestow no word of censure, gentle Harrovian of
modern times, whose superfluous energy finds scope on
the " footer " field, or who shouts to his heart's content

---

* *Parr's Works*, by J. Johnstone, vol. I. p. 21.

when the "cock-house" match has been decided, or
cheers some popular demigod whose place in the eleven
for the match at Lords against Eton is at last secure.
Kindred sympathy should surely not be denied to those
of our ancestors who indulged the ecstasies of youth
according as opportunity afforded; and, indeed, it is
delightful after passing through the mists of darker
ages to emerge at last amidst kindred samples of recognised flesh and blood such as stand prominently forth
from the canvas in 1757, having each a counterpart
amongst us now.   Yes, the time of Thackeray first
opens modern school life to our view, and allows us to
perceive not alone mere shadowy forms pieced together
by means of laborious research, but an image of the
life we all apprise so highly now, and study to preserve
in all its integrity for the sake of those around us, as
also for future generations yet unborn.   This, at least,
will be felt by many faithful Harrovians, some of whom
may peruse these pages and pardon a passing panegyric,
while hailing substantial fame and assured position after
long ages of doubtful struggle.*

The future Bishop Bennet's lines were lengthy, and
we are not disposed, even were we in the position, to
transcribe them in entirety; but the few stanzas given
in Johnstone's *Parr*, vol. i. p. 22, bespeak descriptive
power unusual in a schoolboy of tender years :—

> There, where but one could stand from danger far,
> A neutral chief surveyed the shifting war—
> Richard Ld. Barrymore of Irish race.
> Strong were his limbs and manly was his face,
> But dull his mind to honours fairest charms,
> His spirit mean, and small his skill in arms.

* These records will be found in full in Johnstone's *Parr*,
vol. i. pp. 1–22.

Again,

> Farran his fate by Bennet's bludgeon found,
> And Seward* fell extended on the ground ;
> But e'en in victory Murray's arm we fear,
> And shun to meet him in the walls of war,
> As when the giants on Olympus' height,
> With Neptune, Mars, and Phœbus dared the fight,
> Th' inferior gods with ease from heaven they drove,
> But shrank themselves before the arm of Jove.

And although evincing natural spirit at a becoming age, we must not forget that Sir William Jones had within a month or two of his arrival assisted the youths Parr and Bennet in the composition and acting of a play. Given Archdeacon Thackeray's supervision, and we are not surprised to learn how great was the measure of fame which their reputation as matured scholars brought to Harrow in the day when Dr. Sumner became head-master.

We do not hear of the great home-boarder, Parr, taking an active part in the above-mentioned vagaries, but we learn, nevertheless, that he fought a battle with Lord Mountstuart in defence of a worried cat.†

This chapter would be incomplete without reference to one other pupil of the good Archdeacon's, namely, Richard Archdale, the future friend of Dr. Johnson and Garrick, who helped to raise the standard of scholarship at John Lyon's school to the level at which we shall leave it when we bid farewell to Dr. Thackeray and his excellent works. To Bennet's friendly eye Archdale appeared in the light of a genius ; and there

---

* Seward was a compiler gifted with great discernment, his literary taste being remarkable, while his *Historical Anecdotes* are amongst the more popular books at the London Library in 1884.
† *Parr's Works*, by Johnstone, vol. i. p. 18.

is evidence in our literature which shows that he attained
a high standard in the current scholarship of those days.
It is certain that Dr. Thackeray kept up his noble connections and sustained the level of scholarship, but did
not succeed any more than had others before him in
stemming the apparently inevitable reaction which an
increase of scholars presaged at the poorly endowed
Harrow school.   But on this occasion the rise from
fifty to one hundred and thirty and the decline thence to
eighty was but as the tide that leaves the pebbly shore
glittering in the sun, as an earnest, may be, of inevitable
and speedy return.

Observant critics must have known well that when
Archdeacon Thackeray resigned in 1760 he had once
and for all established the fame of Harrow School,[*]
even if the remembrance of 1721 and Brian's then well-
filled schoolroom had prompted him to put to the touch
a reputation which came unscathed out of the conflict.

Amidst the changes effected during Dr. Thackeray's
regime, we do not find that he by any means discouraged
the foundation scholars, who, living in the neighbourhood, had a prior right to the free education provided
by John Lyon.   The dame system of home elementary
teaching for resident students was by no means abandoned, and in 1747 we read in the Governors' Minutes
of Mary Berry being appointed school-dame in the
hamlet of Sudbury instead of Mary Bliss lately deceased.
But it is, nevertheless, remarkable that in the last century, before modern capitalists became plentiful and
their caste dominant, an intermingling of classes was
found possible in one of the most aristocratic commu-

---

* In May, 1759, was published the first school list.   It is not
extant (Governor's Minutes, 1759).

nities in England, whereas, as later events have shown,
the modern home-boarder has entirely superseded the
once dominant free scholar, who, in presence of others
domiciled at Harrow (who are not by the letter of the
law foreigners), finds refuge on the slopes of Roxey
where probably he gains the very enlightenment designed
for his benefit by John Lyon, bereft, unfortunately, of
such advantages as the name of Harrovian confers. And
the fact remains that despite two, if not three, Reform
Bills and imminent popular rule, English rich and poor
are less disposed to consort together at school than they
were before George III. was king, or the successful
struggle for American independence led men to yearn
for that equality which human nature will not endorse
in the practice of life.

For the closing days of Archdeacon Thackeray's
Harrow sojourn we must again turn to the charming
volume of *Memorials of the Thackeray Family*. From
this volume we learn how, " by his learning as a
scholar and by his abilities as a teacher, Dr. Thackeray
raised the reputation of Harrow School." Himself ever
unwilling to turn one hair's breadth from the line of
what he deemed to be duty, however flattering the
prospects, he was led to adopt a mode of instruction
which condemned his pupils to similar conscientious
abnegation. He would never allow them to hear a word
of praise issue from their master's lips.

Believing praise to encourage vanity and idleness, he
probably carried out this principle to excess, and not a
single encomium on his many promising pupils remains
on record, except the celebrated opinion as to Sir
William Jones, given privately, " That he was a boy of
so active a mind that if left naked and friendless on

Gentlemen

As I am prevented by sickness from attending at your present meeting, I take this method of acquainting you, that I intend to leave the School at Bartholomewtide next.

Permit me to return my thanks to those Gentlemen from whom I have received favours; & to subscribe myself

Their much Obliged
Humble Servant
Thos Thackeray

Harrow May 3d 1760.

Salisbury plain he would yet find the road to fame and riches."

In 1748 Archdeacon Thackeray was made chaplain to Frederic Prince of Wales, the eldest son of George II., with whom, as we have previously shown, he was a great favourite.

In August 1760 he resigned the head-mastership of Harrow in a formal communication to the governors, written in a clear round-hand, which may be now seen amongst the school archives, and a copy of which faces this page, valuable in itself as the letter of one who, Dr. Parr tells us, wrote but sparsely, the little leisure he had at command being employed in attaining the (in those days) remarkable knowledge of modern languages,[*] which, taken together with high classical attainments, striking personal appearance, and polished manners, rendered the Archdeacon a notable instance of the refined clergyman during the days when George II. was king.

"It was expected," writes Mrs. Alicia Bayne, "that Archdeacon Thackeray would shortly be made a bishop,[†] not only on his own merits, but from the royal favour which he enjoyed. George II. was drawing near his end, and the son of Prince Frederick was to succeed him. But it was not to be. He went with his wife and daughters for a short time to London, and there, attended by a most affecting incident, his death occurred. They were lodging in the house of a Scotchwoman. One day the Archdeacon dined with some dignitary, and as was customary in

---

[*] *The Public Schools*, by Etoniana, p. 273.
[†] *Memorials of the Thackeray Family*, p. 18. We continue to quote therefrom.

those days, when the dinners were in the middle of the
day, the company left about 5 P.M. My grandmother
and her daughters had been out shopping, and when
they returned they inquired if Dr. Thackeray had come
back. The mistress of the house replied, ‘ Yes, 1 saw
him pass just now.’ On going up-stairs they found that
he was not there ; but he came in shortly afterwards,
laid down on his bed, and died instantly, as was supposed from some affection of the heart. This was on
September 25, 1760. The Scotchwoman still maintained that he certainly passed by her door, and that she
had seen his *wraith*. He was buried, aged sixty-six
years, in the churchyard at Harrow.”

Dr. Parr composed the following epitaph on his old
master, but it was never placed over his tomb :—

THOMÆ THACKERAY, S.T.P.,
COLL. REGAL. APUD CANTABR. OLIM SOCIO
CHISSELIÆ PARVÆ ATQUE HAYDONIÆ
IN AGRO ESSEXIENSI RECTORI
FREDERICO PRINCIPI VALLIÆ A. SACRIS
ARCHIDIACONO SOUTHRIENSI
SCHOLÆ HARROVIENSIS PER XV. ANNOS MAGISTRO.
VIRO INTEGERRIMO SANCTISSIMO
ET AD JUVENTUTEM LIBERALITER ERUDIENDAM
STUDIO OPTIMARUM ARTIUM ET SUAVITATE MORUM
EGREGIE INSTRUCTO
QUI
CONJUGE SUI AMANTISSIMA
LIBERIS XIV. SUPERSTITIBUS
DECESSIT LONDINI VII. CAL. OCTOBR.
ANNO DOMINI MDCCLX. ÆTATIS LXVII.
ET IN SEPULCRETO HUJUS ECCLESIÆ
A LATERE OCCIDENTALI CONDITUS EST.
NEPOTES EJUS
L L, M, HOC MONUMENTUM POSUERUNT.*

Some Latin verses written by Dr. Thackeray while at
college are to be found in the Cambridge Collections on

* Field’s *Life of Parr*, vol. ii. p. 462, 463.

the Peace of Utrecht, 1713, and on the accession of George I., 1714.

The Archdeacon's will, whereby he left everything to his wife except legacies of £300 to fourteen children, commenced as follows :—" In the name of God, Amen. First and principally, I recommend my soul into the hands of Almighty God, hoping for a blessed resurrection through the merits and mediation of His Son Jesus Christ my Saviour."

The Thackeray family possess two miniatures representing their ancestor dressed in his gown and bands and a small powdered wig. They portray a handsome, benignant man. Another, presented by his grandson, is in the Vaughan Library at Harrow, as well as a copy which Dr. H. M. Butler had done of a half-size portrait in oils. Visitors to King's College, Cambridge, may also see a portrait of this distinguished man in the Master's lodge. The Archdeacon's widow lived on at Harrow until January 23, 1793, attaining the great age of eighty-nine.

The two youngest children of Archdeacon Thackeray and his wife Ann were born at Harrow, the son William Makepiece being destined to give an ancestry of dignity to the greatest master of satirical fiction and judge of human nature in the Victorian age. The adoption by this family of the Harrow arrows amidst their arms led the great William Makepiece in 1859 to celebrate his direct descent from the good archdeacon by reciting to a delighted school-boy audience world-famed lectures on the Georges at the time when Dr. Vaughan held sway at Harrow.

CHAPTER VII.

JOHN LYON'S HOPES REALISED UNDER DR. SUMNER.

The power of thought, the magic of the mind.
LORD BYRON, *The Corsair.*

IT needs a due sense of historical proportion on the part of a writer, if the sudden prominence of Harrow life is to be duly appraised, and yet the individual share of each personal influence on contemporary thought or future culture to remain faithfully fixed on the reader's mind. The converse of men of talent, when the sphere is limited, naturally leads each local luminary to regard his daily counsellor and accepted guide as infallible. This tendency to contract the mental vision as regards externals is, from the nature of the case, more prevalent in school society than in the wider college sphere. Harrow, doubtless, suffered from such contraction of ideas before facility of travel and increased communication of thought, by means of cheap literature and the daily press, had led the wisest recluse to recognise his own infinite littleness in the scale of life. This observation is made because it is vain to deny that, amidst the records of early Harrow scholarship have crept in comments on the qualities of those acting on that remarkable school stage, which must be

accepted with caution, not only because the speakers
had not yet mingled freely in the great world, but
because the literature of their time seemed prone to
extol individual prowess in somewhat sounding tones.
But when all this has been said, and the chaff been
duly separated from the corn by careful winnowing,
there remains enough to show that the standard of
knowledge reached by a remarkable band of Harrovians
was uncommonly high between 1760 and 1771, while
we are inclined to believe that such early development
of talent was largely due to the new head-master
Dr. Sumner's skilful culture of the good seed sown by
Archdeacon Thackeray.

Sumner, indeed, flits like a splendid meteor over
the history of Harrow, but leaves behind little trace of
his personality. We are inclined to accept his pupils'
estimate, eloquently expressed by Sir William Jones,
and state our conviction that, had circumstances allowed
participation in its excitements to Dr. Sumner, the
Senate's thundering applause must sooner or later have
been his, and the niche in Harrow story have remained
unfilled in which he afforded an elevated guidance to
some remarkable minds. And, indeed, to have fired
Sir W. Jones, Parr, Bennet, Halhed, Archdale, and
Warburton Lytton with their respectively high resolves
is no mean outcome of talent which finds no direct
counterpart in the distinguished list of Harrow masters.*

We can find no space here to recount the lives of
men whose literary careers were bound up with the

* Nor should it go unmentioned that Jones was fifteen and Parr
thirteen when Dr. Sumner came to Harrow, so that Dr. Thackeray's share in their training was very considerable. Jones was
deputed by the Upper School to instruct the new master in his
daily routine. See Lord Teignmouth's *Life of Sir W. Jones.*

century in which they flourished.   Their strivings
after classical attainments stood as the perfecting of
ideas which had origin when Harrow School was
founded in 1571, and, although we cannot accept Sir
William Jones, or Samuel Parr, or William Warburton
Lytton, as being representatives of the more practical
spirit which has since advanced England, still we may
see in Dr. Sumner's glowing teaching just that link
which was required to unite eighteenth-century Harrow
with that of its earliest traditions, and connect Herga's
hill with the reputation for learning, without possession
of which John Lyon's hopes could never have been
consummated.

It has ofttimes been recounted how Jones, Parr, and
Bennet, together with other kindred spirits, are said to
have divided the fields around Harrow into imaginary
states, wherein the youthful imagination devised battles,
sieges, and such like accompaniments of ancient political
life.   Had any such tendency to indulge the imaginative
faculty been general throughout the school, one might
have well pined for more modern school regulations,
such as would have relegated Parr and Sir William
Jones to participation in compulsory football, or assigned to the youthful genius of the period a spell of
cricket fagging, of a character that must have left scant
leisure for indulgence in what modern schoolboys would
deem pedantic vagaries.   But at Harrow, in Dr. Sumner's
time, we have, fortunately, evidence of juvenile life
in the full swing of hey-day delight, combined with a
display of culture which was in advance of the age.

Various are the entries in governors' minutes concerning the arrow-shooting under Dr. Sumner.   We
read of such interest being excited by the annual

gathering that the master desired to alter the date,* and to thus mitigate evils which, under a succeeding master, were deemed fatal to the continuance of a most charming pastime. The keeping up of the butts had come to be reckoned an annual item of expenditure for several years before Dr. Sumner's time, and in 1747 the sum of 10s. 4d. was laid out for this purpose, while at the usual competition in August of the following year a single constable sufficed to keep order.† That invasion of the London riff-raff, which Harrow authorities learnt to deprecate, had certainly not commenced at this period.

In the *Gentleman's Magazine* are to be found the following interesting entries. Thursday, July 2, 1761 : The silver arrow was shot for (as usual) by twelve young gentlemen at Harrow-on-the-Hill, and was won by the Earl of Barrymore.‡ And again, on Thursday, July 5, 1764,§ the silver arrow annually shot for at Harrow was won by Master Mee ; while on Thursday, July 4th, 1765, a Master Davies came off victorious in the presence of certain Indian warriors, who, although they thought the Harrow boys shot well, are said to have avowed a belief in their own superiority.||

The competition of 1766 appears to have waxed uncommonly keen, and we have the testimony of the winner's son, Mr. Charles Allix, of Willoughby Hall, Lincolnshire, given in a letter to Dr. George Butler, how intensely desirous of success was a rival whose

---

* The first Thursday in July was substituted for the first Thursday in August.
† *Governors' Account Book.*
‡ *Gentleman's Magazine,* vol. xxxiv. p. 346.
§ *Ibid.* vol. xxxv. p. 344.
|| *Public Schools,* by Author of *Etoniana,* p. 305.

three elder brothers had previously carried off the
prize. We regret, moreover, to add that some partisan was found in whose heart the true horse-coping
instinct must have rested, inasmuch as the week before
shooting, Master Charles Wager Allix's bow was
maliciously broken, so that the winner performed
with a shortened, but, as the event proved, not less
effective weapon.*

But it is clear that the ancient arrow-shooting was
not by any means the sole amusement of the increasing
school, which had at last commenced to make itself
known in the world. One Mrs. Edmonds was paid
annual rent by the governors for a play-field, in which,
we can have little doubt, was pursued the game which,
despite all rivals, has been most permanently connected
with the School on the Hill. We speak of cricket, at
this period fast rising in the popular estimation.

But we turn afresh to the earlier days of Harrow
under Sumner, thence to trace the means whereby this
master mind, through practical attention to sublunary
matters, succeeded in inducing parents to entrust their
children to his care ; for the numbers certainly rose at
Harrow speedily as the school reputation increased.
Nor was such success gained by any subservience to
the aristocratic connection that almost desired to claim
Harrow as its own. The learned Dr. Glasse's boarding-
house, of which we made previous mention, had hitherto
enjoyed an unconstitutional privilege of allowing its
members to absent themselves from calling-over, known
at Harrow as "bill." The cancelling of this privilege
was but the first blow struck at an anomaly which Dr.
Sumner resolved to destroy, being unwilling to brook

* E. Walford, *Greater London*, Cassell & Co., part 6, p. 265.

an *imperium in imperio*, towards which, whatever its excellence, irresponsible power such as Dr. Glasse wielded in Harrow must sooner or later lead. For what was to prevent other unattached individuals from playing the free-lance, and taking pupils without reference to school statutes, so offering free education to the rich and well-provided for, when it was intended for *bonâ fide* residents in the town. Dr. Sumner contended successfully against aristocratic patrons of the school for a Harrow frequented, may be, by those of gentle blood, but yet offering a field wherein no favour should be shown either to peer or commoner, rich or poor.

Dr. Glasse had the sense to perceive that he was engaged in an unequal contest when pitted against Dr. Sumner, and withdrew from Harrow, not relying on the well-meant but questionable support of the Earl of Radnor, who threatened to destroy Harrow School if Dr. Sumner molested this patrician retreat.[*] In justice to the then Lord Radnor, it is fair to state that he had some ground for believing that the authorities had tacitly acquiesced in the arrangements which rendered Dr. Glasse's pupils independent of the head-master's authority out of school. His Lordship's communication to the governors appears in the *School Archives*, and is too long for insertion here, but the following extract states the case from his point of view :

" I must desire," says his Lordship, " this matter may not go off as a matter of no consequence between Dr. Glasse and Dr. Sumner, but be considered, as it is in fact, a question of justice between the parents and the master ; as such I urge it."

---

[*] J. Johnstone, *Parr's Works*, vol. i. p. 58. Communicated by Mr. Roderick, an assistant master.

After appealing against what he called an unjust
regulation, Lord Radnor concluded by stating that he
had received *an assurance* that the privilege of exemption from bill and other school duties was not to be
infringed upon.* Such was the penalty of yielding to
aristocratic influence for the purpose of strengthening
the Harrow connection. It was, in truth, a Gordian
knot that Dr. Sumner so boldly elected to cut. Fortunately, however, the reputation of the little Middlesex
village had been so far established that, with the fates
fighting on his side, Dr. Sumner was enabled to take
up the only worthy ground, when protecting the foundation statutes from being ignored in the first blush of a
triumphant progress, due almost entirely to their wise
latitude, as faithfully interpreted by the governing body.
But Sumner's bold and successful stand left the Harrow
School community struggling in the throes of a difficulty
which—necessity being the mother of invention—was
only foiled by the same wise perception which had
preferred the confronting of present peril to the disin-
tegration certain to accompany a policy of cringing
to the great and subserviency to the strong. Where
and under what conditions was an additional influx of
some 200 boys to be housed? The head-master,
despite the governors' readiness to assist him, could
not board a tithe of this number, while even modern
knowledge of Harrow goes to show how inadequate
must have been the means to provide for the boys'
comfort, when large houses, in the modern sense of the
word, were unknown within the school system, and
when, according to theory, the head-master had a sole

* Letter written from Grosvenor Street, W., on May 13th, 1768.
It is in the *School Archives.*

privilege of lodging foreigners. Under these circumstances, Dr. Sumner hit on the expedient of extending this right to any of the six dames who might be chosen for the purpose, and whose conduct, when employed in imparting the rudiments of religion and learning, had disclosed faculties fitting them to undertake wider responsibilities of a matronly character.

Hence it occurs that, towards the close of their Harrow career, we find Dr. Parr and Sir William Jones located in a dame's house, and sharing the board of one Mrs. King,* in the strange company of George II.'s wild boy, who had been captured in the Black Forest of Germany, and—high tribute to the Harrow dame in question—was sent to that worthy lady as the person most likely to kindle the dormant torch of reason in a totally untutored mind—a task, alas! found to be beyond mortal power. And so the system of female boarding-houses became rooted at Harrow, inheriting the tradition of the six dames who formerly instructed the scholars in religion, reading, and writing. And it is worthy of observation that in some form, either in the person of a master's wife or a skilled matron, such requirement as that perceived by Dr. Sumner still remains a recognised part of public school education, being specially in vogue at Harrow, where in every master's house the general health is as carefully regarded as are the boys' characters and capabilities of mind thoughtfully trained and patiently developed.

We have dwelt upon Dr. Sumner's judgment when confronted by the encroachments of patrician privilege, such as, persisted in, must have paralysed the natural growth of Harrow School, and would add that his dis-

* Field, *Life of Parr*, vol. i. p. 25.

crction was united with the resolution of a strong man.
But we cannot pretend to aver a belief that any exercise
of individual effort was the sole cause of the steady rise
from 80 to 250 scholars, which took place within a few
years of Dr. Sumner's appointment. In the first place,
coincidently with the rise of Harrow, a rebellion against
Dr. Foster's authority occurred at Eton, and seriously
reduced the college numbers,* while a remarkable
immunity from disease had previously allowed it to be
placed on record that between 1753 and 1763 only one
death had occurred amongst the numerous scholars
who had received education at Harrow.† A remarkable
fact this, a parallel to which it might be difficult to find
in days when sanitary precaution was scarcely known.
Yes, and for ever and aye, so long as there is a school
at Harrow, will the fine bracing air of those Middlesex
uplands prove a recommendation in maternal eyes,
when a decision has to be made as to where young
hopeful shall pass his early days.

In the year 1763 occurred a tempest, which, if in its
general fury it sinks into insignificance when compared
with the wind demon that possessed England for a time
in 1702, yet left its mark upon Harrow, whose prominent church-steeple, stricken with lightning, was consumed by a fire which threatened to spread in the
direction of the school buildings, between which and
St. Mary's fane nothing intervened save a small
building that has since undergone sundry additions,
and is now known as the Vicarage. But it is certain

* In 1768 smouldering discontent culminated in rebellion, and
seriously injured Eton. For account of the circumstance, see
Maxwell Lyte, *Eton College*, pp. 333–38.

† Carlisle, *Grammar Schools*, vol. ii. p. 161.

that, with the wind surging in that direction, the
original edifice, which arose after John Lyon's widow
died in 1608, was for a time in danger; otherwise staid
yeomen and old-fashioned gentlemen of the Harrow
governor type would never have consented to vote £10
as a reward for the efforts of those extinguishing a fire
which they believed to have endangered the property
under their charge.*

A careful study of the school archives connected with
this period shows that Harrow history repeats itself.
We find the same intercourse between school and town
which has rendered the place a mart of business; while,
indeed, both in the repairing of the master's house and
the school buildings are found names which a boy at
Harrow would recognise, if he heard them repeated 118
years afterwards. And then that ever-present flow of
apprentices sent forth into the world, who claim the £5
allowed them by the governors, because the recipients
claim to be fellow-townsmen of John Lyon—they, at
least, lead one to realise in some sort how the great
school has never shirked its responsibilities when called
on to provide for the inhabitants in times of need. But,
of course, all minute descriptions of the daily Harrow life
between 1760–71 sink into insignificance when measured
by the fast-spreading scholarship, which included at one
moment Dr. Parr, Sir William Jones, Bennet, the future
Bishop of Cloyne, Nathaniel Brassey Halhed, Richard
Archdale, Mee (the friend of Parr and maternal relative
of Lord Palmerston), Richard Warburton Lytton,
and, last but not least, Richard Brinsley Sheridan,
amongst those who gloried in the Harrow name—yet,
as we have already stated, no space can here be found

* *Governors' Minutes*, 1763.

for biographical notices of those whose history is to be sought amidst the literary records of their times.

It is enough to say of the single-minded and gifted Orientalist, Sir William Jones, that Dr. Samuel Johnson said of him that he was the most accomplished of the sons of men.* Sir William was exceedingly popular amongst his school-fellows, because of the numerous holidays he gained for them through his prowess ; and, indeed, Dr. Sumner is said to have declared that the pupil excelled him in knowledge of Greek, while he was actually master of thirteen languages.† As a judge in India, Sir William Jones's success in inducing the Brahmins to afford him respect was as remarkable as his constancy towards Harrow, to which he ever looked affectionately as the spot upon which he hoped to end his days.*

And if Richard Warburton Lytton was accounted the first Latin Scholar of his time, and will ever be remembered as the grandfather of the great baron, Lord Lytton—not to say the great-grandfather of the first earl of that name, statesman, poet, and novelist (himself an Harrovian)—so was Nathaniel Brassey Halhed famed for proficiency in his own language, which rendered him a worthy contemporary of the refined and learned Bishop of Cloyne, Dr. Bennet, who owed so much to the scholarship which connection with John Lyon's foundation enabled him to enjoy at Emmanuel College, Cambridge, where his name is treasured amongst the most illustrious of their *alumni*.

---

* *Public Schools*, by Author of *Etoniana*, p. 283.
† This eminent scholar has been credited with a knowledge of twenty-eight languages ; but Mr. F. Pincott, an Orientalist of repute, informs me that Sir W. Jones himself appears to have claimed only thirteen.

Nor must we forget the attainments of Richard
Archdale, whose position in the literary world was
probably not the least assured of all these remarkable
boy scholars. When this phalanx of ability was at
Harrow, a wild and wayward youth was observed both
by Dr. Sumner and his assistant, Parr, who had left
Emmanuel College, Cambridge, unable to pay the
expenses of his college career.

The two masters thought they perceived in young
Richard Sheridan glimpses of genius, marred, may be,
by resolute idleness, but still of a character that led
them to employ each magisterial device calculated to
inspire their pupil with a desire for knowledge. On
their failing to arouse any such interest Sheridan was
placed in the unpleasant position of a clever schoolboy,
who, wilfully idle, has the master's eye constantly upon
him. Called on to construe, without any aid but his
own wit, and probably ignorant of the lesson, the future
author of *The School for Scandal* seems to have impressed
Dr. Sumner with his latent powers, but to have passed
through Harrow without enthusiasm for his studies,
even if future success in the Senate may in some sort
be traced to the statesman-like training of Dr. Sumner.*
For it seems almost impossible to have passed under
that remarkable man's immediate influence and not
gone forth into the world with aspirations raised
beyond the ordinary level, whether the student's mind
was turned towards scholarship, or to an interest
in affairs of State, then matter of contemplation at
Harrow.

The teachings of the past were not allowed by Dr.
Sumner to pass without some practical reference to the

* Moore, *Life of Sheridan*, vol. i. p. 6.

present ; and if in application this method of thought
did lead to the adoption of popular politics, the prevalence of such opinions was so purely intellectual that at
this distance of time we can afford to condone what then
appeared to be utterances of a polemical character.
Moreover, the tendency of Dr. Sumner's political
teaching bore fruit in the training of at least two
public characters of considerable merit in the Marquess
of Hastings and John James Hamilton, who was
destined to be created Marquess of Abercorn by Mr.
Pitt in 1790.* Of the former history speaks as a
successful soldier-statesman, whose career as Governor-
General of India between 1812 and 1822 has made his
name famous ; while of the latter we have recorded
Mr. Pitt's opinion, expressed to Mr. Wilberforce, of
the high character of the Marquess of Abercorn's
oratory. "Had he chosen," said the Prime Minister,
"to take to public life as a speaker, he would have
beaten us all."—Letter of Lord Aberdeen in Mr. J. W.
Croker's *Correspondence and Diaries*, p. 299–300.

The tone of Harrow scholarship was undoubtedly very
high at this epoch, and it is possible to conceive the
dismay with which the sudden removal of the mainspring
of the whole machine was received by an enthusiastic
school community, as well as by those who, settling on
their path of life, were spreading the fame of Harrow
throughout England. For Dr. Sumner seems to have
ruled over his subordinates by the force of a gladly
acknowledged superiority, while even Dr. Parr must
yield in Nature's gifts to his beloved chief.

* In Dr. George Butler's selection of Lists of Harrow School,
p. 8, *tempore* 1760, when Dr. Sumner was head-master, occur the
following names : "Fifth Form.—Lord Rawdon, afterwards Marquess of Hastings. Hamilton, afterwards Marquess of Abercorn."

It may be interesting for modern scholars to note the
technical system of teaching in vogue at Harrow under
Dr. Sumner. And we owe it to the late Dr. George
Butler that printed bills dated as early as August 1770,
may be seen in the Vaughan Library, which enables
us to produce them here. According to these lists in
question, John Lyon's three monitors were four in 1770
and six in 1771, and were succeeded by the Fifth Form,
who in turn had below them the Fourth and Third
forms ; all these ranking as an upper school.

The under school arrangements were of a different
character. The Scan and Prove class ranked first, then
the Ovid, the Phœdrus, the Upper Selectæ, the Under
Selectæ, the Nomenclature, the Grammar, and Accidence.
There was also an unplaced division awaiting the development of youthful powers. A scheme of division such as
gave ample scope to the varying conditions of young
minds, and thoroughly warrants the conclusion arrived
at by the author of *Etoniana*, who in his *Public Schools*,
p. 276, instances the above class division as indicative
of that almost unique talent for teaching possessed by
Robert Sumner, which may be said to have founded a
school, and which produced a ripe harvest when the
noble-minded Joseph Drury—himself an under-master
at the time we mention—guided the Harrow fortunes
between 1785 and 1805. Hence it is, that with scant
matter within reach wherewith to perpetuate the most
trivial detail concerning such a man as Dr. Sumner, we
naturally grasp at any characteristic which may enable
us to picture the man as he appeared to his contemporaries. We are told* that Dr. Sumner had such an
admiration for Fielding the novelist, and for his famous

---

* Field, *Life of Parr*, vol. i. pp. 54 and 63.

creation *Tom Jones*, that he used to declare he would at
any time give ten guineas wholly to forget that fascinating novel, for the pleasure of coming anew to the
literary banquet. So far did Dr. Sumner carry his
enthusiasm as to indoctrinate the Harrow staff with his
reverence for the great author.   To London in holiday
time would Sumner, Parr, Wadeson, and Roderick resort,
and meet at the " Hercules Pillar " in Piccadilly, for the
purpose of seeing and possibly conversing with Fielding
himself.*

At Harrow, again, we catch a glimpse of the eloquent
Sumner reading the Burial Service most touchingly
over the remains of his friend's nephew, Mr. Frank
Parr : while the master's daily round of duty was inter-
spersed with high-souled dissertations on critical questions of religion or scholarship.   And at these moments
of relaxation from school toil we find that his companion
was more often than not the sympathetic Parr, who had
access thereby to the innermost thoughts and aspirations
of the man he admired most, and whose habits he ever
sought to emulate.   A constant smoker, when the
habit was by no means common in England, Dr. Sumner
beguiled Parr into a like indulgence ; so that we read
of cloudy symposiums† wherein were discussed maxims
of a Whig tendency, such as doubtless confirmed Parr's
well-known political opinions.

Mr. Maurice, the author of *Indian Antiquities*, has
testified in the memoirs of his own life (part i. p. 62)
that a democratic spirit prevailed at this period in

* William Warburton Lytton used to relate how precedence had
been given to Parr on these occasions, because, although only
twenty-four years of age, he wore a large scratch wig.

† An amusing account of these festive evenings will be found
in Field's *Life of Dr. Parr*, vol. i. pp. 63, 64.

Harrow School, which he ascribes to the love for
liberty which the histories of Greece and Rome, when
interpreted through Dr. Sumner's eloquence, inspired in
young and ingenious minds.   These were the days of
Wilkes,* whose questionable character did not prevent
the noblest men on the popular side perceiving the importance of sounding the trumpet of freedom when the
rights of mankind lay dormant and could hope for little
from a party of privilege such as the sarcasms of Junius
failed to stir into action.   And, indeed, it is notorious
that, during the early days of the reign of George III.,
when Lord Bute was Prime Minister, no high office
in the Church or State could be expected to reward
talent even such as that possessed by Sumner and Parr,
Sir William Jones, or Warburton Lytton, unless the
possessor were classed amongst the King's friends.

Opposition by the American colonists to the obnoxious
Stamp Act in 1765, was destined to set aflame both
Old and New World, opening a vista of hope to poorer
people, who soon wildly sought the promised goal in a
delirium of savage disorder which shook society to its
base, and still causes many liberty-loving men to dread
their goddess' very name.   When, then, Dr. Sumner
inculcated the doctrines of civil liberty at Harrow he
cut from below the feet of his hearers and followers
all hopes of the early attainment of power which their
conspicuous talents would otherwise have allowed them
to gain.

This was notably the case with Dr. Parr, whose reaction from paternal Jacobitism has been described, and
who now gloried in supporting the recalcitrant Wilkes

---

* For a sympathetic and interesting account of these transactions, see Mr. G. O. Trevelyan's *Charles Fox.*

when he stood for Middlesex, conduct which could scarcely be to the taste of old-fashioned governors who overlooked the business matters and chose the headmaster of Harrow School.

Dr. Sumner's end was fearfully sudden. The concluding portion of his life had not been free from anxieties and troubles, which seem to have in some degree embittered a life brightened by the delights which resort to the high regions of classical thought ever affords. Nor can we, after perusing the sparse details of his life, believe him to have left this world unsolaced by the one abiding comfort which mankind can hope to claim. But that a cloud rested over those sadly-shortened last hours no honest historian can deny.*

Something akin to despair seems to have settled over the denizens of the little Harrow republic when they learnt that their chief was indeed gone. Gathered together with the other members of the staff in that chamber of death were Samuel Parr and Joseph Drury, the former representing Harrow scholarship and the latter that benign wisdom which was destined, when ripened through experience, to enable the owner of those attractive qualities to reproduce the salient points of Sumner's teaching, and raise the school to the very acme of prosperity. It is almost impossible to conceive what men's feelings were as to the depth of a loss which could not be accurately gauged in 1771. At forty-one it was indeed difficult to believe that a man's life-work was accomplished, when scarcely a written or spoken record remained of one whose facility of speech rests on hearsay and has left no trace of his penmanship behind.

Out of the many tributes to Dr. Sumner's genius we

* *Parr's Works*, by John Johnstone, vol. 1. pp. 53, 54.

select that of Sir William Jones, which, translated from the preface to his *Poesios Asiaticæ Comm.*, speaks warmly and with discrimination, and is to be accepted as the writer's *deliberate, boná fide* opinion of his old master; because the conscientious Asiatic scholar is well known to have well weighed every written word, and to have stooped to flatter no man.

"If there ever was a man worthy to be honourably remembered, it was he. In him, high powers of mind were united with pure integrity of heart. His dispositions were most excellent, and his manners most amiable. His learning was exact and profound. In the art of communicating and enforcing instruction he was not surpassed by any master whom I have ever known. Such were the sweetness and cheerfulness of his temper, that it would be difficult to say whether he was more the love and delight of his friends or of his pupils. He was deeply versed in Grecian and Roman literature; and though, like Socrates, he wrote little himself, yet none ever displayed more acuteness or more judgment, either in discovering and correcting the faults, or in discerning and applauding the excellencies of other writers.

"If, instead of being placed at the head of a school, the course of events, or the favour of fortune, had conducted him to the Bar or the Senate, few would have ventured to dispute with him the praise of eloquence, even in England, the only country in the world where at this time the art is cultivated. For he possessed all the great qualities of an orator, if not in their full perfection, yet certainly in a very high degree.

"His voice was powerful and melodious; his style was polished, his wit sportive, his memory wonderfully retentive. His eye, his look, his action, were not those

11

of an ordinary speaker, but those rather of another Demosthenes."*

Dr. Parr read the burial service over his beloved adviser, and composed the monumental elegy which, in choice Latin, adorns the tomb of Harrow's brightest light, and which few visitors to the Parish Church will forget.

We have not transcribed Dr. Samuel Parr's above-mentioned famous Latin inscription which adorns Dr. Sumner's monument in Harrow Church, and remain content with the translation of Sir William Jones's eulogy; as this testimony of the high estimate formed by Harrow scholars of their late master is more forcible than the monumental eloquence of a time when *post mortem* adulation was far too common.

Again, when Dr. Parr was called on by Moore to describe Dr. Sumner's peculiar powers, for insertion in his *Life of Sheridan*, he is told of "a critical judgment, alive to the errors of genius, combined with the warm sensibility that deeply feels its beauties."† He speaks, moreover, of the Harrow head-master's "fine voice, fine ear, fine taste." Nor, when combined with such testimony, can we reject the indirect evidence adduced by the Governors' Minutes, which show Dr. Sumner to have combined a resolute will with his well-known good temper and humanity.

Sir William Jones's beautiful eulogy upon Sumner's excellencies was penned some years after the gifted preceptor's death, and may, therefore, be considered to have expressed the abiding conviction of the Asiatic scholar's reflective mind ; while, finally, Dr. Parr's

---

* Field, *Life of Parr*, vol. i. p. 17 f.
† Moore, *Sheridan*, p. 4.

constant lament that he should have been unable to complete Dr. Sumner's biography points to a profound conviction that the high opinion we have transcribed was no extravagant panegyric.

Where, then, are the *written* details of that remarkable life which, as Dr. Parr said (Field's *Life of Dr. Parr*, vol. i. p. 59), only escaped publication because, immersed in much business, the historian could not proceed until a scribe was procured?

11 *

CHAPTER VIII.

DR. HEATH'S REGIME.—CIVIL WAR AT HARROW.

Here, while the Latian echoes ring,
Rome's wandering genius rests his wing.
REV. F. TRENCH.

WHAT would any great school be without the record of a
rebellion to enliven its history ?   Eton, Winchester, and
Rugby have each their story to tell of struggles against
authority, which, with all their futility and foolishness,
present an attractive mixture of romance and comedy to
readers; while many a grave and reverend senior secretly
delights in accounts of exciting barring-outs and other
juvenile riots.

Up to the year 1771 no internal discord seems to have
marred the upward struggle of Harrow.   Magisterial
shortcomings, it is true, had sullied the page of the
school history more than once, and caused a passing
decline in numbers; but nothing approaching seditious conduct on the part of the boys themselves is to
be discerned before Dr. Sumner's death.

Now the man who had been marked out for promotion
by young Harrow in 1771 was undoubtedly the late
head-master's associate and colleague, Dr. Samuel Parr.
Not only did the *vox populi* point to his elevation as
desirable, but the idea was not discouraged by the great

scholar himself, who remained possessed with the belief that Dr. Sumner cherished a design of nominating a successor, and that the fortunate individual was no less a personage than the erudite friend of Sir William Jones and the Bishop of Cloyne,* viz. Samuel Parr.

But despair at the loss of his guide, philosopher, and friend must have blinded Parr to the improbability of Dr. Sumner, a hale and hearty man of forty-one, so far anticipating premature death as to designate one of the staff to succeed him. Neither can we discover one word written or spoken on the part of Dr. Sumner which gives colour to such belief.

Nor, indeed, was a nomination of the deceased headmaster's—had one been made—likely to carry the weight with it which Harrow public opinion believed. For if, as William Warburton Lytton tells us,† his statement being confirmed by the archives, Dr. Sumner and the governors had for some time been at issue on questions of school government; so much the more were old-fashioned men like the Rushouts and Mr. Bucknall likely to look askance on a disciple such as Parr, who had imbibed Sumner's Whig opinions, and not hesitated to support Wilkes for Middlesex;‡ while, from no fault of his own, and in consequence of poverty, the most accomplished scholar resident in Harrow had left Emmanuel College, Cambridge, without a University degree. If, on the other hand,

* Field, *Life of Parr*, vol. i. p. 61 ; *Parr's Works*, by J. Johnstone, p 63*f*.
† In Field's *Life of Parr*, vol. i. p. 62, will be found Mr. William Warburton Lytton's story of how Dr. Sumner resisted the governors' claim to grant holidays at will. Parr, as Dr. Sumner's supporter, is there assumed to have lost the governors' favour.
‡ *Parr's Works*, by J. Johnstone, vol. i. p. 63.

recommended by sundry outside supporters of the
school,* Parr may, nevertheless, be said to have rested
under serious disabilities.   With all his undoubted
genius, force of will, natural kindliness, and amiability,
it cannot be believed that Dr. Parr would have made an
ideal head-master of Harrow School.   His character
exhibited strong contrasts, and admirers of his sterling
merits might well fear his contentiousness and eccen-
tricity.

Any objections put forward on the ground of this
great man's political opinions were nevertheless baseless
and trivial in the extreme.   For who can read Dr.
Parr's expressions of glowing patriotism in 1803, when
England was threatened with invasion,† or listen to the
fair and philosophical analysis of a political opponent's
character, with which he had previously approached
the *vexata quæstio* of American independence, without
feeling that he was endowed with statesman-like spirit
and animated with knightly feeling.

It is probably true that politics were more or less
discussed amongst the masters at Harrow in Dr.
Sumner's time, and that some few studious youths
like Sir William Jones, Charles Combe, Archdale, and
Bennet, did thus early in life imbibe popular opinions;
yet it is ridiculous to suppose the rioters who wrecked
Mr. Bucknall's carriage, on the occasion of Dr. Heath's
election to the coveted head-mastership, were animated
by any such ideas.   They, after throwing stones at
the vehicle in question, drew it down the hill to
Roxeth Common and demolished it, probably on the

* Lord Dartmouth, the Secretary of State for America, supported him firmly.—*Ibid.* p. 57.

† *Parr's Works*, by J. Johnstone, vol. i. pp. 564–8.   The letters
from Mr. Fox have a historic value.

present cricket-ground. The incident was graphically described by Mr. Bucknall's descendant, the present Earl of Verulam, on the occasion of the Harrow School Tercentenary in 1871.

The reason given for this outrageous behaviour was set forth by the ringleaders in the subjoined manifesto, which has, so to speak, a patriot ring about it.

To the Governors of Harrow School.

SIRS,

WE, the senior scholars, as the voice of the whole school, having received intelligence that you propose, contrary to the manifest desire of each of us, to appoint Mr. Heath, or some other person from Eton, as successor to our late Master, Dr. Sumner. . . . . A school of such reputation, as our late master has rendered this, ought not to be considered an appendix to Eton. . . . . . . Mr. Parr cannot but be acquainted with those rules which his predecessor has established, and will consequently act upon the former successful plan. We hope, in your determination, private attachments or personal affections will not bias your minds to the prejudice of the school. A school cannot be supported when every individual is disaffected towards the master.

We have transcribed the main arguments of this anti-Etonian document, which, moreover, evinces a seditious spirit amongst the boys, such as might have appalled the stout-hearted Dr. Keate himself, had the incidents we have narrated taken place under the shadow of Windsor Castle some sixty years later; and if the universal panacea of block and birch, which Keate believed in, ever seemed applicable to the occasion, it was during this crisis at Harrow when poor Dr. Heath had to write to Dr. Demainhay, Horne Tooke's brother-in-law, to allow him to compel young Demainhay to obedience. In Volume I., page 60, of

Johnstone's *Parr's Life* will be found that precious
document, the authors of which could not even plead
the excuse of patriotism when urging an objection to
Etonian rule, without which, in the persons of Horne,
Brian, Thackeray, and Sumner, Harrow might have not
gained its eighteenth-century distinction, even if, as
staunch Harrovians piously believe, fame was, sooner
or later, destined to crown John Lyon's efforts.

Parr has been entirely freed from the suspicion of
complicity in this lawless expression of sympathy,
notwithstanding that enemies were ready to distort and
misinterpret measures adopted and views expressed
when, under the lash of disappointment, the great
scholar accused his judges of unworthy dealing towards
himself, and yet absolved the new head-master, Dr.
Heath, from any share of blame.*

Dr. Heath sprang from a family settled in Exeter,
where, as freemen, they were well known during the
latter half of the seventeenth century.

His father, Benjamin Heath, an eminent lawyer,
excelled also in classical attainments ; so that the
University of Oxford conferred upon him the degree
of D.C.L. in 1752. The learned Town Clerk of
Exeter, for to such dignity was he advanced by his
natal city, left literary labours behind him of no mean
character, for, besides a critical work on the Greek
poets, he was also author, in 1740, of an essay towards
a demonstrative proof of the Divine Existence, and, in
1765, published a Revisal of Shakespeare's text. But
it was, nevertheless, as the initiator of the rare classical
library, yclept *Bibliotheca Heathiana*, which descended to

---

* Johnstone, *Parr*, vol. i, pp. 61-2.

the head-master of Harrow, that Benjamin Heath *pere* will be best remembered.

Our Heath, Benjamin Heath *fils*, received his education at Eton, and thence proceeded to King's College, Cambridge, where he gained a reputation for commune with the muses, such as a matter-of-fact father declined to acknowledge.

" It is my real opinion that you have justice done you to the full in allowing you to be a tolerable versifier, which you owe to the school you were educated in, whereas the character of a Poet implies talents of which you have a moderate share."

So writes the plain-spoken father to a son about to commence a career, which the scholarly erudition and sound classical learning imbibed at Eton and Cambridge was destined to render a conspicuous success, under circumstances, moreover, of considerable discouragement.*

Born at Exeter on September 27th, 1739, Benjamin Heath Junior was thirty-two years of age when he came to Harrow and essayed to guide the juvenile community which a Sumner had raised to such a high level in scholarship, if not in discipline, and to numbers largely beyond any expectation hitherto formed even by the most hopeful well-wishers of Harrow. A search through the school archives of this period has convinced us that the governors' choice, despite the controversy aroused, was inspired by good judgment, and duly justified by results. Common sense and decision seem to be the chief features of Dr. Heath's character, and these

---

* For the above extract, see *Heathiana* (privately printed). p. 12. To this work we also owe these details of the Heath family.

qualities enabled him to live down much obloquy, and
lay down his office a successful man.

In some degree the possession of means assisted Dr.
Heath. Indeed, the governors may well have considered
Parr's poverty as a disqualification in itself. For, no one
can go over the items of expenditure in which a Harrow
master became involved during the years 1771 and 1772
without seeing that if Benjamin Heath had not belonged
to a more or less moneyed race he could not have found
£1,000 to expend on the master's boarding-house, and
so provide for needs made pressing by the retirement of
Dr. Glasse.

Dr. Sumner had proceeded some way on the path of
house renovation when sudden death cut short his
projects, and left a legacy to any new comer which
rendered some investment of capital a *sine quâ non*, if
numbers were to be kept as high as the late master left
them.

Now Dr. Heath was in the position to find this sum,
and, moreover, he remained content with the paltry assistance that the governors were enabled to contribute out
of John Lyon's funds, a large portion of which was so
lamentably misdirected to the maintenance of metropo-
litan roadways. The Governors' Minutes state that Dr.
Heath was to be presented with £50 *per annum* for three
years,* and then receive nothing more in return for
money invested on property not his own. Is it not then
palpable that the needy Parr could never have made a
successful head-master, at any rate at Harrow, and that
lack of accommodation must have marred the stability
which a century's steady advance had at last secured.
Hence, unprejudiced reflection must recognise the

* Governors' Minutes, 1771-72.

wisdom of the unpopular decision which *unanimously** selected Benjamin Heath to sit in the brilliant Sumner's chair.

We have laid special emphasis on the unanimity of choice which hailed Heath's election, because by an error in Carlisle's *Grammar Schools* it has been reported that Drs. Heath, Drury, and George Butler were alike elected after reference to the Archbishop of Canterbury, the number of the governors' votes for rival candidates being equal to those cast for names ultimately chosen. The truth being, that in Dr. George Butler's case alone was such appeal made, while the other two candidates, ostensibly at least, met with no serious opposition.

When Dr. Heath came to Harrow he seems to have adopted a pre-eminently practical course of conduct, and contrived to carry out his views without engendering undue strife, while he preserved an astute silence as regards politics. The governors, at any rate, seem to have trusted most unboundedly in his judgment, for they preserved silence, and so gave consent to the reforms he initiated ; and, indeed, not one word is to be found in the minutes touching the abolition of the arrow-shooting, or the subsequent institution of periodical Speech days. And so it came to pass that Harrow turned once more towards Eton for magisterial guidance. It has been a correct appreciation of the historic relations existing between the two schools which has linked Harrow and Eton together in natural brotherhood. No lingerer beneath the shadow of the unambitious Elizabethan school building on the incline of Herga's hill can

---

* The word *unanimously* occurs in the governing minute announcing Heath's selection.

fail to acknowledge an indebtedness to Eton for sending forth successively a Brian, a Thackeray, a Sumner, and a Heath to labour in the scholastic vineyard of John Lyon's planting, until, by reason of careful training, the fruit borne even rivalled that produced upon the soil of Eton.

The Harrovian must further feel grateful to William of Wykeham for founding his glorious college at Winchester, whence by way of Eton came the monitorial system of school government which the Harrow founder had in the first instance enjoined but not created.

In 1771 Samuel Parr was induced to sever his connection from Harrow, and take to Stanmore such pupils as were allowed to follow him. This secession illustrates the very self-sufficiency and intellectual pride which marred this distinguished man's advancement to the summit of professional honour and profit. He could not brook a check in his career, and would not act as subordinate to Heath after having been known as the friend of Sumner.

Whatever else may be said of Parr and his followers at this period, they did not *then* act as loyal Harrovians. They did all that open rivalry could to injure their old school, otherwise a locality contiguous to Harrow would never have been chosen; and we sympathise with the horror in which, as a Harrow head-master, Dr. H. M. Butler alluded to this episode during the school Tercentenary in 1871, and deprecated the possibility of so ill-omened an event ever recurring, as that an under-master should carry off to Stanmore a practised assistant (Mr. Roderick), together with the flower of his pupils, who to the number of

forty adhered, in 1771, to the man whom at that time
their fathers most associated with Harrow scholarship
and renown as bequeathed by Thackeray and Sumner.
It is, on the other hand, remarkable how, amidst this
portentous convulsion the native worth of Lyon's
institution proved its stability, and rendered itself for
ever independent of aristocratic favour or popular
fashion.*

One notable result of this unfortunate disruption
consisted in the loss Harrow sustained through the
great Marquess Wellesley, then a youth of eleven, being
taken away from the school by his guardian, Archbishop
Cornwallis, and sent to Eton. We read of him impeni-
tent as to his conduct, and entering the venerable
archprelate's apartment waving one of the tassels from
Mr. Bucknall's wrecked carriage, and shouting,
" Victory ! "†

Order seems not to have been restored for three
weeks after Dr. Heath had entered upon his duties,
while, in addition to the forty odd upper boys who
went to Stanmore with Parr and Roderick, others were
also withdrawn by their parents. Yet so strong was
the prestige which surrounded the Harrow name, that
within three years of Dr. Heath's arrival the numbers
were 205 : a wonderful result, considering the crisis
through which the school had passed since Dr. Sumner
died, leaving 232 names in the list.‡

In the year 1772 Dr. Heath was led to suppress the
ancient arrow-shooting. It was a questionable resolve,
prompted, however, as those best informed have

* Lord Dartmouth supported Parr. and sent his sons to Stan-
more.—*Parr's Life*, by Johnstone, vol. i. p. 67.
† *The Public Schools*, by Author of *Etoniana*, p. 280.
‡ Butler Bills, January, 1771, p. 16.

recorded, by the necessity of withstanding a fast
encroaching system of privileges claimed by the higher
boys, which, if unchecked, would have drifted into
exercise of authority altogether foreign to the subordinate place in school economy which the noblest
and wisest must be content to hold when still *in statu
pupillari*.

Dr. Heath had probably seen something during his
under-mastership at Eton which warned him against
toleration of such assumptions of school-boy rights as
the famous " Montem " on Salt Hill served to perpetuate. When at Harrow he found his new pupils
claiming to absent themselves from school duties, not
alone on the occasion of the annual shooting, but also
during practice for that event, Dr. Heath, we are told,
at first suggested certain curtailments of these said
practice days,* and other irregular customs. But as
the boys received his offers of compromise with ill-
favour, and refused to shoot at all, Dr. Heath, with
that quiet decision which seems to have characterised
him, cut the knot by resolving to abolish altogether
what had become somewhat of a Saturnalia. Other
reasons were not far to seek which might prompt
any head-master to act thus decisively in reference
to a picturesque and interesting survival of the sixteenth century, which might otherwise have claimed
every consideration, and been preserved with advantage
through the various phases of manners and customs
which have supervened since Lyon of Preston endowed Harrow. But, to begin with, the competitors
were accustomed to give a ball in the Speech-room, a
kind of enjoyment harmless enough for those of riper

* *The Public Schools*, by Author of *Etoniana*, p. 306.

years, but hardly of a type that parents bargain for
when entrusting their children to a school that shall
fit them for the intellectual battle of life, rather than
encourage premature dissipation of that description,
which comes naturally with the Christmas holidays.
Turmoil and excitement, no doubt, also to some
extent prevailed during a competition the like of which
could not be witnessed around London at that epoch,
which took origin from Elizabethan times; and this
although the single constable who, the archives tell us,
kept order, and the trifling annual expense incurred,
prove that the crowd, however constituted, was at least
manageable.*   Moreover, the late Lord Arden and Mrs.
Arnold, the old Harrow stationer, who in youth had
lived amongst the actors in these scenes, were wont to
talk of some accident, caused by the ill-direction of an
arrow, having brought matters to a climax.   According
to Lord Arden, Goding, a barber, was shot in the eye,
while the octogenarian, Mrs. Arnold, speaking in 1859,
was wont to declare that the fugitive arrow struck the
unfortunate individual in the mouth, destroying two of
his teeth.

The late Rev. Henry Drury, however, writing in July
1838, stated that "he was familiar with a frontispiece
to the School Lists, wherein the village barber is seen
walking off, like one of Homer's heroes, with an arrow
in his eye, stooping forward, and evidently in great pain,
with his hand applied to the wound. It is perfectly true
that this Tom of Coventry was so punished; and I have
somewhere a ludicrous account of it in Dr. Parr's all
but illegible autograph."

This latter story seems to confirm the correctness

* School Accounts in *Archives* for 1771-2.

rather of Lord Arden's recollections than those of Mrs.
Arnold, and yet goes to show that some catastrophe of
the kind did take place before Dr. Heath abolished the
oldest of all Harrow customs.*

Fortunately, sufficient materials exist to enable us to
reproduce something akin to the scene which must have
been yearly enacted on the ancient amphitheatre yclept
yᵉ Butts, mention of which, together with its annual
repair, is made in the earlier school archives, which
record a recurrent item of 5s. for mending the arena in
question.

Let us, then, picture to ourselves the spectacle of
twelve youths,† fancifully attired in white satin trimmed
with green, flowing sashes, and silken caps of similar
hue. They are assembled together on a detached
amphitheatre to the left of the London Road, where,
above them, on a shady eminence, are seated favoured
individuals anxious to witness an enactment which
possessed an interest alike historic and dramatic.

The masters, in full academic costume, stand prominent amongst a group of schoolboys in the knee-breeches
of eighteenth-century fashion, who are separated from a
considerable crowd of outside spectators by a rude but
elevated fence, such as may be seen protecting ground
for purposes of recreation on many a public common at
the present time. Intense anxiety is felt by all as to
the result of a competition which can, it is true, alone
prove the winner to possess local predominance in a
sport long since abandoned by the nation.

---

* For full accounts of the suppression of archery at Harrow,
see *Greater London*, Cassell, part 6, pp. 263–4.
† In Dr. Cox's time, 1731, the number was six, but had been
increased as the school grew.—See *Gentleman's Magazine*, August
1731.

Nevertheless, there is something so purely English in this strife, recalling, as its incidents seem to do, the days of Crecy and Poictiers, that it is scarcely to be marvelled at how closely packed and encroaching are the visitors from London and Windsor, who fill the country streets of Harrow with a motley assemblage in the year of grace 1771, and see the happy boy who has twelve times shot nearest to the central mark proclaimed Victor and escorted up the High Street to the old school by a troup of delighted friends rejoicing in their hero's possession of the famous Silver Arrow.

Amidst the flourish of French horns, and shoutings truly British, may we, indeed, conceive the gladdened youth* to experience emotions similar to those of a successor who, in the second half of the nineteenth

---

* For accounts of the annual archery contests which we have consulted, see *Greater London*, by E. Walford, p. 263; also *The Public Schools*, by Author of *Etoniana*, p. 305. In the Vaughan Library, at Harrow, is the arrow won by Charles Wager Allix, of Willoughby Hall, Lincolnshire, also an embroidered archery dress worn at one of the competitions, being presented by the Rev. J. Read Munn, whose knowledge of Harrow is perpetuated by the author of *Etoniana*, in the account of Harrow which appears in *The Public Schools*, Blackwood, 1867. We copy the subjoined extract from *Greater London*, p. 266:—"With reference to the shooting in 1769, the following interesting anecdote was communicated to the Dean of Peterborough (the late Dr. George Butler), upon the authority of the late Hon. Archibald McDonald: 'On the day of the competition, two boys, Merry and Love, were equal, or nearly so, and both of them decidedly superior to the rest, when Love, having shot his last arrow into the bull's-eye, was greeted by his schoolfellows with a shout, *Omnia vincit amor*. Not so, said Merry, in an under voice, *Nos non cedamus amori*, and, carefully adjusting his shaft, shot it into the bull's-eye a full inch nearer to the centre than his competitor.'" As the name of Love does not appear in the list of shooters for the year, it seems as if a nickname had been fastened upon one of the competitors. It is worth recording that the butts were in existence so late as

century, undergoes an equal amount of effusive congra-
tulation when carried into the Pavilion at Lord's by
eager partisans at the conclusion of a Harrow and Eton
match.

While disposed to regret the abolition of archery at
Harrow, we nevertheless hasten to give Dr. Heath the
κῦδος to which, by establishing public speeches, he is certainly entitled. The fugitive eloquence of Dr. Sumner
had left its mark on the minds of Harrovians, and bade
them desire in some sort to attain proficiency in the
lists of oratory, that fascinating accomplishment without possession of which many a well-favoured youth has
been forced to rest content with a mediocre reputation,
though in other respects qualified for the higher walks
of clerical or political life. Adequate facility of expression is a *sine quâ non* when a man, however well stored
his mind, desires to make an impression on the popular
feeling, and so grasp power. This Julius Cæsar felt
and acknowledged, when he deemed it necessary to
retire to Rhodes to study oratory under a rhetorician,
before he could aspire to control the Roman democracy
or hope to appease Patrician prejudice.

Until Dr. Heath established public speaking at Harrow, Sheridan had been the only public orator of note
trained there; but the practice of repeating extracts
from the classics during annual celebrations instituted
by Dr. Heath soon produced several notable instances
of the self-possession acquired by early exercise of the
voice and memory. Two remarkable instances of this

June 28, 1791; on that date Lord Althorpe, the future statesman,
writes to his father, saying, "I have found a place at the butts
where I can get writing sand."—*Memoir of Earl Spencer,* by Sir
Denis Le Marchant, Bart., p. 39.

faculty are those of Mr. Perceval, whose conspicuous clearness of diction enabled him to lead the House of Commons when Pitt and Fox had left the scene of their triumphs;* and also of the first Lord Harrowby, a strangely underrated statesman. As a speaker the Earl held his own amongst Wellesley, Grey, and Grenville early in the nineteenth century; while he lived to make a most remarkable speech on behalf of compromise when the first Reform Bill convulsed the political world in 1831. Foreign Secretary to Mr. Pitt in his final administration of 1805, Lord Harrowby joined the Governments of Mr. Perceval and Lord Liverpool, supporting the latter Minister as President of the Council between 1812 and 1827, when Mr. Canning became Premier, who also looked to the old Harrovian statesman for his potent aid.

Had not subjection to sudden and disabling headache made it impossible to keep any business appointment with the necessary certainty, Lord Harrowby could have been Prime Minister of England;† while as a diplomatist his talents were fully recognised by Lord Brougham, who met him during a mission in Prussia previous to the battle of Jena in 1806. The Lord of Sandon was

---

* See *Memoirs of R. P. Ward*. Mr. J. W. Perceval, son of the Prime Minister, to Mr. Croker:—" My father was educated at Harrow; he was pupil to Dr. Drury, who afterwards, but not, I believe, during my father's time, was head-master. Lord Harrowby and Mathew Montague were amongst his most intimate friends, and the prize books which he brought away from Harrow, and a number of old exercises of his which I have, together with others by his contemporaries, bear witness that he gave his mind to the studies of the place."—*Croker Correspondence and Diaries*, vol. ii. p. 373.

† He refused the office. This fact was communicated to the author by the late Earl of Harrowby, who also at the same time attested to Mr. Perceval's peculiar faculty of *clearness* in expressing his opinions.

originally selected to represent England at the Congress
of Vienna in 1814, but himself pointed out Lord
Castlereagh as the fittest available man for the post.
To these names we may add that of the then Lord
Hardwick, who filled the Lord-Lieutenancy of Ireland
with credit in 1801–2.

Amongst others at Harrow during Dr. Heath's *régime*
were two sons of Lord Charles Spencer* and the
second Earl Grosvenor, Sir Joseph Yorke, Sir John
Neale, Sir George Robinson, Sir C. Hudson Palmer,
and also Mr. Henry Drummond, the banker, whose
family has continued to support their ancestral school.†

Dr. Heath continued quietly to carry out the policy
which he had conceived, finding in the Rev. Joseph
Drury a sympathetic coadjutor, destined to become
allied to the Heath family by the closest possible tie.
Dr. Heath, being a bachelor, had brought his mother
and sisters‡ to live with him at Harrow, and there the
youngest Miss Heath contracted a marriage with Mr.
Joseph Drury, the future head-master (then one of the

---

* The Hon. William Robert Spencer was born on May 3rd,
1747, and was at Harrow under Dr. Heath. He was a graceful
poet, and a favourite in society. Lord Byron remarked to Lady
Blessington, " His was really an elegant mind, polished, graceful,
sentimental, with just enough gaiety to prevent his being too
lachrymose, and just enough sentiment to prevent his fun being
too Anacreontic." In 1825 he retired to the Continent on slender
means, and died in 1834 at the end of a sad old age. As a poet,
Mr. Spencer's work has been variously appraised, and scarcely
holds the position Lord Byron predicted. But, as the friend
of Henry Hallam, he deserves mention here, the historian speaking of his brilliancy and vivacity of wit, his ready knowledge, his
strong natural acuteness, sweetness of disposition, and a warm
affection for his friends.—Howard Staunton, *The Great Schools of
England*, p. 282.

† *Life of Rev. Dr. Drury* (privately printed), p. 11.

‡ *Heathiana*, p. 16.

assistants), and united the two families together by a link familiar to all who care for Harrow history.

The epoch at which we have now arrived is not marked by any special genius in the scholarship displayed by those educated under Dr. Heath, such as threw lustre over the days of Thackeray and Sumner. But good men, furnished with due requirements for the battle of life, nevertheless, left the school in considerable numbers. The most eminent of these we have just mentioned, so it only remains to say that, in a period full of varied historic interest, school life seems to have passed on at Harrow for several years without any special incident occurring which we can cite as a landmark in that inevitable monotony which sometimes befalls the story of a well-ordered school community. But if the school life itself, between 1777, after Mr. Joseph Drury married Miss Heath, and 1785, when Dr. Heath resigned, was somewhat uneventful, the celebrity of Harrow had attracted to the neighbourhood men of ability and culture, consorting together at Harrow for the sake of one another's society. Mr. Orde, who had been Secretary for Ireland, and was afterwards created Lord Bolton, a man of various attainments, stood prominently forward amidst this gathering of literary and artistic associates. It is not, moreover, generally known that Sheridan, sharing the enthusiasm for Harrow which so many have felt after the tie which bound them to the spot was broken, returned thither about this period (1778), and with his beautiful and fascinating wife (the celebrated Miss Linley), brought new life to the social circle. In the Grove, which the great dramatist, wit, and orator then occupied, Tickell and his wife were frequently seen, also

George Glasse, Earl Manvers, Mr. Page of Wembley, and, towards the close of Dr. Heath's head-mastership, Aloysius Pisani, a Venetian nobleman of taste and high culture, who fled before the threats of revolutionary disturbance so soon to convulse the European world.* We can conceive how a lover of books such as Dr. Heath—even then enlarging his father's library—must have found grateful solace in the literary associations with which Harrow was so bountifully enriched, and that his leisure brought with it delights not always within the weary schoolmaster's reach. And we take it that it was hard work on the part of unobtrusive men like Heath and Joseph Drury, his counsellor, that then sustained the Harrow name against all discouragement, making it so clearly impossible to conduct an opposition school at Stanmore, that even the mighty Parr had to beat a retreat and discontinue an unequal contest, may we say *ludere Parr impar*.

While dwelling upon the literary attractions of Harrow in 1777, we may mention that Dr. Parr gave rein to his natural nobility of character, and, putting away all unworthy regrets, projected a visit to Harrow Speeches before Dr. Heath resigned, and when it must have become evident that the Stanmore venture was doomed to respectable extinction.†

---

* *Life of Joseph Drury* (privately printed), p. 11.

† Dr. Parr's biographer, John Johnstone, M.D., found an undated note amongst his correspondence, proving that Mr. Nicolaides, a learned Greek refugee, had been asked by Dr. Parr to accompany him to Harrow Speech-day. Now Mr. Nicolaides was clearly a *Stanmore* friend (see *Parr's Works*, by J. Johnstone, vol. i. p. 87), and as Dr. Parr left that place in 1777, any visit of his to Harrow Speeches would have been anterior to prolonged sojourn at Colchester, Norwich, and Hatton ; and this although Parr's biographer remarks that he did not *know* of any visit to Harrow Speeches which the Doctor made in Dr. Heath's time

The fact is that Dr. Parr's connections and associations were Harrovian to the core, and if parents, in their plenitude of confidence, were found to allow their sons to follow the great man to Stanmore, and so condone an unquestionable error, yet when the youths in question went out into the world, other members of their families naturally reverted to the time-honoured place of education which John Lyon founded, and over which Dr. Heath ruled with such conspicuous discretion.

The kindness of Mr. William Winckley, of Flambards, Harrow, has furnished us with an account of the daily round of school life which an ancestor of his made note of at the time when he was under Dr. Heath about 1780. At that date there were but seven or eight inhabitants of Harrow who sent their sons to be educated with the some two hundred noblemen's and gentlemen's sons then enjoying a practical monopoly of the privileges which John Lyon meant for rich and poor alike. The foreigner element had swamped almost entirely the forty poor scholars.

Hours of instruction read as follow :—

Prayers were celebrated daily, being repeated to the scholars at 7 A.M. by one of the monitors, such early devotion being followed by first school, which lasted until 9. Breakfast then took place ; and at 11 the boys again went to work until 12, when, after prayers being repeated, an interval of three hours occurred, lasting until 3, when an hour's application was followed by preparation for fourth school, which commenced at 5

(Johnstone, *Parr's Life*, vol. i. p. 90). Archbishop Trench told at the Tercentenary how, in 1824, Dr. Parr had astonished the Harrovians by his scratch wig when at the Speeches in 1825. This visit was paid but a few months before the Doctor died.

and concluded a whole school-day at 6.   A daily round this, brought to an apt conclusion by evening prayer.

We are not told in Mr. Winckley's interesting letter whether the interstices between schools were filled up with the pupil rooms of modern date, or that *monstrum horrendum* yclept extra school, and are inclined to believe that the needs of those days demanded less work from youthful minds, when the battle of life was less keen, and Great Britain numbered some fourteen millions in lieu of the thirty-seven millions known to inhabit the United Kingdom in 1884.   On the other hand, there were only two half-holidays in each week instead of the three which nominally obtain in the Harrow of modern times.

" The scholars were at this time, without any distinction, brought up in the principles of the Established Church, while classical teaching formed the staple of the education afforded."

The modern Harrovian will here recognise the nucleus of a system under which he himself has progressed in mental training, and likewise perceive that recreation and amusement were essentially the same then as now.*

---

* Dr. Kaye, Dean of Lincoln, who was elected to that position 19th November 1783, made during his life sundry tours in England, and kept a diary, which is preserved in the British Museum. He visited Harrow, and recounted his experiences, such notes being taken probably about the year 1780 (see Butler's Bills for that year, when the numbers correspond).   The Dean enjoyed his ecclesiastical supremacy on Lindum Hill until 1809, when he died aged seventy-two.   His remarks we append : " Harrow : The school an old high Hous, about 180 Boys, a Head master and 4 junior masters, Dr. Heath, Dr. Drewry (*sic*) and Mr. Bromley who married his sisters.   His mother.   At the Speeches Mrs. Bromley got up at three to provide custards, &c. which would not keep, clouted cream.   She has the conduct of the whole.   Mr. Drury is most likely to succeed to the school.   On Dr. Sumner's death

To those who remember the Warners, Dick and Billy, who flourished between 1856 and 1860, it will not seem strange that, as the Rev. Read Munn communicated to the author of *The Public Schools*,* a family called *Martin* gained a sort of prescriptive right to purvey illegitimate and questionable luxuries, and laid the foundation of such dominion during the time that Dr. Heath was head-master.

"Dick Martin, we are told, was the individual who first arrogated to himself the right of being put out of bounds by the authorities, and thereby (such is the contrariety of human nature) claiming a certain share of school-boy support when vending painted sparrows, which he called cocky-olly birds." Dr. Heath, according to Mr. Munn, was quite aware of his character, and used annually to give out as a subject for Latin verses, *Alfenus vafer*, under which Horatian *alias* Mr. Martin was well understood to be proposed for poetical treatment.

"Latin verse was more common at Harrow that at the present day, and the wits of the school, we are told, satirised the establishment over which Mr. Martin ruled."

Fancy a modern Harrovian indulging in a classical

He wish'd Mr. Parr to succeed. The Five Trustees of Lyon the Founder chose Mr. Heath from Eton. The Boys wished for Parr. They broke and burnt the Carriage of Mr.   Coll. Legge hissed them. 50 seceded with Mr. Parr to Stanmore. Parr was irregular and unfit, not immoral. He then went to Colchester and afterwards to Norwich."—British Museum, *Additional Manuscript*, 18,556, fo. 22. Tradition has been fully sustained in the matter of custards, as any modern Harrovian can attest. It is worthy of remark that Mr. Joseph Drury was, in 1780, expected to become head-master, and that the governors' adverse decision as to Dr. Parr's claim was endorsed by local opinion.

* *Public Schools*, by author of *Etoniana*, p. 300.

skit on amiable weaknesses possessed by the local
baker, or even stooping to celebrate the feats of those
well-known vagrants who infest the cricket-ground !

But the more youthful portion of the Harrow community will think of the Heath period as that during
which the game of cricket first gained a permanent
footing at Harrow.   It had, doubtless, been pursued in
a desultory way since Dr. Thackeray came from Eton,
both in the school-yard and on the play-ground rented
from Mrs. Edmonds.* But after Sir Horace Mann and
the Duke of Dorset formulated the laws of the game
we are now familiar with, and instituted the M.C.C. in
1774,† there is every reason to believe that pursuit of
the leather came generally into vogue.

One of the first things Dr. Parr's scholars did after
seceding from Harrow in 1771 was to transplant the
game to the uplands of Stanmore, and make use of the
late Duke of Chandos' magnificent bowling-green for
the purpose.   It is, therefore, probable that cricket was
popular before Dr. Heath came to Harrow, as, indeed,
we know it to have been at Eton in 1736.‡   We have
only to regret that all local records connected with the
game at this time should have irretrievably perished.

When in the year 1785 Dr. Heath resolved to take
his well-earned rest, he had sustained the numerical
strength equally with the prestige of Harrow.   And,
indeed, it is a marvel to those familiar with the place to
discover how more than two hundred boys were taught
in the left wing of the school building.   As for the
boarding out, even allowing for a gradual increase of

---

* Governors' Minutes, 1773.
† Old Lord's ground was where Dorset Square stands.
‡ Hor. Walpole, *Letter to G. Montagu*, May 6th, 1736.

the head-master's house, which seems to have grown
up bit by bit, much as the British Constitution, the task
never could have been performed unless the more
reliable school dames had been entrusted with boarders.
And then knowledge of the older buildings in the locality goes to show how easily content were our forefathers, who must have consigned their children to
quarters wherein a working man might *lire* now-a-days,
but so earn the right to grumble, not to say to have an
article written upon his woes in the larger type of the
Daily Telegraph.

We have said that Dr. Heath came into possession of
a portion of his father's choice collection of books.
This having occurred in 1766, the library he possessed
at Harrow was doubtless a remarkable one. But in
1781 King's College, Cambridge, presented the head-
master of John Lyon's school with the Rectory of Walkerne, in Herts, and here it was that the famous library
connected with his name came to be situated.

In 1785 Dr. Heath was elected to an Eton fellowship,
so that easy circumstances conspired with cultured taste
to seduce this lover of books from more active duties.
Dr. Heath's *regime* may be said to have consolidated the
fame of Sumner, and prepared Harrow for the still
greater advance in store under that *beau ideal* ruler,
Joseph Drury. Thirteen uneventful years of daily toil
were passed between 1772 and 1785 at Harrow, during
a time when the passions of mankind were by no
means allayed throughout the realm.

The American Colonists had gained their freedom,
and the younger Pitt stood the champion of the
English Senate; neither event being consummated
without stirring controversy of world-wide fame; while

Sunday schools had been established in England, in 1781, at a moment when Howard the philanthropist was pursuing his mission of mercy in the cruel prison-houses of this half-enlightened country. So stood England when Heath and Drury were counselling one another for improving the education of those destined to wield power at home when the blast of revolution desolated the fair land of France and spread over Europe. Neither should we forget that to men such as Mr. Perceval and Lord Harrowby do we owe it that after Mr. Pitt's death England remained, as Mr. Canning beautifully phrased it, " One kingdom untouched midst the wreck of the world."

It is to the pages of that pleasant volume, *Heathiana* (privately printed), we must turn when contemplating the lettered ease of Dr. Benjamin Heath. There we learn that he shaped his Walkerne library in the form of a capital T ; and Dibdin tells us that never did the eye alight upon sweeter copies. In Dibdin's *Biblio-graphical Decameron*, edition of 1817, vol. iii., will be found not only a detailed account of this paradise of *bokes*, as the old fashion has it, but also a verbal portraiture of Dr. Benjamin Heath in his retirement, with which we propose to close this chapter.

About the year 1807 the rich Eton living of Farnham, Bucks, had been added to Dr. Heath's other benefice, and he stood, therefore, the very type of a cultured ecclesiastical pluralist before the days that accumulations of additional income derived from various Church sources were forbidden. But it is nevertheless pleasant to think that the delights experienced by the ex-Harrow master stood as a reward for good work performed in the world.

Well, however, might Dibdin exclaim (in *Bibl. Dec.*, *loc. cit.*), "Oh, rare and brave for a pastor not being a dignitary. Here lived and here revelled the bibliomaniacal scholar and chieftain of whom we are discoursing. Here he saw, entertained, and caressed his friends, with Alduses in the forenoon, and with a cheerful glass towards evening, hospitable, temperate, kind-hearted, with a well-furnished mind and purse, and with a larder and cellar which might have supplied materials for a new edition of Pynson's *Royal Boke of Cookery and Kervinge*, 1500, 4to."

"It was in this retirement, reader, that old age, which, like time and tide, wait for no man, overtook the worthy character of whom we are speaking."

Dibdin goes on to tell how he became indifferent at last to his once beloved tomes, so that the sale of the library Heathiana ensued, when £9,000 was realised by Jeffreys of Pall Mall, on whose premises the bidding took place. This event took place in May 1810, and in May 1817 Dr. Heath paid the debt of nature, and was buried, aged seventy-eight, at St. Leonards, Exeter, whither in January 1834 were brought the remains of his friend, coadjutor, and brother-in-law, Dr. Joseph Drury, the two Harrow masters resting within a few feet one of the other.*

Dr. Heath will be celebrated in Harrow history as the uprooter of one institution and the founder of another. The man who abolished shooting for the Silver Arrow was destined to establish those Public Speeches since rendered so famous. It is a strange reflection that the archery at Harrow came to an end in 1772, under the auspices of one by no means fitted

* *The Life of Joseph Drury* (privately printed), p. 34.

by temperament for the *rôle* of reformer, while a.kindred
institution, viz. *Montem*, perished at Eton in 1847, by
the hand of another respecter of traditional forms and
ceremonies, in the person of the then Provost Hodgson,
Lord Byron's friend. Truly we frequently know not
the character it may one day be ours to play on Life's
wide stage.

CHAPTER IX.

DR. JOSEPH DRURY.—1785–1805.

What Chief, what Sage, what Hero trained by thee
To Wisdom, first on this delightful isle
Struck his adventurous prow ?—

SIR WILLIAM JONES.

AT last we emerge into the perfect light of day, finding
ample materials ready to hand for compiling a trustworthy account of Harrow school life as it existed
towards the close of the last century, and also during
the first few years of our own. Indeed, so various are
the topics which present themselves that it becomes
necessary to make a judicious selection from available
materials.

The school archives are still a safe guide to the reconciliation of differing statements or the verification of
hitherto assumed facts ; yet there is little to be added
to the information already published about those several
men of genius whose names are entwined with that of
their old school at this epoch. The records in question
fill an important page in the book of nineteenth-century
story, wherein we read of men who exercised a potent
influence over affairs at a time when national independence hung in the balance ; and readers may there
learn how youths trained at Harrow were destined

afterwards to shape in some degree the direction of a wondrous supremacy amongst the nations. We might, then, elect to tell of the after triumph of song which a Byron achieved, or dwell on the political careers of Peel and Palmerston—a task impossible within the limits of these pages.

As the name of Dr. Joseph Drury is associated more especially with these halcyon days of Harrow, a short sketch of his career previous to acceptance of the head-mastership, derived from a privately-printed volume in the possession of the Drury family,* will be acceptable.

Descended from an ancient Norman stock, the Drurys were found settled in Norfolk during the latter half of the seventeenth century, while from a younger son of the then elder branch, who resided at Lesgyat Holt, in the aforesaid county, sprang the preceptor of Byron and Peel. Lesgyat Holt, however, passed from the family before Dr. Drury's father came into this troublous world and started an eldest child on his career with such advantages as a respectable origin and an unblemished name could afford. This son, Joseph Drury, whose life is under consideration now, was born in London on the 11th of February 1750. Educated at Westminster, he was entered at Trinity College, Cambridge, in 1768, and there, under the tuition of Watson, the future Bishop of Llandaff, found a friend who, perceiving his merits, recommended him to Dr. Sumner at Harrow, when that king of living schoolmasters required an assistant, and at a moment, moreover, when Joseph Drury, like Parr before him, found that neither adequate talent nor con-

* *Rev. Joseph Drury, D.D., late Head-master of Harrow.* Privately printed, and placed at the author's disposal by the Rev. B. H. Drury, of Caius College, Cambridge.

stant application atoned for a scantily-filled purse. Despite every effort to make his means suffice, he was forced to leave Cambridge; while the course of our story will show that he was wise to accept Sumner's offer.

An assistant mastership at Harrow was but a poor thing in itself in 1769; but in this case the recipient found exceptional opportunities of acquiring culture and imbibing knowledge, which enabled him to equip himself for the realisation of a teacher's highest hopes. Dr. Sumner was then at the summit of his reputation, his numerous scholars famed alike for knowledge and breeding. Only thirty-eight years of age himself, the head-master's influence over younger men developed itself more naturally than when, as sometimes happens, crabbed age is called on to inculcate its experience on those fresh from University life. We cannot doubt that the glow of Sumner's talents exercised a great and abiding influence on the youthful Drury's future; but we think that the key to that notable triumph of unobtrusive merit was most certainly the possession of remarkable *patience*, made evident in a power of unwearied application. Without this faculty Mr. Drury could never have developed other gifts or been enabled to put into practice the teachings of his chief. But there was not to be a prolonged association between those two kindred minds. Dr. Sumner, as we are aware, died suddenly in 1771, and Joseph Drury had to decide whether he should follow the fortunes of Samuel Parr at Stanmore or cleave to the older institution. His loyalty to the memory of his late instructor and to the old school resulted, as was only just, in his attaining the proud position of a successful head-master.

13

Dr. Joseph Drury, be it remembered, lived before the days of cheap newspapers and popular literature, in the pages of which success has in later years been made manifest to the public. So that the fact is not generally known and appreciated that the system of school government by personal or moral influence was first tried by Drury, who, if he boasted not Sumner's eloquence, yet seems to have stood *facile princeps* in government of youth by the tongue.

We catch more than one glimpse of Joseph Drury in the biographies of Dr. Parr. We see him at the bedside of the dying Sumner, and learn of his hesitation whether or not to follow his associates Parr and Roderick to Stanmore.

We find, however, that when once his decision was in favour of giving Dr. Heath a loyal support, those two instructors of youth became fast friends, and remained so all their lives. Located in the house next the King's Head, which for years was occupied by the late Dr. Hewlett, Mr. Drury worked steadily on. His friendship with Dr. Heath was cemented by a family tie, for in the year 1777 he married Louisa Heath, youngest daughter of the Exeter Bibliophile and scholar, and sister to the Harrow head-master.

Several celebrated men were in some way or another under his tuition during the next few years, but as their names are given *in extenso* in our last chapter, it is enough to say here that Spencer Perceval and Lord Moira were of the number. During this time Mr. Drury's devotion to his professional duties was unremitting and his perseverance perpetual, so that it was with difficulty that he could be persuaded to join the party at The Grove, where for a brief period, as we have said, the beautiful Mrs. Sheridan and her gifted husband resided ; and when Mr. Drury was enticed away from his labours by the irresistible charms in question, he would pay for the delight of listening to Mrs. Sheridan's voice by subtracting an equivalent from his night's rest.*

Such was the man who, in 1785, was pointed out by the general opinion of those familiar with his character as successor to his brother-in-law, Dr. Heath. For, although it is said† that Dr. Parr's claims were again canvassed, there is no trace of the candidature in the minutes, nor is it recorded by Field or Johnstone in their Lives of that celebrity.

Mr. Drury had just completed his thirty-sixth year when he obtained the head-mastership. He had, as his biographer tells us,‡ " been so interwoven with his brother-in-law and predecessor in all their views regarding the studies of the place, that little or no change was made in the system." This is true of the first years of his rule, excepting as regards the development of the system of moral influence. Neither must it be imagined that any great strides were made by Harrow School during the first few years of Joseph Drury's advent to power. The connection seems, however, to have been held together, though after Dr. Heath's retirement a slight diminution in numbers took place ; while, as we are told in Dr. Drury's privately-printed life, any further encouragement was drawn from his own mind, and the opinions of watchful and appreciative friends, who

---

* *Life of Joseph Drury* (privately printed), p. 12.
† The writer of the privately-printed monograph on Dr. Joseph Drury's life states this, p. 13.
‡ *Rev. Dr. Joseph Drury* (privately printed), p. 13.

18 *

cheered him on his path of diligence by prognostications
of a brilliant harvest, in the shape of a Harrow famous
and prosperous beyond previous experience.*   This
belief they based on their knowledge of the head-
master's natural good judgment and great experience.

Accordingly, about the year 1800, Harrow School
surpassed the most sanguine hopes of its friends, both
as regards the number and position of the students.
For a moment, in 1803, it equalled even Eton as regards
size, while—if such be an advantage—no school has
ever shown a greater proportion of the upper classes in
its ranks.† Probably this was, in some degree, owing
to Dr. Drury's fame ; for he seemed to have inherited
much of the benevolence and gentleness and the fire
and genius of Sumner, while he had the advantage of
a knowledge of boyish character which gave him pre-
eminence over other living schoolmasters.   Moreover,
Dr. Drury's success as a teacher was equal to that
which he achieved in the character of guide, philosopher,
and friend.   He held a very equal balance between
Greek and Latin, while he spared his hearers any long
philological dissertations, as unfitted even for the upper
classes of a public school, the right object being to

* Dr. George Butler's printed lists show that in 1796 the
numbers were only 139

† The Bill of 1803 shows the largest proportion of nobility
that could at any time have been counted in any school of the
size. Out of 345 names, there are those of one reigning and three
prospective Dukes, Dorset, Sutherland, Devonshire, and Grafton ;
a future Marquess ; two actual and five future Earls and Vis-
counts ; and besides these, four others who bear the titles of
Lord, twenty-one Honourables, and four Baronets. Two sons of
Rufus King, then American Minister in London, appear in this
list. He professes to have sent them to Harrow because it was
the only school in which no special honour was attached to rank.
—*Public Schools*, by author of *Etoniana*, p. 286.

imbue the mind with a love for the literature of old ;
and Dr. Drury, as his anonymous biographer tells us,
was peculiarly happy in reproducing the beauties of
poetical figure.* Latin prose and English essays were
freely encouraged by Dr. Drury, and he fostered the
custom of allowing promising pieces of English verse
to be read in public, and by so doing stimulated a taste
for poesy when the divine art was at a high level in
England.†

But the most distinctive feature of Dr. Drury's training consisted, as has been said already, in the friendly
intercourse which he held with his scholars, not only by
visiting them in their rooms, but by admitting them to
walk and talk with him. As a well-known kinsman of
the Drurys remarked to the writer, " he was one of those
Qui preceptorem sancti solvere parentis Esse loco."

Although not by any means an old man when he left
Harrow, the venerable appearance of Dr. Drury has been
left on record by an attached pupil,‡ who pictures the
Harrow master as a man whom nobody ever knew to be
in a passion, gifted, nevertheless, with a power of impressing youth deeply by means of simple but graceful
eloquence, delivered with the intelligence of a sage and
the tenderness of a parent.

Such conduct and demeanour captivated the more
generous instincts of Lord Byron, and doubtless rendered them prominent in his Harrow life. The love
that the noble poet bore for Dr. Drury is creditable alike
to himself and to his dignified preceptor. The more

* *Life of Rev. Joseph Drury* (privately printed), p. 18.
† See Appendix F. for tables of a week's work in the Heath-
Drury time, and also in Dr. Longley's.
‡ Letter of an old pupil, copied in *Life of Dr. Drury* (privately
printed), p. 35.

we learn concerning this period of that ever-interesting career confirms the experience of the great Sir Robert Peel, the late Rev. W. Harness, the late Lord Zetland, and others, who were indebted to the wayward child of song either for protection or sympathy in the rough battle of school life. For the noble poet held influence amongst the boys during the latter part of his stay at Harrow; and we owe more than one glimpse of the times there to his inimitable letters. Doubtless at school, as elsewhere, the inquirer is met with strange contrarieties, such as baffle explanation. From time to time the demon within him seems to hold temporary sway even thus early in life, and in turn gives way to sentiments of tender affection towards friends like the Honourable John Wingfield, brother of Lord Powerscourt, who died of fever at Coimbra on May 14th, 1811 ;* Lord Clare, the sound of which name always delighted Lord Byron, and whose chance greeting led him to utter in tender song the love which struggled for expression :—

> If chance some well-remembered face,
> Some old companion of my early race,
> Advance to claim his friend with honest joy,
> My eyes, my heart, proclaim me yet a boy.
> The glittering scene, the fluttering groups around,
> Were all forgotten when my friend was found.

* A stanza in *Childe Harold*, Canto i. 91, runs as follows :

> "And thou, my friend !—since unavailing woe
> Bursts from my heart and mingles with the strain—
> Had the sword laid thee with the mighty low,
> Pride might forbid e'en friendship to complain :
> But thus unlaurel'd to descend in vain,
> By all forgotten, save the lonely breast,
> And mix unbleeding with the boasted slain.
> While Glory crowns so many a meaner crest !
> What hadst thou done to sink so peacefully to rest ? "

And then prominent amidst that inner throng comes the name of Edward Noel Long, with whom Lord Byron was wont to come down and visit his old haunts after he left the Harrow he loved so dearly well.* Nor can we omit the name of Tatersal, celebrated in the *Hours of Idleness* as Davus, or forget Lord Byron's intimacy with the scholarly prodigy Sir George Sinclair, the fourth Duke of Dorset, Hunter, Curzon, Lord Delawarr, Gordon, Wildman (who afterwards bought Newstead), William Banks, De Bathe, and others whose names have crept into those historic records.

We are not disposed, even had we the space or power, to reproduce any complete picture of Byron in his school days, nor to copy out at length lyrical expressions of interest in Harrow from his early poems. They are before the world, and may become familiar to any man or boy with a shilling in his pocket; but it is, nevertheless, part of this story to remind our readers how the poet was wont to nurture his earlier inspiration while meditating over the strange solemnity which characterises the well-wooded pasture lands that lie between Harrow churchyard and the banks of the Thames. There, under the spreading elm of lyric fame, and on a tomb† of the Peachey family, was the bard accustomed to recline, smitten thus early in life, as his written thought proves, with a deep sense of the mutability of man as compared with the immutability of nature.

Lord Byron's own short notices of his Harrow career are supremely interesting, and cannot be all omitted ; the

* " I so much disliked leaving Harrow, that, although it was time (I being 17), it broke my very rest for the last quarter with counting the days that remained."

† Now enclosed in an iron cage to prevent the depredations of the poet's admirers.

more that such memories are likewise bound up with
mention of Sir Robert Peel's school life.

" At school I was remarked for the extent and readiness of my general information, but in all other respects
idle, capable of great sudden exertions (such as thirty
or forty Greek hexameters, of course with such prosody
as it pleased God), but of few continuous drudgeries.
My qualities were much more oratorical and martial than
poetical, and Dr. Drury, my grand patron (our head-
master), had a great notion I should turn out an orator,
from my fluency, my turbulence, my voice, my copious-
ness of declamation, and my action. . . . Peel (the
orator and statesman that is or is to be) was my form
fellow, and we were both at the top of our remove. We
were on good terms, but his brother was my intimate
friend.   There were always great hopes of Peel amongst
us all, masters and scholars, and he has not disappointed them.   As a scholar he was greatly my superior ; as a declaimer and actor I was reckoned at least
his equal ; as a schoolboy out of school I was always in
scrapes, and he never ; and in school, he *always* knew
his lesson, and I *rarely* ; but when I knew it, I knew it
nearly as well.   In general information, history, &c., I
think I was his superior, as well as of most boys of my
standing."*

Byron then goes on to relate how George Sinclair
was the school prodigy, and to tell of having fought
seven battles and only lost one ; the occasion in question being when the youthful poet had ventured into the
regions of an unfriendly boarding-house and been even
refused a second.   Lord Byron's most memorable con-
flicts were with Morgan, Rice, Rainsford, and Lord

* Moore's *Byron*, p. 21.

Jocelyn. He remarks, " I was a most unpopular boy, but led latterly."*

Byron and Peel were contemporaries in real truth, the former being born on January 22nd, 1788, and the latter on the 5th of February 1789. Peel gained high honours at Oxford, entering Parliament in 1809.† He was not popular at Harrow.

A paper in the *Harrovian* of 1828, written by a contemporary pupil who boarded with Peel at the Rev. Mark Drury's house,‡ remarks how his reputation as a clever studious boy had rendered the future minister out of sympathy with the majority of his school-fellows. Contemptuous heedlessness apparently seemed to render the youth impervious to such shallow disfavour. But, as the writer adds, it only *seemed*, inasmuch as during the first few months of Harrow life so keenly was the dislike of his school-fellows felt by young Peel, that his friends debated whether he should not be removed from a sphere where he was so lamentably out of sympathy with his surroundings. As has been the case with many another sensitive youth, it took time for Peel to enjoy the advantages of contact with his fellows at a great school. Like Byron, he learnt to love and appreciate Harrow.§

The fact seems to have been that in early life Peel

---

* It is worthy of note that he fought the then Lord Calthorpe for calling him an atheist.

† The foregoing details are taken from Howard Staunton's *Great Schools of England*, pp. 279–81.

‡ Now occupied by Wilbee, the school bookseller, and by the *Philothletic Club*. Mark Drury was brother to Dr. Joseph. On the wall of this dwelling may be seen two bricks whereon R. Peel has carved his famous name. They should surely be protected from possible injury.

§ See the *Harrovian*, 1828, p. 108.

was not constituted to take part in the pleasures and
undertakings of those equal in age and fortune. "What
am I to do with this youth who is always repeating
Pitt's speeches and living in a world of his own?" said
the old Sir Robert Peel to Sir Thomas (then Mr.)
Plumer, known as Solicitor-General in Perceval's administration. "Why, put him into Parliament," was
the prompt reply of the clever lawyer and acute observer.*
And it needs not the ruling of a sage to tell us why
such a spirit as Peel's was totally out of unison with
the wild rush of youthful life at Harrow.

It is well known that both Lords Palmerston and
Aberdeen were under Dr. Drury at Harrow. Of the
former it is impossible to escape mention, even in the
most cursory sketch of later Harrow life, though few
traces of his stay on Ida's slopes remain beyond the
name "Temple" cut up in the Fourth Form room,
and his privately-expressed assertion that it was a positive pleasure to be reprimanded by Dr. Joseph Drury.
This fact was told to the writer by the Rev. B. H. Drury.
But, as Mr. Howard Staunton observes, in his *Great
Schools of England* (p. 281), "the aroma of scholarship
flavoured his most ordinary sentences." We can
scarcely doubt that he owed this to Harrow and Dr.
Drury rather than to later instruction at Edinburgh with
Dugald Stewart, under whose influence political economy
ruled supreme.

Lord Aberdeen's connection with Harrow came to be
prolonged far into the century, for, as a governor, when
residing at Bentley Priory, he did good service to the
school, thus justifying John Lyon's foresight when look-

---

* This story was communicated to the author by a daughter
of Sir Thomas Plumer.

ing to the neighbouring nobility and gentry for aid in developing his educational hopes, which have been realised or surpassed to a great degree through the efforts of men such as the Gerards of Flambards, the Duke of Chandos (when at Canons), the Bucknalls, Grimstons, and Villiers, hailing from Gorhambury and the Grove, Watford, while last, but not least, has the sojourn of the Hamilton family around Bentley and Stanmore contributed to sustain John Lyon's poorly-endowed school.

Although Lord Aberdeen was a Gordon, his first wife was a daughter of the then Marquess of Abercorn, and her early death threw a shadow over a private life as spotless as was his public career remarkable. The first messenger who brought the news of Vittoria to the Allies in Germany in 1813, Lord Aberdeen was twice Foreign Minister, and his name became famous in every Court of Europe. At home he is remembered as having been instrumental in bridging over the gulf between the Peelites and Radicals, and so making Liberal rule possible; and if some politicians acquainted with the facts believe that such a result was attained at an enormous sacrifice, viz. war with Russia, yet an historian will not fail hereafter to record the excellence of those motives, which, while desiring to banish partisan hatred from the Council Chamber, yet hoped to utilise all available talent for the task of government. Lord Aberdeen displayed a kindred zeal in advocating the establishment of a British Literary Academy* on the French pattern, and decided to allow a free public expression of Church feeling when, although himself a Presbyterian, he per-

---

* The fact was recounted to the writer by the present Lord Houghton.

mitted Convocation to resume sittings suspended during
the Bangorian controversy in 1717.

If these were the achievements of a notable pupil of
Dr. Drury, whose long life allowed his projects to become
matured, much might have been expected from more
than one promising school-fellow of Byron and Peel
who found an early grave.

One of the most promising of these was the Lord
Royston, who met his death by drowning in the Baltic
soon after he attained full age, and had given evidence
of a powerful understanding, combined with scholarship
gained at Harrow such as allowed him to make a
valuable translation of the *Cassandra of Lycophron.* *

The able judge Sir John Richardson, Lord Goderich,
the successor of Canning in the premiership, Sir
Thomas Acland, Sir Charles Pepys, Master of the Rolls,
the Rev. Robert Bland of scholarly repute,† the Dukes
of Devonshire, Sutherland, Manchester, Grafton, and
Hamilton, the Marquesses of Headfort and Abercorn,
the Earls of Verulam, Clare, Bradford, Powlett, Onslow,

---

* *Life of Dr. Joseph Drury* (privately printed), p. 15.

† We learn from the school archives that in 1800 Robert Bland
was one of the Lyon scholars at Cambridge. A pupil of Dr.
Joseph Drury's, Mr. Bland showed early evidence of considerable
ability, and became an assistant master at Harrow. As a contributor to literature, Mr. Bland will be remembered chiefly for
several school books, which, under the title of *Latin Hexameters
and Pentameters*, are familiar to the generation now passing away.
Mr. Bland was also author of some classical translations, together
with Tales and Miscellaneous Poems. His daughter married the
late Baron Heath, Lord Byron's fag at Harrow, who, when the
school tercentenary was celebrated in 1871, was the oldest Harrovian present.—See *Heathiana*, p. 24. The pages of the Rev.
Francis Hodgson's Memoir should be searched for Mr. Bland's
letters from Amsterdam, where, during the Napoleonic supremacy,
he undertook the duties of British Chaplain to the prisoners who
were located there. His career was alike adventurous and
cultured.

Roden, Pembroke, Plymouth, Delawarr, Bandon, Mount
Edgcumbe, Winterton, Jersey, together with Lords
Althorpe (of Parliamentary fame*). Duncannon, Lil-
ford, Calthorpe, Lowther, Powerscourt, Burgheish,
Northland, Poltimore, Raucliffe, Bury, Monson, and
Macdonald were educated at Harrow under Dr. Drury,
who ruled over the most patrician school assemblage of
which record remains. Among the scholars contemporary
with these who gained eminence in after life were several
distinguished Churchmen.

Of course such a condition of things could be but
exceptional when Eton stood as a perpetual competitor,
both amply endowed and furnished with the advantages
which a noble and ancient history confers.

Nor, taking John Lyon's original conception as a
model for Harrow can we pretend to urge that any one
class was therein mapped out for special prominence ;
and probably the Harrow of 1884 is more representative
of the founder's desire than the aristocratic and expensive school which Harrow was between 1785 and 1805.

Other visions of Harrow life at the commencement
of the present century flit before us as we glance over
the contemporary school archives. Daniel Peachey, the
well-known school servant, first makes his appearance on
the scene ; while we read again and again of expenses
for repairing the gallery of St. Mary's Parochial Church,
showing how the school had established a traditional
right thereto during divine service. It was then customary to attend public worship on Fast days ;† but the

* An indifferent speaker, Lord Althorpe nevertheless displayed
much power over men when leading the House of Commons during
the whole time of Lord Grey's administration, and the first period
during which Lord Melbourne was Minister.
† Recollections of Harrow, in *Harrovian* for 1828, p. 143.

Harrow numbers were such between 1800 and 1804
that they must necessarily have encroached far into the
body of the Church.

We may here observe that Dr. Drury was at a manifest disadvantage as regards the inculcation of religion
and morality upon the younger part of the Harrow community, as he had no pulpit of his own from whence to
deliver the teaching which experience bade him impart;
and, indeed, the Harrow head-master did not often
appear as a preacher, but, when in temporary occupation
of the parish pulpit, chose subjects adapted to the needs
and understandings of the youthful portion of his audience.   Enforcing, however, plain principles of the
gospel, he received an attention from his auditors in
striking contrast to the impatience and restlessness of
boys under the infliction of ordinary sermons.   Dr.
Drury's skill in keeping up the respectful attention of a
juvenile audience in school was so remarkable, that we
can quite believe him to have exercised an equally powerful influence when the deeper mysteries of human
existence formed the theme of his discourse.*

Again, in more private admonitions addressed to individual boys, a few well-chosen sentences adapted to the
case of the youth he might be called on to exhort, were
followed by appeals founded on the inalienable principles
of religion and morality.   As a notable result of care,
almost parental, we may certainly instance the case of
Lord Byron, that wild mountain colt, whom Dr. Drury,
gauging the sensitive pride which lay concealed in the
young peer's character, declined to place in the low

* For a description of Dr. Drury's hortatory power in pulpit
and form we are indebted to the *Life of Joseph Drury* (privately
printed), p. 21.

orm which a backward education had otherwise rendered inevitable.* The delay which ensued was fully
justified by the fact that Lord Byron, discursive as his
reading may have been, did imbibe much knowledge at
Harrow, and benefited from contact with a master whose
purity of classical style must in some sort have been
communicated to a favourite pupil. For although he
was on his own showing idle, the great poet rose to be a
monitor at Harrow, and therefore came more immediately under the head-master's influence. "I believe,"
says Lord Byron, in the Notes to *Childe Harold*, "no
one could or can be more attached to Harrow than I
always have been, with reason. A part of the time
passed there was the happiest of my life; and my
preceptor, the Rev. Joseph Drury, was the best and
worthiest friend I ever possessed, whose warnings I have
remembered but too well, though too late, when I have
erred, and whose counsels I have but followed when I
have done well or wisely."

Combined with this personal influence over his pupils,
Dr. Drury seems to have possessed a perspicuity as
regards the latent talents of his pupils, which he mani-
fested by speaking almost prophetically to Mr. Perceval
concerning Sir Robert Peel's future career.† No
wonder, then, that at this period it was found possible
to exempt the Upper Forms at Harrow from corporal
punishment, a measure totally in advance of the times,
as a mere glance at contemporary records of other schools
will show. Indeed, given the perpetual influence of a
presence such as that of the Harrow head-master's

---

* Moore's *Byron*, p. 21. "Not-placed" was a regular school
division.
† *Life of Dr. Joseph Drury* (privately printed), p. 15.

between 1785 and 1805, many have hoped to see the
rod relegated to oblivion, and spoken of only with antiquarian interest ; and yet, although the Drury traditions
have been followed by later masters, it has *not* been
found practicable to exempt younger boys from personal chastisement altogether. But we have, happily,
no saturnalia of flogging wherewith to spice pages,
which, if they contained a questionable sort of interest
could not vie in this particular with other school records
before the world. It would not, however, be fair to
attribute Harrow prestige in 1805 exclusively to the
popularity of its head-master, since much was certainly
due to the co-operation of a sympathetic staff.

Nor could a school three hundred and fifty in number
have been efficiently governed by its masters had not
the monitorial system been in vogue, ten of the Upper
boys standing responsible for the discipline of those
amidst whom they more immediately moved ; and we
suspect that with Dr. Drury's disinclination to make
use of the rod crept in the custom known as "monitorial whoppings" with a cane, the strokes given on the
back of the culprit being limited by the head-master.
And, indeed, we are so far justified in this opinion by
the dictum of Dr. Parr, who, when appealed to by the
new master, Dr. George Butler, after his accession in
1805, replied that the custom in question was not in
vogue when he (Dr. Parr) left in 1771, and must therefore have obtained a footing at Harrow under Heath or
Drury.*

But the time comes when we must bid adieu to Dr.
Drury and his times, during which men had learned the
dangers of a promiscuous and unscientific application

* Communicated to the writer by the Rev. H. M. Butler.

of principles, good in themselves, but which in the
assumed name of Liberty sullied the pages of European
history. We read, however, little in Dr. Drury's life
which leads us to suppose he allowed politics to influence his conduct towards those under his rule ; nor
do we find the names of any who, like Parr, Sir William
Jones, Bennet, and Archdale, became fired with a desire
for achieving the freedom of mankind, caught, may be,
from the classics, and encouraged by their master and
guide, Dr. Sumner, till they adopted something akin
to Republican principles. Dr. Drury seems resolutely
to have avoided any polemical contentions ; and this,
although it would be misleading to suppose that the
young mind of Harrow had then adopted no political
preferences or dislikes. Buonaparte, for instance, found
ardent admirers amongst this miniature world, and
might have claimed Lord Byron as a believer in opinions
which Charles Fox and his Parliamentary followers
were loth to abandon, even when invasion threatened
England.*

It was unfortunate for Harrow that Dr. Drury should
have thought it necessary to announce his approaching
resignation (rendered necessary by his wife's ill-health)
some time before he finally retired. A scantily endowed
school is naturally more dependent upon the personal
character and abilities of its head-master, and, therefore, when it became known that after March 1805 new
hands would be upon the reins, less anxiety was evinced
to travel on the road (royal or not) to learning by the
Harrow coach. Hence came a pause in the course of
unprecedented triumph ; while upon the report that

* See two letters of Charles Fox, written in 1803 to Dr. Samuel
Parr.—Johnstone, *Parr's Works*, vol. i. p. 568 f.

an outsider would succeed, the rebellious spirit was
rising which will be found to have influenced the events
recorded in our next chapter.

We state this fact before closing our account of
Dr. Joseph Drury's career, because it is important to
remember that when Dr. George Butler became head-
master, a slight reaction had occurred already, and
numbers that had been as high as 350 stood at 257.*

During the summer of 1804 the second royal visit to
the town of Harrow and the first to its school was paid,
namely, by George III., under happier auspices than
when his predecessor, King Charles I., stood on the
Hill and gazed over rebellious London. George III.
was driving out from Windsor and alighted at the old
" Crown and Anchor " quite unexpectedly. Charles
Drury, the youngest son of the then head-master, being
senior monitor, showed His Majesty over the school,†
after which the Sovereign visited Lord Northwick at
the Park¦ and admired the prospect stretching towards
Kingsbury and Hendon, expressing his satisfaction by a
handsome compliment.§

There is a story current that Mr. Bliss,‖ the land-
lord of the " Crown and Anchor," thought to exalt
Harrow in the good King's eyes by producing a local
sprig of nobility, and therefore accosted His Majesty

* Dr. George Butler's lists. 350 is the traditional number
given, and, as the lists are imperfect, we cannot say that the story
is correct, but the Butler Bills record that, in 1803, 345 youths
received education at Harrow.

† These details were communicated by the Dean of Ely.

‡ The Park, close to the old site of Flambards Manor, and
very near the head-master's house, has been a boarding-house
since Archdeacon Phelps' time.

§ Life of Archdeacon Phelps (privately printed), vol. ii. p. 89.

‖ See Land for February 10th, 1883. The story is copied into
Harrow Notes of February 24th, 1883.

thus, "The Duke of Dorset, Your Majesty." The
King, who expected to see an adult representative of
the title, appeared surprised at seeing the youthful
patrician whom Byron speaks of as

Dorset, whose early steps with mine have strayed,
Exploring every path of Ida' shade.

The demolition of the old "Crown and Anchor,"
together with Custos' house, may, as *Harrow Notes* suggests, have improved the appearance of the town.   But,
as we are not of the number who desire to see Harrow
"Haussmannised," we hear with regret rather than
satisfaction that such old landmarks have been removed.
Possibly some of our readers who pass by the familiar
ground on which the former hostelry stood, will recall
the above-mentioned incident in Harrow history when
occasion takes them back to the enchanted ground of
early memory.

Dr. Drury, although he dearly loved his work, had
from time to time indulged in holiday recreations, which
proved him to possess the faculty of enjoying a lettered
retirement.   At the house of Mr. Drummond the banker
at Langley Park, near Uxbridge, he had spent more
than one vacation, and there, from time to time consorted with men such as Lord North, the first Lord
Melville, and Lord Harrowby, while in addition to such
intercourse, he indulged his taste for music in company
with Greatorex and other well-known musicians of that
day.*

Nor should it be forgotten that towards the close
of his Harrow career the inclination for farming, which

* *Life of Joseph Drury* (privately printed), p. 18.   Greatorex
was organist of Westminster Abbey, and a well-known harmonist
of Handel's works.

rendered his old age so delectable, had been more or less
indulged in during vacation time, when he sometimes
ran down to his 300 acres of farm-land in Devonshire,
the natal county of his wife, towards the air of which
she turned when hoping to recruit her health.*

Inclination, therefore, in some degree conspired with
a sense of duty to render the resolve final, when in the
spring of 1805 Dr. Drury placed his resignation in the
governors' hands.†

As his biographer relates, "the last closing of the
book of the last day's lesson in the school of Harrow
was a trying scene, not only to his own feelings, but to
those of all assembled around him." In addition to
the Preceptor's natural emotion, he must have keenly
regretted that Lord Byron and Lord Clare, his favourite
scholars, were both to be left behind. The Harrow
boys presented Dr. Drury with memorials of their
affection when he left, in the shape of silver plate ;
and his name remains indelibly connected with the
palmiest days and most stirring associations of the
school. But the tie between a schoolmaster and his
work must be finally severed when the decision to
resign has been arrived at ; and, despite various trips
to London, we only once hear of Dr. Drury revisiting
Harrow. Then, as his grandson the Rev. B. H. Drury
told the writer, " the boys met his carriage at the bottom of the hill, tore out the horses, and drew it up
themselves." This so affected the old head-master that
he suffered absolute distress of mind and resolved never
to return. Like Dr. Newman, when he bade adieu to
the spires of his beloved Oxford, this interesting " good-

* *Life of Joseph Drury* (privately printed), pp. 16, 26.
† *Ibid.* p. 16.

bye " was in Dr. Drury's case to be—in a public sense, at least—for ever.

The governors of Harrow School sent Dr. Joseph Drury a farewell letter, part of which we copy from their minutes :—

" We feel upon this occasion, in all their force, our gratitude for your distinguished services, and our regret that the School can no longer profit by the various and important advantages of being under your approved care and direction.

" We could have wished *upon this spot* (inter has Musarum sedes) to have caught the spirit of composition, and to have been enabled to *grace* the merits which we are anxious to acknowledge. Let us, however, hope that even *this* Testimony of our high opinion and regard will not be unacceptable, and that it will at least be received with that full conviction of its sincerity which *alone* is capable of giving it *some* value.

" We beg leave to subscribe ourselves, with the highest sentiments of esteem,

" Dear Sir,
" Your very obedient Servants,
" CLARENDON.   WALTER WILLIAMS.
GRIMSTON.   SAM. MOODY.
NORTHWICK.   WILLIAM PAGE."

We may add that the governors' action on this occasion did confer a special compliment upon their late master which they themselves were clearly not aware of. The minutes contain no previous communication which offers a precedent for such a compliment being paid to a retiring head-master. Brian, Thackeray, Sumner, and Heath had deserved well of the State, but exceptional expressions of official gratitude are not on record.

Dr. Joseph Drury's retirement was enjoyed chiefly at his pleasant little domain of Cockwood, near Dawlish. But that he was instrumental in establishing Edmund Kean the actor at Drury* Lane, the world would have heard nothing more of one who did so much to mould

* It was regard for the great tragedian, and not, so far as we are aware, any connection between the Doctor's family and *Drury Lane*, which led to the above-mentioned incident.

English character in the early part of the nineteenth century.   He sleeps at St. Leonards, near Exeter, by the side of his friend and brother-in-law Benjamin Heath, also head-master of Harrow.   Dr. Drury's fame and abilities have been fitly perpetuated in the persons of his grandchildren Dr. Charles Merivale, Dean of Ely, the historian, and the late Hermann Merivale, whose career at the Colonial Office was unique in its success.

CHAPTER X.

DR. GEORGE BUTLER'S ACCESSION IN 1805, AND
TWENTY YEARS OF HIS EXPERIENCE.

> The antique casements, black and broken,
> Are sadly flapping to and fro,
> And seem to tell of glad thoughts spoken,
> In summers long ago.
> The racquet ground, the running brook,
> The greenness of the elm-tree shade,
> The place where Byron left his book,
> The spot where Bennet played.
>
> *Harrow in his Time*, by ROBERT ARIS WILMOT,
> *Harrovian* of 1828, p. 225.

BY the original constitution of Lyon's will, an equal
number of votes cast on behalf of any candidate for the
head-mastership caused a reference to be made to the
Archbishop of Canterbury for his arbitration. Archbishop Moore having died in January 1805, it fell to
his successor, Manners Sutton, to make the decision
when the portly second master, Mr. Mark Drury,
received an equal amount of support to that given by
governors to the Rev. George Butler, of Sidney Sussex
College, Cambridge; when these two candidates, together with the Rev. B. Evans, were competitors for
Dr. Joseph Drury's vacant chair.

The following extracts from the governors' minute of April 1805 tell the story of Dr. Butler's election :

" At the request of the Governors of the Free Grammar School in Harrow, the Archbishop of Canterbury has carefully considered the merits and pretensions, so far as he was able to ascertain them, of the two candidates for the mastership of the said school, returned by the governors to the visitors with an equal number of votes. And the Archbishop is of opinion that the interests of the school will be best consulted by appointing the Rev. George Butler, Fellow of Sidney Sussex College, Cambridge, master of the same.

" Mr. Butler attended, his appointment was notified to him, and he complied with the requisitions of the Founder's Statutes."

The new head-master was son of the Rev. Weeden Butler, once amanuensis of the unfortunate Dr. Dodd, to whom he showed unswerving kindness in the hour of ruin. Mr. Weeden Butler undertook what had been Dr. Dodd's cure at Pimlico, and afterwards kept a classical school at Chelsea, where he educated his sons. George turned out a great mathematician, and in 1794 was senior wrangler and first Smith's prizeman, John Singleton Copley—afterwards Lord Lyndhurst—being second to him in both these honours. Some of his friends had expected that he would win one of the Chancellor's classical medals, but a severe illness just before the examination prevented him from being a candidate. But, however excellent Mr. Butler's credentials, the enthusiasm for the name of Drury had so prevailed among the Harrow boys, that they straightway protested as best they could against the archiepiscopal ruling, nor was their resentment kept within the bounds of taste or guided by a proper sense of fairness towards the blameless new-comer.

Lord Byron was led to satirise his new master, and used his monitorial influence to undermine authority which it was part of his duty to support. The poet himself afterwards gloried in making ample atonement for those errors of prejudice, for which the nobleness of his nature made him eager to make amends.

The ex-head-master, Dr. Joseph Drury, had in vain appealed to the boys themselves to give fair play to his successor, and, therefore, when Lord Byron resolved to make his confession of error as notorious as possible, he not unnaturally wrote to his old friend and mentor, and this after paying a formal visit to Dr. Butler to express regret for the injury he had done him. Thus, in June 1809 we find, in a letter to Dr. Drury, that the poet had resolved to suppress all reflections on Dr. Butler when a new edition of the *Hours of Idleness* was published. He desired, he said, to frankly acknowledge himself wrong, and to do so by insertion of the following stanzas :

If once my Muse a harsher portrait drew,
Warm with her wrongs, and deemed the likeness true,
By cooler judgment taught, her fault she owns ;
With nobler minds, a fault confessed atones.

And again, after a tribute to his beloved Dr. Joseph Drury, he adds :

Another fills his magisterial chair,
Reluctant Ida owns a stranger's care.
Oh may like honours crown his future name,
If such his virtues, such shall be his fame.*

* Moore, *Byron*, p. 41.

Nor did the desire to avow his reconciliation end
here ; for when he was on the *Salsette* frigate in May
1810, a message reaches Dr. Butler through Dr. Drury
that Byron is writing with a gold pen which the Harrow
head-master had given him.* He had also previously
announced his intention of taking one Friese as a
servant, whom Dr. Butler had recommended.† Considering all the circumstances, this *amende honorable*
was no more than was to be expected from a youth
whose chivalric instincts, though opposed by many
less elevated tendencies, yet generally triumphed in the
end. Indeed, the boy who, in conjunction with his
friend Wildman, had encouraged the school in its opposition to Dr. Butler, even carrying a loaded pistol, and
tearing down the gratings of the hall windows,‡ could
scarcely do less if he desired to efface honourably the
injury done by conduct which, after due reflection, he
could not uphold.§

Several entries in the school minutes speak of *the
house* where dancing was taught, and it is interesting

---

* *Ibid.* p. 104.
† *Ibid.* p. 89.   Letter from Falmouth, June 1809.
‡ *The Public Schools*, by author of *Etoniana*, p. 288.
§ Lord Byron refused the usual invitation (regarded by the boys
as a command) to dine with the head-master at the end of the half
year, saying that he should never think of asking Dr. Butler to
dine with him at Newstead. Several suppressed satires, were said
to have been launched against Dr. Butler by his gifted but trouble-
some pupil, and to have been current in the school. Ultimately an
absolute rebellion seems to have arisen, during which gunpowder
was laid down in a passage through which Dr. Butler passed. Owing
to the mediation of the future Judge Richardson, no explosion took
place, because, when appealed to not to destroy their fathers'
names on the walls, the boys relented. This part of the story
Captain Medwin declared that Lord Byron told as if he had been
the mediator, whereas the Dean of Ely now says that he heard
from Richardson's own mouth that his word, and his alone, prevented the *dénouement* in question.

Yours ever Byron,—

This was signed in 1806—7b

LORD BYRON'S AUTOGRAPH,

SOON AFTER HE LEFT HARROW.

Given by the Poet to Miss Pigott.

to know from the lips of the late Mr. Webb, who taught him,* that Lord Byron equipped himself for his London career in this then necessary particular. It is well to remember that dancing in 1804 was a somewhat stately art, and associated in our minds with the grave minuet rather than the giddy waltz.

There is no incident in Harrow story less familiar to the world than that of the very serious rebellion of 1808. Probably in some degree an after-wave of the dissensions which prevailed on Dr. Butler's appointment, this *émeute* commenced after the head-master had questioned the legality of certain monitorial innovations, so declared to be by no less a personage than Dr. Parr. Contumacy on the part of the older boys, being followed by resignation of their offices, lapsed into riot and defiance. The school key was taken forcibly from old Peachey, the custodian, the birch-cupboard broken open, and the head-master's chair injured. Under ordinary circumstances a master could have adopted the natural resource of threatened authority, and appealed to the parents of the boys, who, by their intervention, might have prevented matters being carried to an extreme. But on the occasion in question these recusant youths had precluded any such domestic means of subjugation being resorted to by the simple device of blockading the road to London, and allowing no communication, postal or otherwise.

For several days the paralysis of authority was complete. It would seem that the spirit of the French Revolution had permeated into Harrow; for this strange episode had been originally ushered in under the names

* Mr. Webb communicated the fact to Mr. William Winckley. See *Harrow Notes* for June 2, 1883.

of Liberty and Rebellion, such being the motto posted
up in the Fourth Form room. Dr. Butler seems to
have met the crisis with fortitude and tact, for the
number of expulsions which were inevitable did not
reach the total that might have been expected ; while if
the Shell did lose the privilege of exemption from chastisement which Dr. Drury had granted, the change came
as the result of experience it was impossible to ignore.
We may add that not only did Dr. Goodall of Eton
commend Dr. Butler's ruling of the storm, but this
commendation was endorsed by His Majesty George III.,
who averred that no man could have acted better under
the circumstances.   Dr. Butler was deeply sensible of
the debt he owed. to Mr. Mark Drury's judgment and
experience, never more manifest than during this unfortunate episode.*

It appears that one result of this untimely upheaval
was an increased watchfulness on the part of the head-
master over the school discipline and government, such
as could not be maintained in times of general laxity
without arousing some opposition.† But that Dr.
George Butler acted otherwise than in the school interest
when he put down for the nonce blanket tossing, *rolling
in* (during which a new boy had to stand a bombardment of rolls when claiming admission to the hall,
considered at the master's house as a sort of club),‡ it
is impossible to believe.

* These facts are derived, thanks to Dr. H. M. Butler's kindness, from manuscript preserved amongst Dr. George Butler's
papers.

† *The Public Schools*, by author of Etoniana, pp. 314–18.

‡ For account of this rolling in, see *Notes and Queries*, vol. xii.
series 4, p. 307. Two public rooms at the head-master's, called
the hall and play-room, the latter open to all, while the hall was
regarded as a sort of club-room, except at meal-times. This club

That a monitor's whopping for dishonesty was delivered in 1810 with a toasting-fork, instead of the cane
now in vogue, we cannot regard as any special evidence
of cruelty, although probably the gradual extension of the
monitorial system has led to improvement in the nature
of fagging demanded.* Performance of lighter menial
duties for a duly constituted Sixth Form authority has
now neither part nor parcel with what is generally termed
bullying.

It was otherwise, we must allow, when not only had
the fags to prepare their master's breakfasts, to make
coffee, toast bread, go on errands, as at present, but also
to clean their master's shoes and clothes after football
or Jack-o'-Lantern,† or even after actual hunting, for
some ambitious sportsman amongst the elder boys did
now and then steal a day with the hounds, mounted
on a miserable screw hired out by Jem Martin, the
purveyor of all kinds of forbidden indulgences to the
school; so that an unfortunate fag might often be heard
brushing away at five o'clock on a December morning.
Poker and tongs were unknown luxuries in the play-
room at Butler's, and the junior fag at the call of *lag*

consisted exclusively of upper Fifth boys, and the candidates had
to run the gauntlet of *finds* thrown at them, the rolls found by
the household (and so called to distinguish them from what the
boys purchased themselves) going by the mysterious name in
question. One minute's bombardment with this species of ammu-
nition was allowed, while the boy knelt down with his face to the
wall.

* To prove how soon such custom changes, an old Harrovian
of nineteen years later date writes to say that in his time a boy
charged with any disgraceful act was tried, and, if found guilty,
received three strokes on his hand with a post-boy's whip from
each monitor. This was called handing up, and was clearly a
development of the older custom, while its perpetuation never
could have been sanctioned by authority.

† Paper-chases at night, the hare carrying a light.

poker had to rush out in the cold to pull a hedge stake
of substantial dimensions from the nearest fence or
faggot-stack.*   Moreover, positive tyranny seems to
have been sometimes practised in sending fags out
on illegal errands, which, if detection ensued, led to the
almost inevitable penalty of a flogging.†

Dr. George Butler deserves the thanks and admiration of Harrovians generally for having in his time
made a bold and unselfish stand against encroaching
evils such as these ; for he must have known that a
struggle against customary abuses would tend to a
temporary decline in the numbers.   Difficult and delicate, indeed, is the task of a head-master ruling over
one of our great schools.   It is, then, not surprising
that not even Dr. George Butler's resolution served to
commend public schools to the early nineteenth-century
reformers, who would none of them, and outside Eton
nearly caused a national desertion to ensue, which never
ceased until Dr. Arnold went to Rugby.   Hence the
success of the reformers in checking the popularity of
Harrow argues no lack of zeal or ability on the part
of those who, acting in sympathy with the lights presented to them, governed and reformed Harrow
according to the canons which prevailed when they
were in power.

Nothing is more remarkable in Mr. Maxwell Lyte's
admirable history of Eton College than the paucity of
his matter as regards the delineation of school life at
the commencement of the nineteenth century, while

---

* *The Public Schools*, by author of *Etoniana*, pp. 318–19.
Matter contributed by the Rev. J. Reade Munn.

† The Rev. G. Scott, rector of Rhos Crowther, was sent out in
this way by Bishop Ashton Oxenden, who generously confessed
the truth to Dr. Butler, the fag in this case escaping.

in all probability a like sterility would have befallen the
history of Harrow but for the exceptional interest with
which Lord Byron invested the epoch in question; and
despite the poet's many social shortcomings, it cannot
be said that his Harrow career was by any means ill-
spent, as it most certainly reflected honour on the
place. Lord Byron, it should not be forgotten, was a
descendant of an original governor of John Lyon's
school, namely Sir Gilbert Gerard.*

We have stated that Dr. George Butler entered upon
his duties with numbers slightly reduced. But, nevertheless, 257 boys were found in the lists, and, so far as
the school prestige was concerned, no prospect could
have been more hopeful. Yet the new head-master
was soon made aware that a veritable sword of Damocles
was suspended over the prosperous institution, which,
if its shortcomings were many, yet did most certainly
reflect the national manners and feelings of the time.

Encouraged by certain active and enthusiastic men of
business, amongst whom the name of a Mr. John
Foster,† one of the churchwardens, is prominent, the

---

* Sir Gilbert Gerard, Attorney-General to Queen Elizabeth,
was one of the first governors of Harrow, and a grandson of
Sir John Byron, of Newstead, who fought for Henry VII. on
Bosworth Field, and died in 1488.

† *Handbook to Harrow-on-the-Hill*, p. 49. In the Report of the
Committee of Enquiry into John Lyon's Charities, p. 5, is an
account of the way in which the Harrow boys assaulted Mr.
Fisher, the Chairman, and two of his friends. Also how they
absolutely "Boycotted" his family; "his domestics, even his cattle,
were made to suffer." This occurring in February 1808 is clear
evidence of the indiscipline existing amongst the boys, which, cul-
minating in rebellion, gave plausibility to an organized attack on
Harrow which the writer, with all his respect for the townspeople's
rights, cannot but deplore. Mr. Fisher and Mr. Foster, when they
thus brought matters to an issue, failed to secure the approval of
the Bishop of London, named by John Lyon to appoint Governors
when any question of legality of the choice arose; and they further

parish of Harrow had determined to assert what they believed to be their rights, and, if possible, limit the numbers of those admitted to Harrow School under John Lyon's Foreigner Clause. By so doing they hoped to bring about a state of things which would attract tradesmen's children into the school, and so make it possible for purely local inhabitants to profit almost exclusively by prestige which had been the growth of ages, and had its foundation in John Lyon's definite and distinct provision, the character of which it is vain to dispute.

The dissentients in question, however, appealed to the Court of Chancery on the following heads: firstly, for the removal of such of the governors of Harrow School as had not been duly elected; secondly, for the better administration of the revenues of the Charity; thirdly, for an alteration in the then constitution of the school. As regards the first point, technically speaking, some of the governors had resided out of the Harrow neighbourhood, and were therefore assumed to be ineligible, when, nevertheless, by taking the trouble to learn who these men were, anyone might learn that the founder's wishes had been consulted in spirit.

Nor could a person perusing the accounts since 1611 come to any other conclusion than that the roads had swallowed up an enormous sum of money, disbursements being frequent and liberal; while an apprentice never left Harrow without receiving a money present from the school, varying from £2 to £5, a species of liberality regularly repeated when a poor marriage made such assistance desirable.

sustained a rebuff from the parishioners of Pinner (equally interested with Harrow), who unanimously resolved to decline any interference whatever. *Ibid.* pp. 10, 14.

So much, then, for the first two counts in this indictment; while the third, which in effect questioned the
Foreigner Clause and its legality, has been amply discussed, not to say disposed of, by the logic of facts
as related in the earlier pages of this book. And yet,
despite the solidity of the Harrow School cause, it is
certain that the threatened law-suit found the governors
appalled at the possible consequences of any doubtful
ruling, and the whole machine of management seems to
have suffered a passing paralysis. For instance, when
Lord Grimston—an able and active governor—died in
1809, it was thought desirable to seek counsel's opinion
as to the validity of an election promoted by the governors when threatened by legal impeachment; the result
being that Mr. Bell, an eminent counsel, had given an
opinion adverse to any such exercise of power under the
circumstances ; so that the choice of a successor to Lord
Grimston was relegated to the Bishop of London, whose
traditional authority had remained dormant in Harrow
story ever since the consecration of St. Mary's fane by
Anselm.*

When the decision of Sir William Grant was given
in 1810, it was fortunately clear and outspoken as to
the main point at issue, although the interests of the
townspeople were carefully guarded. Sir William Grant
reprobated any future tenancy of school property by
the governors themselves, although as regarded a
special case brought to issue—viz. that of the Vicar
of Harrow, the Rev. Mr. Williams, to whom, when
a governor of the school, part of a Lyon trust
farm had been let—the Master of the Rolls held

* Bishop Porteous chose Mr. John Gray, of Wembley, grandfather of Dr. H. M. Butler.

15

that no personal blame attended the transaction in question.

But as to the Foreigner Clause, Sir William's ruling[*] stands unchallenged to the present day. To limit foreigners, and so alter the character of Harrow, would have injured the inhabitants generally, who depend upon the prestige of the school for their local prosperity, and this although the peculiar privileges of a Harrow inhabitant as regarded free education remained as in 1571, and have ever since been protected. For an understanding of the gulf between rich and poor, which in practice has made it impossible for the two classes to grow up side by side, we must ask our readers to study their English histories, if they wish to elucidate a problem, contemplation of which has led some modern thinkers even to sigh for feudal times.[†]

But Sir William Grant was only called on to state the law as it stood in the year of grace 1810, while we may observe, before taking leave of the subject, that he disclaimed the Court of Chancery's power to interfere with the election to governorship in a body corporate such as Harrow School. Hence the defence was practically triumphant all round.

On the other hand, the subject having been mooted led to a renewed care being evinced on behalf of the Harrow inhabitants, so that the school might keep strictly within the bounds of law. Hence Dr. George

---

[*] For this ruling see Vesey, *Chancery Cases*, vol. xvii. p. 498.

[†] See article on *Rich Men's Dwellings*, by Alfred Austin, *National Review* for December 1883; also opinion of Mr. J. Cowen, M.P., given at Newcastle on Dec. 22, 1883 : " Workmen have many comforts now their fathers had not, but the gap between them and the modern capitalist is greater than that between the old squire and his labourers. We have gained in strength by the new system, but we have lost in sympathy."

Butler was asked by the governors to address leading natives of Harrow as follows :—

Dr. Butler having received intimation from several of the inhabitants of Harrow and Pinner, That it is their wish to send their children, as undernamed, to the Free School established at Harrow by John Lyon, to be educated upon the Foundation of the said School, hereby gives notice to the said inhabitants, That he is willing to examine the said children as to their fitness for admission into the School at the times and in the order following, viz.:—

Monday, 29 April 1811, at half-past one—Wm. Foster, Hy. F. Hill, Jos. Hill, Sam. Honeybun, Hy. Middleton, Js. Gardner.

Tuesday, 30 April 1811, at half-past one —Wm. Childs, Richd. Baxter, Jas. Stockley, Wm. Foskett, Geo. Chalfont, John Page.

Wednesday, 1 May 1811, at twelve—John Deer, Wm. Deer, Jacob Arney, John Slow, Wm. Slow, Jas. Delemore.

Thursday, 2 May 1811, at twelve—Jas. Loosby, Wm. Jackson, Sam Wilson, Jos. Pearce, Hy. Sandilands, Wm. Sandilands.

Friday, 3 May 1811, at half-past one—John Green, Elisha Oldfield, Thos. Sims, John Cox, Wm. Street.

As it will be proper that the Fathers or Mothers attend with their respective children, should the hours above appointed be particularly inconvenient to any one or more of them, Dr. Butler, upon notification thereof, will endeavour to accommodate his Time to his or their convenience.

Signed   GEO. BUTLER, D.D.

Harrow-on-the-Hill,
    27 April, 1811.

Writing of days as to which records of personal experience at Harrow are scarce, we have gladly given prominence to the late Mr. Reade Munn's information, although perforce obliged to again turn towards the archives for guidance in writing this narrative. On December 28th, 1810, we find the then Marquess of Abercorn elected a governor in the place of the Rev. W. Williams, the respected Harrow vicar. This choice had only been deferred because, as his new colleagues phrased it, " previous to the determination of the Master of the Rolls," they did not care to impose a trust fraught with doubts and difficulties upon one who, if given free play, was certain to advance the credit and success of Harrow.

To step back a little, we should not forget to state that in 1809 Duckpuddle was first instituted, and a bathing-place of some description formed on the spot where a tortuous and inviting expanse of water now delights the wearied Harrovian's vision, while contemplating that delightful plunge which most of us envy when we remember what Harrow athletic life is in the summer quarter.

The year 1811 had not found John Lyon's foundation oblivious of the peculiar nature of its origin and the consequent obligation to remain faithful to the Established Church. The six sermons, we read, were still preached on the Martyrdom of King Charles, Ash Wednesday, Good Friday, the Restoration of King Charles II., the King's (George III.) Coronation Day, and the Fifth of November.

A notable alteration in the character of the Harrow surroundings was conceived in the year 1811, when the Regent's Canal made an inroad into the pure vale of Harrow, such as those to whom railways are familiar can in no wise conceive. The present head-master of Harrow was much horrified when, in general conversation, the writer of these pages talked of the aforesaid encroachments as effected by a *canal*, which Dr. Butler's predecessors knew by the shorter name of *cut*, meaningless to one who learnt his experience amidst the whistle of steam engines, and knew not the canal-boat any more than he recognised the Brent as a place wherein to lave his weary limbs,* while information concerning Harrow had been of necessity acquired, not being a family heritage.

The year 1812 at Harrow seems to have been as unfruitful in incident as it was productive of sensation in the world, when Napoleon retired baffled from Russia. Not so the succeeding years 1813 and 1814.

The first of these dates was famous for the erection of a monument in the church to John Lyon, which the governors very properly resolved should be erected by public subscription.† Those who have perused the previous pages of this work will acknowledge that it was in accordance with the fitness of things when the learned Dr. Parr undertook to compose the inscription.

The year 1814 will be remembered by all who love their country as the year during which the tact of England's Plenipotentiaries secured for her the proud position of an arbiter in European affairs, when the whole population of these kingdoms did not exceed fifteen millions. The occasion was not inaptly referred to in the monitor's speech, and the governors replied, " that, at the risk of laxity as regards discipline, they still were unable to refuse a holiday at a period of such unparalleled cause for rejoicing."

National glory, as we all know, reached its climax in the following year, 1815, when, at Lord Northwick's house in Harrow, the governors decided that a week's holiday should be given to the boys in consequence of

* In Lord Byron's time the river Brent was the school bathing-place.
† The monument of marble, by Flaxman. Dr. Parr composed the Latin inscription, above which is a *basso relievo* of a master and three pupils, said to be Dr. George Butler and the three sons of the Right Hon. Spencer Perceval.—*Handbook to Harrow*, p. 35.

the victory at Waterloo. But we have drifted ahead
somewhat too fast, for it is important to notice a local
incident, dramatic in its character, and of interest
outside the scholastic circle, which occurred on one of
the old Speech-days, when fashionable London had not
yet elected to smile on those less festive but then more
frequent occasions.

In the summer of 1813 one of the chief celebrities
present was the first Lord Harrowby, Lord President of
the Council of the Liverpool Ministry, which had succeeded that dissolved by the murder of Mr. Perceval in
May 1812. Lord Harrowby, himself an honour to the
Heath and Drury rule, was much affected when the
eldest son of his old colleague elected to recite
" Wolsey's Farewell," despite Dr. Butler's endeavour
to dissuade him from a course calculated to awaken
memories painful to everyone present. For the murdered minister had been a most enthusiastic Harrovian,
clinging affectionately to the spot where, at all events,
he had escaped party judgment, and been spared the
unjust partisan gibe and slanderous slur, to convey
which so many pens were at work long after the
clear-headed, statesman had gone to his rest.

It is a remarkable fact that, in 1816, when 295
scholars were educated at Harrow, only three free
scholars were found to claim the advantages which John
Lyon designed for the Harrow inhabitants; and this
despite the governors' efforts to keep the numbers up.
Neither Dr. Butler's above-mentioned measures, nor Sir
William Grant's assurance had effected the required
object; and although in 1818 and 1819 the numbers
are returned at ten, the free scholar remained an exotic
in what we may term his own ancestral domain.

It will be interesting to all British readers to learn that in 1818, when the mother and father of Queen Victoria were united in marriage, the Harrow boys secured an extra week's holiday, a privilege which, when asked for on less important grounds by the monitor in his annual speech on June 17th, 1819, was refused by the governors, in a minute which alleged that to gratify so unreasonable and purposeless a desire was inconsistent with duties which they had to discharge to the school and the public.*

The death of the Marquess Abercorn, in the year 1818, had led to the election of the Rev. J. W. Cunningham, Vicar of Harrow, to the vacant post, which he filled as the representative of the Low Church party for many years until, in September 1861, he died, full of years, not without literary honour, " and his parish followed him to the grave like one great family."

The late vicar has been a great link between the Harrow of to-day and that of Drury and George Butler, while he has gained an abiding name in our history by means of the party which he represented, reconciling influential members thereof to a public school system that many did not hesitate to condemn. Nor should it be forgotten that his appearance on the Harrow stage was coincident with a retrograde movement in numbers, which for the next few years averaged about 250, so that Dr. George Butler's scholars were about equal in numbers to those of Dr. Sumner in his palmiest days, an earnest—we regret to state this—of a more serious declension.

It is somewhat strange to read in the governors'

---

* Signed by Clarendon, Northwick, John Gray, J. W. Cunningham.

minutes for 1818 that Dr. Butler should have felt
bound to apply for leave to contract his marriage with
Miss Gray, daughter of the Squire of Wembley, one of
the governors, despite the fact that twice in previous
years had the governors, by deliberate decisions, made
it clear that celibacy was abolished, so far as the power
given them to effect any change could secure such
object.   But in 1818 the school rested under the
apprehension of a possible appeal against Sir William
Grant's decision, and steeled themselves to resistance by
means of careful adherence to the law in its very letter.

Nor must it by any means be supposed that Harrow
had undergone such a crisis as that of 1810 without
suffering in the process to a certain extent. Fathers
called on to select a school were apt to make choice
of an institution like Eton, raised by rich and royal
endowments far above struggles in the law courts,
which threatened to alter the character of the teaching,
and provide companionship of a sort which might be
all very well in theory, but yet stood adjudged impossible in practice. And it was not alone the blight of
an uncertain to-morrow which operated to prevent
Harrow from competing on anything like equality
with Eton at this period of their respective careers.
During Dr. Drury's exceptional popularity as a teacher,
many names traditionally belonging to Henry VI.'s
foundation were found in the Harrow lists, while
between 1819–26 these same families returned to their
Eton allegiance.

A numerous and distinguished assembly was present
on the Speech day of 1820, when the right wing of the
old schools was opened, and the first prize poems of
Dr. Butler's gift were recited in the newly-erected

speech-room by Isaac Williams and others. Amongst the guests on that occasion was Sir Thomas Acland, a popular old Harrovian of Dr. Drury's time, contemporary with Byron and Peel,* and a Whig legislator of considerable popularity.

The new wing had been commenced in 1819, and, including the speech-room, cloisters, and other apartments, cost £10,000, which was subscribed by the governors, masters, and old Harrovians.

There is, we think, some cause for regret that the old red lion, symbolical of the founder, which was erected, according to the archives, in 1704, holding a weather-cock at the summit of the left wing, should have perished amidst the *débris* of building which accompanied its removal in 1819.† But we could raise a like lament on behalf of several objects mentioned in the school accounts, the ancient Bible to wit, which was bought with the chest in 1611, and of which there is no trace within that venerable tomb of all the Capulets which so lately disclosed its contents to the delighted gaze of Mr. Edward Scott of the British Museum, to whom Harrow now owes so considerable a debt.

In 1821 the school-yard was enlarged, while a cupola and clock surmounted the ancient Elizabethan buttresses, the contingent expense being borne by subscription. In fact, the general character of the so-called old school buildings takes date from this epoch, which is likewise to be remembered for the death of Mr. Fladgate, the school solicitor, who had defended the

* Privately printed *Life of Archdeacon Phelps*, p. 42.
† The Dean of Ely's recollections, given at the close of this chapter, will tell its fate.

suit in 1810. He died much regretted by the governing body, who left due expression on the minutes both of Mr. Fladgate's work and of their regret at his loss.

Lord Aberdeen, the distinguished statesman and diplomatist, having become a resident at Stanmore, was in 1823 chosen a governor of the school. His house was on a spot better known in early Harrow history as the locality where formerly stood the priory of Bentley. The modern mansion had been in occupation of the late Marquess of Abercorn before 1818, and then stood famous as the resort of a literary society not yielding even to Holland House in brilliancy. There Sir Walter Scott wrote a portion of *Marmion*, while the banker-poet Rogers was a frequent visitor, and John Kemble with his sister, Mrs. Siddons, were constant visitors.

Nor is an account of the political and literary coterie which frequented Bentley complete without naming Mr. Pitt, the Duke of Wellington, Mr. Canning, Lords Liverpool and Sidmouth, Southey, Wordsworth, Moore, Rogers, Lady Morgan, and Sidney Smith. A summer-house on the lake is traditionally believed to be the spot where Scott wrote part of *Marmion*, while Rogers gave to the world the *Pleasures of Memory* when resting in these placid shades. George IV. as Prince Regent greeted Louis XVIII. here, and part of the Cedar garden is called the Meeting-place of the Four Emperors, said to have assembled there in 1814. Louis Philippe was also a guest at Bentley. Finally, Her Most Gracious Majesty Queen Victoria came to stay with the late Queen Adelaide in 1848.*

* Most of these interesting facts we owe to a writer in the *Illustrated London News* for December 13, 1884.

Nor when taking a final farewell of the eloquent and accomplished Marquess, who so nobly did the duties of host at beautiful Stanmore, should it be forgotten how Sir Walter Scott met him travelling in the North in the old fashion, the ladies and suite having four or five well-appointed carriages, while His Lordship, his breast covered with orders, rode behind on a small pony. This occurred between Carlisle and Longtown; and at every village where they halted, an establishment worthy of a British nobleman's position was maintained, the cuisine being duly cared for.*

Famed for his forensic power, the Marquess also wielded a ready pen, and is said to have added the following to Sir Walter Scott's lines on Fox's death, which occur in *Marmion*, then under revision at Bentley :—

> For talents mourn untimely lost,
> When best employed and wanted most.†

Ballantyne had, however, unfortunately printed this portion of *Marmion* off before the Bentley additions reached him.

Such was a governor of Harrow School in the early nineteenth century.

Lord Aberdeen's connection with the Hamilton family consisted in a marriage with a daughter of the house, whose early death is said to have cast an abiding shade over the Earl's long career. As a Harrovian of Dr. Drury's time, and so connected with Harrow during the very zenith of her renown, Lord Aberdeen well deserved the governors' eulogy, which pointed to the rising statesman as " one of the school's

* Lockhart, *Life of Sir Walter Scott*, vol. ii. p. 37.
† *Ibid.* vol. i. p. 322-3.

favourite sons,* and this although, strange to say, the
compliment was qualified by a request that resignation
should follow departure from the neighbourhood.
Verily, the fear of the law courts was before their
eyes still. However, fortunately for Harrow, Lord
Aberdeen stood to his guns, notwithstanding that, as
Foreign Secretary under the great Duke, he was frequently at Argyll House, where many governors'
meetings are recorded to have been held.

An account suggestive of Harrow life towards the
close of 1822 appears in *Temple Bar* for 1870, vol. 28,
p. 467. There we learn how the physically and
mentally active head-master ruled by means of trusting
to the honour of those under his charge ; for he always
believed a boy's word. Hence, despite strict discipline,
Dr. George Butler's name remained very dear to those
under his charge, some of whom are still amongst us
to speak with enthusiasm of the days of a happy youth.
Nor can a Harrow history be complete without reference
to the prince of tutors, whose name will live on the
hill, much as that of the late Mr. Coleridge's at Eton,
as being *facile princeps* in the art of imparting knowledge in pupil-room, and, as regards scholarship, being
the twin brother of Dr. George Butler. In the year
1820, out of 250 boys, 90 were the pupils of the Rev.
Henry Drury (Harry, as he was familiarly called). He
had the utmost facility in Latin composition, writing
Latin verses faster than most persons could write English. With a remarkable memory he combined a love of
old books only equalled by his knowledge of the library

* In the year 1800, under his title of Lord Haddo, Lord
Aberdeen played *Dido* on Speech-day, while Temple (Lord Palmerston) recited the *Bard*, by Grey.

and its delights. Mr. Drury was a great walker, had an utter contempt for an umbrella, and was quite a hero amongst the boys.*

The writer in *Temple Bar* speaks of a Harrow shut off from the busy world, and draws a picture of the Speech-day attendance quite different from what experience has left on later visitors' minds. One great excitement in the High Street seems to have been the yellow chariot of the then Earl of Clarendon, governor of the school, who died in March 1824, and who is described as a tall, very thin old man, in top-boots and leather breeches. And then that last joyous race to London on breaking-up morning! What a sight it must have been! Gigs, carts, and every species of vehicle stood horsed around the school gates and down the High Street, and, the luggage having been sent on before, such a rush of liberated and expectant boys took place out of first school, that solemn farce on breaking-up morning, still an institution. Black coats and ties were discarded with an alacrity unknown off the stage, and travelling garments of an approved type donned; for young Harrow was to hold his own in St. James's Street that day. And then the race was fast and furious until, the second milestone being passed, the leaders settled down into more sober paces, and soon reached the wished-for haven of even then smoky London. Oh the joy of that spring-time of life, when the blood courses through the veins with a vigour of itself delightful, while the flow of animal spirits leaps, as it were, in harmony with the strength felt within the healthy frame. To some this condition remains

* Letter to the *Harrow Gazette*, September 1872, by Christopher Cooke.

until far into manhood, while most of us, sobered,
may be, by the stern realities confronting all human
progress, have to rest content with memories, precious
because in full accord with our natural instincts, but
very far removed from daily experience.

We cannot approach the conclusion of this chapter
more satisfactorily than by inserting the Dean of Ely's
experiences of the epoch, omitting the account of Dr.
George Butler's election to the head-mastership, because
that has been told at length from the archives. That
several of our researches concerning the early nineteenth century are therein confirmed is necessarily
matter for just satisfaction.

My admission as a scholar at Harrow School dated from January
1818, when I was not quite ten years of age; but my family had
been closely connected with it for nearly half a century, and I was
already familiar with the place and with many of its traditions.
"Sir William Jones, Sheridan, and Bruce the Abyssinian traveller," were the heroic names with which it was associated in my
imagination—"Byron and Peel" had not yet arrived at the stage
of hero-worship to which I presume "Palmerston" is now
admitted. And I will venture here, before giving a few pages to
the history of the school and its master during the seven years
of my time there, to enter my protest against the mythical story
which seems to be now too easily accepted, that Byron saved the
school-house from conflagration, on the occasion of a boy's *émeute*,
by pointing to the names of their fathers on the walls. At least
I can certify that just such a story was told in my early days of
Sir John (the Justice) Richardson, a distinguished and favourite
pupil of my grandfather, Dr. Drury, a fiery soul in a puny body,
to whom it was not inappropriate. Surely Byron could never have
had any such influence with his school-fellows. It is clear that
he was never a leader among them. On the contrary, awkward,
sentimental, and addicted to dreaming or tombstones, he seems to
have been held in little estimation among our spirited athletes.
The remark was once made to me by Mr. John Arthur Lloyd (of
Salop) a well-known Harrovian who had been captain of the

school in the year of the first match with Eton (1805) : " Yes,"
he said, " Byron played in that match, and very badly too. He
should never have been in the eleven if my counsel had been taken."
Mrs. Drury was once heard to say of him : "There goes Byron"
(Birron she called him) "straggling up the hill, like a ship in a
storm without rudder or compass." Jones and Sheridan must
have left Harrow a little before Mr. Drury arrived there in 1770,
but he knew them and often spoke of them. Of Sheridan he saw
a good deal when our famous Harrovian resided for a time, a
fact not generally remembered among us, at The Grove at Harrow.
1 may be allowed to remark that Harrow, under Dr. Drury, is
famous both for its numbers and for the eminence attained by
many of his pupils. The family tradition whispers that at one
moment the list of the school, amounting to 351. was just one
above that of Eton. However this may be, it is worth recording
that Dr. Drury gave us as many as five Prime Ministers. Spencer
Perceval was his private pupil, Peel, Goderich, Aberdeen and
Palmerston, all passed through his hands as head-master. I presume that this distinction is unique.

But I must return to my entrance at the school in 1818. The
head-master at the time was Dr. George Butler, who had obtained
the appointment thirteen years before, and was, it would seem,
in his forty-seventh year, the age which Aristotle marks as the
acme of man's combined bodily and mental vigour. His stature
was somewhat below the middle height, but his limbs were little
and well-set: his countenance, with its keen eyes and curved beak,
was full of expression, but evidently kept under strict control; and
his march up to school at the head of a procession of lagging
and perhaps unwilling assistants, now, I fear, disused, was decidedly impressive. His cropped and powdered hair, and dignified
costume, gave an idea of more years than he really numbered ;
but there could be no doubt of the agility of a man who thirty
years later leapt off his horse to rescue a woman from the river.*

* On the morning of the 9th of January 1843, a woman proceeded to the Grand Junction Canal, and precipitated herself into
the water: the day was intensely cold. Fortunately. the Very
Rev. Dr. Butler, Dean of Peterborough, who is nearly seventy
years of age, was crossing a bridge on his way to Northampton,
and upon seeing the woman floating in the water, he instantly
alighted from his horse, and plunged in to her relief. After con-

After recounting facts concerning Dr. Butler's previous career familiar to our readers, the Dean goes on to describe the master's mode of imparting knowledge. Henceforth, we quote *verbatim* from the Dean's experiences.

He varied the ordinary routine of accidence and grammar with frequent illustration from parallel passages in modern prose and verse, and was remarkable for the readiness with which he supplied day by day the themes or topics which he expected us to expand in our own compositions. Nor did he fail to excite our emulation by the frequent recital of the most approved of these exercises in open school, and I really think the younger ones picked up a good deal from their hearing a spirited copy of school-verses, when they would have little heeded the unattainable excellencies of the great ancient masters. I can now remember the excitement of listening to the effusions of an Estcourt, a Dallas, and an Isaac Williams, which to the most hopeful of us might seem not beyond measurable distance from ourselves. So much in every way may boys learn from one another.

While Dr. Butler undertook the entire daily hearing of the Sixth Form, which might comprise ten monitors, six upper and ten or twelve under-sixth, he made a point of requiring all the lower forms to "say" to him monthly, or perhaps oftener, and this was a crisis to which the juniors looked with some apprehension. At the end of each alternate quarter (there were, of course, *three* quarters in the Harrow year) each Form was critically examined in set subjects, and always by the head-master himself, the result determining the order of the class, which thereupon mounted to

siderable difficulty, he succeeded in bringing her to the bank in a state of insensibility : the countenance was swollen, and of a livid colour. The doctor, with much difficulty, prevailed on the boatman of a barge, passing at the time, to convey the body to the 'Navigation Inn,' where she was attended, and after some time animation was restored."

[The above note is extracted from *Acts of Gallantry*, p. 105, being a detailed account of each deed of bravery in saving life from drowning, in all parts of the world, for which the gold and silver medals and clasps of the Royal Humane Society have been awarded from 1830 to 1871. By Lambton Young, C.E., Secretary, Royal Humane Society.]

a higher Remove. To mount *per saltum*, or take a double Remove, was an exceptional occurrence, a phenomenon like the *Sol geminus* of antiquity, nor did it often occur that any boy, however slow in learning, was kept down below the normal level of the class to which he had been originally attached. It was only in my own day that the school-prizes were instituted. So far were we behind the age that at first the Prize for Greek verse was assigned to a Sapphic ode, and was not transferred to the iambic which Cambridge had recently brought into vogue till a year or two later. The attempts originally made to elicit a good composition in English verse, which had been an ordinary school exercise a generation earlier, was pronounced a failure, and the Latin ode, which has held its place ever since, was substituted for it.

The head-master was ably supported. I am bound on all accounts to mention first my own uncle Henry (or Harry) Drury, who held for many years the amplest boarding-house and the most crowded pupil-room of any. The extraordinary energy with which he coped with the numbers that thus besieged him, and if he was unable to give them all equal attention, at least impressed them with a sense of his constant vigilance, and kept them strictly under his authority, was a matter of general admiration. To the management of those boarders and pupils he added the control of both Removes of the Shell, numbering at least sixty boys. The schoolroom appropriated to this large Form was the whole attic floor of the old building, and a sight it was to see and to remember, the massive figure of the ruler, then in the full vigour of his age, striding from end to end, rolling out awful questions and sonorous recitations, commanding the attention of all and impressing each with the apprehension that he would be himself the next "called up." Harry, I must add, was the tutor to whom most of the cleverest boys were consigned, and it will be found that the Harrow prize-men of the earlier years came, with few exceptions, from his pupil-room.

Meanwhile, however, a younger man, Mr. Batten, was gaining a high reputation as an assistant in a lower Form. When he began to feel his strength he took a lease of the handsome house and grounds, known as The Grove, which constituted a new era in our school economies, which had been hitherto conducted too much on the old rude lines of the olden time. Batten soon succeeded in filling both his house and pupil-room with many

of the *élite* of the school, and his premature death was assuredly a
great loss to it. It was supposed, indeed, that he came to his
post with little preparation for classical teaching ; but he was a
man of much ready ability, and devoted himself earnestly to the
venture he had made. He was said to have trained himself for
training in Latin verse composition, as the surest factor in the
task, by setting himself to learn by heart the whole of *Ovid's
Elegiacs.* The present generation may smile, but they may be
assured that such a feat was quite in keeping with the scholastic
traditions of the time. Harry Drury had thus possessed himself
of the whole of Lucan's *Pharsalia,* and, as he once told me with
much satisfaction, had repeated to himself its 8,000 verses during
a long summer's day walk from Harrow to Eton. I can fancy
him now descending one hill with *Bello per Emathios,* and entering
the Shooting Fields with *Calcanten mœnia Magnum.* I believe he
was almost equally conversant with his favourite *Claudian* and
many others of the less familiar *Poetæ Latini Minores.*

If the objects to which our attention was mainly directed must
seem somewhat strange to modern ideas and requirements, no
less strange was the neglect of others which are now reputed every-
where essential to sound public education. We were wholly
prescientific ; mathematics were limited to a book of Euclid
lightly glanced at by the Sixth Form once a week ; arithmetic, like
writing, was taken for granted ; Algebra was unknown. Our
deficiency in religious, and even, it must be added, in moral training, may cause more painful reflection. When I first came to
Harrow the Fourth Form "did" Greek Testament on a Sunday
morning to the head-master ; but, if I remember right, condign
punishment for defective preparation was deferred to the Monday.
When, however, Mr. Cunningham, Vicar of Harrow, became one
of the governors, he was not satisfied even with a bloodless exercise
on the Holy-day, and the Sunday Greek Testament was dropped,
nor can I affirm from my own recollection that its place was taken
by any other religious teaching in any of the Forms throughout
the week, except that Dr. Butler had the Sixth Form for half-an-
hour on Sundays to read "The Evidences" in his library.

Since writing this an old Harrovian, somewhat junior to myself, assures me that he remembers the Fourth reading Wake's
Catechism on Sunday mornings to Butler. He adds, "One incident
of this school-hour was the entrance of the Custos, who had charge

of the school clock, with a large silver watch open in his hand,
which Dr. Butler set for the week according to a time of his own,
without much reference to Greenwich." There was no Custos in
my early day. I believe he was an institution of the New School
era. Ah! Peachy rang the bell; what an institution was the
cobbler Peachy! There was no school chapel during my time,
nor did the head-master or any of the assistants ever take the
pulpit of the parish church, at which the boys were of course
required to attend on Sundays and Saints'-days. Yet while I
write I seem to have a faint vision of Dr. Butler once preaching
there, probably on some special occasion. Mr. Cunningham was
an able divine of the Evangelical type, and seemed jealous of
yielding his place to anyone but his own curate. He seldom if
ever addressed himself to the boys, while the masters were perhaps
no less jealous of his influence and made no offer to assist him.
The upper half of the school sat in the spacious gallery which
occupies the western extremity of the nave; the remainder were
crowded together over the north aisle, from which Lord Byron
tells us how he used to spell out, as I have spelt it after him, the
inscription to "Daniel Graham Armiger" crowning the south
entrance. At this moment I can but feel shame and contrition
at the hours wasted, and sometimes worse than wasted, in these
gloomy recesses. Let me contend, however, for the undoubted
fact that the low state of feeling at Harrow in my time was
shared by the public schools generally throughout the land.
Even the powerful, though fretful, pleading of Cowper's *Tiro-
cinium* had done little to amend it, and it corresponded only too
faithfully with the feelings of the parents, who were content to
submit their children to it.

In the year 1818 John Lyon's old school building stood alone,
surrounded on three sides by the school-yard, the northern side
abutting, as now, on the Vicarage (Mrs. Leith's) garden. Mr.
Cunningham resided in the house opposite to the old turnpike,
at the corner of the lane to Roxeth; at a latter period he mi-
grated to the villa on the other side of the London Road,
occupied for a time by the Trollopes, and said to be the place
designated by the name of Orley Farm in the novel so called.
The Vicarage, with its extensive garden, which has been resumed
by the present incumbent, was for many years rented by the
"Dame," Mrs. Leith, and was held in great repute for its high

16 *

social character, and especially for its eminence in cricket. "Leith's against the School," was an annual match in which Perry, Wordsworth, and several Halls, Oxendons, Andersons, Davidsons, and Trenches took a distinguished part, which deserves to be historic.

From the public road which leads up to the church, we ascended to the school by a flight of twelve or more broad steps, entering the yard on the left hand, where a line of flags led to the projecting bell-tower, the same which now connects the old with the newer edifice. The entrance was approached from the north, not, as now, from the opposite quarter. Lyon's school-house had then, as now, its three storeys; but these were then all fully occupied as they are not now, with classes and class-rooms. In the great area of the ground floor, now denominated "Fourth-Form room," the Sixth Form occupied the northern portion, on the right on entering, and there it was that all their lessons were carried on. The Third Form and lower removes of the Fourth sate at the same time to the left. The head-master took the pulpit, if I may so call it, at the northern end of the room, except when looking over exercises, for which the big chair and table below were more convenient. Later generations may take some interest in these antiquarian details, and be amused, perhaps, to hear how, on winter mornings, the master took up his wax-taper for his own private convenience, and the boys, for the most part, followed his example, our austere founder having made no provision for throwing light upon our studies. Very chary was he also of warmth. That big schoolroom was warmed by a single faggot— a huge one, certainly—which blazed for five minutes in the monstrous chimney, and served, perhaps, to suck up the damps of parting night.*

The masters of the Fourth and Third Forms filled the grim thrones, now vacant—unless frequented since by the ghosts of Mills and Batten—which face each other below the door and chimney, while that which stands to the right of the entrance was assigned to the Sixth Form monitor, the head-master's official, who, after reading the daily prayers, was excused from the

---

* The smaller rooms above had, I think, no fire at all; but our school-times were seldom an hour long, and often a good deal less.

ordinary lessons of his week, but required, in lieu thereof, to do a copy of verses extraordinary, on a subject of his own choice.

Before the new school with its cloister was erected, the great schoolroom, left open to all comers, was used sometimes as a playground in wet weather. A good deal of rough play went on there. I have seen cricket practised there with great vigour, and racquetballs flew about in plenty. The brill window to the south was put in at the time the new school was built, and it may be observed that the names cut upon the panels round it generally bespeak its date. There is also a panel to the left of the head-master's seat which was inserted about that time, and is occupied by the names of that generation. The names, I beg leave to add, are all *autographs*, at least, if not engraved by each boy for himself, by a more expert school-fellow for him. To employ a professional hand was very rare, and deemed rather shabby.

On the first floor the Fifth met in the central, or governor's room, the Upper Fourth in the southern chamber, while the northern was supposed to be reserved for that mythical personage, the writing-master, or employed for occasional uses. These three rooms had originally constituted the common parlour and private lodgings of the Upper and Lower masters, and the two closets cut off from the passage or corridor behind them had served for their respective bed-rooms. In my time these little corners were fitted with shelves for the reception of the slender store of books which has since expanded into the noble Vaughan Library. Lastly, the long upper chamber, or attic, held, as I have already said, the two Removes of the Shell under their single master. The erection of the new school, or Speech-room, was commenced in 1819, and I was one of the number who marched in procession and trod sturdily on the first stone, beneath which were deposited the coins of the period, and—to be worth many coins whenever it shall be recovered—a bill of the school, written by Bollaerts, and adorned, as I remember, with some graceful flourishes by Isaac Williams, as the two worthiest of the honour.*

---

* Bollaerts, a youth of much ability, and first in his Form. He took but a low degree in the Classical Tripos at Cambridge. Isaac Williams obtained high distinction at Oxford. His English verses enjoyed considerable reputation in later life, but were, perhaps, hardly equal to the promise of his Latin prize poem in illustration of Buckland's geological discoveries.

The school-yard has always witnessed excellent practice in racquets, but in my early days it was the ordinary football ground; and, confined though it was, it afforded good scope for very vigorous and fiercely-contested engagements. The greatest feat, but one not unfrequently executed, was to kick the ball right over the school, from whence I have seen it descend even into the road beyond. Failing to clear the building, it often rebounded from the ridge to the parapet, and there fags were stationed to find and cast it down. This service was cold in the wintry winds, and seemed not a little perilous. I do not recollect my own very tender years having ever been subjected to it. Nevertheless, I was free, while the building was in progress, to clamber by poles, ropes, and ladders on my own account, and I mounted more than once to the rampant red lion (symbolical of our honoured founder), which sustained the weather-cock on the summit of the belfry. I possessed myself of a splinter of this august trophy, the whole of which—and possibly more than the whole—was dispensed among us in the shape of snuff-boxes, and the like. Some of these fragments may still be treasured up by very ancient Harrovians.

Immediately below the school-yard lay, and still lies undisturbed, a narrow strip of level soil known and much used as the fighting-ground. If the name is still remembered, I hope and believe that the practice of the old school-duello has ceased in politer times. From thence, as soon as the Bill had been called, at 2 P.M., on a summer holiday, we rushed down the hill to the cricket-ground, with no such unsightly obstruction as the modern Fives' Courts in our way, and gave ourselves up, as players or spectators, to the queen of sports. The Sixth Form game was the cynosure of the school then as now. Some variations have been made in its manners and customs, which veterans may be allowed to regret; but, on the whole, few such usages have persisted with so little change, for a period of sixty-five years of more than common mutability. One distinction, at least, I may claim for the Sixth Form game of 1823–24, in which I took part myself, namely, that it comprised among its players two Archbishops that were to be, three Bishops, and one Dean, and I venture to challenge the cricketers of any other school to produce such a list.* Perhaps I may be allowed to set this against

* Archbishops Trench and Manning; Bishops Terry, Charles Wordsworth, and Oxenden.

the disparaging view I seem to have taken of our church teaching. *Valeat quantum!*

And one word as to the wielder of so graphic a pen. These records have commemorated several statesmen, more than one poet, but hitherto no historian. The gap, however, is worthily filled by the present Dean of Ely, the writer of the above letter, who is bound to Harrow by every conceivable tie of affection for the place. As Dr. Joseph Drury's grandson, his success in the world of literature has been hailed with pride by other Harrovians besides those who remember him at school, where, as he has himself stated, he entered in 1818. It is almost a work of supererogation to say that he is author of a *History of the Romans under the Empire.*

CHAPTER XI.

TEMPORA MUTANTUR.—1825–1844.

Spot of my youth! whose hoary branches sigh,
Swept by the breeze that fans thy cloudless sky;
Where now alone, I muse, who oft have trod,
With those I lov'd, thy soft and verdant sod;
With those, who scattered far, perchance, deplore,
Like me, the happy scenes they knew before;
Oh! as I trace thy winding hill,
My eyes admire, my heart adores thee, still.
                              LORD BYRON's *Hours of Idleness.*

THERE is a tone of contemplative regret in Lord Byron's beautiful lines which render them applicable to a time when pride, as regards the past, and hope for the future, must have been indulged in by many an enthusiastic Harrovian, who, witness of a decline in the numbers of his school, scarcely dared to exalt the present.

The year 1825 is chosen as an epoch from which to trace this temporary decline of Harrow, because if at that time numbers showed no serious diminution, yet indications were not wanting to convince thoughtful men that public school education generally was on its trial. In the first place, the religious world, as represented by Mr. Wilberforce and his associates, had declared against the then prevailing system; while an idea was abroad, not, unfortunately, totally without foundation, which represented public school life as a rough mirror of the peculiar state of society then existing in England. Eton, it is true, taking refuge under her enormous prestige, might even at this time of day pass unscathed by criticism such as threatened the very being of another school, yet murmurs of discontent were not by any means unheard even as regards the premier seat of youthful training.*

Indeed, as early as 1812 the Conservative instincts of the *Quarterly Review* led its editor to rebuke Miss Edgworth for averring Harrow in particular to be a place where the home influence was soon shattered† by the prevalence of a totally different and, according to the talented authoress, questionable tone. But the complaint, nevertheless, had been formulated. And although the *Quarterly* was justified most thoroughly in demonstrating the high purpose which animated an institution intensely national in its sympathies, yet the private evidence laid before us speaks of a period during which the battle of life was hard, and when the monitorial system did not altogether secure small boys from oppression.

The impression made by this information is further confirmed by the publication of the early experiences of Anthony Trollope, the famous novelist, who was at Harrow between 1822 and 1825,‡ and, after a sojourn at Winchester, returned to the former scenes of his educational misery (for such unfortunately did he esteem it), to repeat four years later experiences such as were doomed from the very nature of the case to be unhappy.

---

* *Edinburgh Review*, vol. lxi. pp. 65–80.
† *Quarterly Review*, 1812, p. 333.
‡ *Autobiography of Anthony Trollope*, pp. 1–10.

That so remarkable a character should have failed to hold its own in youth against the contempt of ignorant and thoughtless companions, when the spirit was lowered by poverty and its hapless concomitants, no lover of literature will fail to regret ; while that Harrow boys should have been so cruel, will call up a blush of shame in quarters where the recital would have been scouted had not it reached us from a source absolutely indisputable.*

But, on the other hand, it is clear from his own showing that Anthony Trollope was a very dirty little boy, or Dr. George Butler would never have told him so ; while that public school life was ill-suited to his temperament, his weary five years at Winchester goes to show. As to Trollope's second spell of home-boarder life at Harrow, it was impossible that he could walk twelve miles

* Lord Bessborough has sent us such an interesting critique of Mr. Trollope's later Harrow recollections that we give the substance of it here: "Anthony Trollope, who was in the same form with Lord Bessborough, averred that Harrovians of his own time learned nothing but Latin and Greek, and that badly. Trollope, I am sure, wrote," says his Lordship, "according to his memory, but he must have certainly forgotten a good deal of his Harrow life. There was, no doubt, great opportunity for shirking work, but anyone who chose to learn had the means to hand, when under Harry Drury, not only of becoming a first-class scholar, but of picking up a mass of curious and useful knowledge, such as many men of eminence in their several callings have gladly acknowledged in after life. Mr. Trollope must have forgotten the weekly English themes which the writer, Lord Bessborough, had reason to remember, because, having taken extraordinary pains with one for which a small prize was to be given, he went anxiously to Dr. Longley for his decision, having, as he believed, done fairly well. ' You did well,' replied the head-master, ' but, you see, Trollope writes better English than you do, at present.' " Lord Bessborough adds, "I was not satisfied then, but acquiesced in the decision in after life." As regards classics, his Lordship reminds us that the Rev. B. H. Kennedy, of Shrewsbury fame, was then a master of Harrow, and "must have been competent to teach a little Latin and Greek to those willing to learn."

a day through the lanes and yet do himself justice.
Every practical person must know this; and it ought
not to escape mention that when in the earlier part of
Orley Farm a comparison is made between the two
friends, one of whom has been educated privately and
the other at despised Harrow, the novelist attributes to
the former youth, one Lucius Mason, a conceit which
public school education would, as the *writer* believed, *not
have created*. So even Anthony Trollope perceived the
bright side of public school training.

The year 1825 was one of dire disaster to the
moneyed classes, nor did the aristocracy pass unscathed
out of a financial crisis totally unparalleled as regards
the ruin it spread, since the year 1720, when the English
people lost their heads over the South Sea Bubble.
Harrow, by no means a cheap school, naturally felt the
shock, and entered the year 1826 with only 214 boys, a
number which by Christmas of that year had decreased
to 193.*

* Archdeacon Phelps' *Diary*, from his Life, privately printed,
vol. ii. p. 47.
   The decline of numbers was almost coincident with that at
Westminster, where, when Goodenough was master in 1821, 300
scholars still attended. But falling in 1824 to 260, numbers gradually dwindled until, in 1831, there were 202 Westminsters, all
told, and, in 1841, only 67.—*Westminster School, Past and Present*,
by F. H. Forshall, p. 113. But the Harrow decline was aided by
local incidents which are not generally known, but were noised
about London society at this crucial moment in public school
history, causing a scandal which injured the character of Harrow
generally. Lord Bessborough heard the details from his naval
brother, then at Harrow, and also from an old pastry-cook, one
Mother Bird, who kept what is known as a "tuck shop," in Hog
Lane. So far as we can learn, the Harrovians were not aggressors
in the disturbance which "originated (as Lord Bessborough
believes) in the ill-treatment of some small boys in the school by
the sons of a blacksmith who kept a forge at the foot of the hill,
near Sudbury. The place may be identified, because it is still
occupied by a man pursuing a like trade. In 1826 the Harrow

Eton at this time, it is well to remember, averaged something over 500 in numbers, which were to increase as the once formidable rival further declined ;* while Rugby, on the other hand, had but lately suffered from the effects of a rebellion, and although under the once successful care of Dr. Wool, was at a low ebb.

Dr. George Butler at Harrow not only strove hard to put down doubtful customs, which the tone of society amongst men and boys then tolerated at schools generally, but he busied himself to get the scanty funds available for scholarships at the universities consolidated in such a manner as to make these institutions worthy objects of competition.

He remembered, possibly, how that neither Dr. Parr nor Dr. Joseph Drury had been enabled to finish their university course when relying on the scanty pittance which a Lyon scholarship afforded. Hence an impulse was given whereby the best-known old Harrovians were encouraged to supplement the scanty endowment which remained available for school purposes out of John Lyon's considerable bequests. Voluntary subscription, it is true, had raised a new wing to the school buildings in 1819-20 ; while Dr. George Butler introduced the institution of annual prizes for Greek Verse, Latin Hexameters, and Latin Lyrics *out of the founder's estate* in 1820. But to Sir Robert Peel is the merit due of becoming the first benefactor proper since the Preston

boys took rough reprisals to compensate for the ill-treatment of their schoolfellow, and absolutely demolished the blacksmith's house. Police had to be summoned from London to put down the riot ; as less extensive disturbances had previously occurred with some travelling tinkers, the effect upon the Harrow reputation can be conceived when the story, exaggerated as such matters usually are, became known in town.

* Maxwell Lyte, *Eton*, p. 405.

gentleman launched his wise scheme in 1571, and the great statesman claimed this honourable memory by becoming founder of an annual gold medal for Latin Prose which was instituted in 1826.*

During the latter year occurred a sad event which it is necessary to record. The only son of Sir Charles Lemon—sent to Harrow in preference to Eton in order that he might avoid that very danger—was drowned in Duck Puddle, having been seized with a fit when bathing. Verily, *l'homme propose mais le Dieu dispose !*

In February 1826 evidence of lack of discipline ap- peared at Harrow, and the governors, in a carefully prepared minute, called on the head-master to take measures which should ensure the scholars remaining in their respective houses after lock-up, and so cease to expose the inhabitants of the parish to interruption and discomfort.† This statement probably had reference to the previously mentioned school and town rows which had stirred up much bad blood and led to considerable disorder.

We have mentioned this matter again to indicate clearly one of the several causes which we believe tended to undermine the school position and alienate its connection. But with Dr. Butler at the helm and fully apprised of the situation, such an evil could but be transient. Not so the inherent difficulties which lack of proper accommodation presented in a school where the under- masters were poorly remunerated for their hard work. The members of the Harrow staff, who had commenced their school duties under Dr. Drury, when John Lyon's

---

* A complete list of Harrow endowments was published in *Harrow Notes*, for Nov. 3. 1883.

† Governors' Minutes, Feb. 9, 1826.

institution swarmed with eager students, were naturally
at a disadvantage when comparatively meagre entries
left them high and dry, and without due chance of other
preferment; brighter hopes having formerly led them to
stake *all* on their continuance under the banner which
bore the crossed arrows on its escutcheon.*   Very properly the head-master had by repeated decisions been
placed in the leading position which his responsibility
warranted, and hence it happened that several of the staff
were divided amongst themselves; the usher appealing to the Lyon statutes to claim a share of the entrance
money.†   Such dissensions must have been most injurious to the school.   Again, more than one of the under-
masters found the liabilities he had incurred to be absolutely ruinous, and the general character of Harrow was
injured thereby.   Nor can we fail to record how a Bill in
Parliament for consolidation of the turnpike trusts on the
northern side of London affected Harrow, whose liability
concerning keeping up the roads to London is well
known. Ultimately, when the Bill passed in the summer
of 1826, several clauses were inserted to preserve the
school interests, but not to guard against flaws in leases
previously granted.   Hence the opinion of Mr. Tindal,
Q.C., was sought; and it being unfavourable, a special
measure was promptly introduced and passed through
Parliament‡ which rendered the leases in question
valid.

At this period of our history general change seemed

* Custom had ruled (exception proving the rule in the persons
of Drs. Cox and Joseph Drury) that the under-masters should not
attain to the Harrow head-mastership.
† Governors' Minute, March 18, 1826. Settled previously in
favour of the master, according to the Minute of April 1721.
‡ Governors' Minutes, June 21, 1827.

to be in the air. Lord Liverpool's administration, after a sway of fifteen years, was dissolved in February 1827, in consequence of the Prime Minister's ill-health ; while a more liberal policy at home accompanied Mr. Canning's popularising of his predecessor's maxims of foreign policy, which, since Lord Byron's death in Greece during 1824, had led men to desire liberty for the enslaved all over the world. Among the domestic institutions threatened at this exciting moment our public schools seemed marked out prominently as destined to embrace reform or endure comparative neglect.

Thomas Arnold, hitherto taking private pupils at Laleham, was elected head-master at Rugby at the close of 1827, to commence in the following year duties the remarkable performance of which led to beneficial change throughout the land. He entered upon his new career just at the time when the reformers of the day were accusing the then established public school system of confining itself to ancient learning, and to but a limited portion even of this ; while in the religious world it was urged that little or nothing was done to give a Christian tone to an education upon which depended the future of so many English gentlemen.* At this time, on the very verge of the great Church movement which commenced at Oxford, John Lyon's institution retained, more than any other school, the confidence of the British religious world. Owing to the Rev. J. W. Cunningham and the influence of his school, the then unpopular principles of Newman and Hurrell Froude never gained footing on the Middlesex hill ; while the

* See *Life of Archdeacon Phelps*, privately printed, vol. ii. p. 2.

school was left free to extract the good out of Arnold's
Rugbeian system, just as the Warwickshire schoolmaster
had previously profited by adapting much then in vogue
at Harrow to the needs of Rugby.* But it must have
shocked the Oxford theologians to learn that but a few
years before the promulgation of the Oxford creed Harrow had so far placed herself out of their pale as to
abolish attendance at Church on Saints' days, a change
which commended itself to the governors' judgment
because, as Dr. Butler phrased it, " at collegiate public
schools there may be some reasons for preserving the
customs of observing Saints' days which do not affect
such a school as Harrow, and I am fully persuaded that
no real benefit on the score of piety and devotion is
actually obtained by this adherence to ancient usage."†

Harrow, however, retained her traditional moderation
as regards polemical discussions, whether religious or
political ; and, despite the temporary decline which we
are compelled to record, retained certain elements of
advantage which rendered a return to prosperity certain
for an institution still reflecting the national life, and
possessing a past the study of which might well reassure
the doubting and inspire the mind of any chosen and
trusted leader. Such a school might well be accepted
as a compromise between the Toryism passing away
and the system about to be inaugurated when Dr.

---

* *Life of Archdeacon Phelps*, privately printed, vol. ii. p. 3.

† Governors' Minute for June 1825. Ash Wednesday, Good
Friday (which occurred in the holidays), Ascension Day, Jan. 29,
George IV.'s accession, Jan. 30, Charles I.'s martyrdom, Nov. 5,
Gunpowder Plot, were the days retained. An old Harrovian of
the date writes to us as follows : "The abolition of church-
attendance on Saints' days was sensible, because, with two half
and one whole holiday a week, little time could be spared from
the necessary studies of the place."

Arnold left for Rugby, resolved to reform the old order of things as tried and found wanting ; and he went there, moreover, speaking distrustfully of evangelical theology as propounded in the newly-established *Record*,* while at the same time he respected the motives of its representatives.

The Harrow numbers fell at Christmas 1827 as low as 148,† a decline which continued to prevail each successive quarter, until Christmas 1828 saw only 127 mustering under the once popular banner bearing for its crest the silver arrows.‡

" The main fact of Dr. George Butler's long reign," writes 'his distinguished son, the present head-master, " was the building up of the (old) Speech-room. It occupied his mind and energies from about 1818 (probably earlier) till 1829, when he left. He was still at work, adding to the long subscription list. Then there was his foundation of the Verse prizes ; correspondence with Sir Robert Peel ; founding Duck-puddle ; rebuilding the head-master's house, whereon he spent £12,000." All these benefits should remain in the minds of our readers when they contemplate a career which, so far as our story is concerned, is about to close.

Under Dr. Butler, during the last few years of his rule, we find the following staff :—The Rev. B. Evans, second master, who had succeeded to the chair of the Rev. Mark Drury when that gentleman retired from his long spell of service ; the Rev. E. Batten, a trusted member of the Low Church party, whose house at The

---

* *Life of Archdeacon Phelps*, privately printed. vol. ii. p. 55.
† At Easter, 1827, the bill-books showed 173, at Midsummer, 160, and at Christmas, 148.—*Diary of Archdeacon Phelps*, privately printed, vol. ii. p. 47.
‡ *Ibid.*

Grove was exceedingly popular; the Rev. Henry Joseph
Drury, the popular mainstay of an old historic connection; the Rev. William Mills; the Rev. John Edwards;
the Rev. William Oxenham of honoured memory; the
Rev. William Whitmarsh Phelps, and Mr. Marillier, who
is known to most old Harrovians under the pseudonym of
" Old Teak." He filled the position of assistant-master,
teaching mathematics from the spring of the year 1826
up to the date of his death in 1876. Two dames' houses
still remained, the system being tacitly allowed to die
out as the impossibility of restoring the free scholar
permanently into modern Harrow received recognition.*

Mother Armstrong, who lived in M. Masson's present
house, received only two boys; but Mother Leith, in
the Vicarage situate between the Church and the old
school, presided over a most famous house. Her boys
looked upon their dame as a perfect lady and treated
her accordingly; while the discipline under good heads
and monitors was better than that of some masters'
houses. Amongst the Leithites of those days was the
present Archbishop of Dublin and his brother, three
Pagets, and the late Marquess of Hertford, whose untoward death from the kicks of a horse so deeply moved
all his friends, causing also the regret of those aware of
the great merits which Prince Albert's friend possessed.
Francis Hugh Seymour, eldest son of Captain Seymour,
had in 1828 no thoughts of his future honours. He
was a cheerful, happy, spirited. good-natured fellow. It
is said of him, as of the friend at whose instance these
details are published, that the future Marquess held the
black tail-coat in abhorrence, and, therefore, clung as

---

* During the year 1825, the free scholars rose as high in
number as 17.—Governors' Minutes, 1825.

long as he could to the jacket which then as now was the alternative raiment wherein it was possible for a Harrovian to garb himself.* As everyone familiar with the subject is aware, entrance into the Fifth Form leaves no option in the matter of dress, so Francis H. Seymour had to repress his objection when, as soon occurred, he attained that position in the school.

It is interesting to trace the career of those who carried off the newly-founded first prizes. The late baronet Sir Thomas Dyke Acland was captain of the school during the summer quarter of 1826, and left in 1827 after winning the first medal founded by Sir Robert Peel for the Latin oration. The governors' prize for Latin Lyrics fell in 1826 and 1829 to Charles Thornton, one of a family attracted to Harrow by Mr. Cunningham's presence in the government, and who was Sir Robert Inglis's ward.

His career at Oxford and as a London clergyman was short, and he is better remembered for his faculty of attracting men to him personally than for any achievement such as his abilities made probable. His friendship with Dr. Newman, Mr. Gladstone, and Mr. Sidney Herbert was warmly reciprocated by those distinguished men.† Edward Thornton, a younger bearer of that name, but claiming no relationship with the above-mentioned, is well known as a philanthropist. He carried off a Peel medal and delivered the Latin oration in the summer of 1829, leaving at Christmas in the same year when captain of the school.

---

* These facts, together with much other matter of interest not directly acknowledged, we owe to the Rev. G. H. Scott, rector of Rhos Crowther, near Pembroke, one of Mother Leith's house.

† For record of Charles Thornton's Harrow career, see *Life of Archdeacon Phelps*, privately printed, vol. ii. p. 79.

To compile anything approaching a list of distinguished Harrovians under Dr. George Butler is not within the present plan ; but we may remind our readers that Lord Shaftesbury, the greatest British philanthropist since Howard, and the Duke of Abercorn, were both pupils of Dr. George Butler. Nor should we forget to mention the great Lord Lytton's elder brother, Sir Henry Bulwer (Lord Dalling), Lord Palmerston's trusted diplomatist. The high-minded and accomplished statesman, Mr. Sidney Herbert, who died Lord Herbert of Lea, was also a prize-winner ; the man, be it remembered, to whom his friend Mr. Gladstone applied the following lines : —

> A sweeter or a lovelier gentleman,
> Framed in the prodigality of Nature,
> The spacious Earth cannot again afford.

In the hour of comparative decline Harrow still retained its questionable pre-eminence amidst expensive schools by the addition of a charge for repairing buildings.* This decision of the governors affords an explanation of items of expenditure such as the paternal mind cannot at first digest. But Paterfamilias had chosen a school scantily endowed, and was obliged to accept such disabilities as the situation rendered necessary. Later efforts have, however, been directed towards rendering a Harrow education less costly, and within reach of ordinary people.

In November 1828 Dr. George Butler lost his father-in-law, Mr. Gray, of Wembley, the place of that gentleman amidst the Harrow governors being filled by a notable benefactor to the school, Mr. Joseph Neeld.

* Governors' Minute, June 26, 1828.

Nor did the head-master defer the resignation much longer which was destined to secure him well-earned retirement, and in December 1828 he announced his intention of leaving at Easter 1829. Very pleasant indeed is the picture drawn by old pupils and other friends of Dr. George Butler's retirement. Possessing a lively sympathy with field sports, he also had a special predilection for the canine species, of whose merits, as regards pointers more particularly, he was a good judge.

In society he seems to have been delightful and unbending, while being, as Archdeacon Phelps described him, a very polished gentleman; he was appreciated accordingly by the fair sex, in whose society he was seen to great advantage. And this, although men never failed to perceive the aroma of that scholarship which, in conjunction with Mr. Henry Drury's peculiar powers, has rendered this epoch representative of modern Harrow scholastic culture, if not equally celebrated for any accrued popularity to the place as one of education.

It is remarkable that the hesitation as regards Dr. George Butler's election was caused by his very pre-eminence. The possibility of a senior wrangler being likewise a notable classical scholar was questioned because of its—to use an expression of the great Paley's—contrariety to experience. Moreover, no classical tripos existed until 1824. Hence the temporary deadlock above described. But that Dr. George Butler's classical scholarship was of a high type, the efforts of *Porson* and *Parr* to secure his election to the Harrow head-mastership stand as undeniable evidence; while a testimonial given by the Cambridge heads of houses and professors, signed by R. Porson and E. Maltby amongst the rest, attested to universal esteem held for Dr. George Butler in such quarters, not only as a man, but also as a scholar.

A refined taste and sound judgment combined to make his general and classical scholarship peculiarly adapted for the instruction of youth, ill-health alone preventing such faculty from receiving general acknowledgment when at College.

The co-examiner at St. Paul's School, for some years with the late Bishop Lonsdale, whom Dr. Goodall declared to be the best scholar he ever turned out at Eton, Dr. Butler was then frequently entrusted with conduct of the examination; while the fact that Lonsdale rested content that the papers should be set by his colleague, speaks for itself to those who have ever been concerned in such matters.

As for the election itself we have the testimony of no less a personage than the Dean of Ely, to the effect that the best man was chosen; and he knew all three.

What the governing powers thought of his work will be seen in the subjoined extract from a letter written to Dr. Buttler when leaving. And it is worthy of remark that the eulogistic tone of the communication in question had only one precedent in the school history, viz. the case of Dr. Joseph Drury.

We desire to express the deep sense which we entertain of that zeal, talent, and conscientiousness with which you have discharged the difficult duties of your office, of the substantial improvements you have introduced into the discipline and instruction of the school, of the singular munificence which you have displayed on all occasions, and especially in the enlargement of the Public School and the Master's residence.* On all these grounds we are

* Dr. Butler expended £12,000 on his house, a sum of money practically bequeathed to the school, in whose possession these premises had been since John Lyon's time.

most anxious to convey to you the sincere and deliberate impression of our high respect, gratitude and regard.

(Signed) NORTHWICK.

J. W. CUNNINGHAM.

C. HAMILTON.

JOHN ROBERTS.

JOSEPH NEELD.

Dr. George Butler has left an abiding mark on Harrow, in that to the ancient motto, *Donorum Dei dispensatio fidelis*, he added that now in general use, *Stet fortuna domus* ; and he so acted because the ancient motto was too lengthy to appear outside the prize-books, but had no idea of abolishing the older sentence, which appears on the outside of this volume. It will be seen there that the crossed arrows were not part of Lyon's original device, which simply consisted of a lion rampant.

Retiring to his rectory of Gayton, in Northampton-shire, to which he had been preferred in 1814, Dr. Butler there spent thirteen remarkable years over an almost ideal parish community, who reverenced him as a friend and parent, until in 1842, when, Sir Robert Peel being Prime Minister, and the Doctor's old rival, Lord Lyndhurst, Lord Chancellor, the Deanery of Peterborough was also given to him. In that historic Cathedral close he died on April 30th, A.D. 1853.*

Dr. Butler's mastership had been signalised by the first dawnings of a literature at Harrow. *The Harrovian* of 1828, now a scarce work, is equal to any contemporary rival, even if it cannot compare with the Eton *Microcosm* under George Canning. But for adequate knowledge of what the school was early in the nineteenth

* *Life of Archdeacon Phelps*, privately printed, vol. ii. p. 47.

century, the publication in question may be searched
with advantage, as the present writer has found. A
lively criticism of the Rev. J. W. Cunningham's sacred
poetry, which created some sensation when it was
written, will be found there, while local details alternate
with articles upon purely classical subjects. *The Harrovian*, moreover, lacks not poets, whose Byronic strivings
seem to indicate the lyrical taste prevailing in 1828.
Altogether, there is literary evidence of the existence
of cultured taste among Dr. George Butler's pupils at
Harrow.*

The Rev. Charles T. Longley, an Oxford first-class
man, who took his degree in the Waterloo year, became
head-master in Dr. G. Butler's room, and was believed
by competent critics to be the man of all others for the
post.†

The aspirations of the various candidates for Dr.
Butler's vacant chair are well described in the *Life of
the Rev. Francis Hodgson*, vol. ii. pp. 183–185. There
we read how a strong Harrow party, supported by influential Etonians and others, were for elevating Harry
Drury; also how local Evangelicals smiled on Mr. Batten's claims. When a stranger was elected, the horror
of Mr. Drury's Etonian connection at such a supersession
of long services is as noteworthy as the defeated candidate's ready acquiescence in the decision. Truly the
Arnoldian theories, if generally recognised, progressed
amidst much obloquy.

Finding common ground in literature and music, of
which Dr. Longley was specially fond, the two masters

---

* *The Harrovian*; a Collection of Poems, Essays, and Translations, in the Vaughan Library.

† *Life of Archdeacon Phelps*, vol. ii. p. 132.

soon became fast friends, and resolved to initiate a regime of moral influence, during which flogging should be almost if not entirely abolished.* The reform in question was never adopted; but the reins of governorship were nevertheless allowed to fall somewhat loosely on the horses' necks during the next few years.

Owing to the prudence of his early management, aided by a favourable reaction due in a great measure to the improvements instituted by his predecessor, numbers advanced, until in 1832, 240, and in 1833, 259 were found in the school.†

We have quoted so often from Archdeacon Phelps' life that it is time to say a few words of the man himself. Mr. Phelps came to Harrow in 1826, and had occupied with a few boarders what was then known as the Pond House. But, following in the steps of Mr. Batten at The Grove, Mr. Phelps was destined to assist in raising the character of boarding economics, but lately of an almost squalid description. Mr. Batten had fitted up The Grove handsomely for the reception of a rather aristocratic class of boarders, and, being of the evangelical persuasion, had laid himself out to form a good connection with that party. In this he was so successful that Mr. Phelps, a clergyman holding kindred views, seized an opportunity afforded when General MacGregor vacated The Park in April 1831, and straightway secured that property as an adjunct to the great school, the importance of which, in the later history of Harrow, it is not easy to overrate. Indeed, we have indicated, during the course of the last few pages, several reasons for the instability of Harrow during the first half of the

* Life of Archdeacon Phelps, vol. ii. p. 93.
† Life of Rev. Francis Hodgson, vol. ii. pp. 183–185.

present century ; and, without withdrawing one reason
we have previously put forward to account for the
reaction which we now are called upon to describe,
it is, we think, clear that, without adequate accommodation methodically arranged, any chance of the
institution flourishing as it had done under the exceptional guidance of Joseph Drury was at an end.
Hence it is that for Mr. Batten of *The Grove* and Mr.
Phelps of *The Park* we claim the honour of adding
permanent strength to Harrow, such as survives at the
present day. For when the race of dames had died out,
and the head-master's house suffered utter destruction
by fire, what would have been the immediate hope of
Harrow but for the existence of these well-adapted
boarding-houses, which still form such an important
portion of the school system ? It would be a prudent
course, if possible, for the governors to become owners
of these two most conveniently-situated residences, as
the diversion of either from their present uses would
be an irreparable inconvenience to the school.

Mr. Batten died suddenly in 1830. Rumour spoke
of him as in some sort a disappointed man, for he had
been a leading candidate for the mastership at Rugby,
which Arnold secured, while, as we have said already,
there were not wanting friends who looked towards
The Grove for Dr. Butler's successor. Nevertheless,
he must be held to have filled an important niche in
Harrow history.

As Mr. Phelps and his diary will continue to guide
us in some sort through the unravelling of the history
connected with the next few years, we will for the
present defer further mention of The Park and its
master.

But of Dr. Longley, the head-master, the course of events bids us speak. One who owned a peculiar power of attracting mankind towards himself, Dr. Longley is seen at his best when ruling over those of mature age, for this reason—that boys are apt to take advantage of the charity which hopeth, believeth, and endureth all things. Dr. Longley's early prestige at Harrow was, nevertheless, gained in the teeth of difficulties of no ordinary nature ; and this although many believe that his early success might have proved permanent, had not the Harrow head-master earned the cognomen of "Good-natured Longley." A tendency to benignant judgment when independent decision was possible naturally prompted the school monitors to adopt similar easy-going methods of rule, and, as some say, led them to doubt whether they would be supported in exercise of their authority. But Dr. Longley was so courteous and bending to the staff of masters that, though not a strict disciplinarian himself, he nevertheless gave way to the most experienced of them as regards making rules and enforcing obedience, so that delinquents by no means always got off scot-free. But the moral fibre of the school became loosened, and it is agreed on all sides that too mild an exercise of authority had led to a mischievous laxity in discipline.

But it is fair to the memory of that universally-beloved man who then governed Harrow to point out how manifest were the disadvantages under which he laboured. Public opinion was then calling on school rulers for the inculcation of a high moral tone amongst their pupils, such as Dr. Arnold, with matchless influence, had succeeded in infusing more or less into Rugby. Dr. Longley apprehended this early in his career, and,

as his pupils tell us, endeavoured to bring more religious
teaching into the Harrow system. But how was this
to be effected at all in accordance with Arnold's ideas,
if there existed no school chapel, and custom did not
allow of the Harrow head-master occupying the pulpit
except on special occasions.*

Readers of Stanley's *Life of Arnold* and of *Tom Brown's
School-days*, with other Rugbeian literature dealing with
Dr. Arnold's system, know how much the great teacher
relied on the Sunday's sermon for communicating his
ideas to the lower school, who, as Dean Bradley tells us,
were not altogether under the magician's wand.†

Mr. Batten's successor at The Grove had been the
now celebrated Benjamin Hall Kennedy, well known to
the world as Dr. Kennedy of Shrewsbury, who, as all
familiar with the epoch agree, exercised a remarkable
intellectual influence over the school during his stay at
Harrow ;‡ but the evangelical connection seems to have
followed Mr. Phelps to *The Park*, for at the end of 1831
Zachary Macaulay, Hannah More, and Sir Thomas

---

* Dr. Joseph Drury laboured under this disadvantage, but
appears to have preached more frequently to the boys than his
successor, Dr. George Butler, whom Dean Merivale says he cannot
remember in the pulpit of St. Mary's Church, but who, according
to a writer in *The Harrovian* of 1828, preached a remarkable
sermon on the death of Dr. Parr in 1825, while the Author has
seen in the British Museum a discourse of his which commemorated the Princess Charlotte's early death. At Rugby a chapel
had been built in 1814, and was served by a chaplain, an office
which Dr. Arnold undertook with his other duties.

† "*My School Days*, 1830 *to* 1840." By Dean Bradley. *Nineteenth Century* Magazine for March 1884, p. 465.

‡ It is not generally known that Dr. Kennedy's house at the
Grove was nearly consumed by fire in 1833, the present front
alone remaining. The record has been merged in memories of
the greater disaster at Dr. Wordsworth's in 1838.—*Life of Archdeacon Phelps*, vol. ii. p. 114.

Acland were all found recommending this then recent acquisition to the school accommodation.*

Nor did the old patrician connection fail to perceive the advantage which such a spacious residence afforded, so that the Duke of Grafton, Lord Aberdeen, and Sir Robert Peel were amongst Mr. Phelps' supporters.

We have availed ourselves of certain data placed in our hands by the head-master of Harrow, which indicate the changes made in the general course of study between Dr. Joseph Drury's head-mastership and that of Dr. Longley,† and will help to dissipate many misapprehensions which exist concerning the school curriculum at this period. Before Dr. Arnold went to Rugby mathematics and foreign languages were at a general discount at our large schools ; while as regards Harrow in particular, we have seen a report of an amusing speech by Mr. C. R. M. Talbot, M.P., Lord-Lieutenant of Glamorganshire, who in 1872 spoke of his 1822 experiences as follows :—" It was in my time absolute heresy for a master to attempt to teach anything but Greek and Latin. Mathematics and French were not allowed. It is quite true there was a French master, but he lived the life of a dog ; and there were also writing and arithmetic masters, but whenever they appeared they were received with hallooing and hooting."‡

Mr. Talbot was doubtless speaking generally when he gave these amusing experiences to the world; but public opinion, nevertheless, partly pointed at that time to some unsatisfied needs in the Harrow system.

Yet men of great ability, some amongst us still, have

---

* *Life of Archdeacon Phelps*, privately printed, p. 93.
† See Appendix F.
‡ *Life of Archdeacon Phelps*, privately printed. p. 98.

an affectionate memory of their young days on the hill. An old Longleyite writes as follows of his times :—" My old master, Evans, was one of the most charming old men that any boy could chance to live under. It was, indeed, a happy time until the old man died in 1833, deeply regretted by everyone. The list of old Harrovians dating from that time proves that a great deal might then be learnt besides Latin and Greek. Mr. Evans, for instance, used to point out the desirability of reading English. 'Read a number of the *Spectator* of a morning at breakfast, and begin to get up some modern history of Europe. Don't forget your Shakespeare.' When Mr. Evans died he had but just received from the boys a piece of plate to commemorate fifty years' service as a Harrow master." Of Mr. Mills, who took many of Mr. Evans's pupils after that venerable teacher died, our informant writes :—" He lived next door to the 'King's Head,' was a strict disciplinarian, and a just if severe master, who, nevertheless, possessed the confidence of pupils, whom he always treated like gentlemen." Of old Harry Drury, almost worshipped by the boys, he remarks on his great powers of teaching. The old Harrovian also tells a good story of a long sermon in St. Mary's Church. The two old-fashioned discourses of Mr. Cunningham, the respected Vicar, were scarcely ever alternated by those of the masters, but occasionally an evangelical light seems to have shed radiance on the scene. For instance : " Baptist Noel came once and preached above an hour. At the end of about that time, he said, 'And now— ' on which the whole school, including head-master and the tutorial staff, rose with the usual noise of a general move. But when it subsided the preacher said, quietly, 'I will proceed to another branch of the subject.' We all sat down, and heard a loud groan from Old Harry."

One notable pupil of Harry Drury's exemplified in life the value of his uncle's teaching; we mean Mr. Herman Merivale.* The *Edinburgh Review* for October 1884, p. 564, commenting upon the privately-printed *Memorials of the Merivale Family*, contrasts the advantages thus gained at *Harrow* with the mental isolation which assailed the great John Stuart Mill, Mr. Merivale's friend and contemporary in after years; thus bearing witness to the value of public school training in its less effulgent hour. In the Merivale papers we read of literary symposiums at Old Harry's, where Byron and Denman met in 1807, while the poet's biographer Moore paid a visit to the Harrow tutor *par excellence* —Harry Drury—in 1824, when materials were being collected for the Harrow poet's life.

The above-mentioned view taken by the *Edinburgh* as regards Harrow education is confirmed by perusal of *Notes from Past Life*, by the Rev. Francis Trench, pp. 13–19, where letters from Harrow between 1819 and 1824 speak of considerable culture amongst the higher boys, and likewise bear testimony to the great character of the school.

Herman Merivale finds mention as "by far the

---

* The Brother of the Dean of Ely, Mr. Herman Merivale, cleared the board of prizes, both at Harrow and Oxford, where he became Professor of Political Economy, and was subsequently a voluminous writer, and a contributor to the *Edinburgh*, whose Whig politics were to his taste.—*Edinburgh Review*, October 1884, pp. 564–5. Mr. Herman Merivale died Under Secretary of State for India in 1861, having previously established such a reputation at the Colonial Office that an observant official there with forty-two years' experience told the writer that no one, not even Sir James Stephen, equalled Merivale.

cleverest fellow at Harrow at a time when those in contact with Harry Drury's teaching derived much solid
information outside the scope of the school curriculum.
A vivid picture is drawn of the master in question pacing
up and down the new Shell-room, which, with the rest
of the right wing of the old school, had been built in
1819, and spouting forth verses to his full satisfaction.
Politics seem to have shared with literature the youthful
attention, for we read of the Harrow boys being enthusiastic partisans of George IV.'s unfortunate Queen in
1820, donning white cockades and illuminating their
studies, feelings shared by the great Harrow man Dr.
Parr. Boy politics were not, however, favoured by
Dr. Butler, who possibly remembered how in 1808 those
revolting against his authority had taken *Liberty* as
the motto wherewith to cement *Rebellion*.

In the above-mentioned *Memorials of the Merivale
Family* (privately printed) it is said Mr. Merivale was a
man of sense, as he shows in being pleased by the
looks and behaviour of his sons, one of whom came
home from Harrow with a black eye from fighting with
a boy of his own age. If the latter incident were the
cause of paternal satisfaction, it may serve to illustrate
the feeling of the times, not, perhaps, in accord with
later ideas. And, indeed, at Harrow in 1884 milling
is considerably at a discount.

The topography of Harrow, studied for the purpose
of discovering where, between 1833 and 1835, the
smaller houses were situated, is discussed by Mr.
Christopher Cooke, an old Harrovian of that date, in
the *Harrow Gazette* for September 1867. He there
tells us that Mr. Evans' house was at the top of the
cricket-ground, and Mr. Gepp's nearly opposite. Mr.

Mills lived in the large white house near the "King's Head." Mr. Evans died in 1833, and Mr. Henry Drury then became second master. For persons who could swim, the ponds at *The Park* and *The Grove* were both available, but a majority of the boys frequented the canal yclept the Cut, and even penetrated to the Elstree Reservoir. Duck Puddle, which had hitherto been an institution of a muddy type in 1826, was not popular until May 1836, when it was filled from the Pond.

Those, moreover, who remember the place in 1836, speak of it as far more wooded as regards the neighbouring lanes and farms than we know it now. So much timber has been cut down, that Harrow is scarcely the shady summer retreat it formerly was. Otherwise, in regard to general appearance, Harrow and its surroundings suffered little change during the first seventy years of the nineteenth century; and we know this as the result of concerted observation by the late Baron Heath, the late Mr. Marillier, and Lord Bessborough. The experience of the three men reached over seven decades, and in general features the country surrounding Harrow remains much as Baron Heath remembered it when, as he was wont to narrate, he fagged for Lord Byron, and surreptitiously brought tarts for the poet's consumption after nightfall. We mention this in the hope that those in power will restrain any such injury from being inflicted at least on the school property, and that a rigid resistance may be organised against the advance of the speculative builder, who doubtless is a very good sort of person, but will, if he can, speedily take away from us the little virgin country still surviving. Fortunately, the district between Harrow and Uxbridge produces the best hay in England, as that

in the so-called Pure Vale did the best corn in the
days of Queen Bess, so there is some security for the
view from the churchyard being preserved intact.

Reverting to Mr. Phelps' diary, we find that Harrow
continued to flourish fairly until 1835, when a decline
in numbers became apparent. In that year the school
had the support of the most distinguished of all its
alumni, Sir Robert Peel, the late Conservative Minister,
and then leader of the Opposition in the House of
Commons,* finding time to run down for Speech-day,
and at the moment we speak of nothing seemed more
secure than that same family support in which Harrow
rejoiced. But a change was destined to come over the
scene. We have reached that period of our narrative
when many actors in the events described survive, and
from Dr. Longley's elevation to the newly-founded See
of Ripon in 1836 the pen of the historian proper falls
from the writer's hands, and readers must content
themselves with such outline as is necessary for purely
narrative purposes. As we have, however, undertaken
to tell of the decline of Harrow, we will proceed in
as few words as possible to sketch the situation, and the
results which followed thereon. But before so doing, it
behoves us to glance at the notable personage who was
taking leave of Harrow.

The first Bishop of Ripon was destined, as we all
know, to become Primate of all England. It is said
that his mother discouraged his desire to become a
clergyman, as she had a large family and no church
influence. His success as an Oxford tutor was
remarkable, and there sagacity seems to have vied with

---

* Sir Robert Peel's first ministry resigned in April 1835.

benignity in forming a well-earned popularity. He was (according to Mr. Christopher Cooke) familiarly known in the University as " Rose Longley." At Harrow the *suaviter in modo* seems to have been more prominent than the *fortiter in re*. Yet we by no means believe that Dr. Longley's *régime* can with truth be termed a failure.

Had not public opinion placed an unusually searching eye on schools generally during Dr. Arnold's career at Rugby, quiet acquiescence in the old order of things would have been a matter of course, and the system of pretending not to see when rules were broken have remained a part of the recognised custom. For instance, boys would smoke in the street, both at Eton and Harrow, flying, it is true, before the approach of a master, but secure in the knowledge that pursuit and consequent detection were not likely to ensue. Such laxity of discipline cannot, however, as regards Harrow, be directly charged to any individual head-master, but must be considered part of the times which men had not all realised were really changing between 1829–36.

Several good stories are extant concerning Dr. Longley's benignity of character. A boy is said to have abstracted the inside of a pie from the preceptorial larder, leaving but the crust wherewith to regale a party of the master's friends, whose feelings of mingled amazement, amusement, not to say disappointment, may be imagined when it transpired that a pilferer had been at work. The good Doctor seems to have had his suspicions—not incorrect, as it proved. But on a confession being made by a penitent and apparently terrified youth, certain solemn threats as to an interview in the Fourth Form room gave way to the mercy which

the good Doctor could not find it in his heart to
withhold.*

We have heard, moreover, of a ludicrous scene
wherein the future Archbishop was hauled up towards
the upper storey of his own house by young miscreants,
who believed a basket of forbidden provender to be
attached to the rope.   Rumour has it that a recalcitrant youth dropped the rope in horror, exclaiming in
his surprise, "By Jingo, it's Jacob!" a nick-name
borne by the head-master owing to his fondness for a
parrot of that name.

Nor is it possible to leave unrecorded the story of an
old pupil whose devotion to the Longleian memory is
boundless.   The master had suddenly asked the youth
in question whether he was concerned in a breach of
discipline, and on the spur of the moment had received
a negative answer, which, if strictly true, did not satisfy
the sensitive conscience of this young Harrovian.
Running after Dr. Longley, he said, "I told you
wrong just now. Morally I had to do with the matter"
—or words to such effect.   "I am so glad you told
me," kindly replied the head-master, as, with an
approving smile, he passed on.   That boy loved Dr.
Longley, and, as a man, now reverences his name.

Again, "Jack-o'-Lantern" was abolished by Dr.
George Butler, but reappeared in Dr. Longley's time
as one of those forbidden pleasures so dear to youth.
Always played in the evening, and originally by suf-
ferance of the authorities, the game in question was
simply a run across country after a lantern carried by a
swift-footed boy. Oftentimes would the luckless hounds

---

* We are indebted for these details of Dr. Longley to the
letters of Mr. Christopher Cooke, and other old Harrovians.

be enticed into some slough of despond, and the performers return in a condition of mud which may find its
equal on a wet football day or a paper-chase forty years
later, but yet present no adequate idea of the confusion
caused by the return from "Jack-o'-Lantern" of thirty
or forty boys at night when in ordinary clothes. It
is one of the most distinct evidences that indiscipline
existed when we read of such a proscribed saturnalia
having occurred after lock-up in Dr. Longley's time.
But the fact has been communicated to us by Harrow
men whose word is indisputable.

The newly-elected head-master of Harrow was the
Rev. Christopher Wordsworth, of Trinity College, Cambridge, senior classic and senior classical medallist in
1830. A contemporary schoolmaster of Dr. Arnold's,
he has lived to exercise an influence over another
generation, while what he did for Harrow is only
known to those specially cognisant of her peculiar
needs between 1836 and 1844. Some have spoken
glibly of Dr. Wordsworth's so-called failure at Harrow,
as if numbers were the sole test of success in a task
undertaken when the school was in the downward
course, to arrest which without removing the sources of
distrust was not so easy as some seem to suppose. In
striving to restore discipline, which on all hands was
allowed to have been defective, Dr. Wordsworth necessarily drew attention to the fact of such imperfection
existing at Harrow. When it was known that the
cream (so termed by Dr. Whewell) of Trinity College,
Cambridge, in the persons of Dr. Wordsworth and the
Rev. T. H. Steel,* were engaged in combating with the

* Introductory Biography to Mr. Steel's *Sermons*, by Professor
Henry Nettleship, p. 26.

evil in question, sapient parents not unnaturally elected
to send their children elsewhere. Men certainly are
found to differ as to the judgment displayed on this
trying occasion, while the older masters, to use Mr.
Phelps' words, felt fettered under alterations of the
Harrow system, which seemed to them to diminish their
influence.* Whether Dr. Wordsworth and his advisers
initiated their reforms not enough on the lines of the
constitution, so to speak, thus alienating the connection *pro tem.*, we do not propose to attempt to decide.
But the subsequent depression is a fact which needs
some explanation beyond the commonplace theory that
the authorities were to blame entirely. To begin with,
at the outset of Dr. Wordsworth's *régime* numbers rose
speedily from 165 to 190, which was the highest point
attained. But when ordinary means for restoring a
spirit of order and obedience had failed, Dr. Wordsworth, who was no respecter of persons, caused several
youths, sons of influential people, to leave Harrow,
thereby doubtless giving increased stability to the body
politic, but also adding for the moment to the dis-
satisfaction which an outside public felt with Harrow.

At this juncture, although the old-fashioned could
take shelter at Eton under Hawtrey, and those infused
with more modern ideas satisfy their cravings at Rugby,
where Arnold reigned supreme, it should be remembered
that no attempt was made to meet such severe competition by altering the expensive character of Harrow.

Had the governors elected to place its education
within the reach of the middle class, there is every
reason to suppose that a fresh element might have
been attracted, and the numerical decline at least hin-

* *Life of Archdeacon Phelps,* privately printed, vol. ii. p. 133.

dered. For when at the very lowest ebb, a prestige
accrued to Lyon's school, associated as its name was
with the memory of Sumner, Heath, Drury, and Butler
as masters, while the fame of Perceval, the wisdom of
Bennet and Parr, together with the glories of Sheridan,
Sir William Jones, and Byron, had become reflected on
the scene of their boyhood.

A search through the school papers of this period has
confirmed what we had elsewhere gathered from the
evidence of others, viz. the extraordinary capacity for
work evinced by Dr. Wordsworth. The correspondence concerning the erection of a chapel proves how
thoroughly the success of this project was due to the
future Bishop of Lincoln ; while it sets forth reasons
such as demonstrate the impossibility of exercising the
kind of influence which is connected in men's minds
with the names of Arnold, Vaughan, and Temple, unless
the master supremely responsible is in absolute possession of a school pulpit.

But in thus strengthening a Master's good influence
over his scholars, Dr. Wordsworth laid his policy open
to attack in a direction where quarter was hopeless.
The Evangelical party when they read in Froude's
Remains, published in 1839, that their overthrow was
designed by the Oxford theologians, grew suspicious to
a degree of each and every religious change ; and so
in certain quarters it was whispered about that Dr.
Wordsworth was favourable to the new opinions, and
was about to erect a church wherein a party policy
might be substituted for the time-honoured spirit of
compromise in Church matters, such as John Lyon
himself seems to have favoured, and which was calculated to render the school as national in religious

matters as it had hitherto been unbiassed as regards
politics. Without expressing any opinion as to the
wisdom of their fears, we have to state that some of the
Evangelical connection deserted Harrow, owing to their
distrust of Dr. Wordsworth's theology.

But the climax of adversity was reached when on the
22nd of October 1838 the head-master's house was
burnt down, the neighbouring tenement rented by the
late Dr. Colenso suffering in a like degree.* Henceforth
—and until a new edifice should rise from the ashes of
the old historic pile wherein so many generations had
been nurtured—a distinct hiatus was perceived in the
Harrow system, such as could but accelerate the school
decline. Men whose forefathers had listened to Sumner's eloquence, revered the wisdom of Heath, or learnt
to love Joseph Drury, sullenly concurred in absolute
change such as a choice of Eton afforded. For, in the
minds of many such, the old masters' house was indeed
the school itself. And yet there was no avowed de-
spondence about Harrow until the Peel connection were
found to have deserted the place, Laurence Peel and

---

* Mr. Colenso had hitherto looked after Dr. Wordsworth's
house, and so relieved the head-master of duties which left him
comparatively free to indulge his scholarly instincts. Hence the
confusion ensuing was two-fold. Dr. Wordsworth lost many
valuable books on this occasion, and the old house, redolent of
memories connected with Sumner, Heath, Joseph Drury, and more
especially Dr. George Butler, was consumed. The traditions of
school-boys are not generally reliable; but the story current
amongst the Harrovians twenty-five years ago was, as the author
has since discovered, correct in the main. A most exciting scene
seems to have been presented, the lurid glare of the conflagration
penetrating to the metropolis, and bringing sight-seers from miles
around. The only water available was that in the Grove pond,
and a line of Harrow boys was organised by the late Archdeacon
Phelps to convey the buckets from hand to hand until the scene
of action was reached. A lively description of the disaster appears
in the *Harrow Gazette* for November 1861.

his brother Arthur, the present Speaker of the House of Commons, being sent to Eton; and this although, as Mr. Phelps tells us in his interesting diary, the three elder brothers, Robert, Frederick, and William, had all followed in their great father's footsteps and received their education on the hill.

In 1841 Sir Robert had the pleasure of seeing the medal which he had founded in 1826 carried off by his second son Frederick, who in 1840 and 1841 also carried off the governors' prize for Latin Lyrics. We may learn also from Mr. Phelps' journal how the young Robert Peel got seventy-five runs at cricket in 1838.

The greatest Harrovian then alive would frequently go down to Speech-day, and at other times allow Lady Peel to represent him.* Love for Harrow had survived the memory of his own hard life when a voluntary student; and it was argued that unless the Prime Minister had grave doubts as to the condition of his own school he would never have chosen even royal Eton for his younger boys.

Some there are who look upon the advent of railways as concurring with other causes to deal a heavy blow to the old-world Harrow. Why not penetrate further into the country if change of scene and good air is desirable, and accept the benefits offered by cheaper education than that available at Harrow? Such was the question which presented itself to the paternal mind. But Rugby had made its most important advance before this period;

---

* Sir Robert was present at Mr. Phelps', the Park, in June 1835 and 1839, while Lady Peel lunched there on a like occasion in July 1837. Harrow may well be proud of Sir Robert's son, Sir William Peel, the hero of the Naval Brigade, who also distinguished himself in the Indian Mutiny. He died in 1858.—*Life of Archdeacon Phelps* (privately printed), vol. ii. pp. 129, 139.

and if Eton and Winchester were brought within easier reach, any strength that they might gain thereby would not have perceptibly injured Harrow had not the variety of reasons we have indicated combined to create distrust.*

But before the lowest depths of depression were reached notable changes took place in the *personnel* of the teaching staff. Mr. Phelps resigned in the summer of 1839, and in 1841 the famous " Harry Drury" died, having been engaged in tutorial duties at Harrow for forty-one years.

Harrow had not for many years been without a Drury. One of Mr. Henry Drury's sons, viz. Benjamin Heath, is the respected President of Caius College, Cambridge, who is known as a trusted colleague of Dr. Vaughan's. Another, Henry, was the editor of the *Arundines Cami,* and died Archdeacon of Wilts at the age of fifty. A third is a distinguished admiral. The Latin oration was delivered by a Drury in 1804, 1807, 1809, 1814, and 1830.†

When in March 1836 Mr. Kennedy entered upon his duties at Shrewsbury, his house at *The Grove* was taken by the Rev. Thomas Henry Steel, Dr. Wordsworth's friend and colleague, who had accompanied him from Cambridge. Mr. Oxenham was the new second master, while Mr. Colenso's connection with Harrow terminated in 1842.

---

* Mr. Phelps thus describes the first trains which he saw, July 31, 1837. First saw train at the Weald, August 1837. "It is a great diversion to go down to the railroad station and see the arrival of a train. We saw about 400 persons brought up at the rate of 30 miles an hour by one train and engine . . . . . My friend Hunter was whisked down from London in half an hour by the steam carriage, and spent the day with us."

† *Life of Archdeacon Phelps,* vol. ii. p. 96.

It was Dr. Wordsworth's privilege to have introduced into the Harrow staff G. F. Harris, Esq., who followed Mr. Phelps in his occupation of *The Park*, and was a tower of strength to the day of his death. In September 1839 the new chapel was consecrated by Archbishop Howley, and formed, so to speak, the germ from which Sir Gilbert Scott's fine building has grown, but the design stands as a monument of the head-master's forethought and munificence.*

The last few years of the future Bishop of Lincoln's rule present a melancholy record of progressive diminution. The several Forms came to be mere skeleton battalions, and the very notoriety of the numerical collapse prevented those who would otherwise have sent their sons to Harrow from making choice of a school temporarily under a cloud, so that when Sir Robert Peel elevated the head-master to a Canonry at Westminster in 1844, numbers were as low as 70.

However, it is not pretended here to explain fully why Harrow in 1844 fell to such a degree that Mr. H. E. Hutton, the present Harrow master, when he first came to school at Harrow in 1844, heard the Sixth Form in his house deploring their luck at the new comer being placed too high for fagging purposes.†

---

* In the year 1840 Richard Gregory founded a Scholarship of £100 a year, tenable for four years.

† Mr. A. Haygarth, the well-known cricketer, sends the following contemporary jottings concerning the decline of numbers between 1841–43. They have an obvious historical value: "It will be remembered that only 15 boys came to Harrow during football quarter in 1841; only 11 during racquet quarter, 1842; only 5 during cricket quarter, 1842; only 10 during football quarter, 1842; only 3 during football quarter, 1843; and only 3 during cricket quarter, 1843!" Mr. Haygarth adds, "The grass grew in the streets of Harrow during this period."

Nevertheless, we venture to believe that future generations will admit the good work done at Harrow by Christopher Wordsworth between 1836 and 1844. We now hasten to a more cheerful portion of our story.

CHAPTER XII.

CHARLES JOHN VAUGHAN.—1844–59.

> Pass not unblessed, the genius of the place.
> *Childe Harold*, Canto 4.

READERS of *Arnold's Life*, by Dean Stanley, will remember how the great counsellor of youth addressed several interesting letters to a favourite pupil then at Cambridge. This promising collegian was destined not to belie his honoured master's hopes, but was bracketed Senior Classic with the late Lord Lyttleton in 1838, and elected head-master of Harrow three years after Arnold had been laid to rest in Rugby Chapel. He entered on his duties when Harrow was at a lower ebb than had ever been known since Dr. Cox's laches brought the numbers down to fifty in 1745.* But in Dr. Vaughan, Arnold seemed in the eyes of many almost to live again, and new boys came to Harrow from time to time on that account ; add to this that the head-master accepted loyally the traditions of the place, and made no flourish of trumpets heralding reform for its own sake. He doubtless knew that Dr.

---

* The privately-printed memorials of the Thackeray family mention 50 as the number which Dr. Thackeray found at Harrow. In 1721, under Dr. Brian, the numbers had been up to 144.

Arnold, the brightest spirit of the nineteenth-century educational world, though he had challenged what he deemed obstructive conservatism, yet by no means designed any wholesale destruction of old institutions which he found established at Rugby itself.*

Hence, when they found in Dr. Vaughan a sympathising spirit as regards Harrow custom, combined with a reverence for her great past, it was natural that the old connection slowly but surely returned to its allegiance, the swing of the Harrovian pendulum once again taking the upward direction.

Conversations with several inmates of the different houses during the first few quarters of the Vaughan *régime* have not completely elucidated the secret of the chief's peculiar faculty for government. Hence it is that we shall record the Doctor's own experiences. But his practice of addressing the boys themselves *from the pulpit*, and striving to improve each passing event, was a leading feature in his system. Those who have listened to Dr. Vaughan's school sermons will need no efforts of ours to recall their influence; to others less fortunate we despair of conveying an idea of this preacher's power. The influence due to a quiet consciousness led onlookers to take success as a matter of course because it seemed so naturally to follow in the wake of the master's well-arranged dispositions: for of Dr. Vaughan it may indeed be said, in quietness and confidence was his strength.

When Dr. Vaughan first conceived the idea of standing for the Harrow head-mastership, he had only been defeated for the similar position at Rugby by a single

* "*My School Life between* 1830–40," by Dean Bradley, *Nineteenth Century*, March 1884.

vote, given by an old-fashioned trustee, who dreaded to entrust Laurence Sheriffe's school to so young a man. Mr. Vaughan returned from a visit to Harrow, fired with interest in an institution which did not then stand high in the estimation either of Rugbeian or other educational circles. The followers of Arnold thought and talked of the Middlesex free school as a small and inferior Eton, while similar misapprehensions were felt by men such as the late Bishop Turton, then Dean of Peterborough, who accompanied a testimonial asked for by Mr. Vaughan with a warning not to throw himself away at Harrow.

Nor had misapprehension of this sort been limited to non-Harrovian circles, inasmuch as even Dr. George Butler deliberately selected Rugby for his son Montagu, whose abilities gave promise of a brilliant future. But for the intervention of an elder brother,[*] and the courtesy of Mr., afterwards Archbishop, Tait, then headmaster of Rugby, Harrow would not have educated her present gifted and energetic ruler.

Mr. Vaughan did not receive much encouragement from Mr. Cunningham, the influential vicar, when he first unfolded his scheme, and, indeed, the Evangelical party had their eye on the future Bishop Chapman, of Columbo, then leaving Eton. When, however, the coast was clear for Mr. Vaughan's election—rendered probable by a knowledge of the great Dr. Arnold's high opinion of his old pupil—an after-wave of opposition had to be reckoned with, an influential governor doubting the policy of entrusting Harrow School to what was deemed youthful guidance.

The struggles of the school to arise from its untoward

---

[*] Now Canon George Butler of Winchester, who recounted this incident to the writer.

subsidence into a condition which might promise a return
of public favour is to be discovered in the pages of the
Harrow Calendar, Vols. I. and II. Dr. Vaughan informs
us that Harrow School never absolutely fell lower than
seventy, because, although he only found sixty-eight of
Dr. Wordsworth's pupils, other boys came with the new
master.*

In those gradually increasing school lists may be
learnt the story of modern Harrow success, for the
securing of which Dr. Vaughan takes scarcely his meed
of credit, putting it down to a combination of trust in
the boys worthy to be so treated, and to a stern resolve
to tolerate none of the lawlessness which was in full
swing when he came to Harrow. And, although some
severity was of necessity resorted to, the need for stern
measures soon decreased when it became apparent that
a strong man sat in the seat of Sumner and Joseph
Drury.

We append the increase in numbers during the three
first years of Dr. Vaughan's *regime*. The great difficulty
henceforth consisted in the arrangement of a school
which was not equally divided into Forms, the Shell
greatly predominating.† However, this temporary
congestion being dissipated, Harrow drifted into the
condition which it attained some twenty-five years ago,
before the Public Schools Act passed, the numbers being
then between four and five hundred. It is well worth
remarking how steady was the increase after Dr.
Vaughan's advent.

---

* The Bill-book for January 1845 showed a total of seventy-
eight.

† These facts are communicated by the Dean of Llandaff
himself.

Numbers ran as follows :—

January 1845 - - -	80
June 1845 - - - -	110
September 1845 - - -	117
January 1846 - - -	138
June 1846 - - -	173
September 1846 - - -	221
January 1847 - - -	264
May 1847 - - - -	273
September 1847 - - -	315

Nor did this steady revival take place without a conspicuous return to their allegiance on the part of the
old Harrow connection, the names of such families as
were formerly known at Harrow reappearing in a most
remarkable way.

Looking forward three years, we find that Harrow
had increased to 376 in 1850, while henceforth the
difficulty was to keep numbers low enough to receive
adequate accommodation on the Hill.* Harrow has
since risen to over 500, Dr. Vaughan leaving 438 names
in the Bill-book when he resigned in 1859. But
efforts had even then been consistently exercised to
limit the size of the school.

Dr. Vaughan is profoundly impressed with the mistake that has been made by modern opinion, when, as
he believes, in some sort the efforts of our forefathers
are underrated, and, therefore, reverencing the aims of
those who lived in the last century, as well as the earlier
portion of this, he never deals roughly with an institution which has done good since. Thus at Harrow he
worked steadily on with the means he found to hand,
only limiting his tolerance of custom when it was evil,

* See *Harrow Calendar*, vol. i., 1845–52, published in 1853 by
Crossley and Clarke, School booksellers.

and then resolutely did he determine to grapple therewith. Like Dr. Heath attacking the archery celebration, he was soon led to initiate a reform.

The boys had been wont to keep the Fifth of November on the cricket ground after lock-up under care of the monitors, who had been previously unable to prevent what should have been an evening of harmless mirth from degenerating into orgies. Knowing this, Dr. Vaughan promptly abolished the custom, doing so in November 1845, when only fifty boys had previously enjoyed the privilege which it had been adjudged necessary to abrogate.

With these facts before them, our readers will be enabled to judge whether the opinion arrived at as regards Dr. Vaughan's *régime* is a sound one, to wit, that it owes its great fame to a personal influence over the Sixth Form boys, such as not even Dr. Arnold—at whose feet the secret was learned—ever possessed in a greater degree.

No head-master ever more thoroughly studied the monitorial system than the Dean of Llandaff; and although fully aware of its weak points, he considers that, be it well directed, there is no alternative so efficacious. Broadly speaking, Dr. Vaughan holds that the master is responsible for morals and the monitor for manners. His letter to Lord Palmerston on the Platt and Stewart case should be studied for information on this subject.*

The occasion for this letter arose in 1852, when an infringement of the punitive monitorial rights brought on a public controversy in the papers, which, but for

* See Appendix I.

Dr. Vaughan's lucid exposition of the system in question, might have led to another falling off in the Harrow popularity. But the head-master's letter to Lord Palmerston satisfied those ready to look fairly into the matter. Given the monitorial system, its regulation must rest with the head-master, who should possess the power of abrogating ill-used privilege.

But Dr. Vaughan evinced no pedantic dread of reform when it seemed needful. For instance, the high charges, which had hitherto rendered Harrow exceptionally expensive, were as much as possible reduced. Again, as numbers rose, the monitors were increased from ten to fifteen.

But, as we have seen it stated that the Rugby præposters were at this period imported into Harrow, truth bids us aver that those who were at the school in 1844-5 testify that this idea is utterly erroneous. On the contrary, Dr. Vaughan was far too wise to disregard the prejudices of those by means of whose co-operation he hoped to gain influence, even if the monitorial mode of rule had not existed at Harrow since 1571.

As a matter of fact, Dr. Vaughan felt his way carefully, and although he doubtless profited by his school experience under Dr. Arnold, and strove to rule by moral influence, yet he was never rash enough to import a foreign system into Harrow when the original constitution of the school afforded the very means of government required.

The fact that *Dr. Arnold's Life*, by Arthur Stanley, the late Dean of Westminster, was published about this time is a notable circumstance connected with Dr. Vaughan's early prestige, for those eloquent pages made it known with what unusual interest the great

19 *

teacher lately passed away had watched his pupil's
Cambridge career, and it was naturally believed that
one whom Arnold esteemed so highly would elevate the
moral tone of any community over which he ruled.
The moderate party in the Church, moreover, trusted
Dr. Vaughan implicity. We may add that his resolve
to render Harrow a place of work was appreciated by
many in high social position; while Nonconformists
were found to accept the liberal-minded teaching which
characterised this memorable head-mastership.

Although it may be urged that Dr. Vaughan's success
was gained when public school education had once more
become popular, it should not be forgotten how strong
was the competition which prevailed directly a demand
set in for the peculiar kind of education which large
schools afforded. Not only had Harrow to cope with
her ancient rivals at Eton, Westminster, Winchester,
Charterhouse, Shrewsbury, and Rugby, but at Marlborough (1843), Rossall (1844), Cheltenham (1841),
and Wellington (1853) were arising new proprietary
establishments, whose rulers had decided on providing
cheaper teaching for the children of gentlemen than that
in vogue even after the Harrow expenditure had been
reduced to the point which seemed to Dr. Vaughan
advisable.*

We cannot learn that the earlier years of Dr.
Vaughan's head-mastership were characterised by any
gratuitous mental activity on the part of the school.
No local literature existed, while music studied as an
art was unknown. However, the school services in
chapel were remarkable for their heartiness, as well as

* Harrow Governors' Minutes.

for the unity which prevailed in the singing, favourite
tunes both of chaunt and psalm being joined in fer-
vently by the boys generally ; so that a passing tribute
to the devotion of Mr. Tillard, the organist, is not out of
place even now when Harrow has advanced so notably
in her musical training.

On November 16th, 1848, Her Majesty Queen Victoria suddenly notified her intention of passing through
Harrow and seeing the buildings. Like the previous
visit of Charles I. to the town, and that of George III.
to the school, this resolve was unpremeditated, being
made while the Queen and Prince Albert were at Bentley
with the Queen Dowager. However, sufficient time was
given to enable the people, young and old, scholars and
townsfolk, to evince their loyalty to the full. It must
have been an imposing sight when the royal party, being
received at the school gates by Dr. Vaughan and the
masters, were conducted to the Speech-room ; where the
whole school was collected, and bill called over, so that
the Sovereign might be aware which of her youthful
subjects benefited by Lyon's benevolent and wise forethought. Of course the royal party saw the Church,
and Byron's tomb, leaving their joint signatures as a
momento in the Monitors' Library, then situated in the
Old School. It is to be sincerely hoped that Her
Gracious Majesty may repeat her visit to Harrow, which
she has never seen decked in the summer foliage which
elicited from her grandfather George III. special expressions of admiration.

While Dr. Vaughan ruled over Harrow a disposition
to second the founder's original efforts at last became
perceptible. From 1571 to 1819, when the newer portion of the schools was designed, there was an absolute

blank in the record of benefactions, which was at last succeeded by Sir Robert Peel's efforts to encourage classical scholarship, and subsequently by the institution of the Sayer, Gregory, and Neeld scholarships.

Quickened by Dr. Wordsworth's efforts to secure a place of worship for the Harrow boys, the spirit of liberality henceforth animated masters, scholars, and friends of the school. The master's house was rebuilt in 1845, the school bathing-place was enlarged and improved in 1851 at Dr. Vaughan's expense ; while in 1855, not only was a new school building erected, but the chapel was transformed by means of a chancel and north aisle as a memorial to Harrovians who fell in the Crimean war, the chancel being one more monument of the head-master's liberality.*

The years 1844–59 will be remembered on the whole for a steady progress (which even out-stripped the general national advance) in the standard of morals, learning, and discipline ; while, with the single exception of the above-mentioned Platt-Stewart case, public controversy was unheard in connection with Harrow.

Dr. Vaughan would be the first to insist that the services of his assistants should be fully recognised, whilst the weight of such men as Mr. G. F. Harris, Mr. B. H. Drury, and Mr. Steel by influence on the community is necessarily acknowledged more openly when the loss is realised. Nor should the effective aid rendered by younger men be forgotten.

Keeping pace with the times, and resolved to supply acknowledged popular needs, Harrow fulfilled her destiny. Change, however, was gradual ; and when Dr. Vaughan left his post education was looked at from a

* These details we owe to *Harrow Notes* for November 3, 1883.

different standpoint than that of the year of grace 1884,
so that, for instance, the *dullard* was tolerated in hopes
that what little he learned might benefit him in the
future.

Probably no youth in educational contact with Dr.
Farrar or Mr. Bowen could fail to learn something ; but
we are inclined to believe that the now prevailing system
which requires an adequate standard of moderate knowledge before entrance on public school life, will free
many a boy from the haunting conviction of inferiority
when such a condition is the result of circumstances, not
by any means an inherited disability. The agonies of
an ill-grounded boy at a large school, where the daily
task is from no fault of his own beyond the natural
scope, can never be understood unless such experience
be undergone ; nor can the atmosphere created by these
shortcomings be that of truth, or indeed of genuine
industry, when desperate efforts must either be expended
on vain struggles to go the recognised pace when hopelessly clogged by defective knowledge, or still more often
end in idle despair. It is but a partial satisfaction,
under such depressing circumstances, to be frequently
designated by the poetic title of "Grass upon the
House-tops," even if any such pictorial truism issue
from the lips of a rhetorician second to none in
England. We venture to advance these considerations
not by any means unconscious that Sir Robert Peel's
opinion to the effect that boys are sent to Harrow to
learn,* not to be presented there miniature scholars,
has something to be said for it, even when, as is now
the fashion, youths go to Harrow so *much later* than
they did in the great statesman's days.

* Spoken in the hearing of Sam Hoare, the School-custos.

It is somewhat strange to reflect that despite the prominent advantages, of which an Harrovian boasted during Dr. Vaughan's last years of office, yet no school of literature associated itself with the school name, although several members of Mr. Harris's house did conduct a periodical designed to provide an outlet for the youthful pen. We find much tolerable writing and several specimens of English verse which do credit to the composers. But, alas! the *Triumvirate* failed to gain support from Harrow boys generally, and consequently met the fate which has awaited so many like efforts at Eton, Rugby, and elsewhere. With the single exception of the *Microcosm* at Eton, when supported by Mr. Canning's pen, we can call to mind no genuine boyish literary success taking its initiative from a school source; and, indeed, in modern times so close is the pressure of duty, that spare time, when it exists, is naturally spent in the open air, and employed in contemplating, if not in actively pursuing, the variety of diversions which a public school life offers.

But we can urge on behalf of the *Triumvirate* that its authors have collected various striking facts; and without reference to what we consider a fairly high literary tone, it may be said that the publication is one from which even at this day something may be learnt of Harrow life under Dr. Vaughan.

Having alluded to the religious influences extant during Dr. Vaughan's head-mastership, it is impossible to pass by the manifold good works performed by the Rev. John Smith, to whose precept and example many young Harrovians owe the higher impressions which have enabled them to battle against the manifold dangers and temptations of a rough world.

Lucky the schoolboy thus early helped gently and with all the magical power of sympathy upon his path. Who that has ever enjoyed the spring morning walks across the Pinner meadows with Mr. Smith to his mother's house, where, with appetites such as boys alone possess, an ample breakfast was discussed, Harrow being regained in time for second school, will forget these charming experiences, or cease to honour the man who designed them, or the hosts who dispensed such hospitalities. On these pleasant excursions Mr. Smith's pleasant talk and kindly advice made his young companions feel that in him they possessed that best of blessings—a true friend in time of need.

Such, as many knew him, was John Smith, whose tender care for his pupils was at this time in Harrow story seconded by stirring pulpit appeals from Mr. Farrar, his dazzling periods being only approached from an oratorical point of view by certain passages of Mr. Steel's sermons, which have become classical in the records of Harrow literature. Over the whole community, nevertheless, was the head-master's influence supreme. This paramount authority was consecrated to the loftiest of all purposes, so that the wiser of his hearers ever thankfully remember the Sunday evening's sermon at Harrow, and still mould their aspirations by the God-fearing and sapient maxims therein propounded.* A sojourn in such an atmosphere left on the mind the impression of membership in a community which made religion a rule of life, and did not merely regard its

---

* Several Harrovians have told the writer that Dr. Vaughan's pulpit request to his pupils that, however weak their faith and infirm their purpose, they would, as a favour to him, *never* forget to bend the knee in prayer before retiring to sleep, *sank into their memories*, and was followed accordingly.

teachings as part of a formal system. It would, of
course, be an imperfect account of Dr. Vaughan's moral
supremacy at Harrow which overlooked his obvious
faculty for organization, based, as such a talent must
be, on recognition of the power which a well-arranged
division of labour confers.

In the management of boys equally with that of
men a special gift of this character is needed if anything approaching success be desired, and, indeed, a
very few years sufficed to demonstrate at Doncaster,
before all England, one of the several reasons why
Dr. Vaughan was so pre-eminent as a public schoolmaster.

Previous head-masters of Harrow had equalled his
learning, but few if any vied with Dr. Vaughan in tact
and intuitive knowledge of mankind, and this, although
it is probably true that the youth benefiting from John
Lyon's forethought in 1884 has a brighter life than
obtained a quarter of a century ago. Music was not
then a part of education, and the *Triumvirate's* piteous
and subdued appeal on behalf of the soothing art tells
its own tale. Occasionally the routine of cricket,
racquets, and football might be broken by such a visit
as that of the late Mr. Thackeray, who read his lecture
on the Georges to an appreciative gathering who had
been forgiven fourth school; while Speech-day itself
provided some change for all, and entertainment of
an intellectual class for those who could appreciate
declamatory power of a high order when George Otto
Trevelyan proved himself a worthy nephew of England's
most brilliant historian. Nor should the narrator fail
to mention these other names—leading members of the
Conservative party—who were at Harrow under the

Dean of Llandaff, viz. Earl Lytton, Lord Rowton—
the Earl of Beaconsfield's chosen friend, the Hon. E.
Stanhope, and Sir Matthew A. Ridley, a notable friend
to the school.

In the last few pages we have striven to indicate what
to a mover in the scenes themselves was the effect of
Dr. Vaughan's influence over Harrow—that man whom
nobody ever saw in a hurry, seldom ruffled in temper ;
hedged in, in the eyes of youth, with a majesty befitting
his position. But the Harrow boys themselves were
destined to see this great man unbend, and acknowledge,
as it were, his liability to the heartaches and shrinkings
which accompany a severance of old ties and a launch
into a new career.

Those present in the old Speech-room during the
ceremony of Dr. Vaughan's final farewell in 1859 can
never forget the scene. Each youth who grasped the
extended hand and heard the half-suppressed farewell,
passed into the great world a willing witness of the
wisdom that raised Harrow out of misfortune and
guided her truly in prosperity.

It had long been noised about that Dr. Vaughan
believed that after fifteen years of service the work at
Harrow for which he was specially fitted was done, and
that another could enter into his labours there while he
could make the best of his peculiar powers in a new
sphere of activity ; while it is no secret that, after
Henry Montagu Butler, the brilliant son of a former
head-master, was chosen to occupy the historic seat
of Sumner, Heath, Drury, and Wordsworth, Dr.
Vaughan's natural anxiety for his beloved Harrow
became tempered by a trustful faith in the future.

Acceptance of a mitre, although the offer came from

a Harrow Premier, Lord Palmerston, was, after due deliberation, refused ;* and although from time to time rumours have been repeated as to Dr. Vaughan's having been induced to undertake this and that position of honour, it was not until the Deanery of Llandaff fell vacant that titular preferment accrued to one of the greatest English churchmen of the Victorian era. We say *great* advisedly, because, tried by contact with those of acute intellect and shrewd intelligence, close familiarity enhances rather than diminishes their respect for his integrity and admiration for his talents. The nearer you get to him the greater he appears.†

During Dr. Vaughan's head-mastership Lord Palmerston stands pre-eminently as the Harrow minister of his times, fulfilling in the eyes of the school generally that place which in Dr. George Butler's closing years of office, and during the whole of Dr. Longley's, was occupied by the great Sir Robert Peel. No school function of importance was complete without Lord Palmerston's presence. His opinion was sought when a knotty question stood for decision, or a point of monitorial etiquette required adjusting; while the strength gained by the

* The writer of these lines remembers Mr. Farrar granting a school to his Form on the ground of the head-master's elevation to a bishopric; but, alas! before the glad hour arrived, Dr. Vaughan's *nolo episcopari* was known, and the boys lost their leisure hour.

† In the opinion of his friend, namesake, and admirer, the Rev. James Vaughan, of Brighton, it is the humility of the Dean of Llandaff which, combined with his conspicuous gifts, has enabled him to gain notable power over young Englishmen fortunate enough to have passed under the spell of his influence. The value put upon his training by the relations of those about to enter the Church is notorious, and is not only endorsed by public opinion, but justified by the success of younger men who have profited by his instruction in the vicinity of the Temple between the time they left College and took Holy Orders.

knowledge that he approved the course of modern
Harrow is inconceivable to those who forget what popularity surrounded the stalwart Premier's name. Harrow
men, however, be they Whig or Tory in sympathy, will
never do this, and the name of Palmerston will recur
when the halcyon days of the Vaughan rule are described,
as they doubtless will be, by one with materials purely
historical before him. At present we must rest and be
thankful for smaller mercies.

CHAPTER XIII.

THE HARROW RENAISSANCE.   1859-1884.

> Her structures rise
> As from the stroke of an enchanter's wand.
>
> *Childe Harold*, Canto iv. Stanza 1.

OUR readers must often have heard doubts expressed
whether boys at school ever really held regard for their
master, who, in old English idea, was wont to be thought
a natural enemy.   Even enthusiastic Rugbeians brought
up under the glamour of what we may term the school
revival, never averred that small boys low down in the
Rugby Forms shared Vaughan's or Bradley's enthusiasm
for the great genius who effected so much between
1828 and 1841.   Neither would it be true to state that
Sumner, or even Joseph Drury, ever inspired each new
Harrow boy with a tithe of the adoration poured forth
at the shrine of school devotion by scholars such as
Jones, Bennet, and Parr.   But the latter trio had been
under the wizard's wand, and their hour of enchantment
had not passed in vain.

In the same way we cannot claim for Dr. Vaughan
unlimited devotion throughout his career from all the
500 boys who owned his sway.   It would be contrary
to truth were we to allow so much.   But we may state,
on the other hand, that not only did a large average

of the tyros, to use an old phrase, yield to the silent spell of wisdom and benignity which characterised Dr. Vaughan's rule ; but before he left Harrow scarcely an individual could be found whose sympathies were not raised on behalf of the striking personage who with such manifest tenderness was severing the bond between these adopted children, so to speak, and his own life. And the revulsion of feeling would have been such, in our opinion, as to have rendered the task of any chance new comer, however worthy and talented, well nigh hopeless, had not the idea been bruited abroad freely that Harrow was to yield obedience to a favoured friend and pupil of the late chief, that choice being rendered specially palatable by the fact that Henry Montagu Butler was Harrow to the backbone. Senior Classic at Cambridge, the young aspirant to magisterial honour (for he was only 28), had wielded his bat as deftly as he has since used pen and tongue.*

His fame for all-round knowledge had been such that when Mr. Mozley, author of the famous *Oxford Recollections*, was in Rome, he noted the advantages which breadth of general reading gave the young Harrovian, then revelling in the glories of the fallen capital of the European world, since recrowned with a diadem less costly, but, we trust, more permanent, as centre of a united Italy.

Those present when the election of a head-master was pending in 1859 will remember how, amongst those who thought about the matter at all, there was anxiety that the Harrow candidate should be successful, such as afterwards drifted into enthusiasm when it was known

* 41 lbw. b. Reay, had been Mr. H. M. Butler's score against Eton in 1851.

who had been elected. No less a doughty opponent than Bishop Barry was in the field, as well as several other men skilled in the teaching of youth.

Save and except that Dr. Butler perceived the necessity of showing that his yea must be yea and his nay nay, when the school had been agitated by a change of rule, there is little in the first nine years of his pre-eminence at Harrow to distinguish the period historically from Dr. Vaughan's time. The Public Schools Commission and the Act which followed put a different complexion on events.

Despite the fact that by reason of John Lyon's politic provision there was little at Harrow out of accord with public opinion, yet masters and their management had to run the gauntlet of inquiry, together with other institutions dating from the Middle Ages, or owing existence to founders of later origin. Practically the only changes of moment which ensued were, firstly, the establishment of a Modern side, and, secondly, Admittance of Nonconformists to the governing body.

This latter change was resisted by the Archbishop of York in the House of Lords, who thought the clause contrary to the founder's intentions. Based, however, on the Church Settlement of 1559, John Lyon's institution represents the opinions in vogue when Elizabeth, insulted by Paul IV., turned to the Genevan exiles for support, and by recalling Dr. Cox, Rector of Harrow, 1537–44, and others, gave a Protestant colour to the Anglican theology. Therefore it is that any marked ignoring of the nineteenth-century Nonconformists when the government of Harrow School was about to be placed on a fresh basis would have been as foreign to Lyon's intentions as a separation from the Church of England, under whose tolerant *teaching* the founder clearly intended the school to remain.

We are so fully conscious of the impossibility of contemporary history being satisfactorily recorded in detail that we shall certainly attempt no analysis of modern school government, which has not been without its critics who rise superior to all difficulties when in the self-appointed judgment seat; but it is necessary to recount the fact that changes in the course of study have obtained a large accession of class honours at Oxford and Cambridge. Harrow boys having ceased to be called on to give undue importance to original classical composition, but rather to practise the translation of English into the dead languages in the form adopted at the universities, have done more than hold their own.

Dr. H. M. Butler's time will, we believe, when its *history* is fully written, be commemorated as a period of notable advance all along the line. But the event which will ever be connected with this epoch is the Tercentenary Celebration of the school foundation, which took place in 1871. Technically speaking, the authorities were correct in thus dating the commencement of school studies at Harrow, as marking the date when Queen Elizabeth granted the charter; although it has since been discovered that grammar was taught in the Church house at Harrow some years before. The ceremony which was held on this occasion was no mere cold formality, patronised by a few smoke-dried old Londoners, who prosed over the days when they were young, without contributing information or interest to the matter in hand; but, on the contrary, nearly every living Harrow celebrity within hail of the metropolis

20

found his way down to the little Middlesex town.   John
Lyon's memory, we are glad to narrate, came in for
much enthusiasm from the younger part of the community, who seemed almost personally familiar with the
founder, thanks to the soul-inspiring songs of Mr. E. E.
Bowen, set to charming music by his coadjutor, the
modern Farmer of Harrow Hill.

And, indeed, within the compass of those few rhymes
may be learnt nearly all that until quite lately we knew
of John Lyon, whose prescient forethought, as narrated
in these pages, received a worthy acknowledgment when
so many hundred voices were uplifted in his honour, the
echoes of the choruses reaching up to St. Mary's
Church, where the old landowner sleeps the long sleep
of all.

At Harrow on that memorable day were two former
headmasters, Dr. Wordsworth, Bishop of Lincoln, and
Dr. Vaughan ; the then oldest living Harrovian, Baron
Heath, who entered the school in 1798, and was subsequently fag to Lord Byron ; together with the Duke of
Abercorn, Lord Spencer, Lord George Hamilton, the
Hon. F. Ponsonby (now Lord Bessborough), the late
Hon. Robert Grimston, and a long roll of names, whose
fervent love of their old school was as notorious as they
themselves were in most instances useful members of
society.

Not the least interesting feature was the pregnant
oratory of the head-master, both when speaking from
the pulpit and on the platform, telling his hearers of the
days wherein, one hundred years before, the school had
sprung into acknowledged fame under the guidance of
Drs. Thackeray and Sumner, the former spoken of as
second founder, while the latter's great abilities, as

acknowledged by contemporaries, are known to have deeply impressed Dr. Butler.

But certainly there never were three more cultured teachers who ever wielded John Lyon's magisterial wand than the head-master and his two predecessors present on this occasion, and altogether the celebration of the 800th anniversary of the school foundation will not be forgotten by the Harrovians lucky enough to be present.

Prominent in later nineteenth-century Harrow history stands the establishment in 1883 of a mission for the spiritual and temporal needs of the poor in the suburban district of Latimer Road. Following the good precedent elsewhere set by Eton, funds were collected from Harrow men and boys, who undertook to maintain the missioner, the Rev. W. Law, whose popularity at Harrow has since repeated itself wherever duty called him.

The project was consecrated by an interesting address from the old Harrow philanthropist, Lord Shaftesbury, who in the summer of 1883 addressed an enthusiastic gathering at St. James's Hall, the result being that funds were forthcoming to support the good work.

It would be purposeless to dwell longer on the Harrow of to-day, with its consistent prosperity. Numbers are at present alone limited by design, and the 528 present at Easter 1884 represent rather those whom the masters chose to teach than the boys whose parents would feign let their children profit by the education afforded. Nor, despite almost unlimited competition, do we believe that Harrow is ever likely to undergo the decline which awaited her in 1843-4, when older ideas had not given way to the age. But we nevertheless deprecate Harrow undertaking to keep up many more expensive buildings,

20 *

which a poorly endowed school in time of only comparative depression might find it difficult to maintain.

It is a crying shame that a visitor to the fashionable church of St. George's, Hanover Square, should read high up in the list of benefactions that of John Lyon for repairing Oxford Street, when all valid excuse for keeping up such a road as a highway between Harrow and London was scattered to the winds directly the railway came from Euston.* It is doubly anomalous now that an alternative iron road is open between Baker Street and the hill itself. But unless some Parliament man, himself an old Harrovian, will find time to bring the matter forward, we may grumble (as we are fully aware) in vain. Moreover, as a natural means of sustaining the school prestige, we hope to see the historic Harrow families with strength of mind enough to forego fashion and adhere to the old place once and for all.

In an hour when each institution has to stand on its own basis, and therefore in the case of a public school rest its future mainly upon the fidelity of its children, the narrow and unsympathetic opportunism which dictates that the past is to count for nothing is to be deprecated. Therefore we claim for Harrow the Grimstons, Ponsonbys, Drurys, and Butlers of the future, urging that as their forefathers have helped to make us what we are, so should the rising generation benefit by their liberality and inherit their patriotism.

We have spoken of the Harrow Renaissance, associating this period with the epoch during which these records were compiled. The new Speech-room and Vaughan Library stand by no means alone to represent

* Mr. Howard Staunton, the famous chess-player, went fully into this subject in his *Great Schools of England*. His verdict is in accordance with that recorded here.

the architectural needs of the time. Possibly professional, not to say æsthetic, eyes may see defects which a general nobility of outline nevertheless redeems. But we are not far wrong when claiming for the school a noble room worthy the forensic triumphs of any future Peel or Palmerston, and a library amid the variety of whose treasures the archæologist may rest content, and the lover of history revel. For we venture to predict that shortly few more perfect modern libraries will exist around London than that at Harrow, where every branch of literature will be represented. Nor do we hesitate to claim for the Renaissance period a revival of literature, imperfect from the nature of the case, but still fully equal to that in vogue amongst the youth of England generally.

We allude to the *Tyro* and the *Second Harrovian*, two school publications which, if they provide scant matter for a future inquirer, still bear witness to an intellectual life amongst the boys themselves. In the pages of the *Tyro* Mr. W. J. Courthope first published poems, which possess generally acknowledged merit, even if they do not, as we believe, display originality and genius of no mean type. During the last two years (1883, 1884) a literary old Harrovian has welded together the available talent, past and present, besides providing matter chronologically arranged as to incident, which will assist the historian who undertakes to tell posterity something of Dr. H. M. Butler's headmastership. *Harrow Notes* has deserved well of Harrovians generally.

In music Harrow stands *facile princeps*, her ascendancy being due mainly to the presence of Mr. Farmer. That gentleman came to Harrow a poor and friendless Not-

tingham man.   Dr. Butler, gauging the truth of his
character and the extent of his musical power, after
due consideration, gave him a confidence which once
proffered is never unduly withdrawn.   Mr. Farmer has
requited this trust by raising the musical education to a
height which could never have been reached, unless the
scholars themselves had been imbued with the teacher's
own enthusiasm, and, in some instances, shared a portion of his genius.   Some, however, are found to doubt
whether music studied to the extent now in vogue at
Harrow is not taking a place which should belong more
exclusively to the leisure hour.

Of Mr. Farmer we may record that he has declined
lucrative positions elsewhere, indignantly declaring that
money would never tempt him from Harrow; while,
despite such fidelity, he is making his way to the front
of the musical world, where the oratorio *Christ and His
Soldiers* and the opera *Cinderella* are, we believe, but the
heralds of future triumphs.   For proof of the high
character of music which has been performed by the
school musical society under Mr. Farmer's auspices we
refer our readers to the abstract given in Appendix H.

The Renaissance period will be also memorable for a
sanatory advance all along the line at Harrow, illness
being in the first instance prevented, and, if unhappily
incurred, treated by scientific method.   A laboratory
and a gymnasium are both to be found at Harrow,
while the present racquet-court and the new fives-
courts date from this period, during which, be it noted,
an athletic revival proper has succeeded that initiated
at the Universities twenty years ago.*   Nor should we

* The writer can remember the school mile being run on the
Pinner Mile, when the starter and judge, setting their watches

forget the improvement of the school bathing-place,
now rendered classical by Mr. Robertson the present
master of Haileybury's popular lyrics which adorn the
sheds.

Although the sovereign has not repeated her visit to
Harrow since Dr. H. M. Butler became head-master,
the Prince and Princess of Wales have twice received a
warm greeting from the boys and the inhabitants. On
the 30th of June 1864, soon after their marriage, horses
were removed from the carriage in which the heir to
England's throne and his beautiful bride were driving,
the equipage being guided up the awkward ascent to
the school-yard by the stalwart arms of Herga's most
athletic sons. Their Royal Highnesses came again in
1871, when on the 6th of July they attended the Tercentenary Speech-day. The royal party drove from
London, entering Harrow under two triumphal arches,
and amid cordial expressions of loyalty. Passing
through the lines of the boys' Rifle Corps in the school-
yard, they were received by Dr. Butler, and after hearing
the speeches, lunched at the head-master's house, where
the Prince of Wales, in one of his terse, clear, and

together, compared notes after the race was over, before announcing the official time. This method of time-keeping resulted in
the register of more than one sensational performance, which the
unlucky hero was vainly expected to repeat. *Times* are changed
now, and the stop-watch is recognised here as elsewhere, although
further reform seems to be demanded in circles purely athletic.
To ask boys to run on wet clay was, of course, destructive of
speed. Modern athletes are not in danger of having their fame
prematurely extinguished now that the sport is popular, but the
author, with some title to speak as being the *first* Cambridge
Secretary of the Inter-University Sports, wishes to register his
belief that J. D. Burnett was a remarkable boy runner at Harrow
in 1858. His swiftness of foot was wonderful, and, if equalled
by other boys—like J. T. Ridley of Eton, who was amateur
champion quarter of a mile when at school—still those who knew
Mr. Burnett at the time in question will endorse this statement.

sensible speeches, summed up the causes of Harrow holding her head so high at the end of 300 years by stating that she marched with the times.

Another notable ceremony was the laying of the foundation-stone of the aforesaid new Speech-room in 1874, by the Duke of Abercorn, just before he resigned the Lord-Lieutenancy of Ireland.

Students of Harrow story should not omit to visit the building overlooking the cricket ground, where John Lyon's poor scholars, as they are called in old Harrow phrase, receive at small cost the education which the founder designed for those dwelling in the locality; the institution in question being styled the "Lower School of John Lyon," the names of its members appearing in the Bill-book under this title. Whether or not they rank as Harrovians proper it needs a lawyer to decide. When it became practically impossible to pass through Harrow School without incurring considerable expenses, some such *pis aller* was rendered a necessity; the more because Harrow town had ceased to benefit by the money formerly given from the Lyon funds towards forwarding apprentices in their trades, and aiding poor people when they entered into matrimony.

In recounting school experiences, we have been enabled to give no adequate idea of the services rendered by under-masters generally. Probably at the present time, when the range of subjects taught is so much more extensive, this aspect of school life is of greater importance; and the individual silently employed in duties such as those of the highest culture can alone perform, has to rest content with moderate pecuniary reward. Hence Dr. Butler would wish to see acknowledged the efforts of colleagues like Mr. C. F. Holmes,

Mr. Hutton, Mr. A. G. Watson, Mr. Bull, and Mr. Bowen, veterans in the educational profession ; and he doubtless appreciates the presence of a historian like Mr. Bosworth Smith, or a rival poet to Mr. Bowen in Mr. Howson.

Nor is it possible to reflect upon the suppression of the ancient title of under-master without observing that, at the Rev. W. Oxenham's death, in the year 1863, the office in question had been held by four men of note throughout the century, namely, Mark Drury, the house-master of Peel, the Rev. Benjamin Evans, Harry Drury, the famous tutor, scholar, and lover of books,* and last, but not least, by one of the most beloved of all Harrow teachers. To speak of reverence and affection inaptly describes the feelings of many living pupils, distinguished in their various walks of life, for William Oxenham's memory.

Amongst other minor changes lately adopted at Harrow we may mention the abolition of the time-honoured *exeat*,† held by the authorities to be unsettling and therefore reprehensible, so that leave of absence for a few hours is now occasionally granted as a substitute, while on exceptional occasions the privilege receives moderate extension.

It has been very generally believed that the head-master of Harrow was for many years purely autocratic, but that one result of the Public Schools Act was to place the governors in a position of authority they had not occupied since the school became famous. This is so far true as regards the changes which date from

* Both Mr. Henry Drury and Mr. Evans were 41 years masters at Harrow.
† *Exeat* was leave of absence for the night or longer.

1869, because since that time the governors have been
in particular force. For instance, we trace to their
initiation a certain unpopular superannuation rule which
rumour charged solely on the head-master.*

But the preconceived notions concerning an assumed
paralysis of the governing body in earlier times has
altogether been exploded by means of the school
archives. From time to time those in charge of the
revenues had considerable influence, and often initiated
measures which bore upon the future of Harrow most
markedly. The Gerards, as we know, between 1571
and 1660 helped materially to reconcile Government
to the infant institution, when from time to time
revolution threatened every endowed property in the
land. Again, the Duke of Chandos renovated Harrow
completely, when early in the eighteenth century he
utilised his business capacity in her behalf; while to
recount the services of the Rushouts to Harrow would
be to repeat a portion of English history during Sir
Robert Walpole's pre-eminence. Nor can we forget that
the efforts of these men were supplemented by those
of successors who displayed wills of their own when
Samuel Parr missed his mark and saw Benjamin Heath
elected head-master. If, as has been declared, the
governors were nonentities, would they ever have made
the wise choice of preferring Joseph Drury in 1785, or
stood boldly to their guns when the *vox populi* declared
against Dr. George Butler in 1805.

It is doubtless true that some specially strong men
burst the bonds of otherwise unhindered power by a
sheer force of will which must have stood them in

* This fact was communicated to the writer by one of the
Governors.

stead in the Senate or promoted them to affluence at the Bar. And as it is not given to every head-master to possess the genius of a Sumner, so would the school fare ill that relied *altogether* on individual effort for its prestige. It is therefore right to point out how great in Harrow history have been the services of its governors. Drawn, as these men have been for the most part, from local sources, they have nevertheless a roll of fame of their own, as may be gathered from our former chapters. We therefore express a fervent hope that if ever the time comes—long be the day deferred!—when it has to be decided afresh who shall rule Harrow School, the power of the present governors may be conferred on men imbued with the same spirit that has hitherto upheld independence and resisted class aggression ; thus preserving Harrow very nearly in the shape that John Lyon must have approved had his far-seeing mind been allowed to note the signs of times beyond his ken. Joyfully would he then, we believe, have exclaimed " *Stet fortuna domus.*"

Dr. H. M. Butler's head-mastership, if not free from all controversy, will be noted because for a quarter of a century no serious scandal has ever threatened the school prosperity. And this is the more remarkable because an absolute indifference to consequences when principles are at stake constitutes the very mainspring of the system now in vogue in this prosperous institution, whose life we have traced from 1571 downwards.

It is impossible that any educational foundation can remain altogether unscathed by criticism, of which it is certain Harrow has its fair share; but, nevertheless, truth bids us remember that the very worst is always known concerning the school and its shortcomings. No attempt at concealment is ever made when bad influences, the heritage of a common mortality, have to be combated, so that condoning evil is absolutely unheard of. This policy, undoubtedly wise and straightforward as it is, and not universally followed by kindred institutions, does not always engender popularity amongst those who think school a place wherein to sow very juvenile wild oats, and spend a few years merrily. But the battle of life is before all, and the current Harrow doctrine would seem to be that duty confronts masters and scholars alike. This tendency to unveil its very innermost self before the world is doubtless calculated to strengthen a community permanently, but renders it from time to time the gossip of London *salons* and the passing talk of suburban tea-tables. And yet the Harrow reputation is as high as it is well deserved.

The writer is fully aware that the inditing of contemporary history is well-nigh impossible, such work being at the very best but on a par with the high level of modern journalism, wherein not one single item of current events escapes mention, and he therefore leaves to some future narrator to describe in fulness, because armed with knowledge of the secret springs of action, a period which, being a halcyon one in modern school story, owes much of its fame to the head-master who still happily presides over destinies not yet fully shaped. In Lord Bessborough's stirring lines we will conclude this chapter.

> Long may she flourish, scene of rural beauty ;
> Long may increase her green and glorious age ;
> Long may her sons for every Briton's duty
> Foremost be ranked in History's swelling page.

CHAPTER XIV.

HARROW CRICKET.

Read my name upon the panels,
Carved in gold along the boards,
See myself arrayed in flannels,
Batting for the school at Lords.
School Song, by E. W. HOWSON.

STUDY of the best chroniclers* will convince our readers
that modern cricket is an offspring of the " Club ball,"
which in various forms may be traced back, as an English sport, even to the fourteenth century.

John Lyon in his statutes directs his scholars, amongst
other diversions, to *toss a hand ball*, a form of exercise
mentioned as early as 1477,† when *handyn and handoute*
was forbidden to the soldiery on the ground of being
an incitement to gaming; and which must have had
some affinity to cricket, as the term *hands* was retained
in that game up to 1740.‡   But beyond this early reference, we can adduce no proof to show Harrow to have
been in any way a nursery of the national game before
its popularity had been assured in several parts of the
kingdom.   And, indeed, the topography of the neighbourhood could not have favoured a game which required
open space, before even the school-yard was levelled,

---

* *Cricket Scores and Biographies*, vol. i. p. 1; Pycroft, *Cricket
Field*, pp. 1–8; also *Cricket Notes*, by William Bolland, pp. 1–10.
† 17 Edward IV.
‡ Pycroft, *Cricket Field*, pp. 1–9 (quoting Barrington).

and when rough and unreclaimed common land alone stood around the hill.

Cricket in a rude form became localised in Hampshire, Berkshire,* and Kent early in the eighteenth century. In the latter county it was clearly popular in A.D. 1708, when, in the diary of a Kentish farmer resident near Canterbury, we read of a victory over Ash Street village close to Sandwich.†

The Harrow archives are alsolutely silent on the subject of cricket, while again and again reference is made to shooting at the butts ; so that we are led to conclude that the contemporary form of the game "Club ball" or "handyn" must have been pursued in a desultory manner, if at all, until the Eton mode of education became fashionable on the hill.

Dr. Brian, who for forty years swayed the Harrow fortunes, retired in 1730, when, as Horace Walpole testifies, cricket was popular at Eton.‡

Dr. Thackeray, who avowedly ruled Harrow on principles learnt under the shadow of Windsor Castle, may be supposed to have introduced Eton pastimes with the system of mental training there in vogue. This view is borne out by the purchase of a play-ground, the business arrangements concerning which are frequently alluded to after the year 1746 in the school archives.

---

* The Earl of Bessborough tells us that Lord Fred. Beauclerk maintained that the game originally struck root in Berkshire, where, however, in his time, play was poor.

† Egerton MS., 2609, British Museum, folio 108B. Thomas Minter of Canterbury's *Diary*, " Wee beat Ash Street at Creekits, June 23, 1708."

‡ "I could tell you of Lord Mountford's making cricket-matches, and fetching up persons by express from different parts of England to play matches on Richmond Green." June 25, 1745.— Horace Walpole, *Letters*, vol. ii. p. 169 (Cunningham, 1857).

The pastime is not noticed in any of the local biographies or histories before 1771. We first learn that when Dr. Parr seceded to Stanmore, his scholars, who were nearly all Harrovians, secured the Duke of Chandos' bowling-green for the purpose of cricket.

With the establishment of the Marylebone Club in the year 1779, and after the annual shooting for a silver arrow had been for eight years abolished, cricket may be believed to have issued from the earlier stage, which the pictures extant tell us involved hook-shaped clubs, and hitting almost exclusively to the on, where fieldsmen were mostly placed.*

For earlier Harrow cricket records we are perforce led to take refuge in the region of tradition. It is said that at the commencement of the nineteenth century, when Westminster and Eton ceased their rivalry on the green sward, matches were played between Eton and Harrow. They did not take place every year, and the interest felt in the contests must have been limited, because when the old Lord's Pavilion was destroyed by fire, these records are said to have perished,† duplicates being perserved neither at Eton nor Harrow.

The earliest score extant is that of August 2nd, 1805, and this match seems to have been a pick-up contest, played on *old* Lord's ground where Dorset Square stands, Harrow suffering a defeat, compensated for by the participation of Lord Byron, who was never in the Harrow eleven proper, and would not have been selected on this occasion had the late Mr. C. Lloyd had his way.‡ It is, however, remarkable that whereas

* *Cricket Notes,* by William Bolland, p. 11.
† *Ibid.,* p. 61.
‡ See Dean Merivale's *Recollections,* p. 239 of this volume. The following epigram is said to have been sent by Eton to

Lord Byron did score 7 and 2, bowling one wicket, his pitiless critic obtained the 0 and 0 which, in cricketing parlance, entitled him to spectacles. The representative character of this match having been questioned, Etonians agreed to leave it out when counting their victories, while Harrow gave way in like manner concerning a game won at Lord's in 1859, when the teams contained more than one cricketer who had left school.

It is certainly unfortunate that we have no *bonâ fide* score of the Eton and Harrow match until 1818, when the wicket-keeping and batting of G. T. Vigne enabled the school to beat their collegiate opponents by the narrow majority of thirteen runs. Mr. Vigne had another brother, a celebrated traveller, who was also a cricketer, and the two seem in some degree to have in-doctrinated those who came after them with the enthu-siasm that has had its sequel in the days of Ponsonby and Grimston.

Before Harrow and Eton commenced their annual matches in 1818 cricket had entered into the scientific phase which had succeeded one of comparative confu-sion, and henceforth it became the object of Harrow to attain a correct style of play, such as, by means of old boys coming down from time to time, may be said

Harrow after their defeat in 1805. We append it, together with the Harrovian reply:

ETON TO HARROW.

" Ye Harrow '*boys* ' of cricket you've no knowledge,
  Ye played not cricket but the fool with ' *men* ' of Eton College."

HARROW TO ETON.

" Ye Eton wits, to play the fool
  Is not the boast of Harrow School ;
  No wonder, then, at our defeat,
  Folly, like yours, could ne'er be beat."

to have kept the school in touch with Lord's. This, it must be allowed, has given Harrow an advantage over other schools where there are not the same frequent opportunities of seeing good players. Practically, this comparative disadvantage has been overcome in the case of Eton, as many old boys are ready to make any sacrifice of time required to compass the distance from London to Windsor; while at present the college boasts a ruling power in Mr. R. A. H. Mitchell, still able to demonstrate the precepts it is his delight to instil.

But Harrow will nevertheless profit hereafter by her propinquity to the metropolis. We were almost in despair at an inability to add any fresh details concerning the Harrow cricket giants of old, when Lord Bessborough (better known to Harrovians as the Hon. Frederick Ponsonby) placed his Recollections at our disposal, and to some extent filled up this vacuum. Our informant's father, the popular Irish statesman, and his two brothers were at Harrow; while a family friendship with Lord Grimston, the father of the present Lord Verulam, and his lamented brother, the Hon. Robert Grimston, led to his early youth being, so to speak, steeped in Harrow traditions. To a considerable extent, he tells us, they were those of cricket. From a brother, who was at Harrow before going into the Navy, he heard of Charles Wordsworth's (the Bishop of St. Andrews) grand style of hitting half volleys; of the Pophams, Davidsons, and other good cricketers, as well as of a boy called Ward, who during an M.C.C. match at Harrow caught one of his opponents whilst leaping over the old railings of the cricket-ground. In this case Mr. Ward caught the ball "when he was in the air," his feat being distinct from that of R. Daft, the Not-

21

tingham cricketer, who some years afterwards leaping these same railings landed on *terra firma* and then secured the ball. Mr. Ward's name does not, however, appear in any of the school matches in which Harrow engaged between 1805 and 1830, and he must be one of those heroes the records of whose deeds have been consigned to the flames. We gladly revive his memory here.

Despite frequent worstings at Lord's from Eton, which were destined to occur about this epoch, the Harrow cricket could not have been so bad in 1823, inasmuch as the previous year's victory at Lord's was followed by one at Oxford, when the Oxonian old Harrovians beat the University on Bullingdon Common in one innings. Clutterbuck of Merton and Calvert of Exeter were the Harrow batsmen who did honour to their school on this occasion, putting up 100 for the first wicket, a great feat in those days.[*]

Although the Harrow eleven of 1824 failed to hold its own with Eton, the strength of the team had been recognised by no less an authority than Mr. Ward of M.C.C. renown, who, after the M.C.C. match at Harrow, backed them for £10 to overcome Eton at Lord's. The bowler of the Harrow eleven was Mr. Francis Trench, brother of the Archbishop of Dublin, from whose letters we have derived this fact.[†] In 1823 his house, viz. the Leithites, beat the school.

It is a remarkable fact that when a decline in Harrow numbers occurred about 1826 the general average of the cricket advanced, while individual players of merit came to the fore.

[*] *Public Schools*, by Author of *Etoniana*, p. 310.
[†] *Notes from Past Life*, by Rev. Francis Trench, p. 4.

Despite a crushing defeat from Winchester in the last-mentioned year, when Mr. Meyrick carried his bat for 146, Harrow cricketers well sustained their reputation.

A great bowler appeared in the person of Mr. Charles Harenc, who, if his services to Kent surpassed those he was able to render his old school, still deserves a niche in the cricketers' Temple of Fame. Originally an under-hand bowler of the old-fashioned type, Mr. Harenc, when captain of the Harrow eleven in 1828, began to practise what was then called throwing bowling by some and scientific by others.

" He became very efficient in it,* and for some years after that date he was the crack bowler of his native county, Kent. His pace was slow, but the ball left the ground with extreme rapidity, and was always about the knuckles of the batsmen. The famous old Lillywhite is reported to have said, ' I bowls the best ball in England and Mr. Harenc the next.' "

Lord Bessborough fully seconds these remarks of Mr. Bolland, and remembers Mr. Harenc as one of the very best slower-paced bowlers he met during his active career as a cricketer. But Mr. Harenc's Harrow cap-taincy is likewise famous, because it marks an era when the game underwent its most abiding change, which makes it almost impossible to realise how that half a century back round-arm bowling was unknown in the rural cricket centres of England.

Harrow was at that moment entering on the portion of its cricket career which has left the most permanent results behind it. Ponsonby and Grimston were in the school, while Lord Verulam and his brother the Hon.

* *Cricket Notes*, W. Bolland, p. 60.

21 *

Edward H. Grimston, who was the finest bat in the family, were enrolled under Mr. Harenc's banner. The days were approaching when the names of Broughton and Frederick Ponsonby were to be succeeded by those of Nicholson and A. Haygarth, whose defence to fast bowling was probably unequalled when he played for the Gentlemen v. Players.[*]

But it is not so much the excellence of the play that deserves record in a history of Harrow, but rather, as Sir Robert Peel, in his eloquent eulogium on the Hon. Robert Grimston at the Westminster Palace Hotel in May 1884, phrased it, " the spirit of enthusiasm breathed into each small Harrow boy which a well-wisher would desire to perpetuate." Mr. Grimston was never in the Harrow eleven, although he was destined to become a tower of strength to the Gentlemen of England by reason of his patient defence.[†] But he nevertheless

[*] Mr. R. Thoms, the experienced umpire, who has seen much cricket and appreciates a good defence, never talks of Harrow cricket without a word of praise for Mr. Haygarth.

[†] There was a cricketer by name of Fagge, who could generally get a ball past Mr. Grimston's straight bat. On one occasion, in the depths of gloom consequent upon such a disaster, the batsman gave vent to a sentiment which evinced a desire for the triumphant bowler's permanent absence from the scene. "Why Bob! you would not wish him any harm?" said a friend. "No," was the prompt reply, "but I wish they would make him Archbishop of Canterbury." Nor must we forget Henry Vernon, one of the brightest stars of Harrow cricket, who played for the school five years. Dying in youth at his Harrow friend, Mr. C. O. Eaton's, home, his reputation is not equal to its merit. By this we mean that in the days when grounds were rough, and a good defence was a *sine qua non*, Mr. Vernon was a good off hitter, and so impressed Mr. Roger Kynaston, Hon. Sec. M.C.C., that after seeing him bat in the M.C.C. match at Harrow, the veteran pronounced the young aspirant to be "an accomplished player." Many larger scorers at Harrow have been adjudged by Messrs. Ponsonby and Grimston to be inferior to Mr. Vernon, who was a bowler and a good field. Mr. Thoms, the above-named umpire, fully seconds the late Mr. Kynaston's opinion of Mr. Vernon's

shares with his friend Frederick Ponsonby the merit of being not only the moving spirits of the period embraced between 1828 and 1884, but guides of the Harrow that is to be, provided that the boys elect to follow their best and soundest traditions.

We are neither compiling lists of accomplished Harrow cricketers nor recording their struggles for supremacy at Lord's, but we are perforce called on to mark each epoch by the names of those who rendered themselves most notorious in the Harrow cricket world. Deserving of special mention are F. D. Longe, the resolute and powerful hitter, afterwards M.P. for Chippenham; Reginald Hankey, for a time the best gentleman batsman; together with W. B. Marillier, son of the master, whose fielding was unsurpassed in his day. He was contemporary with A. H. Walker, the first of the Southgate Harrovians and an immediate predecessor of V. E. Walker, the best all round cricketer who ever learnt to play on the hill side. For had his slow bowling not been on a par with that of Clarke, and his activity in the field past all belief,* yet without any such support Mr. V. E. Walker's powers as a batsman would alone have placed him amongst the few great gentlemen cricketers of his time; while, when a critic is called on to name the best captain of a side he knows, to V. E. Walker is the premiership assigned almost

merits. In 1842–43, when the school was at a low ebb as regards numbers, W. Nicholson as a wicket-keeper and H. Gathorne (little Gathorne, as he was called) as a slow bowler, were *facile princeps.* A mere stripling, Gathorne had a great twist, and, being accurate in pitch, was frequently very effective. He performed the great feat of bowling at Lord's against Eton and Winchester in 1842 and 1843 without ever being taken off—a feat quite unique.

* W. Caffyn, the Surrey professional cricketer, deliberately expressed this opinion.

universally. Fortunately Mr. Walker's knowledge and experience are exercised both at Lord's and the Oval, where no important matter is decided without taking his opinion.

In the Harrow eleven with Mr. V. E. Walker, were the late Mr. C. D. Crawley (whose 100 in the town match is historical ; and, strange to say, the performance has since been repeated by his son H. E. Crawley, captain in 1884), and also Mr. K. E. Digby, a powerful batsman, who, according to tradition, learnt his off-hitting in the old yard of The Grove, where any other hit resulted in lost ball, and by special agreement a consequent resignation of the bat.

But we find ourselves discoursing of A.D. 1853 without having made good our ground as regards the early part of the current century. For we desire to impress on our reader how difficult Harrow School found it to establish any unchallenged right to a definite ground whereon they might practise and play matches.

In Dr. Joseph Drury's time the eleven played on a field near where Mr. Holt's residence now stands, situated, so to speak, on the brow of that part of Harrow Hill which you ascend when coming from Sudbury and London, about half a mile from the school centre. Judge Richardson, when at school, is said to have hit a ball nearly to the first milestone on the London Road, but it must be remembered that the ground was then open and steep, being afterwards raised to the gradual slope with which a traveller is now familiar.*

* These facts were communicated to Lord Bessborough by the first Earl of Verulam. S. Hoare, the School Custos, attests to this eminence above Sudbury being the locality where cricket was played, the fact being communicated by his father, an old Harrow resident, who was Custos in 1819.

But in 1803 an Act of Parliament was passed which
allowed the school to enclose part of Roxeth Common,
the privilege being, however, stoutly disputed by the
townspeople. Indeed, the Harrovians had to fight for
their cricket-ground during the first fifty years of the
nineteenth century.

Mention is made in Moore's *Byron* of rivalry that
took effect in quarrel, while the *chaws*, so-called in Harrow parlance, frequently gathered together and obstructed
the club-keepers when about to pitch wickets for their
respective games, the fags being sent into Harrow to
call " Row! row! row!" so that reinforcements might
appear on the scene of action in the shape of bigger
boys ready and able to hold their own. About the year
1832 the more respectable inhabitants repudiated the
conduct of their would-be representatives, and the feud
died out, giving way to a better feeling between the
school and town.*

There has been gradual improvement in the ground
since the days when, as the Dean of Ely tells us, he
played in the Sixth Form game during 1818 in such
goodly ecclesiastical company. But it still remains difficult in comparison to others, because it slopes, and is also
on clay, which becomes fiery in dry weather, sticky and
treacherous in wet. Twenty runs on the Harrow ground
represents, as cricketers know, more than at first sight
men are likely to credit. Still the best care available
has never been withheld, nor has there been any lack of
liberality on the part of Harrovians generally, who have
never shrunk from expense when an improvement was

* These facts were communicated by Lord Bessborough, who
himself has seen sharp blows given and received in this strange
quarrel.

deemed desirable.   The names of old Chadd and Gilby
are honourably associated with the safe keeping of the
Harrow cricket ground.

Old Chadd, familiarly styled Pipes, because his legs,
encased in white, gave the impression that the good old
man was supported by two tobacco pipes, was quite an
institution.   He was a great favourite with the boys,
being an honest simple-minded man, with a good deal
of character about him.   For some years he was a
useful medium-paced underhand bowler.   He lived to a
great age, and is buried in the churchyard.

His successor, the well-known Gilby, resigned his
position in 1871, to the regret of every cricketer who
knew him.   He kept the Sixth Form ground for many
years in order which more than satisfied his employers;
while as a slow bowler he was rated very highly by those
best able to judge.   Mr. C. F. Buller, for one, holds the
highest opinion of his capacity in this department of the
game.   Shortly before leaving Harrow, Gilby appeared
in the Middlesex county eleven, but by no means did
himself justice.   Impending physical weakness was even
then beginning to sap his powers.

It is, indeed, fortunate that the vacant position should
again be so efficiently filled, as it now is, by W. Clarke,
who was secured for the school by Mr. I. D. Walker
during one of the Harrow Wanderer tours.

For a short interval during 1855–56 Harrow had no
public school matches at Lord's, as the authorities at
Winchester and Eton put a stop to them; but was perforce obliged to rest content after a colourless contest
with the M.C.C. in London.   During this period, however, the brothers Lang, Henry Arkwright, W. C.
Clayton, G. Hodgson, and others were learning the

cricket which was to give Harrow supremacy when in 1858 a *bonâ fide* contest was once more arranged. In the year 1857, during the summer vacation, a quasi-Harrow-and-Eton match was arranged, in which the embargo of the authorities was evaded by the device of playing only nine scholars with two old boys on each side. Harrow won by ten wickets.

The hero of this triumph as regards batting was Mr. John Carpenter, now Mr. John Carpenter Garnier, M.P. Two brilliant performers at Harrow, not heard of more in the cricket field, were E. Humphreys and R. D. H. Elphinstone. The former, of a *physique* quite remarkable, played in excellent style and utilised his great strength. The latter, for brilliant off-hitting equalled even Daniel or I. D. Walker on their best school form.

For an adequate comparison of the cricket twenty-five years ago and that of the present day, we must refer our readers to a short *critique* placed at the writer's disposal by one specially competent to decide, but who elects to be nameless on the present occasion :—

In comparing Harrow cricket of the present day with that of twenty-five years ago, it will be as well to consider separately the three departments of the game ; and we take batting first as being that branch which, whether rightly or wrongly, undoubtedly receives most attention at the present time. During the period of which we are now treating, batting at Harrow, as elsewhere, has made considerable strides; a man might put his finger on some one particular eleven a generation ago equal perhaps to the best of recent days, but, taking the average year by year, it must, we think, be admitted that there are more batsmen capable of making consistently good scores than was the case, say, from 1855 to 1865. And this may be accounted for in two ways: firstly, the improved state of the ground on which the batsman is taught to develop his art; secondly, the increased attention given of later years to the tuition of younger members of the school. This last remark naturally recalls to mind those two gentlemen whose names are household words wherever cricketers congregate; assuredly, whether we consider their many years of labour, the well-nigh unintermittent nature of those labours, or the energy and remarkable judgment brought to bear, nothing approaching the services rendered by these great twin brethren (one of whom, alas! alone remains) has been recorded elsewhere in the annals of school cricket. With regard to individual play, there were giants of old who would not suffer by comparison with any of a later date. Twenty-four years have now elapsed since that popular and widely-regretted cricketer, A. W. Daniel, wielded the bat for Harrow, and he would be a bold man who should assert that his superior had been seen among any of his distinguished successors. Perhaps the four names that stand out most prominently during the period under review are those of Daniel, Buller, Webbe, Greatorex, though that of Money should hardly be denied a place. We speak, of course, of cricketing powers developed while still at school.

When we come to consider the two remaining departments of the game, we are unable to note the same general advance. Arkwright and Plowden (more especially Henry Arkwright) among slow bowlers, Lang and Linton among fast,* were doubtless superior to their later successors; although at intervals several slow bowlers of average merit have appeared, there has been a singular dearth among their faster brethren. Indeed, in the records of the last twenty years, two only, Cobden and Shand, stand out prominently.

Nor can it be contended that the general fielding of the teams has improved during this period; rather should we be inclined to say, more especially in the all-important matter of holding catches, that it has deteriorated. In this, Harrow cricket closely follows the lines of English cricket generally; for, whereas the batting, so far, that is, as the number of good batsmen is concerned, has made rapid advances, the bowling, by general consent, is certainly not better, and accurate fielding and catching probably inferior to what was witnessed by our predecessors two decades ago.

---

* Linton had the easiest style imaginable, bowling with a sling, but with an accuracy truly enviable. At Harrow he was a tower of strength to the eleven in 1856–57, afterwards bowling for Oxford University. He died young.

From these few remarks it might be gathered that we think somewhat undue importance is given to the science of batting, as opposed to that of the two other departments of the game; and to a certain extent this is true. At schools and universities alike a greater number of professionals are engaged to bowl to the rising talent than was the case some twenty years ago; and it is only natural that advantage should be taken of their services. Still we think it would be an advantage to Harrow cricket in the future if the boys were encouraged to bowl more frequently to each other (though never too long at a time) : and, above all, it cannot be too constantly impressed upon them to study fielding as a science, remembering that no truer cricket maxim has ever been handed down than that which tells us that "the good fieldsman always scores runs, though the best batsman may sometimes be unfortunate in not making any."

While as a whole admitting this thoughtful expatiation on twenty-five years of Harrow cricket to be unexceptionable, we yet claim more credit than this distinguished critic will allow for the Harrow fieldsman of later years. If the opinion of the writer, as one who has watched the cricket of his old school carefully for some years, is not adjudged to be superfluous, it amounts to this : Dark Blue will come up to Lord's strengthened on the whole, provided that more level space can be provided for the smaller members of the Harrow community to practise in extreme youth the several branches of the game, proficiency in which can alone come by experience, together with the strength and stamina that time will duly bring. Hence it is that in memory of the late and, in Harrow eyes, great Bob Grimston, we hope that not only will the Philathletic field be enlarged, but likewise, from a cricket point of view, improved.

About the time that Dr. Vaughan resigned the Harrow head-mastership, the matches between the two great

schools at Eton and Harrow became specially interesting.
Two notable drawn matches occurred in 1860 and 1861,
but in 1862, the Etonians, after a strange lapse in their
long record of concurrent capability—for individual
prowess always existed amongst the light blue cricketers
—came once more to the fore at Lord's, and beat
Harrow after a well-contested struggle. The Etonian
delight may be read of in Mr. Brinsley Richards' *Seven
Years at Eton,* a tribute being thereby paid to the prowess
of their opponents, which Harrow cricketers will appreciate. And it would appear as if the sting of defeat
stimulated to the full the cricketers, who, learning
their batting on a hill-side, were assumed to be more at
home on the slopes of old Lord's than those trained on
the smooth level which constitutes the playing-fields at
Eton. Be that as it may, in 1863 the match was left
unfinished ; and then on three several occasions, viz. in
1864, '65, and '66, did the light blue eleven suffer
crushing overthrow, succumbing relatively in one innings
and 66 runs, one innings and 51 runs, and one innings
and 136 runs. And while by no means prepared to
assume that such figures faithfully reflected the difference
between the schools, it is, we take it, safe to believe
that on the whole triumphs gained by means of W. B.
Money's* slow underhand bowling, were won by the
better men.

A long-scoring game followed in 1867, to finish which
two days proved inadequate ; and then, as the result of
R. A. H. Mitchell's coaching became apparent (Messrs.
G. H. Longman, A. S. Tabor, Lord Harris, Ridley, and
the Hon. A. Lyttelton being found in one team in 1870),

---

* The present Vicar of Weybridge, Surrey ; after he left
Harrow, one of the finest batsmen in England.

the tables were twice turned, Harrow losing decisively in
a single innings and 19 runs to spare in 1869; while
next year a struggle ever memorable resulted in a second
lowering of the Crossed Arrows, who lost by the small
margin of 21 runs. But the style of the Harrow boys
was not thought by the *cognoscenti* to have then declined ;
and despite the after excellence of the Etonians, there
was probably practical equality between these two elevens
in that memorable year, 1870.

It was otherwise in the succeeding summers, when,
although disgrace did not accompany failure before
prowess such as is seldom associated in school elevens,
there was yet lamentable lack of steadiness in the
Harrow defence, combined with strength either mis-
applied or wanting in force, such as led partisans to
charge all on the aforesaid unpopular superannuation
rule, which demanded due progress in school work, or as
an alternative prescribed dismissal to the sturdy youth
burning to gain that distinction before the M.C.C. at
Lord's, which lack of early training, or, in some few
cases, entire distaste for work, had denied him in pupil-
room. And then, to make defeat, as it were, inevitable,
Harrow fielding got slow, while indifferent boy bowling
was not backed up by the sure catching we are on
the whole accustomed to associate with elevens which,
win, lose, or draw, leave no stone unturned to represent their school with credit. But the marvel to a
writer who studies the subject is why more capable
bowlers have not resulted from the careful training
which at any rate has sustained Harrow credit in other
departments. And this although we are free to admit
that numbers of moderate boy bowlers may be cited
who did good work, but whom even their warmest admirers

cannot have destined for future fame. Exception to the
general rule may be claimed for the fast bowlers Cobden
and Shand ; while Money and Carnac sustained the older-
fashioned underhand. But although fair length slow
round-arm has from time to time done good service,
W. F. Maitland to wit, yet we have not lately been
able to boast of a Henry Arkwright or a Plowden.

In batting, so far as style is concerned, the palm must
be conferred on C. F. Buller, who has played several
unsurpassed innings. But it is on I. D. Walker, the
captain of the eleven which lost the historic match in
1862, so nearly pulled out of the fire by the fine batting
of W. F. Maitland,* that the burden of sustaining the
Harrow name has devolved ; and in a long career the Middlesex captain has more than upheld fame early earned at
school, and fully justified the opinion expressed by George
Freeman, the famous Yorkshire bowler, who, writing in
John Lillywhite's *Guide*, stated Mr. I. D. Walker to be
the best timer of fast bowling that he has encountered
during his varied experience. His brother, Mr. R. D.
Walker, on the other hand, was the best batsman on a
difficult wicket that Harrow produced between 1856 and
1861. Nor can these sketches be concluded without a
reference to the most popular figure in the Lancashire
cricket world, Mr. A. N. Hornby, who first evinced his
great hitting power on the hill-side at Harrow.

It is certain that any complete list of Harrow
cricketers would find a counterpart at Eton, where a
long roll of fine players stands unsurpassed by those
trained at any other school. †

---

* M.P. for Breconshire, 1880–84.

† Mr. Herbert Jenner is one of the first Etonians who took high
place in the cricket world. He excelled as a wicket-keeper, using
no gloves, and standing up on the most bumpy and treacherous

The pride of Harrow should nevertheless consist in the fact that when adverse fortune frowned, and the

ground to all the bowling of his time. He played for Eton in a winning match with Harrow in 1823, and is now enjoying a hale old age in Gloucestershire. Lord Bessborough has expressed to us his high opinion of the Etonian cricketers of 1825-26, who overcame Harrow in the days of Edward Grimston. Mr. C. G. Taylor, it is well known, learned his cricket in the playing fields of Eton, and contended at Lord's against Harrow in 1834. An all-round cricketer who adopted a fine style of batting, and excelled beyond all his amateur contemporaries (see Bolland, *Cricket Notes*, p. 58), Mr. Taylor will be known to future generations of cricketers, not alone as a leading proficient, but as a coadjutor of the Hon. Frederick Ponsonby, in his efforts to retain a Gentlemen and Players match in the M.C.C. programme. Mr. Charles Taylor scored 89 in 1843 against the Players, while in 1846 he made 23 and 44 (*ibid.* p. 35). These triumphs gained at that epoch against Lillywhite, Hillyer, and Clarke, speak for themselves. In the Eton eleven with Mr. C. G. Taylor in 1834, we find a popular evangelistic prelate, the Bishop of Liverpool, J. C. Ryle, and Mr. H. Kirwan, the famous amateur bowler, whom Mr. Pycroft (*Cricket Field*, p. 213) saw displace a bail, sending it 30 yards. As early as 1835 the name of Pickering becomes prominent in Etonian cricket, while, as a set-off against that of J. C. Ryle, the eleven benefited by the assistance of A. D. Wagner, the High Church leader and Tractarian Minister of St. Paul's Church in Brighton. In 1837 a remarkable bowler hailed from the banks of the Thames, Mr. W. de St. Croix, combining with the Captain, Mr. W. Pickering, to win many of the Eton matches, while, four years later, conspicuous prowess was displayed by the team that boasted a bowler like Mr. G. Yonge, and a captain such as the Rev. Sir Emilius Bayley, at present an incumbent in Paddington. In the Eton and Harrow match of 1841 this gentleman scored 152 runs, thereby entailing a crushing defeat on his opponents. We hasten on to times within the ken of many living when these lines are written. Of Harvey Fellows, the fast bowler in 1842, whose pace was such that a legend very lately existed at Harrow to the effect that the old Etonian was not allowed to take a run—and this on the score of danger to the batsman's person. We can credit the danger when ground was not scientifically prepared, as it now is at Lord's, but batsmen had to take their chance in the *mêlée*. Bishop Patteson, who perished in pursuit of duty in Polynesia, had been a member of the Eton eleven in 1843-44, after which we meet with the names celebrated in English society to the present hour; J. W. Chitty, the judge; Mr. W. S. Deacon, the well-known city banker; Mr. E. W. Blore, late Tutor of Trinity College, Cam-

school had fallen below 100, high spirit and steady
resolve was most prominent.   It was in the year 1843

bridge, lately elected to the presidency of his University Cricket
Club. Judge Chitty is best known amongst Etonian cricket
records as an excellent wicket-keeper; Mr. Deacon, as a successful batsman, whose average in the Public School matches
was 35 and 5 over for 7 innings; while Mr. Blore was an excellent bowler, whose name was the terror of Wykehamists and
Harrovians alike. These cricketers were in their school eleven
between 1845 and 1848, and the two following years a bowler was
found in the person of Mr. C. Thackeray, who lowered the dark-
blue flag two years running at Lord's. In 1851 Mr. G. R. Dupuis,
the famous Etonian mentor, played for the place of his education,
and since his time the Etonian cricketers have continued to rein-
force the University elevens, and get more than their share of
places amidst those Gentlemen selected to cope with the Players.
T. E. Bagge and Mr. F. H. Norman were amongst the leading batsmen thirty years ago, while the present Lord Lyttelton and Mr. R.
A. H. Mitchell have been unsurpassed as batsmen before or since.
Probably more competent cricketers asked to name a second to
Mr. W. G. Grace will name R. A. H. Mitchell, than render such
tribute to the professional genius of George Parr, Carpenter, or
Hayward, while none will deny that when C. G. Lyttelton did
play an innings it was a rare treat for the beholders. The
triumphs of Alfred Lubbock (whose style rivalled C. F. Buller's),
of the late C. J. Ottaway, the most scientific batsman who of late
years hailed from Eton, of A. S. Teape, the fast bowler, of Lord
Harris, a notable English champion against the Australians, G.
H. Longman, A. Tabor, A. W. Ridley, F. M. Buckland, the
brothers Edward and Alfred Lyttelton — C. I. Thornton, the
hardest hitter of whose doings any reliable record remains—W.
F. Forbes, the Hon. E. Bligh, Mr. C. T. Studd and his two
brothers, are as household words in English cricket circles. As
at Harrow, few great bowlers have of late years learned to play
cricket on the ground which, Mr. Pycroft tells us (in the *Cricket
Field*, p. 130), has always, from its easy character, favoured a free
style of play. Such, as above described, were the opponents against
whom the Harrow elevens have waged, on the whole, an equal contest, the general average of the rank and file being about on a par,
even if more brilliant batsmen have hailed from Eton. It is a
remarkable fact that the last three matches between these two
schools have been unfinished. That in 1883 was left drawn in
the favour of Light Blue, who were baulked of their victory by
the joint aid of Greatorex and the weather. Eton had no great
player to rely on when engaged in an up-hill game in 1884, also
stopped by rain. But it is due to an eleven mostly made up of
beginners to recall the fact that they had previously redeemed

that Bob Grimston spoke of the victorious hill, Eton
and Winchester having both lost their matches by a few
runs. Yet at that moment the shadow was nearly at its
deepest which temporarily obscured the Dark Blue
prestige.

Enough has been said to indicate that nothing approaching perfection is claimed for Harrow even at the
game more particularly her own. Other schools have
equally well sustained themselves in the mimic strife,
while the number of first-class cricketers trained on the
hill has varied more than might be expected, when such
results are taken as the outcome of careful practice conducted amidst much enthusiasm. But be the reason
what it may, cricket at Harrow continues to foster the
feeling of brotherhood—we had almost said patriotism
—which animates each young Harrovian, and which
Lord Bessborough and the late Mr. Grimston have
done so much to foster.

It is notorious that this unity has been not the sudden growth of any particular period, and that these
patrons of the noble sport have re-invigorated and sustained it by means of their own character and popularity.
In Mr. Grimston's case, the combination of truth and
courage which stood out so prominent was specially
engaging to youth. A man of few words, the guardian
of the philathlet, as Mr. Bowen has called him,* could

their position when playing Winchester, after having failed utterly
in the first innings. The Harrow bowling seems, however, to have
been beyond the average in 1884, and the batting and fielding fair
all through.

* R. G.
Still the balls ring upon the sunlit grass,
　　Still the big elms, deep shadowed, watch the play ;
And ordered game and loyal conflict pass
　　The hours of May.

22

nevertheless rebuke the vanity he despised, or encourage
the honest strivings with which he sympathised, in the
shortest sentence imaginable.   And, indeed, the sympathy would often arise when least hoped for and
most desired ; while even disapproval was rendered

But the game's guardian, mute, nor heeding more
   What suns may gladden, and what airs may blow,
Friend, teacher, playmate, helper, counsellor,
   Lies resting now.

" Over "—they move, as bids their fieldman's art ;
   With shifted scene the strife begins anew ;
" Over "—we seem to hear him, but his part
   Is over, too.

Dull the best speed, and vain the surest grace—
   So seemed it ever—till there moved along
Brimmed hat, and cheering presence, and tried face
   Amid the throng.

He swayed his realm of grass, and planned, and wrought ;
   Warned rash intruders from the tended sward ;
A workman, deeming, for the friends he taught,
   No service hard.

He found, behind first failure, more success ;
   Cheered stout endeavour more than languid skill ;
And ruled the heart of boyhood with the stress
   Of helpful will.

Or, standing at our hard-fought game, would look,
   Silent and patient, drowned in hope and fear,
Till the lips quivered, and the strong voice shook
   With low glad cheer.

Well played.   His life was honester than ours ;
   We scheme, he worked, we hesitate, he spoke :
His rough-hewn stem held no concealing flowers,
   But grain of oak.

No earthly umpire speaks, his grave above ;
   And thanks are dumb, and praise is all too late ;
That worth and truth, that manhood and that love
   Are hid, and wait.

Sleep gently, where thou sleepest, dear old friend ;
   Think, if thou thinkest, on the bright days past ;
Yet loftier Love, and worthier Truth attend
   What more thou hast !

1884.   (E. E. Bowen, Esq., on the late
                                 Hon. R. Grimston.)

more palatable by the timely jest, delivered with a humour quite unapproachable, and with effect such as those who knew not the man can never understand.

Those old Harrovians who chanced to be present at one of the autumnal goose matches,* under the presidency of Mr. C. O. Eaton, will not forget the scene, when, after hearing a certain song, Mr. Grimston announced that he had found a melody forgotten for thirty years. "Why, it's the long lost tune, and belongs to the Tie match." This was announced with all the gravity which those well-known tones could assume.

The narration of an incident, trivial may be to the chance reader, must be excused on account of its characteristic nature, which will be appreciated by those who have been under the spell of the friend we of Harrow School all honoured so much in life, and now desire to cherish in memory. For what is history if it contain not the record of those who influenced their fellow-men in ages past, and whose fame and good deeds, apparently notorious for all time, would, if not placed on record, be but sparsely appreciated, if remembered at all, when the sun of present notoriety has set ?

Hence in a Harrow Cricket chapter, we make more than passing allusions to the life of the Hon. Robert Grimston. Mr. Grimston's enthusiasm for Harrow was such that he was latterly quite unable to witness a contest which in former years he had inspired by his well-known presence. The popular idea at Harrow was that Mr. Grimston spent the time at the neighbouring church of St. John's Wood; but as a matter of fact he

* The Goose Match is the last game of cricket played in the year at Harrow. A goose dinner follows.

generally went into the country, ill at ease until he
knew the best or worst, as the case might be. On
one occasion, as he informed the writer, he tried Buxton.
Boys are not unnaturally prone to admire courage; and
if any one virtue predominated in this Harrow cricketer's
character, it was contempt for pain. We remember two
several occasions when R. D. H. Elphinstone and, in
later times, W. B. Money struck him violently when
standing on the off-side of the practice wickets. Although
the blows would either of them have sent ordinary people,
aye, and young ones, too, limping to the Pavilion, all that
escaped Bob Grimston's lips was the laconic expression,
"What fine off-hitting!" And here we take the opportunity of correcting the impression still held by some
onlookers at Lords, who believed that Bob Grimston
stopped the boys from hitting freely. On the contrary,
he condoned even unscientific hitting if it was good.
But he did resolutely set his face against half-formed
boys, who could scarcely wield a full-sized bat, attempt-
ing prematurely to emulate Buller or Hornby.

It has been erroneously assumed by those unacquainted with Harrow that Messrs. Ponsonby and Grimston were in the habit of choosing the school eleven.
The mistake is a fundamental one, inasmuch as not only
was the matter in question religiously left to the head of
the eleven, but successive captains will attest how difficult it has been to extract an opinion from these experts
as to the merits of competing cricketers. We ourselves

---

* Mr. Grimston, having inculcated the principles of cricket,
expected his pupils to exercise due resource in the application.
To a too-confiding aspirant, who asked, "How, Sir, should you
play a shooter?" the mentor replied, "Put my bat in the block-
hole and lean on it." A perfect receipt, supposing the ball were
warranted not to rise suddenly. The good-tempered sarcasm will
be appreciated by every cricketer who knew Mr. Grimston.

have seen Mr. Grimston on the Saturday afternoon
before Lord's anxiously awaiting the decision as to who
was to fill the last vacancy in the eleven. If choice fell
upon one of his game, the great mentor would
chuckle with satisfaction, and look with renewed hope
to the coming struggle. It followed, nevertheless, in
the very nature of things, that any promising colt
singled out by Mr. Grimston had a fair trial; and the
same may be said of Mr. Ponsonby's selections. But
the boys themselves were never in leading-strings. Of
Mr. Grimston, as a cricketer, it is said that in old days,
when grounds were rough, he went by time rather than
by runs, which, nevertheless, came in due proportion.
Mr. Grimston went in first against the Players in 1849,
and in a winning match scored 18 against Wisden,
Clarke, Lillywhite, and Hillyer.

Such considerations as have led us to dwell on Mr.
Grimston's influence, also cause us to recount the services of Henry Anderson to Harrow cricket as being
worthy of preservation in the opinion of those able to
judge. Towards the latter part of Dr. Longley's time an
idle Harrovian passed through school without making the
mark that his abilities warranted. But he, in common
with other gifted minds, cherished a strong devotion to
Harrow; and this, as he was a good cricketer, took the
form of joining in the boys' games and helping them to
prepare for the ordeal at Lord's. To effect this, he
would frequently, when residing at Barnet, walk over
with his friend Henry Ashley (brother to Lord Shaftesbury) and play in the games. Somewhat of a Bohemian
by choice, Mr. Anderson had occupied his leisure by
observation and reading, so that in general information
he had few superiors; excelling to a high degree in

knowledge connected with sport and natural history, in which he was almost a second St. John.

Naturally a character of a type so taking to youth generally attracted the Harrow boys, who learnt to know him at cricket. Despite the above-mentioned restless nature, Mr. Anderson's devotion to the old school was so marked that he became the *Fidus Achates* of no less a personage than Bob Grimston himself, who always spoke of him with affection, and rejoiced that before he died prematurely Henry Anderson's life was solaced by the joys of family life, a compensation in his case for a somewhat troublous career, such as is frequently the lot of those whose dispositions are too generous, and who act too much on impulse.

In the view of old Harrovians such as Lord Bessborough and Mr. C. O. Eaton, Mr. Anderson has claims to mention in the story of Harrow cricket. Lord Bessborough's influence in the cricket world, originating from his Harrow boyhood, is unique. But for his steady resolve that the Gentlemen should not allow their annual match with the Players to lapse, there was a time when it might have been abandoned and dire calamity have been thus brought on the cricket world, which had to dread indifference from its votaries when great matches depended upon long subscription lists.[*] Discussing the many cricketers he has known on the Middlesex hill-side, Lord Bessborough has said that he can remember " several good players, but only one who stood out beyond all others, viz. the famous physician, Dr. Bence Jones. A tall powerful lissom young fellow, Mr. Bence Jones was a natural cricketer, and, moreover, applied his strong intelligence to working out the prin-

[*] Bolland, *Cricket Notes*, p. 29.

ciples of batting." It was in converse with Mr. Bence
Jones that Lord Bessborough learned the science which
he has imparted to the younger generation. He was then
taught, he says, the difference between the drive and
the hit, the cut and the off-hit; how and when to play
back; also the proper length for balls of various paces.

To those acquainted with the almost magical faculty
which Lord Bessborough possesses for imparting knowledge as regards cricket in the space of a few days, it
will be interesting to learn how the teacher himself owed
the groundwork of his knowledge to a brother Harrovian,
famous in a more serious walk of life, but not hitherto
known as one of a roll of fame on which are blazoned
the names of Ponsonby, Grimston, Nicholson, Daniel
Lang, and Walker.

Mr. Bence Jones lived as a boy in Ireland, and, leaving
for home before his companions, never represented
Harrow at Lord's. He gave the game up when at Cambridge University. But the unimpeachable testimony
of his grateful pupil and friend bids us acquaint other
Harrovians how highly the sage doctor of medicine
excelled at cricket in the spring-time of his life.

Later cricket records, more or less worthy of repeti-
tion, are so numerous that they can find no complete
mention here; but as the Harrow bowlers have been
somewhat scarce, we are constrained to speak of the
few who in the last thirty years have done great things
for the school. Prominent amidst this category stand
the brothers Lang—George and Robert, the latter bearing the palm as the straightest boy bowler of his great
pace who ever came from Harrow. Judged by public
performances he stands in the category with Jackson and
Tarrant, whose contemporary professional pre-eminence

is notorious. The writer will not forget how, at a Surrey eleven match on Kennington Oval, H. H. Stephenson threw Mr. Lang his cap when the old Harrovian fast bowler lowered three wickets in succession.

Nor would it be just to forget what F. C. Cobden's fast bowling did on behalf of Harrow, or to leave unmentioned his great success when he pulled the University match out of the fire for Cambridge, earning a renown which will not fade.

There is a story that a small Harrow boy, talking of F. C. Cobden, was asked by his parents what relationship his hero claimed to the great Cobden. The lad indignantly replied, " He *is* the great Cobden."

Another notable Harrovian covered his school and his own name with laurels at Lords ; but destined to a short life, he lies in the beautiful cemetery at Cannes. The writer, for one, did not stand unmoved at the grave of the Hon. J. G. Amherst.* And, indeed, it is remarkable how many young ardent spirits have been quenched, as it seems to ourselves, prematurely, several leaving behind them reputations which entitle them to an honourable mention in the archives of Harrow cricket. We have incidentally mentioned Henry Arkwright and A. W. T. Daniel, the former the first, as he was the best, of that long list of slow round-arm bowlers who did battle for Harrow. An Alpine accident caused the death which his many friends deplore. Mr. Daniel, on the other hand, famous

---

* Reference to the success of Harrow fast bowlers would not be complete were the name of G. H. Hodgson omitted. In 1858 he scattered an Eton eleven at Lords, winning the match for his side. Again, Shand, who, in the darker days of Harrow cricket, bowled so pluckily against the best Eton elevens of later years, must not be forgotten, the more that the gallant fight he made for his school has not been followed by the leisure which would otherwise have gained him a high place in the cricket world.

for his great innings of 112 not out against Eton in
1860, was a veritable Crichton amongst his compeers;
but a sudden change in the habits of life, entered on
that he might cultivate his remarkable powers of mind,
proved fatal to a delicate constitution. The names of
these true sons of Harrow are perpetuated in her school
chapel; while that of W. C. Clayton, of the 9th
Lancers, the active all-round cricketer and good wicket-
keeper, is commemorated by a stone in the parish
church-yard. Despite an abiding renown gained as one
of the more promising British cavalry officers, he was
not the man to underrate the affection of old Harrow
associates. He met his death in India at polo.

Prominent amongst younger men stands Mr. A. J.
Webbe, whose single combat (for the fortune of war
rendered it almost so) with Eton is remembered as by
no means one of the least honourable defeats undergone
at Lord's. With the single exception of W. F. Maitland's innings in 1862, when an up-hill game was well
played under more than ordinary difficulties,* we can
remember no individual success more remarkable than
Mr. Webbe's. Very properly he straightway became
canonised as a hero amongst the Harrow worthies,
school and town, so that when Lord George Hamilton,
the popular Harrovian M.P. for Middlesex, advising his
supporters in 1880 how to cope with proceedings on the
part of his opponents, which he deemed disingenuous,
exclaimed amidst great applause, "*As a boy called Webbe*
used to meet sneaking underhand bowling, by hitting
hard with a straight bat," the allusion brought down
the house.

---

* It rained hard over-night, so that the Harrow innings was
completed on wet ground.

The actual results of the various school contests it would be foreign to our scheme to give in detail. Suffice it to say, that out of 24 matches with Winchester Harrow won 13, and the Wykehamists 11 ; while 57 games with the Etonians show that each school has won 24, while 9 have remained unfinished.* Defeat—while every effort to

---

* On one occasion the Wykehamists were seen on the Harrow ground. This was in 1837, and, though defeated, they were meeting their foes at a disadvantage. 1842, 1843, 1848, 1849, 1853, and 1854, were the only years in which Harrow won *both* their matches at Lords against Eton and Winchester. The earlier games with Eton do not seem to have yielded much incident. In 1822 the dark blues ran 15 short runs, while there was some tall hitting in 1827, Lord Grimston (the present Earl Verulam) scoring three fives, and his brother, the Hon. E. Grimston, three threes off an over of 6 balls delivered by a Mr. Broadhead. In 1838, Harrow beat Winchester by an innings and 54 runs, Eton beat Harrow by an innings and 30 runs, while Winchester defeated Eton by an innings and 34 runs. In 1855, George Lang, bowling for Harrow, disposed of 7 Etonian wickets for 17 runs. His analysis showed also that he bowled 66 balls and had 6 maiden overs ; all seven wickets were clean bowled. In 1856 and 1857 the Etonians were not allowed to play. We have recounted the later matches elsewhere, and it only remains to say that, in 1877, Mr. H. E. Meek (the hardest hitter the author has ever seen in a Harrow eleven) scored 27 in seven minutes, and that four Etonians (1841, Sir E. Bayley, 152 ; 1869, C. J. Ottaway, 108 ; 1871, A. W. Ridley, 117 ; 1876, W. F. Forbes, 113) have obtained over a hundred against Harrow, while A. W. T. Daniel stands alone amidst the Harrovians for his 112 not out, in 1860. (These details we owe to the Supplement of *Harrow Notes* published July 10, 1884). It should not be forgotten that Mr. W. Meyrick scored 146 not out for Winchester against Harrow in 1826. Several elevens seem to have deserved well of Harrow, but the crown of honour should on the whole, we think, be given to those two teams which came to Lords in 1842 and 1843, when numbers were down to 87, and literally swept the board, Eton and Winchester each returning beaten. Mr. Haygarth tells us that the Etonians in 1842 were, he thinks, stronger than Harrow, but Gathorne's bowling, backed up by W. Nicholson's wicket-keeping, pulled their side through. Ground, our informant adds, was rough compared to that in vogue now, while tubular gloves had not been invented. Pads even were small. Mr. Haygarth cannot say much for the second eleven strength in those days, and ascribes this double overthrow of the large school at Eton to the teaching of Ponsonby and

avert it should be exercised—is by no means the chief cloud in the horizon of Harrow cricket. We dread much more than even any succession of disasters a decline of the spirit inculcated by Ponsonby and Grimston—a carelessness as to practice and an absence of steady resolution under ill success and discouragement. And to ensure this, not only must first principles be studied and adhered to so far as the game is concerned, but the fellowship between past and present, which is the secret of all brotherhood, as well as of enthusiasm, and hence of much good cricket, will, we hope, survive. Neither men nor boys will strive hard to gain that which their compeers appraise sparingly, still less will any abiding anxiety be evinced to become one of an eleven whose style is bad, and does not, therefore, arm the members with an ability to hold their own in London and the universities. "How did you *play?*" was Mr. Robert Grimston's constant answer to the young Harrovian who narrated a batting triumph which the mentor knew must have in some sort have been due to the luck of our national game.

How to keep alive the better traditions of Harrow cricket is not, fortunately, far to seek. We have read again and again eloquent prose periods, and tenderly-expressed thoughts in verse, which tell of the schoolboy's sorrow when he throws aside the bat and bids farewell to his old school for ever. Now fifty per cent. of us fortunately need do nothing of the kind. Thanks

Grimston, which was even then paramount. The Eton elevens of 1842-3 wore light blue rosettes bearing their time-honoured motto, *Floreat Etona*, which, after the second defeat in 1843, a disrespectful Harrovian is said to have translated "Eton's floored." We do not hear that he was sent to extra school. That eminent scholar, the late Sir A. Grant, was in the Harrow elevens of 1843 and 1844.

to the contiguity of London, those desirous of renewing
the experiences of their youth can do so, provided they
have an hour or two of leisure; while overlooking the
cricket-ground stands the Old-Harrovian Club, a place
of greeting, where, if the welcome be but homely, it is
none the less pleasing.

Nor, speaking from experience, do we find the better
Harrow cricketers desert the green sward prematurely,
men like Messrs. W. H. Hadow, F. E. R. Fryer,
Spencer Gore, and W. S. Paterson, for instance, finding
time to keep up their reputations amidst the duties
and occupations of life. We hope a similar attachment
to the game will keep M. C. Kemp, the enthusiastic
and successful Oxford Captain, in the cricket world.

The Harrow Wanderers offer an annual inducement
not to quite forsake bat and ball. Numerous old, but
we fear, not any present Harrovians amongst our
readers have had the opportunity of joining one
of the Harrow Wanderer tours. Beginning in the
South, they have passed Northwards, and rejoiced in
the warm welcome annually given by friends at Leeds,
York, Durham, Lincoln, and Derby. Nothing has
struck the present writer more than the enthusiasm
with which the team is always received.

To some degree, the hospitality thrust upon the Wandering and, to coin a word, *fast-bowlerless* Harrovians is
due to the prestige of certain names well known on
the green sward; but we venture to suggest that the
hill itself has something to do with a popularity such
as individual character, however high, cannot command.
Englishmen are proverbially proud of their institutions,
and the Wanderers themselves would take it as a far
higher compliment were they sure that their friends

desired—as we believe they *do*—to honour the Harrow name rather than that of any individual reputation.

The Harrow Wanderers date from Dr. H. M. Butler's epoch, Mr. H. St. Leger and Mr. C. J. Smith being those originators who, handing the post of Secretary over to the writer, have since seen their efforts fructify under Mr. I. D. Walker's popular care.

We have but one criticism to make as regards present management, and it is this—Let the dates be so arranged that Harrow boys *in statu pupillari* may join in the tour, when their cricket abilities are such as to allow of their being chosen. An institution will then have been founded, not a delightful gathering of old school friends organised. It is due to older Harrow that we should state how this prosperous club is the outcome of a former effort of the same description, for which Lord Bessborough wrote the song, from which we have already quoted, but which boasts the following stanza :—

> Though some may feel that age is stealing o'er them,
> Still here at least they can heart and voice unite
> With those whose lives are opening out before them,
> For, old and young, we are all Harrow boys to-night.

And, indeed, the Harrow Wanderers welcome all ages into their ranks.

We have prolonged these remarks far beyond our intended scope, but they speak of the very life of modern Harrow existence, leading, as we believe, to an apt fulfilment of the duties of life, because the boy has contracted habits of self-control and obedience, and, above all, of patience, which is a necessary virtue in the world into which each school-boy passes.

CHAPTER XV.

HARROVIANA.

H allowed pile our fathers raised,
A ncient fane where God is praised,
R esting-place of saints of old,
R efuge of the living fold,
O h may ages yet to come
W orship in this sacred home!

C rown of all the neighbouring lands,
H igh and lifted up it stands;
U nto Heaven its lofty finger
R aised, forbids us here to linger;
C alling with its silent voice,
"H eaven or Hell awaits thy choice."

Edward Scott, Esq.

THE elevated spire of St. Mary's can be seen from
every point around London whence a view of Harrow is
obtainable, and is, therefore, more associated with the
spot in the public mind than even the venerable Elizabethan school building. Thus it is that Mr. Edward
Scott's inspiring lines head this chapter, destined as
the closing portion of the book is to present Harrow in
some of the various phases which have escaped direct
mention during the narration of our story. As we have
shown in Chapter I., the earlier records all point to an
ecclesiastical connection as the cause of local rise from
obscurity.

To the learned Dr. Parr's mind the name of his old school suggested a joint idea, scriptural and classical, the hill " shining, in his imagination, with the united glories of Zion and Parnassus."*

Although the readers of this book will probably carry away no such glowing images, they may possibly connect Harrow more with the history of their country, acknowledge its connection with literature, and establish in their minds a link with the past, not bounded even by mediæval chronicles, but having origin in the mists of antiquarian research.

Seeking for such affinity between the present and past, the reader of John Lyon's Will alights on mention of the common chest, wherein was to be deposited the school archives, consisting of deeds, evidences, and writings. This ancient depository of Harrow secrets

* Field, *Life of Parr*, vol. ii. p. 336. This being our last allusion to Dr. Parr, we take the opportunity of giving the following story, which the writer heard from an old pupil of Dr. Butler of Shrewsbury. Dr. Parr received an invitation to dine with his brother scholar and pedagogue, and when he arrived, having brushed and washed, he was conducted to Mrs. Butler's presence. Now the visitor was monstrously fond of roast goose, and certainly thought that he detected the familiar flavour ascending from the lower regions. On his way upstairs he met the housekeeper, whom he thanked for remembering his weakness. " Oh, Sir," said Biddy, " Mrs. Butler has done this to surprise you, for I never saw the goose." When a similar remark from the lady of the house led the good Doctor to bestow the grateful outpourings of his soul upon the cook, he received for reply the crushing rejoinder, " No goose has been cooked in this kitchen." Whence, then, was the savoury odour which impregnated the whole house? " Why, the doctor's scratch wig is burnt bald!" cried an excited domestic who chanced to enter the ante-room and witness a holocaust ridiculous to contemplate, but which explained the mystery. He had unfortunately left that appendage too near the fire. Dr. Parr was accustomed to tell his Shrewsbury friend: " Porson is the first Grecian; everyone knows the second; you, Butler, are third."

was for the first time archæologically examined in the autumn of 1883, by Mr. Edward Scott, and he has thus rendered our present task possible. There stood the wood and iron-work as contracted for in 1611 ; while, as the event has proved, the old chest was the depository of one of the most interesting collections of school archives that the British Museum authorities have ever deciphered.

Having recorded such Royal visits to Harrow and its neighbourhood as have occurred during the progress of our story, a notable omission would be made if Queen Elizabeth's sojourn at Osterley, Sir Thomas Gresham's stately home, escaped mention. Within six years after Her Majesty had granted the charter to Lyon (viz. in 1577), a magnificent entertainment was given by the City magnate to his Queen, whereat a play was acted,[*] not, we may feel sure, without the presence of neighbouring gentry, faithful to the throne, amongst whom we know none stood higher than John Lyon of Preston. The Virgin Queen appears to have been delighted with her reception, but said that the court before the house would look better divided with a wall. Whereupon Sir Thomas Gresham sent for workmen from London, who during the night made the addition according to royal suggestion, the Sovereign and her courtiers expressing much surprise when they awoke next morning, although one of the household was heard to say " that it was no wonder that he who could build a 'Change should so soon change a building."[†]

* Lyson, *Environs of London*, vol. iii. p. 26, quoting Fuller, Nichol's *Royal Progresses*, and a pamphlet by one Churchyard.
† The story occurs in Fuller's *Middlesex Worthies*. We need hardly add that Sir Thomas Gresham built the London Royal Exchange.

As Osterley Park is within a drive of Harrow, and is close to Heston—that part of the Pure Vale celebrated for its wheat—it is worthy of consideration whether the occupants of the mansion contributed towards the Free School expansion between 1571–84.

Sir Thomas Gresham was succeeded at Osterley, according to the Heston parish register, by Lord Justice Coke, whose daughter was christened in the church in 1597. Again, George, Earl of Desmond, and his Countess inhabited the mansion in 1639, while Sir William Waller, the Parliamentary General, died there much respected in 1668.

A very clever man, and a great projector as to coinage, who held a controversy with Locke on the subject, one Dr. Nicholas Barbon, dwelt at Osterley during the closing years of the seventeenth century, after which Sir Francis Child restored its civic traditions, which in the present owner's Lord Jersey's hands are allied with noble connections.* The late Dowager Duchess of Cleveland died there in 1883, over ninety years of age. The Villiers family, who gained Osterley by an alliance with the Childs, have by no means eschewed Harrow as a place of education, although the present Earl is a distinguished Etonian.

We have striven to apportion the interest of the Harrow papers between the various periods of history to which they belong, and, therefore, few addenda remain for production here ; but we are so impressed with the support rendered by certain well-known families to Harrow and its surroundings, that we cannot forbear from making mention of some of the more prominent

* These facts will be found narrated in Lyson, *Environs of London*, vol. iii. pp. 24–30.

names, which if not mentioned before in detail, yet connect themselves with our story. For instance, the last
glimpses of the Gerard family are necessarily interesting.
The school archives tell us that the Lady Gerard on
the decease of her lord, a school governor in 1704,
found in his cupboard two separate sums of £3 6s. 3d.
and £55 12s. 9d., and handed them over to the
Harrow School governors, one of whom was the last
baronet of the Gerard family, viz. Sir Cheek Gerard.

Henceforward the Rushout name appears as a
main support of Harrow fortunes. They had by
purchase and intermarriage become owners of Flambards, and as the chief people in Harrow exercised
the influence which naturally pertains to any lord of the
manor in a country town. Natural capabilities accen-
tuated this in the case of Sir John Rushout, the opponent of Sir Robert Walpole in Parliament, whose
energies found scope for performance of his duties connected with the guardianship of John Lyon's Free
School.

The elder branch of the Roualts—for so the Rushout
family were called in France—were possessors of large
estates in Picardy and Normandy. Related to the
Dukes of Normandy, they retained their property until
the French Revolution. A cadet of the family, after
residence in Flanders, came to England in James I.'s
time, and was created a baronet by Charles II. Sir
John Rushout, however, could not conscientiously
requite the Stewart king's favours by supporting
James II. at the close of his reign, when, deeming
liberty at stake, Sir John Rushout raised a regiment in
support of William III. This baronet married a Miss
Pitt, of Harrow, and so became possessed of Flam-

bards, which his wife's family had purchased of the
Gerards.* He was Member for Evesham during thirty
years (except in the Convention Parliament, when he
sat for the county of Worcester). In May 1697, Sir
John was appointed Ambassador to Constantinople, but
died before leaving England. His son was the school
governor, with whose services to Harrow the minutes
literally teem. After Sir Robert Walpole's fall in 1742,
Sir John Rushout became Lord of the Treasury, and
then Treasurer of the Navy. Being of remarkable amiability, he flourished to a green old age, dying ninety-one
years old in 1775. His son, fifth baronet, became Lord
Northwick in 1797 ; and the family has never ceased to
serve Harrow School to the utmost of their abilities.
The second Lord Northwick resided more at The Park,
Harrow, than at Northwick Park, Worcester. He was
an antiquarian and munificent patron of the fine arts,
his picture gallery at Thirlestane House, Cheltenham,
being justly celebrated.† Born in 1770, this venerable
nobleman died a bachelor in 1859. The third Lord
Northwick, re-chosen governor after the Public Schools
Act became law, still holding the office, was born in
1811.‡

Considering that by statute the governors of Harrow
were obliged to be drawn from the neighbourhood, it is
remarkable how many distinguished families are mixed
up in the history of the school and its surroundings.
The Waldos, for instance, have a story which we cannot
find space to tell at length, but it is of deep interest.

* Dodd, *English Peerage*, pp. 463–64.
†.This nobleman was known in Harrow for affability to his
neighbours and kindness to the boys. See *Harrow Gazette*,
February 1859.
‡ For above information see Burke's *Peerage*, p. 833.

During the last two centuries it has ever had one or
more of its members distinguished as city dignitaries, or
eminent in the law, the Church, the army, or science.
Descended, according to tradition, from Thomas Waldo
of Lyons, who in the twelfth century denounced the
Roman Church, one Peter Waldo is believed to have
been the first of the family who came to England,
fleeing from Alva's tyrannies, which rendered the Low
Countries intolerable to men of intellect. In a house at
Mitcham, Surrey, may still be seen a carved chimney-
piece whereon is cut " Peter Waldo, 1575 " or 3 (the
last figure being imperfect). A grandson of this refugee,
Daniel Waldo, married at Harrow in 1625 (the family
settling in that neighbourhood), was one of the school
governors; and we find him signing minutes in 1660, the
year before his death.   But his brother, Sir Edward, was
a more prominent character. Purchasing Daniel Waldo's
property in Cheapside, he erected a large messuage there.
On the 29th of October he was knighted at his own
house in Cheapside by Charles II., on his entertaining
the Sovereign, together with the Princesses Mary and
Anne and the Duchess of York, who, from a canopy of
state in front of his house, saw the Lord Mayor's Show
pass through Cheapside on its way to Guildhall.*

Sir Edward had a country house near Pinner, and
was one of the Harrow School governors up to the
close of the seventeenth century. Dying in 1707, aged
seventy-five, Sir Edward Waldo was buried at Harrow,
where a marble monument is erected to his memory.
An intermarriage with the Sibthorp family occurred in

---

* These details are taken from *Notes on the Family of Waldo*,
p. 6, printed for private circulation. The account of Sir Edward
Waldo entertaining the Royal family is in Strickland's *Queens of
England*, vol. vii. p. 37.

this generation. Hence the name Waldo-Sibthorp inherited by the well-known Colonel, for thirty years
Member for Lincoln, and being likewise known as a
popular Harrovian.

The next family claiming our notice is that of Bucknall, again and again appearing in the school records.
As forming an alliance with the Grimstons, and so producing a race of faithful Harrovians, they deserve more
than passing attention. We have elsewhere told how
the carriage of a governor bearing the name of Bucknall was wrecked by the Harrow boys in 1771 because
after Dr. Sumner's death he was supposed to favour
Benjamin Heath rather than Samuel Parr as Harrow
head-master.

The second Lord Verulam told the assembled company at the Tercentenary Festival in 1871, how his
ancestor, when in conclave with Dr. Heath, the unpopular choice of 1771, had to learn that his carriage
had been filled with faggots and sent blazing down the
hill.* The Grimstons, however, requited this questionable service by steady support rendered to Harrow. The
earlier bills in Dr. George Butler's famous lists are
never without a Grimston ; while a later generation can
and will tell what it owes to the Gorhambury family.

Amongst distinguished Harrovians hitherto unmentioned we may mention Malthus, the writer on Population, who was a pupil of Dr. Sumner's in 1770 ;
Baron Chedworth, a well-known literary character in
the later eighteenth century (the title became extinct in
1804); William Sotheby, the poet, and the Rev. T.
Gisborne, whose literary position in the religious world
was notable. Nor should the famous Sir Frederick

* *Harrow School Tercentenary,* p. 38.

Cavendish Ponsonby be forgotten, whose gallantry at Waterloo is a household word amongst Englishmen.

As diplomatists are recorded the names of *David Morier*, who at Frankfort and in Switzerland represented England during the Revolutionary Wars, and George, third Earl of Tyrconnel, Aide-de-camp to the Duke of York, who died from cold and fatigue when accompanying the Russian army in the capacity of military diplomatist during its pursuit of the French in December 1812.

Both Theodore Hook, the famous wit, and Charles Buller, the popular politician, whose power of attracting men was equal to his knowledge of colonial affairs, were at Harrow. Furnished with qualities which developed themselves early, the school life of these youths possesses more than ordinary interest. But despite its well-worn character, the career of Lord Byron at Harrow stands out specially attractive to the world, so that each and every incident is devoured with avidity.

Twenty-five years ago, towards the close of Dr. Vaughan's sojourn, there were several inhabitants of Harrow who knew him well. The noble poet seems to have fraternised with the townspeople; for instance, with old Mrs. Arnold, the stationer, whom the boys familiarly called "Polly." She was never tired of praising the consideration which his lordship showed for those with whom he came in contact. There was a certain family called Greentree, who kept what in modern parlance is known as a tuck shop, where Byron was wont to regale. When Mr. Greentree died, the poet, in response to the widow's desire, wrote an epitaph which was placed on Isaac Greentree's grave under the spreading elms of Harrow church-yard. The closing lines ran as follows :

A time shall come when all green trees shall fall,
And Isaac Greentree rise above them all.

A sure evidence that Lord Byron at Harrow was a believer in the truths of Christianity. Considering that the writer was only thirteen years of age, one hereby gains some idea of what Lord Byron's ability was at Harrow.*

We are not able to decide the *vexata questio* whether Byron, as he imagined, ever led, in the athletic sense of the word, at Harrow, but there is undoubted evidence that he used his monitorial position and maturing strength for the purpose of protecting weaker boys. The cases of Harness and Peel are well known ; while we owe it to the kindness of him who, alas ! it is now necessary to speak of as the late Bishop of Ripon, that the following anecdote is rescued from oblivion.

The third Earl of Zetland, lately deceased, was at Harrow in 1804, when only nine years old, and in common with many other tenderly-cherished children found the battle of school-life rough and unpalatable. One great hulking bully was the plague of his life ; and from the tyranny which contact with his enemy engendered, the little Yorkshire boy could alone take refuge in flight. Lord Byron one day chancing to see young Dundas running in terror before his pursuer, promptly caught the persecutor by the collar, and turning to his would-be victim, said, " Now I shall pull his ears until you laugh." A delicate way of remitting the chastise-

---

* The lines are obliterated from the wooden memorial surmounting the grave.

ment, because the culprit's contortions were such as to speedily excite ridicule on the part of the future Lord Zetland, who to the day of his death never forgot Byron's generous intervention on his behalf.*

But it is impossible to finish these old Harrow jottings without saying that many visitors, English and foreign, who see the Vaughan library, ask eagerly for records of Sir William Jones, whose reputation has survived the 124 years since Dr. Thackeray declared that turned naked on Salisbury Plain he would yet have made his way to fortune and reputation.

A story has lately passed current concerning Sir William Jones at Harrow which requires verification, inasmuch as, although appearing in an amusing publication called *Tit-Bits*, it received prominence in *Harrow Notes* for December 13, 1884. It is said that when Samuel Parr, Warburton Lytton Bennet, and Sir William Jones, parcelled the fields around Harrow into ancient Greek territories, that the future Orientalist went by the name of "Old Ulysses," and, as leader of the aforesaid band of ancients, sallied forth at *dead of night* to rescue a poor fruiterer's donkey out of a pound where it had been placed by an offended cleric. Where, we ask, was Dr. Sumner's authority, when the choicer spirits of the school could thus defy all rules, and turn night into day with impunity? Moreover, we have failed to find mention of this incident in Lord Teignmouth's *Life of Sir William Jones*, and, although by no means incredulous, wish that a reference had been appended to an undoubtedly interesting anecdote.

---

* This anecdote was told to the second Bishop of Ripon and retailed to the writer.

The anxiety to glean knowledge concerning so
remarkable a genius as Sir William Jones will not
surprise those who have studied his career.   One
Harrovian, however, much beloved and honoured by
this remarkable man himself, has not received the
chronological mention which high character and powerful talents deserved. We mean Sir John Parnell, a
pupil of Dr. Sumner's, who became in after years
Chancellor of the Exchequer in Ireland.   A scholar
and a refined gentleman, he was a worthy member of a
famous band. We are quite in accord with general
opinion as regards Sir William Jones, but nevertheless
believe that fifty years hence more people visiting
Harrow will strive to gather details concerning Lord
Palmerston than we who live so soon after him can
believe. A great flood of opinion will seat him on the
pinnacle of boy hero-worship.

The man who at eighty, as Mr. Ashley tells us, was
in the habit of riding from Cambridge House, Piccadilly, to Harrow town within the hour (anyone familiar
with the road will know what that means), and who
delighted in any function held in dear old Harrow, was
also the Premier of England, hopelessly elevated above
the reach of enmity, whether from one group of politicians or the other.

How he did love to break a lance on behalf of his
dear Harrow boys constantly in disgrace for the stone-
throwing he himself declared that he and his compeers
indulged in, but which, pursued far into the nineteenth
century, when Drs. Longley and Wordsworth ruled,
gained Herga a bad name, such as it required all Dr.
Vaughan's tact and firmness to dissipate ! But geolo-
gists said that the place had been an old sea-beach,

and as the stones were round, Lord Palmerston had thrown them in his day, and, notwithstanding his years and Premiership combined, stood ready to condone the boyish offence. Like Peel, Palmerston was Harrow to the back-bone, and claims such honour as we can give. Fancy a bolstering match between two future Premiers! Such an event nevertheless occurred in Dr. Joseph Drury's time, when the late Rev. T. Rooper* saw Lord Aberdeen driven into his study by that after-opponent in Foreign policy whom men learnt to know as " Pam."

Benefactors to Harrow have proceeded from all directions, because contact with the place is alone needed to kindle enthusiasm for her past, and inspire hope for the future. Therefore it is that complete justice cannot be done here. But the masters seem to deserve more than ordinary consideration at the historian's hands—men who have silently toiled and given of their best. Take for instance Canon Westcott. What a religious and intellectual influence he must necessarily have possessed over any community in the midst of which he lived and, in the case of Harrow, wisely counselled! Mr. Pears, Mr. Warner, and Mr. Edwin Vaughan also did good work in an inobtrusive way. Nor, as regards townspeople, can we forget the liberality of Mr. Leaf, no longer resident on the Hill, which nevertheless profits from his bene-factions to this day.

It should be likewise told how freely has Harrow thrown open her portals to the children of all nations.

* Butler Bills for 1796. Mr. Rooper's son, the Rev. W. H Rooper, communicated this fact to the writer.

The sons of Rufus King, a distinguished American minister, early in the nineteenth century were Harrovians, sent to the hill because social distinctions were there unknown ; while Harrow education was also afforded to the young Lievens, children of the Czar's ambassador. Nor do we trace any falling off in Herga's tendency to spread her culture over the world when we learn how within the last few years the Italian Duke of Genoa donned the dark blue ; while Tewfik Pacha of Egypt, according to the *Times*, expressed his desire in April 1884 that the princes of his family should be sent to Harrow.

We do not pretend to furnish in *Harroviana* any complete list of notable incidents of famous lives, and we may well leave modern records to those more prepared to enter on such task.* Nevertheless, it is within the scope

---

* We are constrained to make one exception in the case of a modern Harrovian, Mr. C. S. Calverley, whose traditional fame amongst the boys has been continuous ever since he left the tutelage of Dr. Vaughan, during the earlier days of that great teacher's rule at Harrow. If, accustomed to look on these boyish stories as presenting a somewhat mythological character, it is a surprise to find that Mr. C. S. Blayds (who changed his name to Calverley) really did jump from the top of the school steps to the bottom. Allowing for the fact that a slight alteration has been made in the conformation of these steps, still the feat would seem to be an impossible one, but for its performance having been vouched for by credible persons, one being the head-master of Harrow in 1884. Blayds is said to have leapt into the milling-ground over the school-yard wall (being not the only deluded youth who has chanced the attendant shock), and also to have cleared an iron-bound table of great breadth at his tutor's. Probably his activity of body was as unique as that of his mind. Courageous to a fault he is known to have been. But it is as a wit, inditing the best English of the style he adopted, that he will be remembered, rather than as a Balliol Scholar at Oxford or Second Classic at Cambridge, for his career embraced these double academical honours, together with the Craven Scholarship. For humour the famous alphabet in rhyme will, we believe, become a

of our narrative to recount what seems to have been
one of the most picturesque events of the epoch, illus-
trating the connection between modern Harrow and the
days that are no more, when old Colonel Wildman,
Byron's friend, who bought Newstead, and who fought
at Waterloo, came in September 1872 to look again on
the panel whereon his name is carved by the side of
that great poet whom he loved so well.

A strange reminiscence of Harrow in the first thirty
years of the nineteenth century was recounted by Lord
Shaftesbury when presiding at the Harrow Triennial
Dinner on June 18th, 1884.   "He recalled the case of
a master who, being himself a bad sleeper, frequently
called up his Form—the Shell—at four o'clock on a
winter's morning, and relieved the tedium of the night
by this very early first school."   The venerable philanthropist also spoke with horror of the unpleasant state of
Duck Puddle in his time, when it swarmed with insects,
reform having been brought about by the Earl's own
ingenuity in selecting the subject for Latin verse composition.

Nor were other speakers without interest, Sir John
Kennaway testifying to the toning down of party
asperity in the House of Commons by old Harrow ties.*

---

classic, while as a ready versifier his reputation is as high as that
of his genial good-fellowship, which gained Mr. Calverley as many
friends as admirers. *Harrow Notes* for March 15th, 1884, has an
appreciative notice of his career which, humanly speaking, must
be thought to have prematurely closed at fifty-two. It should
remain on record how both the late Mr. William Spottiswoode and
the late Sir Alexander Grant were Harrovians, and pupils of Dr.
Christopher Wordsworth.

* The writer of these lines was himself at Harrow between 1856
and 1860, and watched the early part of the Right Hon. G. O.
Trevelyan's career, acting as fag to that eminent Cabinet Minister.
To satisfy the doubts of anxious parents who dread to expose their

The head-master spoke of days in the memory of some
then present when a batch of Harrow boys might be
seen on Epsom Downs during the Derby day, and early
morning fishing visits to Ruislip reservoir were constant.
Comparing with the past a present, when scholarship
was by no means waning, he claimed also the sustenance of a manly vitality for the school, such as
the substitution of other pleasures and employments
had by no means dimmed. Nor did Dr. Butler close
without bearing well-deserved testimony to the Harrow
Mission in Latimer Road as overlooked by the popular
missioner, the Rev. W. Law. Sympathy with the poor,
when struggling to avoid the pitfalls which threaten to
degrade their existence, has been liberally evinced by
old and young connected with John Lyon's school.

The writer would fain, however, have seen the
authorities take a step further, and, on the principle that
charity begins at home, offer social recognition to the
town's-children who enjoy that education the founder
designed for them. In a small building above the new
Pavilion on the cricket-ground youths are taught with
the school money, but share little of the prestige which
the name of Harrovian brings. Their names do, however, appear in a class by themselves in the bill-book of
the great school, into the courts of whose tabernacle
they may, nevertheless, not trespass. An anomaly
this which it was found difficult if not impossible to
remove at the time of the Public Schools Act, despite

darling to the performance of menial offices, it may prove a conso-
lation to learn that a hungry boy who cleared away the tea-things,
when the stentorian voice of Macaulay's nephew summoned him
by the word "bo-o-o-y!" (a prolongation which Harrovians will
understand), often received as a reward a capital hot meal and
always a kind word for his pains.

the desire of many liberal-minded men to compass this
end.*

But other forms connected with more recent Harrow
life rise up before us.

Some there are now alive who remember old Peachy,
who in Dr. George Butler's earlier years kept the key
of the school, and rang the bell up from the head-
master's house before school.   Peachy was a shoemaker
by trade, and had been a free scholar under Dr. Sumner
in 1771, his name appearing in the Butler bill of that

---

* The services of the Winckley family to Harrow are worth
recording.   They have filled the office of Vestry Clerk for 116
years, a century's service being completed on April 15th, 1868.
The duties are at present performed by Mr. William Winckley of
Flambards, who has occupied his position since 1844, succeeding
Thomas Bland, who had been Vestry Clerk for many years prior
to April 15th, 1768 (*Harrow Gazette*, May 1st, 1868).   Mr. Winckley's personal knowledge of Harrow, past and present, is probably
superior to that of any other inhabitant.   He wrote to *Harrow
Notes* on May 8th, 1883, stating how the late Mr. Webb, the
school dancing-master, had imparted his art to Lord Byron (this
fact being told to the writer by the master in question), and this
despite the noble poet's club-foot.   While recording this incident
as evidence of Mr. Winckley's association with those of the earlier
nineteenth century, it becomes a duty to tell how a business
supervision given to the Harrow Waterworks Company rendered
modern scholastic pre-eminence possible.   But for a continual
flow of water being placed within reach of Harrow School, bracing
air and natural salubrity would have passed for little value
in the paternal (or, more important still, in the maternal) eye
It is true that the Colne Valley Water Company, being able to
offer a softer water—which medical men prefer as less likely to
encourage rheumatism, and other kindred maladies which residence on a clay soil engenders—has persuaded the Harrow share-
holders to part with their privileges, and so allow the neighbourhood to be supplied by the best available source.   But the services
of those who rendered Harrow habitable before such an arrangement was possible should, we opine, receive recognition when the
matter (as it must shortly do) comes before Parliament for its
formal approval.   For, with all parties agreed as to the desirability
of a sanatory change, little opposition may be feared in high
quarters.

year. Peachy was assisted by his so-called devil, old Stag Iles, who flourished in Harrow up to Dr. Longley's time, and of whom Custos possesses a characteristic portrait. Many reading these pages will not have forgotten the Warner family, Billy and Dick. Scarcely any have been at Harrow since 1830 without carrying away memories of Custos.

Sam Hoare was born in 1818. His father filled a similar situation for some time, and several Recollections of his are scattered about this book. At Eton, Mr. Maxwell Lyte tells us, " Custos " was the dunce of the form. At Harrow the word bears a different signification, implying that the bearer is in charge of the buildings generally and of the school in particular.* Custos' den in the old schools has been the resort of two generations, at least, who have there conned their *rep* before going up to form; chosen bats or racquets, of which Sam has always a plentiful supply; or cracked a grim joke before facing the head-master's tribunal when, sitting in *banco*, that dignitary had there and then to decide whether one of those lithe and compact birchrods, for the manufacture of which Sam stood responsible, was or was not to be shattered in a conflict wherein the assailant had the field to himself. But in another sense fulfilling the duties of his office, Sam Hoare was during Dr. Vaughan's *régime* at least looked on as guardian of the milling or fighting ground. By which we mean that when two boys had agreed to settle their differences in single combat, Custos would, after a short skirmish, dissipate the pugilistic gathering by means of a kindly chaff which rendered his pacific

* The first regular Custos at Harrow was a man called Hope, who performed the duties between 1817–19.

efforts palatable alike to principals, seconds, and onlookers. Nevertheless, it is true that within the memory
of living men, stout conflict has taken place on the
circumscribed ground below the school-yard, which the
Dean of Ely tells us was early in the nineteenth century
at least devoted to this questionable purpose. Captain
Fred Burnaby will probably one day tell us something
of pugilistic Harrow, should his literary recollections
ever, as it is to be hoped they one day will, see light.
Custos was no mean cricketer and bowled with effect,
and to this hour his opinion on the merits of the Harrow
eleven is eagerly sought by those who know best where
to become informed. His mind is a repository of Harrow experience, which he pours forth readily to those in
his confidence, and which at the same time it is impossible to reproduce in entirety. We have little doubt
that he could pass an examination on the nineteenth-
century history of Harrow generally, which would put
to shame many a college don who owes his early culture
to a residence on the hill. Custos knows and appreciates
the good points of the various masters who have done
their meed of service to Harrow. He is enthusiastic
for Dr. Wordsworth and Mr. Harris, venerates the
Drurys generally, honours Mr. Oxenham's memory,
recounts how Dr. Longley promptly forgave him for
accidentally bespattering the preceptorial person with
mud, which in a scuffle with a young Harrovian had
been thrown on the magisterial toga; while it is possibly more interesting still to listen to earlier memories
which embrace a period when at eleven each morning
the then head-master, Dr. George Butler, would march
up to school in solemn procession at the head of his
assistants.

The changes that Custos has seen from time to time effected at Harrow are so manifold that, with all his belief in the monitorial system, he counsels a zealous watchfulness over questionable innovations which, if not disputed at the outset, come to be reckoned as institutions privileged because believed to be ancient, when frequently they are of mere mushroom growth.

We are not, for instance, aware of the origin of what was formerly termed *the Squash* at election of cricket club keepers, but it is difficult to adduce any conceivable object gained by a purposeless disturbance such as rendered exercise of a privilege dangerous and unpleasant to the most combative. The two monitors who registered votes given for rival candidates stood near the head-master's chair in the Fourth Form room, while the friends and opponents of the several would-be club-keepers occupied the space between the door and the aforesaid magisterial throne, beyond which Squash* was

* In reference to Squash, it is said of the late Rev. Robert Middlemist, when desiring to confer a favour on a pupil whom he liked, that he said sententiously, not to add sarcastically, "Shall I sign you for the *Squeeze?*" A man of few words, Mr. Middlemist was nevertheless a severe master, apt, be it noted, to scent what he was pleased to term *conspiracy* amidst his scholars. And yet those who knew the man best were the most prepared to extol his merits. It was believed by Harrovians generally that Mr. Middlemist was incapable of being disconcerted, at least on this side of the river Styx. It was said of him that, when travelling in Italy, he was attacked by robbers, who, desiring to learn the name of their captive, received for reply, "Robert Middlemist," and they fled—so at least the master told the tale. The last three words, be it noted, have no necessary connection with that proper name which seems to have frightened these Robert Macaires of the marshes. Public school men will know that if a master's sayings and adventures are as household words, the man himself is probably popular amongst the boys. Take, for instance, Mr. Marillier, or "Old Teak," as many remember him. Nor will the biographer of the Rev. T. H. Steel fully perform his task unless he tells us the current Harrow gossip con-

24

not allowed to extend. Within these limits, however, the battle waxed sore, and with the result of much personal discomfiture to the boys coming and going to support their House candidates for the coveted guidance of the several games of cricket, and this despite help rendered by friendly onlookers. Squash has gone the way of public milling or fighting, and, latest change of all, of the time-

cerning old Tommy, whom, if the boys laughed *with* (for he always saw a joke), they nevertheless loved very dearly. Mr. Steel was wont to rebuke his erring pupils in the first person, and on one occasion said, "*We* will write out one hundred lines." He is said, however, to have scarcely appreciated the joke when fifty lines were sent up instead of the full quota. Nor can we forget the story of Aladdin and his wonderful lamp—an Harrovian who rejoiced in a nick-name which most of his fellows recognised, had been reported in the hearing of Mrs. Arnold (elsewhere mentioned as Polly) as being the culprit who consistently broke a lamp between the school and Mr. Steel's house, The Grove. The real wielder of the sling, being a veritable David, was in truth a noble Earl of Whig proclivities, whose popularity at school was on a par with that he now enjoys in more mature life. But Mr. Steel seized on the clue afforded, and in solemn conclave after supper sent for the suspected individual and solemnly uttered the words, "*Aladdin and his wonderful lamp.*" The puzzled schoolboy left the magisterial presence in confusion, and when accosted in like terms next day, asked for an explanation, which was refused with contumely, and with assurances that, if the hint were not taken, dire evils would ensue. At last, in despair, the accused party threw up the cards and wrote the lines allotted to the culprit, only to be told how Aladdin's lamp was the parish gas-light outside The Grove, which a boy called —— (the nick-name) daily broke. Mr. Steel ever treated the person in question with great kindness, but, so long as truth allowed him to do so, spoke of "the *boy* who broke the lamp." Mr. Steel's death followed swiftly on his resig- nation of Harrow duties. His House, past and present, combined to give him evidence of their respect and affection in the shape of plate, as well as by assembling in large numbers. As a ripe and general scholar, as well as a remarkable linguist, Mr. Steel made a mark in the world. Learning Welsh at seventy is no joke. When he came to Harrow with the Bishop of Lincoln, Dr. Words- worth, Dr. Whewell remarked that Harrow had gained the cream of Trinity. But Mr. Steel died suddenly in his new Oxford home. His blue umbrella was a feature at Lord's during the Eton and Harrow match for many years.

honoured *exeat*,* for which a few hours' leave of absence has been substituted, such as the improved communication with London renders possible. To place on paper one tithe of the memories which crowd upon us when bringing these notes to a close would be impossible within reasonable limits ; but acknowledging the fact that Harrow under Dr. H. M. Butler has improved her scholarship, held her own at rifle shooting and racquets, marched with the times in athletic sports and football,†

* *Exeat* was an oasis in the midst of the term, which allowed a youth to visit his parents or accredited friends for one or two days.

† Some of us will remember when a catch was followed by the right to *throw* the football after taking three yards. Harrow football has been played under greater disadvantage than Harrow cricket, because, although the old Sixth Form turf is dangerous in drought, and in wet weather difficult, the summer steps in and renders the practice tolerable, and (given men like Clarke and Gilby to keep the ground) a fair cricketing wicket is found. But in the winter, amidst prevalent south-west wind, the low-lying fields at the bottom of the old Flambards slope are in a perpetual slough. Here football has been pursued for many years. Under these circumstances a heavy ball has been found to be the best, because the game does not become so fast as with a smaller and lighter object of pursuit. Flesh and blood could not possibly follow closely under such conditions as would then be prevalent. Of late years a game has been devised in London by an association so named, who with a light ball agree to abrogate in all its strictness the so-called off-side rule, which means in plain English that a clever loafer near the enemy's goal may find divers opportunities for dashing fresh into the fray when his intervention may powerfully aid his side. He need not be in tip-top condition, and yet gather laurels denied to the steady and plodding. However, when football assumed such phase in the Metropolis, it was certain sooner or later that desire would be expressed for an approach to be made by the Harrovians to a system which had become almost general outside Rugby football circles. But, despite the obvious advantages of being enabled to compete on equal terms with the others, the innate Conservatism of the modern Harrovian came to the front when the question assumed the proportions of a controversy in the autumn of 1883 and the winter of 1884, for a fair account of which the reader should look at his *Harrow Notes*. In the writer's opinion, the objectors made a very good case, and they certainly were those

24 *

as well as kept up her social prestige before the world,
we pass to the concluding pages of our work.

Within a few months of this volume seeing light
there passed away an Harrovian who exercised a great
influence over his own generation, and a still firmer one
over that now rising to manhood. At a moment when
the life of Harrow was mirrored forth in her cricket,
the Hon. Robert Grimston ever inculcated honest and
patient striving to attain a knowledge, the habits formed
in securing which were of a nature to help the man

most competent to speak ; A. J. Webbe, S. W. Gore, H. O. D.
Davidson, and the Rev. W. Law strongly deprecating any hasty
alteration of rules adapted to the ground on which the game is
played. Mr. Davidson's phrase seems best to formalize their
views : " Instead of ' Follow up,' we shall say, ' Pass it on.' " It
is worthy of note that Mr. M. C. Kemp, the Oxonian cricket
captain, adopted the wise *rôle* of moderate reformer. No handling
is allowed in the Harrow game except when a ball can be caught
off the foot, when a run of three yards is allowed and a free kick
given. The poles are open, no bar being placed across. We have
not heard of any leading change, so suppose that the football
Tories have it. Mr. A. F. Hill's letters put the reformers' side
with great clearness. Mention of football leads us to two other
spheres of philathletic action, viz. rifle-shooting and racquets.
At the former, thanks to the spirit breathed into the corps by the
late Mr. Templar and his family, Harrow came to Wimbledon
but to conquer. It is otherwise now when a reaction has set in,
and the shield knows its Vaughan library niche no more. With
regard to racquets, the traditions of Dyke, Ainslie, Daniel, R. D.
Walker, and Clay, are so well sustained that since 1868 Harrow
has won the competition on ten occasions, becoming absolute
possessors of the original cup in 1873, and securing the second
one presented in 1881. Eton stands second on the record with
six victories, Rugby winning in 1870. Excellence at sports generally seeming at Harrow School to go hand-in-hand with a similar
spirit in the town (in the matter of the Rifle Corps this tendency
being specially evident), it is with considerable pleasure that we
hear of a recreation ground being about to be acquired on the
right of the Pinner road. The property will be placed in trust
for the use of the Harrow inhabitants, and Harrovians generally
should support the scheme, and so help to raise a bar against the
building encroachments which threaten to leave few green fields
around the old hill-side.

to grasp such higher prizes of life, as the mimic strife of the play-ground had prepared each boy to claim. *Truth* was Mr. Grimston's motto ; *thorough* his mode of conducting affairs, whether his business had reference to the telegraph system of the kingdom, or the sustenance of a high tone and correct style amongst Harrow cricketers. It was characteristic of the respect which his undeviating frankness inspired that when in 1869 the late Baron Martin was at a loss to decide whether or not the letter and spirit of law had been, as regards a special transaction, outstripped during Mr. W. H. Smith's first election contest for Westminster, the bewildered judge decided to refer the thorny question to Mr. Grimston's word. The two men differed in politics, but the judge knew that he had appealed to a faithful witness.

It is the fidelity evinced by the old Harrow families when men such as the venerable and respected governor, Lord Verulam, brother of Mr. Robert Grimston, together with Lord Bessborough, *the most popular living Harrovian*, stand stoutly by their old school, that gives us good hope for the future. Nor has the Peel connection, despite a temporary desertion, discarded the dark blue for Etona's more fashionable colour, inasmuch as reference to the present bill-book will show that the Speaker of the House of Commons, himself one of the two Peels who were not educated at Harrow, has adopted the family tradition, and chosen his great father's school for a son bearing a name specially honoured in these annals. For say what we will, Harrow, like most other schools, must appeal to the devotion of her children, if prevalent prosperity is to be preserved intact.

It is neither possible nor desirable to despise such

family connections. It is a remarkable fact that when last April the third baronet, Sir Robert Peel, was elected to Parliament, and before the Hon. G. H. C. Leigh met his lamented death, Sir Robert's selection raised the number of Conservative Harrovians in the House of Commons to thirty-two, a precisely similar number having been returned to support the popular side in politics. And, indeed, it is a matter of universal observance in Parliamentary circles that the acerbity of party politics is mitigated by the public-school element, because a man will never remain long angered against an old school friend, no matter what the subject of contention.

Sixty-three legislators is a large quota to be provided by the members of any one school, and should go to prove that the mode of education at Harrow has not on the whole been at fault. " Stability, as applied to a school, means progress," said Dr. Vaughan (when he revisited Harrow for the first time after his surrender of office) ; and upon such lines alone can a successful future be relied on. But we nevertheless would desire to mark how consentient is the opinion of men who have looked into the matter, that Dr. H. M. Butler has been conservative of all that is noblest and best in the Harrow system.

And here, with the expression of his heartfelt conviction that if John Lyon's foundation is to flourish, independent of external change, social or political, the little state must ever be administered in a similar spirit of reverence for her time-hallowed institutions, the writer concludes a labour which has from first to last been one of love. As, however, important discoveries concerning the earlier history of Harrow have been made since our opening chapters were printed, we must ask our readers to study the Appendices with more than ordinary attention. Specially do we desire that Dean Vaughan's analysis of the monitorial system as set forth in Appendix I. (which he endorses after thirty years' contemplation) should receive from parents such attention as the experience and ability of the writer deserves.

APPENDICES.

APPENDICES.

APPENDIX A.

WE had intended to produce in full and in its original monkish Latin the *Inquisitio* 18 *Edward III.*, to which reference is made on p. 10, but its length and obscurity has led to our adopting the subjoined abstract made by Mr. Sims of the Manuscript Department, British Museum.

"An Inquisition, *ad quod damnum*, held 14 July 18 Edw. III. [1344], before John de Cogeshale, Escheator of Co. Midd.

"The jurors say that it would *not* be to the detriment of the King, if Robert de Wodehous, Archdeacon of Richmond, assigned to John [Stratford] Abp. of Canterbury, a messuage and lands in Harrow, which the said Robert held of the said Abp. for service of 65s. 5¾d. at his manor of Harrow.

"They further say, that there remain to the said Robert, lands in Willesden, held of the Dean and Chapter of St. Paul's, and lands at Kings holt and West Tybourn, held of the Abbot of Westminster, sufficient for the customs and services, which the said Robert was accustomed to sustain."

THE GOVERNORS OF HARROW SCHOOL, WITH

Extracted from the

19 Feb. 1571: Sir Gilbert Gerrard, Attorney-General.	19 Feb. 1571: William Gerrard, Gentleman.	19 Feb. 1571: John Page of Wembley.
17 Mar. 1592: Sir Thomas (afterwards Lord) Gerrard.	3 Jan. 1586: William Gerrard, his son and heir.	20 Feb. 1624: John Page, his son.
2 Nov. 1617: Gerrard Booth of Harrow.	29 Aug. 1609: Sir Gilbert Gerrard, Bt.	15 Dec. 1654: John Page of Uxendon.
28 May 1638: Edward Claxton.	31 Jan. 1669: Wm. Page of Uxendon.	27 Sept. 1667: Tho. Smith.
24 Sept. 1658: William Greenhill.	7 April 1690: Richard Page, who declining,	24 June 1687: Cheek Gerrard.
6 Sept, 1667: Sir Edward Waldo.	7 Aug. 1690. Ed. Waldo.	12 March 1715 (6): Sir John Rushout, Bart
2 Mar. 1707: Sir Thos. Franklyn, Bt.	12 June 1707: Peter Waldo.	2 June 1775: James Brydges, Esq.
22 Oct. 1728: Francis Herne	8 Feb. 1745: Lancelot Charles Lake.	22 July 1790: Earl of Clarendon.
9 June 1777: Lord Grimston.	4 May 1751: Charles Palmer.	15 March 1824: Charles Hamilton of Sudbury.
24 Mar. 1810: John Gray of Wembley.	27 June, 1774: Richard Page.	3 July 1834: Marquis of Abercorn.
5 Nov. 1828: Joseph Neild, Jun.	26 Dec. 1803: Wm. Page.	
9 April 1836: Rev. J. E. Gray of Wembley, who declining,	17 June 1824: Col. Mark Beaufoy.	
21 April 1836: George Carr Glyn, M.P. who became Lord Wolverton, and retired when the Public Schools Act took effect in 1871.	14 May 1827: Rev. John Roberts.	
	4 Sept. 1841: Thomas Henry Sutton Sotheran, afterwards Sotheran Estcourt, M.P.	
	14 July 1870: William Henry Stone.	

The following Governors were elected under the Public Schools Act of 1868 on November 22, 1871, viz. The Right Hon. Mountague Bernard, who, dying in 1882, was succeeded on the 23rd October 1882 by H. F. Pelham, Esq.; Professor Westcott, Charles Savile Roundell, Professor Tyndall, and Vice-Chancellor Sir J. Wickens, who died in 1874, and was succeeded by F. Vaughan Hawkins, on January 14th 1884.

In November 1884 the Governors stand as follows :—

The Earl of Verulam (*Chairman*).

W. H. Stone, Esq. (*Deputy-Chairman*).

The Duke of Abercorn, K.G.

The Earl Spencer, K.G.

The Lord Northwick.

The Rev. Professor Westcott, D.D.

Professor Tyndall.

C. S. Roundell, Esq., M.P.

F. Vaughan Hawkins, Esq.

Henry F. Pelham, Esq.

Dates of Election.   Arranged in direct Succession.
Archives (1571–1885).

19 Feb. 1571. Thomas Page of Sudbury Court. 3 Jan. 1586. Henry Page. Appears in 1615: Thomas Page. 12 Jan. 1648: Sir Francis Gerrard, Bart. 10 Jan. 1650: Sir Charles Gerrard, Bart. 5 May 1701: Sir Francis Gerrard, Bart. 16 Sept. 1704: Tanner Arnold, who declining. 12 Oct. 1704: John Page of Harrow. 29 Nov. 1715: John Page of Wembley. 16 Jan. 1727: Thomas Graham 5 June 1731: James Lightbourn. 18 May 1733: Daniel Graham. 11 May 1761: John Rushout, afterwards Lord Northwick. 5 Feb. 1801: 2nd Lord Northwick. 11 Feb. 1859: 3rd Lord Northwick.	19 Feb. 1571: Thomas Reding of Pinner. 3 Jan. 1586: William Greenhill. — 1613: Lord North. 22 Jan. 1666: Edward Fenn. 30 June 1670· John Anderson. 2 Sept. 1672: Sir Gilbert Gerrard. 10 Nov. 1683: William Fenn. 24 June 1701: Warwick Lake. 2 June 1718: James Brydges, afterwards Duke of Chandos. 1 April 1740: The Marquis of Carnarvon, afterwards Duke of Chandos. 21 April 1747: Rev. Francis Saunders. 9 June 1777: Rev Walter Williams. 8 Jan. 1811: Marquis of Abercorn. 14 Feb. 1818: Rev. John William Cunningham. 8 Feb. 1862: Earl of Verulam.	19 Feb. 1571: Richard Edlin of Woodhall. 18 July 1604: Richard Page of Uxendon. 7 Dec. 1642: Daniel Waldo. 23 May 1661: Daniel Waldo. 28 Aug. 1691: John Anderson, who declining, 1 Sept. 1691: Samuel Finch. 6 April 1693: Richard Page. 29 June 1715: William Bucknall. 17 April 1742: John Bucknall. 8 June 1797: Samuel Moody of Carpenters. 8 Mar. 1823: Earl of Aberdeen. 18 Jan. 1861: Earl of Clarendon. 14 July 1870: Earl Spencer, K.G.

To those who think that John Lyon's will was infringed on both in letter and spirit by the Public Schools Bill of 1868, it will be consolatory to know that by an Act passed in 1873 the governing body were incorporated by the old familiar name, viz., *The Keepers and Governors of the Possessions, Revenues, and Goods of the Free Grammar School of John Lyon.* These titles were resumed on the 10th June 1874 at a meeting of the Governors.

APPENDIX B.

LETTER of the KEEPER of MSS. BRITISH MUSEUM, regarding the probability of there having been a school at Harrow before Lyon founded the present institution in 1571.

" British Museum, 10 Oct. 1884.

"DEAR MR. THORNTON,—With regard to the words *de novo erigere*, &c., in the Harrow Charter, I cannot think that they mean anything but to set up afresh some more ancient school. The creation of Lyon's school as practically a new foundation is recognized clearly enough in the several clauses of the deed ; but *de novo* would scarcely have been used had not some older establishment existed—otherwise the words would be superfluous.

" It is only natural to suppose that some old school existed in the place in old times.

"Believe me, yours very truly,
"E. MAUNDE THOMPSON.

"PERCY THORNTON, Esq."

This letter has received unexpected support from several quarters. The following entry has been discovered amidst the Caius College papers, and is communicated by the President, the Rev. B. H. Drury :—

" Gerarde (sic) Richard, son of William Gerard, Gent., of Harrow Mi.ldlesex School, Harrow, four years, age 15. Admitted scholar litt : grat : Nov 4. 1567."

Now, it is clear that eight years before John Lyon gave of his substance to endow the institution which very properly claims him as its *Founder*, there was a school established on Harrow Hill. Hence the *de novo erigere* of the Charter, and the *Old House* of the school account-book, *tempore* 1611, while John Lyon's anxiety in 1571 that a house should be forthcoming when the germ he was about to nurture should spring into new life, at last receives adequate explanation. It does not refer to the temporary beneficence which arranges that in Lyon's lifetime thirty poor scholars are to be taught free, but rather to an ancient educational establishment, dating in all probability from the earliest sojourn of the Archbishops at Harrow, when Mother Church did for England what the combined influences of an Established Church and a School Board essay to accomplish in 1885.

The William Gerard mentioned in the Caius archives was one of Lyon's first Keepers and Governors. It is, moreover, remarkable that the connection between Harrow and Caius College belonged to the ante-Lyon period; while both Dr. John Caius at Cambridge in 1558 and John Lyon at Harrow in 1571 were bent on reviving ancient institutions. That on the banks of Cam dates from 1348, when Edmund Gonville created the college; that at Harrow being shrouded in the mists of ecclesiastical antiquity.

The subjoined letter was given us by the Rev. W. H. Rooper, representative of the aged writer's family. It presents an interesting picture of English life under the Tudors.

"Bridgwater, May 25, 1626.

"To my worshipful Cozen,

"I rec^d your letter by M^r. Dange when he came from the last Term wherein you desire me to set down what I know of mine owne knowledge of our kindred. Indeed Cozen I can say little but of my father's and mother's uncles and wh lived in my tyme for I was but a stranger in my Father's County of Derbyshire.

"I and my 5 brethren were all borne in Hide Park by London in the Lodge neere Knightsbridge. My Father's name was Richard hee was servant to King Henry VII. and to King Henry VIII. and was a Pentioner and much in their favor as I have heard my Mother and many others say; and soe it sh^d seeme for King Henry VIII. gave him the keeping of Enfield Chase Hide Park and Maribone, and the King gave him good gifts ever and anon, and my Father put keepers in and out at his pleasure, but hee lived beyond it and he left us all unprovided for. I was not above 8 or 9 years old when he

died as I take it. I remember Queen Mary came into our
house within a little of my Father's death and ffound my
Mother weeping and took her by the hand and lifted her up
—for she neeled—and bad her bee of good cheer for her
children sh^d bee well provided for.

"Afterward my brother R^d and I being the two eldest *were
sent to Harrow to school and were there till we were almost men.*
Sir Ralph Sadler took order for all things for us there by
Queen Mary's appointment as long as she lived, and after
Queen Elizabeth for a time she gave order to bind my brothers
William, Ralph, Henry, Hugh, Apprentices, and sent for us to
the Court and said she would give us good places, but wee
were put to be of her guard which I think killed my mother's
hart for shee would always say that my ffather was of a great
stock and little lookt for such place for his sonnes. I've often
heard her say shee thought we fared the worss that Queen
Mary was so kind to us.

"Queen Elizabeth had not raigned long but my Mother
died. She was one Mr. Hanshaw's daughter, belonging to the
law. My Father had too brothers. Henry was the eldest and
your great grandfather.

"His wife was d^r of one Fetherstone. For my part I married a widdow here by Bridgewater. I had good means by
her while she lived, and it was all the good I gott by my
mistress Queen Elizabeth, but indeed by her means I gott
my wife.

"Cozen you must pardon mee for I wrote not this with mine
own hand. I have not writt a letter this 7 years my eyes are
so bad. I am above four score years old but I made this to
be written after my owne very words and the Writer reade it
once again to mee. Worthy Cozen the Lord of Heaven bless
you. It joyes my hart when I hear from you, and therefore I
beseech you let me receive a letter from you now and then.

"I shall not live long for I am almost done. God prepare
me for Himselfe for I have beene a great Sinner.

"I rest your loving Cozen till Death,

"G. ROPER.

"Cozen if you look upon the seale of this letter you shall
find I have my Father's seale still. My brother Richard gave

it mee he w^d say it had been long in the name, and after my death ıt shall be yours, but I will never part with it while I live."

Under the copy of the original of the above letter is written :—

"This is a true copy of the originall in my Custody, who am the only surviving heir male of that Branch of the family, given under my hand and seal above mentioned 6th April 1679."

The seal is of silver, with upright handle and cross. It contains the arms, and the motto

"Sigillum Fulberti le Rooper."

When Mr. Patrick Fraser Tytler, the Scotch historian, saw this letter, he remarked on the amiable vein thereby proved to have existed in Queen Mary's character, a quality which Mr. Tytler always believed the Queen to have possessed, despite the public savagery associated with her name.

In a Lyon deed dated 1596 the then established place of teaching on Harrow Hill is described as *the now School or Church House*, being in all probability Shakespeare's *Charge* house on the mountain or hill mentioned in *Love's Labour Lost*, Act v., Scene 2, and referred to at the commencement of this work. *Church* has been possibly corrupted into *Charge*, causing divers speculations as to the meaning. Mr. Edward Scott has little doubt "that Charge house was the place where the archbishops had carried on the village school in pre-Reformation times," reminding the author of another quotation from Shakespeare—that in *Twelfth Night* :—

"Like a pedant that keeps a school i' the church."

Thanks to the literary assiduity of Mr. William Winckley, the following extracts have been taken from the Harrow Parish Minutes of May 25th, 1724. They show that an old house was removed from the churchyard a hundred years before Dr. Vaughan came to Harrow. It was in all probability the ancient church school-house, and its *débris* probably forms the foundation of what is now known as Mr. C. W. Wood's Sanatarium, which is said to have been erected on the site of the after-mentioned House of Maintenance.

EXTRACTS FROM THE MINUTES OF VESTRY OF THE PARISH OF
HARROW-ON-THE-HILL.

" May y⁰ 25ʰ 1724.

" 'Tis this day ordered and agreed upon, at a Vestry held in
the Church the day and year above written, That a New House₎
be erected for yᵉ better providing, maintaining and employing
the Poor of this Parish.

" Nem That the House in yᵉ Churchyard be taken down, and
the Materials employed towards yᵉ building of yᵉ House of
Maintenance.

*   *   *   *   *

" Nem That the thanks of this Vestry be returned to Sᵣ John
Rushout, Bart., for the trouble He has taken upon Himself to
recommend the erecting a House of Maintenance for yᵉ Poor,
and that He be desired (if He pleases) to see it brought to
Perfection.

" (Signed)   J. RUSHOUT.
                W. BUCKNALL.
                HUMF. HENCHMAN, Vicar.
                JOHN HIGHLORD.
                THO. BRIAN.
                JAMES COX.
                PHI. BENNET.
                JOHN PAGE, and others."

It is clear that Harrow was not a Free School before 1571,
and therefore John Lyon is the absolute Founder of the present
Institution.   Had not an influential and moneyed supporter
appeared when the Reformation measures destroyed the old
educational system, previous prestige would have availed
nothing at Harrow.   John Lyon's forethought and wisdom,
therefore, become the more apparent.

APPENDIX C.

CHRONOLOGICAL LIST OF TITLE-DEEDS OF JOHN LYON OF PRESTON IN HARROW, FROM 1356 TO 1580.

Edward III.
Anno 30=A.D. 1356.
,,   44= ,,   1370-1.
,,   44= ,,   1371.
,,   44= ,,   1371.

Richard II.
Anno 4=A.D. 1381.
,,   16= ,,   1393.
,,   18= ,,   1395.
,,   18= ,,   1395.

Henry IV.
Anno 2=A.D. 1400.
,,   3= ,,   1402.
,,   8= ,,   1407.
,,   10= ,,   1409.
,,   13= ,,   1412.
,,   13= ,,   1412.
omisso= ,,   1400-12.

Henry V.
Anno 6=A.D. 1418.
,,   6= ,,   1418.
,,   9= ,,   1422.
,,   10= ,,   1422.

Henry VI.
Anno 5=A.D. 1427.
,,   19= ,,   1440.
,,   19= ,,   1440.
,,   23= ,,   1445.
,,   24= ,,   1446.
,,   34= ,,   1455.

Edward IV.
Anno 2=A.D. 1462.
,,   2= ,,   1462.
,,   2= ,,   1463.
,,   7= ,,   1467.
,,   9= ,,   1469.
,,   16= ,,   1476.

Henry VII.
Anno 1=A.D. 1486.
,,   7= ,,   1492.
,,   11= ,,   1496.
,,   23= ,,   1508.

Henry VIII.
Anno 2=A.D. 1510.
,,   5= ,,   1513.
,,   5= ,,   1513.
,,   7= ,,   1515.
,,   9= ,,   1518.
,,   10= ,,   1518.
,,   10= ,,   1518.
,,   15= ,,   1524.
,,   20= ,,   1528.
,,   20= ,,   1528.
,,   21= ,,   1529.
,,   21= ,,   1529.
,,   25= ,,   1534.
,,   28= ,,   1536.
,,   30= ,,   1539.
,,   30= ,,   1539.
,,   32= ,,   1540.

25 *

Chronological List of Title Deeds of John Lyon—*continued.*

Anno	36=A.D.	1545.			*Elizabeth.*	
,,	36=	,, 1545.		Anno	2=A.D.	1560.
,,	37=	,, 1545.		,,	2=	,, 1560.
,,	38=	,, 1546.		,,	3=	,, 1561.
				,,	6=	,, 1564.
	Edward VI.			,,	7=	,, 1565.
				,,	7=	,, 1565.
Anno	1=A.D.	1547.		,,	13=	,, 1571.
,,	1=	,, 1547.		,,	14=	,, 1571.
,,	3=	,, 1549.		,,	14=	,, 1572.
				,,	16=	,, 1574.
	Mary.			,,	16=	,, 1574.
				,,	16=	,, 1574.
Anno	1=A.D.	1554.		,,	17=	,, 1575.
				,,	17=	,, 1575.
	Philip and Mary.			,,	17=	,, 1575.
				,,	22=	,, 1579.
Annis 2 & 3=A.D.		1556.		,,	22=	,, 1580.

TITLE-DEEDS TO LANDS OF JOHN LYON OF PRESTON IN
HARROW-ON-THE-HILL FROM 1356 TO 1580.

1. Extract from roll of Court held at Harrow on Thursday
next before Ascension-Day, 30 Edw. III. [A.D. 1356], wherein
John Alis of Preston is admitted to lands at Preston surrendered by John Hoby and Isabell his wife, daughter of William
Hogges of Preston.

2. Extract from roll of Court held at Edgeware on Wednesday on SS. Philip and James' day, 44 Edw. III. [A.D. 1370],
wherein John Lyoun is admitted to Lands at Kingsbury surrendered by Richard Sanders and Isabel his wife.

3. Duplicate of No. 2.

4. Extract from roll of Court held at Edgeware, on Wednesday, on SS. Philip and James' day, 44 Edw. III. [A.D. 1370],
wherein John Lioun is admitted to lands surrendered by Agnes
Tromes, who inherited them on the death of her mother Lucy.

5. Roll of lands belonging to William Rother, Sen. of Malden
[Co. Bedford], headed:—"Obitus Wilhelmi Rother apud
Maldon Senioris anno domini Mlmo. CCCLXXVIII." Among
the items are "Terra assignata vendi per Aliciam relictam
Willielmi North," and "Terra que deberet vendi per feoffatos
ex assignacione Willelmi Cateran in campis de Malden."

6. Extract from roll of Court held at Hargh [Harrow] on Wednesday on SS. Philip and James' day, 4 Rich. II. [A.D. 1381], wherein William Bokeberd is admitted to lands at Preston surrendered by William Popler and Letice his wife.

7. Grant from Thomas Woodward to Richard Musach of lands, tenements, rents, and services in Harwe [Harrow], Co. Middl., inherited from his mother and grandmother Margary and Agnes Dyket. Dated at Harwe [Harrow] 15 June, 10 Richard II. [A.D. 1387].

8. Extract from roll of Court held at Harrow on Tuesday next after S. Mark's Day, 16 Richard II. [A.D. 1393], wherein Agnes Lyoun is admitted to lands at Preston surrendered by John Wytleseye and Joan his wife.

9. Extract from roll of Court held at Edgware on Saturday, SS. Philip and James' Day, 18 Rich. II. [A.D. 1395], wherein John Lyoun, Sen. is admitted to lands surrendered by Agnes, widow of Andrew Lyoun.

10. Extract from roll of Court held at Edgeware on Saturday, SS. Philip and James' Day, 18 Rich. II. [A.D. 1395] wherein John Lyoun of Kingsbury is admitted to lands surrendered by John Wrench.

11. Extract from roll of Court held at Harrow Hill Rectory on Monday next after St. Denis' Day, 2 Henry IV. [A.D. 1400], wherein Philip Kirkman and Petronilla his wife are admitted to lands surrendered by Robert Sexteyn.

12. Grant from Thomas Godelakes, Esq., Citizen of London, to John Lyon, Sen., of Harugh [Harrow], of land called Smale Wythyes in Kyngesbury [Kingsbury]. Dated at Kingsbury on the Conception of the B. V. Mary, 2 Henry IV. [A.D. 1400].

13. Will of Joan Bucberd of Preston in Harwe [Harrow], dated XVI^c Kalendas Maij [16 April] 1401, wherein she bequeaths her soul to God, Blessed Mary and all the Saints, and her body to be buried in St. Mary's graveyard at Harrow. To the high altar there 4d. To the Vicar there 6d. To Dom. Andrew, Dom. William, and Dom. John, Celebrants there, 6d. a-piece, and the residue of her goods to her husband William Bucberd, whom she names her executor. Probate granted by the Dean of Croydon at Norton, 6 May 1401, with *seal* of his office attached.

14. Extract from roll of Court held at Edgeware on Monday,

SS. Philip and James' Day, 3 Henry IV. [A.D. 1402], wherein Andrew Lyon is admitted to lands surrendered by Henry Waryn and Agnes his wife.

15. Extract from roll of Court held at Harrow on Tuesday, St. Margaret's Eve, 8 Henry IV. [A.D. 1407], wherein William Lyoun and Rose his wife are admitted to lands surrendered by John Vpperyght.

16. Extract from roll of Court held at Edgeware on Wednesday, SS. Philip and James' Day, 10 Henry IV. [A.D. 1409], wherein William Lyoun, brother and heir of Andrew Lyoun, is admitted to lands of which his said brother had seisin at his death.

17. Notification by Robert [Hallum] Bishop of Salisbury that he has admitted to Subdeacon's Orders by letters dimissory from the Pope and on the title of St. Nicholas' Hospital at Sarum, John Sambrok, of Lichfield diocese, Accolyte. Dated Saturday in Easter week, 2 April, A.D. 1412.

18. Supplication of John Hurlegh, Master of St. Nicholas' Hospital, Salisbury, and from the Chaplains of the same House, addressed to the Archbishops and Bishops of the Realm of England, that they would admit John Sambrokes, Clerk Acolyte of Lichfield diocese, to all such Orders as he has not yet obtained on the title of their said House. Dated in the said Hospital on Monday next after the Feast of Easter, A.D. 1412.

19. Extract from roll of Court held at Edgeware on Saturday, SS. Philip and James' Day, Henry IV. [A.D. 1400–1412], wherein William Hobcokes is admitted to lands surrendered by Ralph Kelham, who acquired them from John Lyon. *Mutilated.*

20. Extract from roll of Court held at Harrow on 5 April, 6 Henry V. [A.D. 1418], wherein William Lyon is admitted to lands surrendered by John Vpryght.

21. Extract from roll of Court held at Edgeware on Monday next before SS. Simon and Jude's Day, 6 Henry V. [A.D. 1418], wherein Thomas Dawe quitclaims lands to John Dawe.

22. Extract from roll of Court held at Edgeware on Tuesday next before the Feast of St. Peter in Cathedra, 9 Henry V. [A.D. 1422], wherein John Lyoun, son of William Lyoun, is admitted to lands surrendered by John Lyoun of Le Wroo.

23. Extract from roll of Court held at Edgeware on Thursday

next after the Annunciation of the B. V. M., 10 Henry V.
[A.D. 1422], wherein John Lyoun, son of William Lyoun, is
admitted to lands surrendered by Richard Gardyner and Alice
his wife.

24. Extract from roll of Court held at Edgeware on Monday
next before St. Barnabas' Day, 2 Henry VI. [A.D. 1424], when
William Wynge and Elizabeth his wife surrendered half a
virgate of land lately held by Richard Lorchon, of which the
said William was thereupon seised on condition of paying in
full all the debtors of the said Elizabeth.

25. Grant from Robert Blake of Harrow to William Lyon of
Harrow, of one messuage in Harrow Hill. Dated at Harrow
24 Febr., 3 Henry VI. [A.D. 1425]. With *seal* of arms.

26. Extract from roll of Court held at Kingsbury on Saturday, on the Feast of the Invention of the Holy Rood, 5 Henry
VI. [A.D. 1426], wherein John Lyon is admitted to lands surrendered by John Dawe, son of John Dawe.

27. Grant from Robert Lyon, Husbandman of Hendon, co.
Middlesex, to William Chalkehill, Gentleman, of Kingsbury,
and to John Lyon, Husbandman of Harrow, of all his goods
and chattels in the village and plains of Harrow and elsewhere
within the realm of England. Dated Harrow, 10 January, 14
Henry VI. [A.D. 1436].

28. Extract from roll of Court held at Harrow Hill Rectory
on 15 Oct., 19 Henry VI. [A.D. 1440], wherein John Trumen
is admitted to lands at Harrow surrendered by John Kyrk and
Thomas Colbronde.

29. Extract from roll of Court held at Harrow Hill Rectory
on Tuesday next after the Feast of the Conception of B. V. M.,
19 Henry VI. [A.D. 1440], wherein John Croft is admitted to
lands surrendered by Philip Martyn.

30. Extract from roll of Court held at [Harrow] on Tuesday
next after St. Mark's Day, 23 Henry VI. [A.D. 1445], wherein
Thomas Pernell is admitted to lands at Preston surrendered
by John Lyon.

31. Extract from roll of Court held at [Harrow] on Tuesday
next after St. Matthias' Day, 24 Henry VI. [A.D. 1446], wherein
John Trum and John Cauche are admitted to lands at ——
surrendered by John Croft, for the anniversary of the said
John Croft to be kept annually in Harrow Church.

32. Extract from roll of Court held at Edgeware on Saturday next after Michaelmass Day, 25 Henry VI. [A.D. 1446], wherein John Lyon of Preston is admitted to one quartron of land in Edgeware.

33. Extract from roll of Court held at Harrow on Wednesday next after the Feast of the Purification, 34 Henry VI. [A.D. 1456], wherein John Lyon is admitted to lands at Roxeth surrendered by John Grenehill.

34. Extract from roll of Court held at Harrow Hill Rectory on Thursday 30 Sept., 2 Edw. IV. [A.D. 1462], wherein William White is admitted to lands at Harrow Hill surrendered by John Trum.

35. Duplicate of No. 34.

36. Letters of administration granted by John Crabb (Licentiate in Decrees of Thomas Kemp, Bishop of London and Commissary General in the City of London and the Deaneries of Middlesex and Barking) to William Lyon and Matildis his wife, as executors of the Will of Isabel Myles, Widow, of Little Greenford. Dat. 10 Febr. 1463[4].

37. Extract from roll of Court held at Harrow Hill Rectory on Wednesday next after Ascension Day, 7 Edward IV. [A.D. 1467], wherein reseisin of lands on Harrow Hill is granted to Agnes Cache, Widow, with remainder to (a) Pleasance Cache, Widow of William Cache, (b) Margaret, wife of William Chester, daughter of the said Pleasance, (c) Isabel, daughter of John Cache, Jun., and (d) the guardians for the time being of the goods of Harrow Hill Parish Church, to be sold at as high a price as possible, and the money thus obtained to be distributed for the souls of Agnes and John Cache, late her husband, viz.: one moiety to be expended on the goods of the said church, and the other moiety in repairing and mending the King's highways within the said parish.

38. Extract from roll of Court of Master Robert Kyrkeham, Clerk, Keeper of the Chancery Rolls and Rector of Harrow, held at Harrow, on Monday 9 Oct., 9 Edw. IV. [A.D. 1469], wherein Isabel Segnore, Widow, quitclaims to John Trume, Fuller, a tenement lately belonging to Richard Barkeley, and previously to Ralph Mushache, and at the same Court John Trume abovesaid surrenders the said tenement to the use of Robert Shelton.

39. John Sextene surrendered three acres of land to the use of John Bugberd, 13 Edward IV. [A.D. 1473-1474]. And it is found that John a Grenehill is son and heir of Robert a Grene-hill *alias* Bukberd, and of full age, whereupon he is admitted to his father's lands.

40. Lease from John Ely, Draper of London, to William Edwardes, Husbandman of Kingsbury, and to Margaret his wife, of three tenements in Alperton in the parish of Harrow Hill. Dated at Alperton 4 June, 15 Edward IV. [A.D. 1475].

41. Extract from roll of Court held at Edgeware on Monday, SS. Simon and Jude's Day, 16 Edw. IV. [A.D. 1476], wherein John Lyon, son and heir of William Lyon, is admitted to all the lands in Kingsbury and Edgeware formerly held by his father.

42. Extract from roll of Court held at Harrow on Tuesday next before the Epiphany, 1 Henry VII. [A.D. 1486], wherein John Lyon is admitted to lands at Preston surrendered by John Redyng.

43. Bond from John Lyon, Husbandman of Harwe super le Hill to William Dundy of the same place in five marks payable on the Feast of Purification next ensuing. Dated 11 September, 7 Henry VII. [A.D. 1491].

44. Extract from roll of Court of Master Thomas Wylkynson held at Harrow Hill Rectory on 15 June, 7 Henry VII. [A.D. 1492], wherein John Banys is admitted to a granary adjoining the Perpetual Chauntry at Harrow Hill surrendered by Ivo Chalkhill.

45. Extract from roll of Court held at Harrow Hill Rectory on 12 April, 11 Henry VII. [A.D. 1496], wherein John Grene-hill, Administrator of the goods and chattels of Robert Shelton, acquits William Heth of the rent of a tenement at Harrow Hill: save always a rent of 11s. 8d. due during life to Joan, widow of the said Robert.

46. Lease from Margaret widow of Richard Hubert, formerly wife of William Edwards, Husbandman of Kingsbury, to John Cowper, Brewer of Paddington, Richard Thomas of Harrow Hill, John Edwards of Hendon, John Canou of Harrow and John Braynt of Hendon of three tenements in Alperton in Harrow parish, which the said Margaret together with her late husband, William Edwards, had by lease from John Ely,

Draper of London, to be held in trust to carry out the last Will of the said Margaret. Dated at Harrow 20 April, 19 Henry VII. [A.D. 1504].

47. Extract from roll of Court of Master Thomas Wylkynson, Rector of Harrow Hill, held at the Rectory on Monday, 8 May, 23 Henry VII. [A.D. 1508], wherein John Webbe, William Wende and William Clerk are admitted to lands surrendered by William Heth and Alice his wife.

48. Extract from roll of Court of Master Thomas Wylkynson, Rector of Harrow Hill, held at Harrow Hill Rectory on Monday next after St. Lucy's Day, 16 Dec., 2 Henry VIII. [A.D. 1510], wherein John Skynner and Juliana his wife are admitted to lands on Harrow Hill surrendered by John Webbe, William Wende and William Clerk.

49. Extract from roll of Court held at Harrow Hill Rectory on Monday 11 Oct., 5 Henry VIII. [A.D. 1513], wherein William Hering is admitted to forfeited lands formerly belonging to John Herte and Matildis his wife, and previously to John Ball.

50. Extract from roll of Court of Master [Cuthbert] Tunstall, Rector of Harrow Hill, held at Harrow Hill on Monday 11 Oct., 5 Henry VIII. [A.D. 1513], wherein Thomas Grenhill is admitted to lands in Harrow Hill surrendered by John Grenhill.

51. Extract from roll of Court of Master Cuthbert Tunstall, Rector of Harrow Hill, held at the Rectory 19 Nov., 7 Henry VIII. [A.D. 1515], wherein Agnes Heryng is admitted to forfeited lands surrendered by William Heryng, her late husband, with remainder to (a) Elizabeth, daughter and heir of the said William, and (b) the heirs of Roger Pawtur.

52. Extract from roll of Court held at Harrow on Wednesday, 14 April, 9 Henry VIII. [A.D. 1518], wherein John Lyon, son and heir of John Lyon, is admitted to all his father's lands formerly surrendered by his father to the use of his wife Joan.

53. Extract from roll of Court held at Edgeware on Saturday, SS. Philip and James' Day, 10 Henry VIII. [A.D. 1518], wherein John Lyon, Jun., son and heir of John Lyon, Sen., is admitted to lands at Kingsbury, within the lordship of Edgeware.

54. Extract from roll of Court held at Edgeware on Saturday SS. Philip and James' Day, 10 Henry VIII. [A.D. 1518], wherein Joan, widow of John Lyon, is admitted for the term of ten

years (with remainder to William Lyon their son) to lands in Kingsbury in the lordship of Edgeware.

55. Grant from John Edwards, Yeoman of Hendon, to Thomas Roberts, Richard Hawkes, John Breynt and Nicholas Marshe, a tenement in Alperton in the parish of Harrow Hill, inherited from his parents William and Margaret Edwards, to be held in trust for the performance of his Will. Dated 27 January, 14 Henry VIII. [A.D. 1523].

56. Extract of roll of Court of William Bolton (Prior of St. Bartholomew's Priory, in West Smithfield, London, Commendary and Rector of Harrow Hill) held at the Rectory on Tuesday, 19 April, 15 Henry VIII. [A.D. 1524], wherein Henry, son of William and Margaret White, is admitted to lands surrendered by William White and previously by John Trum.

57. Extract from roll of Court held at Edgware on Friday, SS. Philip and James' Day, 20 Henry VIII. [A.D. 1528], wherein John Lyon, Jun., is admitted to lands at Kingsbury surrendered formerly by John Lyon, Sen., to the use of Joan his wife, with remainder to William their son, and on his dying without heirs to his brother John.

58. Duplicate of the above, No. 57.

59. Extract of roll of Court of William Bolton (Prior of St. Bartholomew's Priory in West Smithfield, London, and Commendary and Rector of Harrow Hill) held at the Rectory on the Monday next after Michaelmas, 4 Oct., 21 Henry VIII. [A.D. 1529], wherein John Jenyns, Vicar of Harrow Hill, is admitted to lands at Harrow Hill surrendered by Juliana Skinner, Widow.

60. Extract from Roll of Court of William Bolton, Prior of S. Bartholomew in West Smithfield, London, Commendary and Rector of Harrow Hill, held at the Rectory on Monday next after Michaelmas Day, 4 October, 21 Henry VIII. [A.D. 1529], when presentment is made that John Ffynche by the hands of Thomas a Grenehill and Henry Page, Tenants, surrendered to the use of John Huslok, Sen., a tenement in Harrow Hill formerly held by Jno. Chalkhill, with a right of way called "a ffotey waye" to the pond of Henry Page, late of Jno. Chalkhill, opposite to the messuage belonging to the Perpetual Chantry of Harrow Hill, and a right of taking water at their will therefrom at the rent of a halfpenny a year.

61. Terrier of lands of John Strachyn in Maldon parish, co. Bedford, made 25 Henry VIII. [April 1533—April 1534].

62. Extract from roll of Court held at Harrow on 14 April, 25 Henry VIII. [A.D. 1534], wherein it appears that John Lyon, tenant of 2 half hides of land, died since the last Court, and that John Lyon is his son and heir and over twenty years of age, and seeks admission to his father's lands, but is respited until the next Court.

63. Extract from roll of Court held at Edgeware on Monday, 1 May, 28 Henry VIII. [A.D. 1536], wherein John Lyon is admitted to lands in Kingsbury surrendered by John Kebyll and Joan his wife.

64. Extract from roll of Court held at Harrow Hill Rectory on 14 April, 30 Henry VIII. [A.D. 1539], wherein William Jenyns is admitted to lands surrendered by John Jenyns, Clerk, with reserve to Joan Lyon, widow, of a chamber adjoining.

65. Duplicate of the above, No. 64.

66. Extract from roll of Court held at Harrow Hill Rectory, 8 Dec., 32 Henry VIII. [A.D. 1540], wherein Richard Page is admitted to lands at Harrow Hill surrendered by William Jenyns.

67. Extract from three rolls of Courts held at Harrow Hill Rectory, (a) by Master Richard Leyton (LL.D., Dean of York and Rector of Harrow Hill) on 6 June, 34 Henry VIII. [A.D. 1542], wherein William Knight is admitted to lands surrendered by William Jenyns; (β) on 14 April, 36 Henry VIII. [A.D. 1542], wherein William Burton is admitted to the above lands surrendered by the said William Jenyns; and (γ) on the same day, wherein Richard Hurlocke is admitted to the same lands surrendered by the said William Burton. The lands are leased, with the exception of a chamber belonging to Joan Lyon, widow.

68. Extract from roll of Court held at Harrow Hill Rectory on 14 April, 36 Henry VIII. [A.D. 1545], wherein Mark Fynche, son and heir of Richard Fynche, son and heir of Robert Fynche, is admitted to his father's lands in Harrow Hill.

69. Extract from roll of Court held at Harrow Hill Rectory on Tuesday in Pentecost week, 26 May, 37 Henry VIII. [A.D. 1545], wherein William Jenyns is admitted to lands surrendered by John Parson, son and heir of Robert Parson.

70. Extract from roll of Court held at Harrow Hill Rectory

on 3 May, 38 Henry VIII. [A.D. 1546], wherein Sir John Wyllyams is admitted to lands surrendered by William Jenyns.

71. Grant from William Kydley, Sen., of Maldon, co. Bedford, for thirty shillings to Thomas Cole of Maldon of an half acre of meadow in•Maldon at the yearly rent of one penny. Dated at Maldon, 7 June, 38 Henry VIII. [A.D. 1546].

72. Extract from roll of Court held at Harrow Hill Rectory on 6 July, 1 Edward VI. [A.D. 1547], wherein Richard Page and William Belamy are admitted to lands surrendered by Mark Fynche.

73. Extract from roll of Court held at Harrow Hill, 6 July, 1 Edw. VI. [A.D. 1547], wherein John Agyrnell and Joan his wife are admitted to lands surrendered by Sir John Wyllyams.

74. Grant from William Kydley of Maldon to Thomas Cole of Maldon of a messuage in Maldon. Dated at Maldon, 5 November, 2 Edward VI. [A.D. 1548].

75. Bond of William Kydley of Maldon to Thomas Cole of Maldon in ten pounds for performance of Covenants. Dated 5 Nov. 2 Edward VI. [A.D. 1548].

76. Extract from roll of Court held at Harrow by Sir Edward Northe on 7 May, 3 Edward VI. [A.D. 1549], wherein John Lyon, eldest son and heir of John Lyon of Preston, is admitted to 2 half hides of land at Preston formerly held by his said father.

77. Lease from Henry Fortescue, Esq. of Fawborne, co. Essex, to John Gryffith, Gentl. of Esynden, co. Hertford, of a capital messuage in the parishes of North and South Mimms in cos. Hertford and Middlesex, for forty-one years at the yearly rent of twelve pounds, or payment of one hundred pounds within the next twelvemonth.

78. Bond from William Tooke, Esq. of Popes in the parish of Kings Hatfield, al. Hatfield Bishop, co. Hertford, and John Griffithe, Gentl. of the same place, to Henry Fortescue, Esq. of Ffawbourne, co. Essex, in one hundred marks for payment of fifty pounds before 9 February next. Dated 28 November, 4 Edward VI. [A.D. 1550]. On the *dors* is the receipt of " Harre ffortescue " for the above sum, dated 8 February, 5 Edward VI. [A.D. 1551].

79. Sale for £140 10s. from John Warner of Ikleton, co. Cambridge, to William Page of Harrow Hill of a messuage in

Alperton in the parish of Harrow, lately held by the said John Warner's grandfather John Edwards, Yeoman of Hendon, co. Middl., deceased. Witnesses, John Lyon and others. Dated 10 August, 6 Edward VI. [A.D. 1552].

80. Bond from John Warner of Ikleton, to William Page in two hundred pounds for performance of Covenants. Dated 10 August, 6 Edward VI. [A.D. 1552].

81. 82. Fine for recovery of a messuage in Harrow Hill by William Page to John Warner and Elizabeth his wife at Westminster in the Court in Michaelmas Term, 1 Mary [A.D. 1553], before Richard Morgan, Humfrey Brown, and Edward Saunders, Justices of the Queen's Bench. (Two copies.)

83. Extract from roll of Court held at Harrow Hill Rectory on 18 April, 1 Mary [A.D. 1554], wherein a composition is made in the suit pending between John Agyrnell, Plaintiff, and Richard Myllett and Henry Agyrnell, Defendants, for payment of rents of customary lands in Harrow Hill.

84. Extract from roll of Court held at Harrow Hill Rectory on 29 April, 2 & 3 Philip and Mary [A.D. 1556], wherein Richard Hurlocke is admitted to lands surrendered by John Hacche and Elizabeth his wife, daughter and heiress of William Heryng.

85. Copy of the Will of Wyllyam Page, Yeoman, of Uxenden, dated 12 January, 4 and 5 Philip and Mary [A.D. 1558], wherein he bequeaths to each of his children, Katherine, Dorothy, Mary and Audrey, forty pounds a piece, and to Katherine also his house and freehold land at Alperton, and to all his said daughters two beasts and a score of sheep, all on their attaining eighteen years, &c., and the residue of his goods to his wife Agnes Page, whom he makes executor.

86. "A rentall of the proffets belonging to the house callyd Herthes, and nowe William Burtons." Sum total, 6s. 4d.

87. The rentall of Harrow Hill, n.d. Two Copies, temp. Elizabeth. The first tenant's name is "John Lion" or "Lyon," and he pays the largest rent, "nineteen shillings." The third tenant is "Sir John Parrat," i.e. Perrot, who died in A.D. 1562 and he pays eleven pence half-penny.

88. Terrier of Richarde ffaldos lands in Maldon, co. Bedford, n.d. 16th Cent.

89. Copy of a deed whereby John Marshe, Brewer of Chipping

Barnet, co. Hertford, for the sum of £9 17s. 11d. enfeoffs
Edward Taylor, Esq., in his lands in Barnet, all being parcel
of the possessions of the late dissolved Monastery of St. Albans,
and pertaining to the Office of the Cook called "Le kytchiners
holde." To be held on the same terms as the said John Marshe
had them by a grant from the late King Philip and Queen
Mary dated at Westminster, 6 November, 5 and 6 year of their
Reign [A.D. 1558]. To be held as of the Royal Manor of
Greenwich in socage and not in chief. With power of attorney
to Francis Shakerley, Gentl., to deliver seisin thereof to the
said Edward Taylor. Dated 22 December, 1 Elizabeth [A.D.
1558].

90. Bond from Gilbert Gerrard, Esq. of Gray's Inn, co.
Middl., Attorney General, to John Lyon, Yeoman of Harrow
on the Hill, in five hundred pounds, n.d. post 1560. On condition of performance of Covenants in a bond from William
Tooke, Esq. of Popes in Hatfield Regis alias Bishops Hatfield,
co. Hertford, to the above Gilbert Gerrard. Dated 6 May, 2
Elizabeth [A.D. 1560].

91. Extract from roll of Court held at Harrow Hill on 8
May, 2 Elizabeth [A.D. 1560], wherein Henry Hurlock, son and
heir of Richard Hurlocke, is admitted to his father's lands at
Harrow Hill, under the wardship of Thomas Hurlocke, he
being a minor of 12 years of age.

92. Grant for ten pounds from Thomas Cole, Miller of
Maldon, to Richard Ffaldo of Maldon, of a messuage and half
an acre of meadow in Maldon, which the said Thomas lately
had by feoffment from William Kidley of Maldon, deceased.
Dated 1 July, 2 Elizabeth [A.D. 1560].

93. Bond from Thomas Cole of Maldon to Richard Ffaldo,
in twenty marks, for performance of the above Covenants.
Dated 1 July, 2 Elizabeth [A.D. 1560].

94. Settlement by John Tamworth in dower on Christian
Walsingham his wife of lands in Lyllstone [in Marylebone],
co. Middl., and Waltham Holy Cross and Hallyfeld [Holyfield],
co. Essex, lately quitclaimed by John Doddington and John
Jackson to the said John Tamworth. Dated 10 February, 3
Elizabeth [A.D. 1561]. Copy examined by William Dodington.

95. Extract from roll of Court held at Harrow Hill Rectory

on 30 April, 3 Eliz. [A.D. 1561], wherein William Jenyns is found to be the only son and heir of William Jenyns, who died seised of lands at Harrow ; the said William, Jun., is now but 14 years of age, and therefore the wardship of him and his lands is committed for seven years to — Ogylthorpe.

96. Sale for £266 13s. 4d. by John Tamworthe, Esq., Groom of the Queen's Privy Chamber, unto William Golightlie, Esq. of St. Martin's in the Fields, co. Middl., of the close Myllne-felde in Lyllston [in Marylebone], co. Middl., being parcel of Lyllston Manor, which premises the said John Tamworthe lately bought of John Dodyngton, Gentl. of London, and John Jackson, Yeoman of London, having been granted to them by Qn. Elizabeth. Dated 25 November, 4 Elizabeth [A.D. 1561].

97. Duplicate Copy of No. 96.

98. Sale for £210 from William Golyghtlye, Sergeant Farrier of the Queen's Stables, to Edmunde Roberts, Esq., of all the lands in Maryborne [Marylebone] Parish, co. Middl., held by William Randyson and by William Thatcher. Dated 19 February, 4 Elizabeth [A.D. 1562].

Recognizance taken before John Guybon, Master in Chancery, 15 April, 4 Elizabeth [A.D. 1562].

Enrolled on the *dors* of the Close roll in the Chancery, 16 April, 4 Elizabeth [A.D. 1562], by Edward Ridge.

99. Receipt of Sir Edward Capell, late Sheriff of co. Hertford, and of William Hamond, late Undersheriff, for six pounds from Hugh Griffithe, Gentl., for licence with Henry Ffortescue, Esq., on a plea of conveyance of the Manors of Powershall, *alias* Porrishall, and Wally Hall in Wytham, Ffawborne, Terlinge, Fferisted and Revenhall, co. Essex, and of the Manor of Bowltons, in North Myms and South Myms, cos. Hertford and Middl. Dated 22 February, 5 Elizabeth [A.D. 1563].

100. Extract from roll of Court of Sir Edward North and Dame Margaret his wife held at Harrow Hill Rectory on 26 April, 6 Eliz. [A.D. 1564], wherein John Lyon and Joan his wife are admitted to lands in Harrow Hill Manor surrendered by John Grenehyll ; license being at the same time granted to the said John and Joan Lyon to lease the above lands to Richard Rede for twenty-one years.

101. Sale for £700 by Edmonde Robertes, Esq. of Neasdon,

in the parish of Willesden, co. Middl., to Allen Horde, Gentl. of Ewell, co. Surrey, of

(*a*) lands in Marylebone parish, co. Middl., purchased by the said Edmonde of William Golightly, Serjeant Farrier of the Queen's Stable, who purchased them of John Dodington, Gentl. of London, and John Jackson, Yeoman of London, to whom they were granted by Queen Elizabeth.

(*b*) of a messuage in Pynner, in the parish of Harrow-on-the-Hill, held by John Sheryn.

(*c*) the reversion after the decease of Ursula, wife of Benjamin Gunston, Esq., of a tenement in Northall [Northolt] parish, held by Robert Ffrynde, and the lands in Northall and Harrow parishes held by Willyam Gerrard, Gentl., and a farm in Roxsey (Roxeth), in Harrow parish, formerly held by John Hawkyns, deceased, and now by Richarde Shepparde. Dated 10 September, 7 Elizabeth [A.D. 1565].

Recognizance taken before Thomas Yale, Master in Chancery, on the same date.

102. Extract from roll of Court of Dame Margaret Northe, widow, held at Harrow-on-the-Hill on 29 Oct., 7 Eliz. [A.D. 1565], wherein John Lyon is admitted to lands at Northfield surrendered by William Belamy, Katharine his wife, and Richard their son and heir.

103. Extract from roll of Court of Dame Margaret Northe, widow, held at Harrow on 29 Oct., 7 Eliz. [A.D. 1565], wherein license is granted to John Lyon to enclose Common lands at Preston.

104. Extract from the roll of Accompts of the Subsidy, wherein acquittance is rendered to John Lyon, Collector, for the second payment of a certain subsidy granted by the laity to Queen Elizabeth in the eighth year of her reign [Nov. 1565–Nov. 1566] in the Hundred of Gore, co. Middl. (as certified by Edmund [Grindal], Bishop of London, and Sir William Cordell and the other Commissioners of the Treasury and the Barons of the Exchequer). The sum collected amounting to £99 0*s.* 6*d.* less £2 9*s.* 6*d.* the amount of his fees, on 21 May, 10 Elizabeth [A.D. 1568].

Examined by Thomas Hyde.

105. Inquisition *post mortem* into the estate of William Ffaldo, Gentl., taken at Bedford, co. Bedford, 27 April, 8 Eliza-

beth [A.D. 1566], before John Colbeck, Esq., and Thomas Beddells, Gentl., Commissioners, which estate consists of lands in Maldon, Higham Gobyon, Pulloxhill, and Okeley, co. Bedford, and descends by hereditary right to Richard Ffaldo as son and heir of the said William, aged thirty-five years and upwards. The said Richard, and Margaret Ffaldo his mother, wife of the above William, have received the rents accruing from the said William's death to the time of this Inquisition.

106. Sale for £250 from Wylliam Golyghtely, Esq. of St. Martins-in-the-Fields, co Middl., to Wylliam Sheryngton, Citizen and Haberdasher, of London, of lands in Marybone parish, co. Middl. Dated 20 May, 8 Elizabeth [A.D. 1566]. With bond of the same date from Wylliam Golightely and Wylliam Downes, Citizen and Merchant Tailor of London, to William Sherington by a recognizance in £400.

107. Copy of the above indenture, endorsed " Copye deed for Mr. Lyon."

108, 109. Fine of £20 taken in the Court of Queen's Bench at Westminster on Trinity Monday, 8 Elizabeth [A.D. 1566], from William Sherington to William Golightely and Elena his wife, for lands in Marylebone.

110. Sale for 20s. from Henry Samwell, Miller, of Flitton, co. Bedf., to Richard Ffaldo of Maldon, of one "hollman" of meadow in Maldon. Dated 23 September, 8 Elizabeth [A.D. 1566].

111. Sale for £3 6s. 8d. from William Albany, Citizen and Merchant Tailor of London, to Richard Ffaldo, Gentl. of Maldon, of one holme of Meadow in Maldon. Dated 28 November, 9 Elizabeth [A.D. 1566].

112. Sale for £563 6s. 8d. from Richard Ffaldo, Gentl. of Maldon, co. Bedf., to John Lyon, Yeoman of Preston, in Harrow-on-the-Hill parish, of his mansion house and lands in Maldon. Dated 3 July, 10 Elizabeth [A.D. 1568]. Signed by Richard Ffaldo. Recognizance taken before David Lewes, Master in Chancery, and signed by him.

113. Bond for £700 from Richard Ffaldo to John Lyon for performance of the above Covenant. Dated 3 July, 10 Elizabeth [A.D. 1568)].

114. Lease from John Lyon, Yeoman of Harrow Hill, and Johan his wife, to Andrewe Ffeilde, Yeoman of Upbury in Pulloxhill parish, co. Bedf., of a capital messuage and cottages

in Maldon, Ampthill, Flitton, and Clephill, co. Bedford, for forty years at a rent of £20 a year and ten quarters of good and sweet malt. Dated 22 July, 10 Elizabeth [A.D. 1568].

115. Paper Copy of the above lease.

116. Lease from John Lyon and Johan his wife to Valentine Norrys, Yeoman, of Chipping Barnet, co. Hertford, of four tenements in Chipping Barnet, to hold for 80 years at £9 a year. Dated 20 October, 10 Elizabeth [A.D. 1568]. Signed " be my John Lyon."

117, 118. Fine in the Court of Queen's Bench at Westminster, Michaelmas Term, 10 Elizabeth [A.D. 1568], between John Lyon, plaintiff, and Richard Ffaldo and Amphilla his wife, deforciants, for a messuage with lands in Maldon, Ampthyll, Flytton, and Clephill, co. Bedf.

119. Lease for £200 from John Lyon and Johan his wife to William Eles, Husbandman, of Wembley in Harrow parish, of a capital messuage in Northemymes (North Mimms) parish, co. Hertf., for seventy years (to begin at the expiration of a lease of the same property from William Toke, Esq., of Popes, co. Hertf., and Alice his wife, to William Spryngam, Yeoman of Blewclosse, co. Hertf., for twenty-one years, made 19 October, 1 & 2 Philip and Mary [A.D. 1554]), at the yearly rent of £21. Dated 18 April, 11 Elizabeth [A.D. 1569]. On the *dors* is a memorandum of the receipt of £60, being the last instalment of the above £200, dated 30 June, 14 Elizabeth [A.D. 1572], and signed by John Lyon.

120. Paper Copy of the above indenture.

121. Bond for £40 from William Eles to John Lyon for performance of the above Covenant. Dated 18 April, 11 Elizabeth [A.D. 1569].

122. Acquittance for £6 from Thomas Belamy, Gentl., late of Preston in Harrow-on-the-Hill parish, to John Lyon, Yeoman of Preston, the said Thomas having by negligence lost the bill obligatory for the said sum. Witnesses, Jack Straw and Wat Tyler. Dated 3 July, 11 Elizabeth [A.D. 1569].

123. "Beddford Maldon. A Terror of all suche landes and tenements as Richarde Ffaldo solde to John Lion lyinge in Maldone made the Xth daie of Januarye in the XIIth yere of the Raine of ower sovereigne Ladie Quene Elizabethe, 1569 " [1570]. Parchment Roll.

26 *

124. Paper copy of the above.

125. Sale for £51 from John Hyll, Brewer of Southwark, co. Surrey, to John Lyon, Yeoman of Preston in Harrow-on-the-Hill, of a messuage in Harrow, to be surrendered at or before the next Court of Harrow Hill Manor. Dated 22 May, 12 Elizabeth [A.D. 1570].

126. Extract from roll of Court of Dame Margaret Northe, widow, held at Harrow Hill Rectory on 26 April, 13 Eliz. [A.D. 1571], wherein John Lyon and Joan his wife are admitted to lands at Harrow surrendered by John Hill, of Southwark, co. Surrey, and Maria his wife, and previously by William Gennyns, son and heir of William Gennyns.

127. Covenant between William Gerrard and Henry Burton made on 11 November, 13 Elizabeth 1571 containing surrender of lands in Roxeth and Harrow Hill, and grant from the said William to the said Henry of lands in Roxeth to hold for four years without rent.

128. Extract from roll of Court of Dame Margaret Northe, widow, held at Harrow Hill Rectory on 4 Dec., 14 Eliz. [A.D. 1571], wherein John Lyon and Joan his wife are admitted to lands at Harrow Hill surrendered by William Gerrard and Dorothy his wife, and previously by Henry Burton and Dionisia his wife.

129. Bond of William Downes, Citizen and Merchant-Tailor of London, of St. Martin's parish, Westminster, and of Philip Downes, his son, to William Sherington, Citizen and Haberdasher of London, in £100 for fulfilment of indentures between them. Dated 26 Febr. 14 Eliz. [A.D. 1572]. Witnessed by Gyles Sheryngton, Thomas Finche, and Humfrey Rilandes. With two seals.

130. Lease from John Lyon and Johane his wife to Hugh Ffelyskyrk, Shoemaker of Harrow, of a messuage and garden in Harrow village, now divided into two dwelling-houses, one occupied by Hugh Ffelyskyrk, the other by William Seldon, and of a croft of two acres within the Manor, to hold for 21 years at a yearly rent of £3. Provided that if at any time John Lyon be minded to take William Seldon's house and to convert the same to be a dwelling-house or lodging for a "scole maister," then John Lyon may resume the same into his own hands; and also the said John Lyon shall at all tymes have a convenient

stable and house room to set his horse in whenever he or his wife have occasion to come to Harrow village on horseback. And if the said Hugh and Isabell his wife die childless during the term of the lease, then this lease shall be utterly void. Dated 14 March, 14 Elizabeth [A.D. 1572]. Signed by John Lyon with seal bearing a stag passant.

131. Counterpart of the above indenture, signed with the *mark* of Hugh Ffelyskyrk.

132. Sale for £140 from Richard Nicoll, Yeoman of Haywood Hill in Hendon parish, and Katheryne his wife, daughter and heir of the late William Page of Vxenden in Harrow-on-the-Hill parish, to John Lyon and Johan his wife, of a messuage in Alperton in Harrow parish, which the said William Page bought of John Warner of Ilcleton, co. Cambridge, on 10 August, 6 Edward VI. Dated 14 October, 14 Elizabeth [A.D. 1572]. Recognizance taken 24 October 1572.

133. Bond for £200 from Richard Nicoll to John Lyon for performance of the above Covenants. Dated 14 October, 14 Elizabeth [A.D. 1572].

134. Fine made in the Court of Queen's Bench at Westminster, in Michaelmas Term, 14 Elizabeth [A.D. 1572], between John Lyon of Preston, in Harrow parish, and Joan his wife, Plaintiffs, and Richard Nicoll of Haywood Hill in Hendon parish, and Katharine his wife, Deforciants, concerning a messuage in Alperton in Harrow parish.

135. Copy of the above.

136. Extract from roll of Court of Dame Margaret Northe, widow, held at Harrow Hill Rectory on 21 April, 16 Eliz. [A.D. 1574], wherein William Gerrard is admitted to lands at Harrow Hill surrendered by Jerome Belamy, Katharine Belamy his mother, and his brothers Robert, Bartholomew, and Thomas.

137. Extract from roll of Court of Dame Margaret Northe, widow, held at Harrow Hill Rectory, 21 April, 16 Eliz., wherein license is granted to William Gerrard to lease lands at Harrow Hill now occupied by William Pedley.

138. Extract from roll of Court held at Harrow Hill Rectory by Dame Margaret Northe, widow, on 21 April, 16 Eliz. [A.D. 1574], wherein Henry Page, son and heir of Thomas Page, is admitted to his father's lands.

139. Lease from William Gerrard, Esq. of Fflambreds in

Harrow-on-the-Hill, to Robert Pedley, Yeoman of Harrow, to
hold for 21 years at a yearly rent of £5. Dated 28 April, 16
Elizabeth [A.D. 1574].

140. Memorandum of the sale for £45 from Henry Hurlock,
Citizen and Grocer of London, to John Lion of Harrow-upon-
the-Hill, of two tenements in Harrow. Dated 2 July, 16 Elizabeth [A.D. 1574].

141. Extract from roll of Court of Dame Margaret Northe,
widow, held at Harrow Hill Rectory on 13 April, 17 Eliz. [A.D.
1575], wherein John Lyon and Joan his wife are admitted to
lands at Harrow Hill surrendered by Henry Hurlock, Citizen
and Grocer of London, son and heir of the late Richard
Hurlock.

142. Extract from roll of Court of Dame Margaret Northe,
widow, held at Harrow Hill Rectory on 13 April, 17 Eliz. [A.D.
1575], wherein John Lyon and Joan his wife are admitted to
lands surrendered by Henry Page, son and heir of Thomas Page.

143. Extract from roll of Court of Dame Margaret Northe,
widow, held at Harrow Hill Rectory on 13 April, 17 Eliz. [A.D.
1575], wherein John Lyon and Joan his wife are admitted to
lands at Harrow Hill surrendered by William Gerrard.

144. Lease from John Lyon and Johanne his wife to James
Mayho, alias Maye, Husbandman of Alperton in Harrow, of a
messuage in Alperton for twenty years at a yearly rent of
£6 13s. 4d. Dated 16 May, 17 Elizabeth [A.D. 1575].

145. Bond for £40 from George Tanner, Husbandman of
Alperton in Harrow, to John Lion and Joan his wife, for performance of Covenants. Dated 16 May, 17 Elizabeth [A.D. 1575].

146. Extract from roll of Court of Dame Margaret North,
widow, held at Harrowe on 24 May, 17 Elizabeth [A.D. 1575],
when John Lyon surrendered two half-hides of land in Preston,
to be re-granted to the said John and Joan his wife, and to the
heirs of the said John lawfully begotten, and in default of such
with remainder to the use of Gilbert Gerrard, Esq., Attorney-
General, William Gerrard, Gentl., John Page of Wembley,
Thomas Redinge of Pinner, and Richard Edlyn of Woodhall
in Harrow, Keepers and Governors of the possessions, revenues,
and goods of the Free Grammar School of John Lyon, in the
village of Harrow, and of their successors for ever, the above-
mentioned Governors paying every twenty-first year after the

death of the said John and Joan fifty shillings in addition to the usual rents and services. Which re-grant took place and seism was thereupon given to the said John Lyon, and he gives nothing in the way of fine, because the Lady forgave it at the special request of the above Gilbert Gerrard.

Examined and found agreeable to the Court-roll by Henry Clerke, Steward of the Manor Court, 29 March 1590.

147. Duplicate of the previous. Examined by William Gerrard.

148. Extract from roll of Court of Dame Margaret North, widow, held at Harrow Hill Rectory on 24 May, 17 Elizabeth [A.D. 1575], when John Lyon of Preston resigned all his customary tenements, &c. within the said Manor, to be re-granted to the said John Lyon for his life, and after his death to remain to the use of the Keepers and Governors of the possessions and goods of the Free Grammar School of John Lyon in Harrow village and of their successors for ever. Which re-grant took place on condition of the said Governors paying every twenty-first year after the death of John Lyon fifty additional shillings, and seisin was thereupon given to John Lyon.

149. Lease from John Lyon and Joan his wife to George Tanner, Husbandman of Alperton, of a messuage in Alperton for fifty years at a yearly rental of £6 13s. 4d. Dated 16 May, 17 Elizabeth [A.D. 1575].

150. Sale for £340 from Alan Hoorde, Gentl., of Ewell, co. Surrey, to Gylbert Gerrard, Esq., Attorney-General, and William Gerrard, Esq., of Harrow-upon-the-Hill, of closes and lands in Marybone parish, co. Middl., lately bought of Edmund Roberts, Esq., of Wyllesden. Dated 6 June, 21 Elizabeth [A.D. 1579]. Recognizance taken in Chancery, 20 June 1579. Enrolled on the dors of the Close Chancery roll, 6 July 1579.

151. Bond for £600 from Alan Horde of Ewell and Thomas Horde, Esq., of Seint Johns Strete, co. Middl., to Gilbert Gerrard, Esq., Attorney-General, and William Gerrard, Esq., of Harrow Hill, for performance of the above Covenant. Dated 6 June, 21 Elizabeth [A.D. 1579].

152, 153. Fine taken in the Court of Queen's Bench at Westminster in Trinity term, 21 Elizabeth [A.D. 1579], between Gilbert Gerrard and William Gerrard, Plaintiffs, and Alan Horde and William Dodyngton, Esq., and Christiana his wife, Deforciants, for lands in Maribone [Marylebone, co. Middl.].

154. Sale from Sir Gilbert Gerrard, Attorney-General, and his brother William Gerrard, Esq., of Harrow, to John Lyon and Joan his wife, and to the Keepers and Governors of the possessions, revenues, and goods of the Free Grammar School of John Lyon in Harrow town, of a meadow grounds in Marybone parish, lately bought of Alan Hord, Gentl., of Ewell, on 6 June, 21 Elizabeth [A.D. 1579]. To be held by the said John and Joan Lyon for their lives, and after their deaths by the said Governors to the sole intent that they shall employ the whole yearly rent therefrom to the repair of the high road from Edgware to London, and any surplus to be devoted to the repair of the high road from Harrow to London. Dated 6 July, 21 Elizabeth [A.D. 1579].

155. Duplicate of the above indenture.

156. Triplicate of the above indenture, with Recognizance taken on 6 July 1579. Enrolled on the dors of the Close roll of the Chancery, 15 July 1579.

157. Fragment containing the first page of a draft on paper of the above indenture.

158. Extract from roll of Court of Sir Roger Northe held at Harrow, 22 Dec., 22 Eliz. [A.D. 1579], wherein license is granted to John Lyon to enclose Common lands at Preston, for which he had previously sought a license at a Court holden on 29 Oct., 7 Eliz. [A.D. 1565]. See No. 103.

159. Quitclaim from Alane Hoorde of Ewell to John Lyon, Jone his wife, and the Keepers and Governors of the possessions, revenues, and goods of the Free Grammar School of John Lyon in Harrow, of all his rights to the meadow lands in Maribone parish, lately sold by the said Alan to Sir Gilbert Gerrard and his brother William Gerrard, and by them sold to the said John Lyon, Joane his wife, and the said Governors. Dated 3 May, 22 Elizabeth [A.D. 1580].

160. Extract from roll of Court of Sir Roger Northe held at Harrow Hill rectory on 5 May, 22 Eliz. [A.D. 1580], wherein a Memorandum was enrolled that at a Court holden on 6 May, 21 Eliz., license was granted to John Lyon, Joan his wife, and the Keepers or Governors of possessions, revenues, and goods of the Free Grammar School of John Lyon at Harrow-on-the-Hill, co. Middl., to lease for 41 years lands at Harrow Hill.

161. Lease from John Lyon and Jone his wife and the Keepers or Governors of the possessions, revenues, and goods of the free Grammar School of John Lyon in Harrow town, to Thomas Ffynch, Yeoman of Harrow, of a messuage and capital tenement in Harrow for forty-one years at a yearly rent of fifty-three shillings and four pence. Dated 20 June, 22 Elizabeth [A.D. 1580].

162. Acquittance by William Cosyn of the audit of the accompt of John Lyon, " Præpositus " and " Bedellus " of Harrow-on-the-Hill Rectory Manor, for one whole year ending at Michaelmas, 22 Elizabeth [A.D. 1580].

163. Sale for £321 10s. from William Sherington, Citizen and Haberdasher of London, to John Lyon of Preston, in Harrow parish, and Joane his wife, and to the Keepers and Governors of the possessions, revenues and goods of the free Grammar School of John Lyon in Harrow Town, of certain lands in Marybone parish, co. Middl. held in lease by Philip Downes, and of other lands in Lillston, also held by the said Philip Downes, lately bought by the said William Sherington of William Golightly, Esq. To be held by the said Governors after the decease of the above John and Joane for the sole purpose of repairing the Highway from Harrow Town to London City through Harlston [Harlesdon] and Padington. Dated 19 Dec. 25 Elizabeth [A.D. 1582]. Recognizance taken 20 Dec. 1582. Enrolled in Chancery, 16 January 1583.

164. Duplicate of the above Indenture.

165. Bond for 500 marks from William Sherington to John Lyon for performance of the above Covenants. Dated 19 Dec. 25 Elizabeth [A.D. 1582].

166. Appointment by John [Aylmer], Bishop of London (according to the trust reposed in him by the Foundation Charter of the free Grammar School of John Lyon in Harrow Town), of three new Governors of the said School in place of three lately deceased, viz. in place of William Gerrard, Gentl., his son and heir William Gerrard, of Flamberds in Harrow, in place of Thomas Page of Sudbury Court, his son and heir Henry Page, and in place of Thomas Reding of Pinner, his son-in-law William Grenhill of Roxheth, alias Roxey, in Harrow parish: the above appointments having lapsed to the said

Bishop in consequence of the surviving Governors having neglected to fill up the vacancies within six weeks after death. Dated 3 January, 28 Elizabeth [A.D. 1586].

167. Lease from John Lyon, Johane his wife, and the Keepers and Governors, &c. to John Eeles, Yeoman of Boltons in Northmyms parish. co. Hertford, of their Capital messuage called Boltons, to hold for ninety-nine years at a yearly rent of £21. Dated 22 June, 32 Elizabeth [A.D. 1590].

168. Lease from the Keepers and Governors, &c. to Philip Gerrard, Gentl. of Gray's Inn, co. Middl., of the reversion of two half hides of land in Harrow, a messuage at Preston in Harrow, and lands in Kingsbury, co. Middl., immediately on the death of Johanne, widow of John Lyon, for thirty-one years at a yearly rent of £20. Such lease to be granted at any time within seven years after the decease of the said Joane, on notice given by the said Philip Gerrard *at the nowe Schoole or Church house of the parish of Harrowe*. Dated 2 November, 38 Elizabeth, 1596. Signed by the Governors, and sealed with the Corporation seal of the School bearing a Lion rampant and the legend " Donorum Dei Dispensatio Fidelis."

169. Bond for £200 from the Keepers and Governors, &c. to Philip Gerrard, Gentl. of Graise Inn, co. Middl., for performance of the above Covenants. Dated 2 November, 38 Elizabeth [A.D. 1596]. Signed by the Governors. The Corporation seal has been torn away.

170. Award made by Sir Philip Boteler and Rowland Lytton, Esq., after taking Counsel's opinion of —— Houghton, Esq. of Lincoln's Inn, by which Anthony Maynard, Gentl., on receipt of fifty pounds, shall assure unto Richard Ffrancklyne, Gentl., Johane Lyon, Widow, and the Keepers and Governors of the possessions, revenues and goods of the free Grammar School of John Lyon in Harrow town, co. Middl., and to Richard Wyat, Citizen and Carpenter of London, the title of lands and tenements in Barnett and East Barnett, co. Hertf. in so far as they are claimed in divers shares by the above parties ; being parcel of the Manor of Barnett and East Barnett, granted on or about the 25 March, 7 Edward VI. [A.D. 1553], by the King to John Maynard, Grandfather of the said Anthony, and to John Goodwyne, and to the heirs of the said John Maynard. The said lands being claimed by the above Richard Francklyne, Johanne

Lyon, the Governours and Richard Wyat, under the title of a Patent made thereof on or about 6 November, 5 and 6 Philip and Mary [A.D. 1558], unto William Rolfe and John Marshe. Dated 20 September, 42 Elizabeth [A.D. 1600].

171. Feoffment from Anthony Maynard, Gentl., of South Mimms, co. Middl., to Joan Lyon, widow, and to the Keepers and Governors of the possessions, revenues, and goods of the Free Grammar School of John Lyon in Harrow town, of four messuages and two closes of land lying in Chipping Barnett. Dated 26 September, 42 Elizabeth, 1600.

172. Power of attorney from Johan Lyon to Thomas Rotherham, Gentl., to receive seisin of the lands above enfeoffed to her for her lifetime. Dated 29 September, 42 Elizabeth, 1600. Signed by Johan Lyon with a cross, with her seal bearing a lion rampant.

173. Memorandum of the receipt by Anthony Maynard from Thomas Rotherham, Gentl., of £26 13s. 4d., parcel of £50 awarded him by Sir Philip Boteler and Rowland Litton, Esq., on behalf of Widow Lyon and the Governours of the free School of Harrow and of Mr. Wiatt, of London, Mr. Francklin's part not being paid yet, because it is not yet agreed how much shall pass between them. Dated 15 October, 1600.

174. Quitclaim from Anthony Maynard, Gentl., of South Mimms, co. Middl., to Joan Lyon, widow, and to the Keepers and Governours of the possessions, revenues, and goods of the free Grammar School of John Lyon in Harrow town, of his right and title to four messuages and two closes in Chipping Barnett, co. Hertf. Dated 15 October, 42 Elizabeth, 1600.

175. Assignment by Edward Ffynch, Citizen and Grocer of London, for £25 to Robert Hexam, Yeoman of Cheeswich [Chiswick], co. Middl., of the lease made on 20 June, 22 Elizabeth [A.D. 1580], to his natural father Thomas Ffynch, Yeoman of Harrow, by John Lyon, Yeoman of Preston in Harrow, Johane his wife, and the Keepers or Governours of the possessions, revenues, and goods of the Free Grammar School of John Lyon in Harrow town, of a messuage and four acres in Harrow for 41 years at a yearly rent of fifty-three shillings and four pence. Which lease the said Thomas on 20 January, 41 Elizabeth

[A.D. 1599] assigned to his natural son the said Edward.
Dated 18 May, 44 Elizabeth, 1602.

Since this abstract was compiled, various documents have
been discovered in the archives confirming the view expressed
in this work that John Lyon, Founder of Harrow, was a local
squire, and a landowner of considerable importance in other
parts of the country. And the said documentary evidence has
received confirmation from other sources. We subjoin those of
more manifest import.

Prepositus et Bedellus may not convey any elevated idea to
one animated with a dread of modern bumbledom; but nevertheless a Collector of Subsidies, who likewise managed all the
parish matters in the wide-spreading Harrow district during
Queen Elizabeth's halcyon days, deserves all the prestige that
a chosen ruler of men can under such circumstances claim. The
man, moreover, who (as a lately-deciphered school-deed shows)
could in 1568 purchase a *mansion* in Maldon, county Bedford,
for no less sum than £563 6s. 8d. (or £6,760 of our money),
must have been indeed favoured by Providence with this world's
goods. We are disposed to think that some accrument of
fortune came to the Harrow founder's family between 1522 and
the above-mentioned epoch, because when Wolsey ordered a
return of those taxed at £20 per annum in Harrow parish, the
Pages then were found to be the more wealthy family—two of
the name paying £30 per annum, two £20, while John Lyon's
(the Founder's father) taxes were paid at the latter rate. For
the latter information we are, in the first instance, indebted to
Brewer's *Calendar, Henry VIII.*, vol. iii. part 2, p. 1051. Reference was there given to a deed at the Record Office, which,
being perfect so far as the Harrow returns were concerned, it
was possible to inspect. This return, however, by no means
gives any indication of the family position when so much was
owned by them in other places; but it is worth recording here.

And now, having shown how temporalities were held by the
Preston Lyons, far in excess of those usually enjoyed by those
of yeoman rank (at least in 1568), we pass on to the more important question of position. For even Shylock's ducats did
not elevate the owner in the social scale off the Rialto. And
in this particular the close friendship with Sir Gilbert Gerard,

guardian of Queen Elizabeth's life, will be, to the mind that realises the circumstances, quite convincing.

The then Mr. Gilbert Gerard's able advocacy had so utilised the condemned Sir Thomas Wyatt's careful exoneration of the Princess Elizabeth, that her royal sister Queen Mary was unable to compass her destruction when the Kentish knight's conspiracy was foiled in 1554. After that period Elizabeth must have felt that she owed her very existence to that sage and learned counsellor, the chosen friend of John Lyon— Gilbert Gerard. Not only was the Harrow Founder jointly bound (£500 each) with Sir Gilbert, but we have seen (p. 70 of this work) how careful the knight was to shield his friend from public exaction when purposing what must have been a design dear to both, viz. the Foundation of Harrow School. Otherwise Sir Gilbert would never have taken the trouble to save the infant institution from incipient pauperism, threatened most certainly if its originator were unduly mulcted for national purposes, nor would the acute lawyer have undertaken the onerous position of an original governor. But the friend and ally of such a man as Gerard must have partaken in some sort of his social status. And that such a position was very high in Elizabethan society it is not difficult to conceive.

As the Gerards play so important a part in this book, we append a short résumé of their history.

William Gerard married a daughter of Sir J. Byron, knight, of Newstead, who gained that honour on Bosworth Field, and whose family afterwards received a grant of Newstead Abbey in 1540.

William Gerard's son James married a Holcroft. They had issue—

Gilbert Gerard, an eminent lawyer, reader, and joint treasurer of Gray's Inn, together with Nicholas Bacon. When the Princess Elizabeth was brought before the council, Mr. Gerard advocated her cause so ably that he was committed to the Tower. Upon the accession of Elizabeth he was released and constituted Attorney-General. He was knighted and made Master of the Rolls when he had been twenty-three years Attorney-General. He erected a stately mansion in the county of Stafford, and was one of the first governors of Harrow School. He married a Lancashire Ratcliffe.

His son Thomas was created, in 1603, Baron Gerard, of Gerard's Bromley, Stafford.

Sir Gilbert's younger son William lived at Flambards, married a Ratcliff of Lancashire, and had issue Gilbert Gerard of Flambards, who represented Middlesex in Parliament and was created a baronet by James II. in 1620. He afterwards joined the Parliamentary party during the Civil war.

His son Sir Francis Gerard of Flambards married Isabel, daughter of Sir T. Cheek, and his three sons were successively baronets, viz.:

Sir Charles Gerard, whose daughter married Warwick Lake, and was grandmother to Gerard, Lord Lake ;

Sir Francis, brother of the last baronet ;

Sir Cheek, brother of the last baronet, at whose demise, in 1715, the baronetcy became extinct. Flambards devolved on—

Elizabeth, the last-mentioned Sir Charles Gerard's daughter, and was sold to one Francis Herne.—Burke, *Extinct and Dormant Baronetcies*, p. 216.

John Lyon's friendship with the Bellamies stood on a different footing from that with the Gerards. The former were such close neighbours that it was next to impossible to live in such contiguity, and yet refrain from amicable relations between the families. Fortunate indeed was the unsuspected household by the side of Brent's meandering stream—so fitted for the once thriving religious house located there—when in 1586 the Babington conspiracy had made the ruling powers eager for the blood of suspects. Who can doubt that the charter of Harrow School was then to a degree due to Lyon's innocence.

Every Harrovian should wander across the fields to Preston, see the founder's home, and, making his way to the Brent, realise where Uxendon farm-house formerly stood—for, alas ! the quaint old building succumbed to modern vandalism in 1876—and return home wiser, if not really better, for silent converse with the earlier characters in Harrow story.

The latest outcome of Mr. Scott's search through what was lately a veritable chaos of dusty and sometimes nearly illegible manuscript has been the knowledge, not only of the time and occasion when the school-yard was purchased, but also its actual limits.

Number 130 amongst the School Deeds describes a lease from John Lyon to Hugh Feliskyrke, shoemaker, of Harrow, of a messuage and garden in Harrow village, lying between the Vicarage lands on the north, the lands of the late John Dolt on the south, abutting on the high road on the east, and other lands of John Lyon on the west; the said messuage being now divided (we quote verbatim from the Deed) into two dwelling-houses, one occupied by the said Hugh, the other by William Seldon. If, however, at any time John Lyon be minded to take William Seldon's house and to *convert the same into a dwelling-house for a school-master*, he could resume possession of the property by taking it into his own hands.

A further proviso gives us a glimpse into the personal habits of the founder and his wife, because he reserves the right to have stabling and horse-room whenever he and his better half *ride* into Harrow village.

We can conceive that an occasional change from the quiet of Preston to the bustle of Harrow at market time must have been grateful.

This aforesaid Deed is signed by John Lyon, and is stamped with his seal bearing a stag passant.

When the Harrow archives tell us of a school-house older than the Charter, and the Caius College muniments disclose the fact that scholars passed from Harrow to Cambridge before that date, we are led to claim antiquity beyond expectation for the School on the Hill. Moreover, the mention of Church House, which occurs in a Lyon Deed, A.D. 1596, proves that this pre-Lyon establishment was of ecclesiastical origin. The governors were then letting the *reversion* of the Preston property after the founder's widow's death to Philip Gerard, at a rental of £20, the said rent to be paid at the *now school or Church House* every year.

We have referred to these disclosures in Appendix B., but their importance must stand as excuse for a further mention.

There is a strange coincidence to which the author desires to call attention.

In 1833 the Harrow Parish Vestry issued a pamphlet dealing with the school generally and its bequests to the Parish, also setting forth certain matters of general interest. From some source unnamed they produced a rental of the Harrow School property in 1590, wherein, as will be seen by the copy, *Walden* occurs.

Now Walden in Essex was the source whence the Lyon family was traced by Mr. Philippe, the Rolls Office expert, who made a pedigree for Mr. Amos Lyon, the American claimant to founder's blood. On the other hand, no mention of Walden occurs in the School archives, whereas *Maldon* in Bedfordshire is mentioned again and again, while John Lyon's direct ancestors are proved to have lived at Preston in the 14th century. The significance of Walden's absence amongst the muniments will be understood when it is known that 176 deeds in the Harrow chest date from periods anterior to James I.'s accession, while 126 are older than John Lyon's foundation in 1571.

RENTALL OF THE FREE SCHOOLE LANDES, WITH LIST OF
THE TENANTS, 1590.

The Rents of Harrowe.

	OLD RENTS.		
	£.	s.	d.
Robert Marsh	05	00	00
Henry Platt	01	00	00
Edward Claxton, Esq. . . .	01	13	04
Widowe Wyld	00	13	04
Andrew Gowlett	00	13	04
John Archer	00	13	04
John Harris	05	00	00
Gabriel Ffisher	00	10	00
Adam Hooper	00	10	00
John Wylde	00	10	00
Mary Jones	08	00	00
Humphrey Thomas	00	16	08
John Reade	02	00	00
Gabriell Maynard	01	00	00

The Rents of Alperton.

Andrew Wright . . .	13	06	08

The Rents of Preston.

Thomas Walter	40	00	00
The Land at Walden . . .	29	00	00
The Land at Minmes . . .	20	00	00
The Land at Barnett . . .	09	00	00
Mr. Johnson for Land at Kilborne .	20	00	00
Mr. Finch of Watford for Land at Paddington	20	00	00
In 1590, the totall sume is	179	06	08

APPENDIX D.

THE LYON PEDIGREE.

The portion of this pedigree to the left of this mark ✠ is extracted from the Lyon deeds contained in the Harrow School muniment chest. That on the right presents the result of the late Mr. C. E. Long's labours, during which he had access to the genealogical collections at the Herald's College. We give it *tentatively*. In one essential this pedigree differs from Mr. Long's research when not supplemented by the light thrown by the school archives. Thomas Lyon, father of Sir John, could not have been an elder son, because his brother John is described as *heres et filius* several times in the Lyon deeds.

John Lyoun, 1370.

Andrew Lyoun = Agnes, *ob.* 1395.

John Lyoun, 1396.

Andrew Lyoun, *ob. s. p.* 1402. | William Lyoun = Rose, 1409–22.

John Lyon, 1422–55.

William Lyon = Matilda, *ob.* 1476.

John Lyon = Joan, *ob.* 1518.

William, *ob. s. p.* 1522. He resided at Horsington Hill, near Harrow, where an old moated house is shown as his residence. His younger brother John was executor to his will. | John = Joan.

Thomas Lyon, of Perivale, who was in trade, and a member of the Grocers' Company.

Sir John Lyon = Alice, Lord Mayor of London, 1554. Sir John married, secondly, Mary, relict of Alderman H.nde, but left no issue. | who predeceased her husband.

John Lyon, who died before his father, in 1560, the Lord Mayor and Knight, Sir John Lyon, dying in 1564, his nephew Richard, son of his uncle Henry, was left by will his heir.

Henry, who died unmarried.

a daughter, who became Mrs. Randall, and left issue one daughter, who married into the family of Adrian, of Kingston-on-Thames.

John Lyon, the Founder, *nat. circ.* 1514; *ob. s. p.* 1592.

Henry Lyon, of Ruislip.

Richard Lyon = Isabel,* who by Sir John Lyon's will inherited his property in 1564. Richard Lyon died in 1579, and was buried at Twyford.

George Lyon, who died before Sir John Lyon.

Dorothy, to whom Sir John left a sum of money on the condition of the road between Harrow and Uxbridge being kept in good order. She died before Henry Lyon, her heir-at-law, and Thomas Page of Sudbury Court was called on to administer her estate.

Alice, who became Mrs. Middleton, and left no issue.

John Lyon, who lived at Twyford Abbey, according to Norden (Lyon, Baronrows of London, vol. ii, part 2, p. 806), inherited Richard Lyon's lands in Berks, and died in 1633.

Henry Lyon = Mabilla. of Harrow-on-the-Hill, *ob.* 1560.

George Lyon, to whom his uncle John left the manor of West Twyford for life, and after to his son. *ob.* 1636.

Richard, who inherited the Horsington Hill property, which his uncle John left to him. The date of his death is not recorded.

Etheldred, afterwards married to William Gifford, buried at Twyford in 1601.

Dorothy, married to Humphrey Hyde.

Elizabeth.

George, who sold the manor of West Twyford in 1647. He died unmarried in 1647.

* Richard Lyon married, first, Agnes Smith, but had no issue. His second wife, Isabel, was a M'Gett, a family well known in Twyford and Harrow during the seventeenth century. Henry Lyon, who died in 1608, had married Mabilla Dunnel, of Thornbarne, co. Lincoln. (These statements we owe to the after-named Rolls Office Research.) The

Some years ago, Mr. Amos Lyon, an American, believing himself to be of Founder's kin, employed an official at the Rolls Office (one Mr. Philippe) to trace the family pedigree. This was done in a few weeks by the expert employed, who fell into the error of merging the Walden family of Lyon, who had been established in Essex since 1226, into that of Lyon of Preston, whose presence at Preston can be proved in 1370. Although inaccurate as regards earlier times, this Rolls Office pedigree contained much interesting information, and bore out Mr. C. E. Long's belief that the Founder and Sir John Lyon were first cousins. The author of this book purchased the Rolls Office researches, and has had their conclusions tested by careful comparison with the Wills of Sir John Lyon and his kinsman John Lyon of Twyford. This tentative pedigree will, it is hoped, be fully discussed, so that if any imperfection exist it may be rectified hereafter. Although Mr. Amos Lyon had not the satisfaction of tracing his descent from the Harrow Founder, it by no means follows that his title to membership with the Lyons of Preston is ill-founded. In the same way, the writer believes that the long-standing tradition which connects the Smiths of Eastbury with the Founder's family, through marriage with Anne Lyon of Ruislip, is too deeply rooted to be ignored.

The records from which this pedigree have been compiled fail sometimes to give the name of the families into which members of the Lyon connection intermarried, but their general accuracy has been tested by the will of Sir John Lyon (who died in 1564), and also that of John Lyon of Twyford Manor, dated 1615. Substantially Mr. C. E. Long's conclusions are thereby justified ; and we give them with the greater assurance.

The Lyons of Walden were possibly a collateral branch, but no documents connected with that place have been found in the school archives. It has been suggested that John Lyon, the Harrow Founder, had two daughters—Mary, buried at Harrow, December 13th, 1558, and Joan, buried at Harrow, May 13th, 1559. Two such entries of burials do certainly appear in the Harrow parish registers under the name of *Lione,* but there is no evidence to show that they were children of John Lyon.

The family position of Zachary, the Founder's son, is, on the other hand, claimed by reason of his presence on the Lyon

27 *

brass before it suffered mutilation. Competent witnesses
attest that the lost effigy represented a boy. A tracing of the
brass in question shows an outline thereon clearly that of a child,
which may be deciphered between the putative parents, John
and Joan Lyon.

On the other hand it is right to say that experts disbelieve
in Zachary as the Founder's child, for the following reasons :—
The Harrow parish registers commence in 1558, but from
that time until 1583, the date of Zachary's death, there is no
entry of his baptism, therefore he must have been over twenty-
five years of age at his decease. There is nothing in the entry
of the burial to connect him in any way with the Lyons of
Preston, whereas John and Joan Lyon, his supposed parents,
are both fully described as of Preston. Again, Sir Gilbert
Gerard's letter in 1579, now in the Record Office, distinctly
says twice over that the Founder had no children, and that for
that reason he had been *for some time* buying lands to endow a
school at Harrow. As the Founder was born in 1514, it is
considered unlikely he would have a child born so late as
between 1579 and 1583, when nearly seventy years of age, and
when Joan was probably past child-bearing also. In not one
single instance among the Lyon deeds in the school chest is
there any mention of the Founder's issue, and therefore it is
held to be more probable that he had one son in early life
who perished prematurely, as denoted by his brass plate, than
that Zachary Lyon, who died in 1583, was his child, or, indeed,
any heir to the Founder.

Mr. C. E. Long's conclusions as regards the Lyon pedigree
are taken from the *Harrow Gazette* for March 1861. It is
remarkable that neither the Heralds Office nor the Rolls Office
experts have succeeded in *tracing* the Lyon family later than
the seventeenth century. Strong evidence of the relationship
existing between the Founder of Harrow School and Sir John
Lyon of Perivale consists in the fact that the family property
at Horsington Hill, once in the possession of William Lyon,
the Founder's brother, came into the hands of John Lyon of
Twyford Manor, representative in 1633 of the Perivale and
Ruislip branches.

We must remember that, although believed to be correct so
far as it goes, this pedigree does not pretend to be exhaustive,

and other branches of the family stem may yet gain recognition. It will, not unnaturally, be asked why in the chapter "Founder's Kin," the tradition connecting the Smiths of Eastbury with the Lyons of Ruislip, and thence with the Founder's family, has attracted our attention, when so many claimants to the kinship in question have come forward. The answer is this. The Ruislip parish registers give colour to the belief held so generally in the neighbourhood itself. The subjoined extracts speak for themselves. The Rolls Office pedigree has it that one John Lyon emigrated to America in 1619, William Lyon following him to the New World in 1635; but as no direct reference is given for such statement, we relegate such statement to the regions of tradition, which none the less has its place in ancient history; and, indeed, we are of the number of those who desire to learn that the American, Mr. Amos Lyon, does succeed in tracing back his ancestry to a contemporary branch of the Founder's family, because the great people beyond the sea have an equal part and lot in early Harrow life with ourselves. Their ancestors were free to benefit from John Lyon's endowments, and doubtless some of them did so, while it is a fact that from time to time visitors from across the Atlantic come to Harrow and, calling on the Head Master, attest how an undying family interest links them to the hill whereon their ancestry had both learned and played. As regards the Ruislip branch of the Lyons, it should be remembered that the family may have possessed property there before the Founder's uncle Henry Lyon's time; and that, therefore, if Mr. C. E. Long was right in holding his male descendants to be locally extinct, still there may have been others to perpetuate a name which survived at least to the close of the eighteenth century.

EXTRACTS FROM THE RUISLIP REGISTERS.

Marriages.

John Lyon and Mary Anderson, Feb. 26, 1700.
John Joell and Eliz. Lyon, 1763, 13th Dec. N.B.—Eliz. Joell bur. Feb. 21st, 1783.
Joseph Moores and Mary Lyon, Aug. 28, 1768.

Burials.

Sarah, daughter of John Lion, Jan. 8, 1718.
John Lion, bur. Oct. 23, 1724.
Mary, widow of John Lion, Dec. 17th, 1724.
Anne, wife of John Lion, March 26, 1735.
James Lyon, buried Sep. 6th, 1739.
William, son of William Lyon, July 11th, 1750.
Mary Lyon, May 2nd, 1759.
Elizabeth Lyon, Oct. 26, 1770.
Mrs. Martha Goodson, Feb. 18th, 1781.
Mr. Joseph Goodson, April 24, 1781.
William Lyon, Feb. 15th, 1784.
Sarah Lyon, — 22nd, 1784.
James Lyon, aged 84, March 24, 1791.

Baptisms.

James, son of John Lyon, and ⎫
Hanah, his daughter   .   . ⎭ Twins, Jan. 26th, 1708.
William, son of John Lyon, May 9th, 1713.
Sarah, daughter of John Lyon, March 28th, 1718.
Ann, daughter of John Lyon, March 26th, 1729.
Mary, daughter of William Lyon, March 1st, 1740.
Anne, daughter of William Lyon, Nov. 11th, 1744.
Hannah, daughter of Wm. and Sarah Lion, Nov. 30th, 1746.
William, son of Wm. and Sarah Lyon, June 3rd, 1750.
Jane, daughter of Wm. and Sarah Lion, Feb. 24th, 1754.

The Ruislip registers commence in 1689.

We have previously alluded to the possible contingency that
the name of Lyon was adopted by one marrying into the female
line, and proceed to indicate other features in this partially
elucidated enigma. Our readers will observe the record of a
marriage between Joseph Moores and Mary Lyon on August
28th, 1768. It is said that in addition to the Smiths of Eastbury, of whom the representative is the Rev. George Smith,
Vicar of St. Paul's, Bunhill Row, there are others now living at
Harrow who claim descent from the Founder's family, as being
members of the aforesaid Moore family—the Andrewes, to wit.
Thus two independent households claim to have Lyon blood
in their veins, and the tradition in each community points to

membership of the Ruislip branch; and, indeed, we know of
no other way in which such blood could have been transmitted.
Some accounts have it that earlier generations than the Founder's
uncle settled in Ruislip, which was an adjoining parish to
Harrow and Perivale, where once dwelt Lyon of Preston,
creator of Harrow fame, and his cousin Sir John. All records,
however, have it that relations of the Founder settled at Ruislip.
The opponent of the claim advanced for the Smiths of Eastbury, Claxtons, Winckleys, Moores, and Andrewes of Harrow
must, therefore, overthrow Mr. C. E. Long's researches, as also
those of the Rolls Office official, Mr. Philippe, and also explain
away the Ruislip registers, if the assumed kinship with John
Lyon be discredited.

While upon the subject of Ruislip, it is well to mention
here the fact that a search into the archives of Caius College,
Cambridge, have failed to bring to light any knowledge of the
intimacy believed to exist between Dr. Caius and John Lyon,
who, being neighbouring owners of property in Middlesex,
probably consorted together in their educational projects.
Hence, as has been hitherto assumed, the two Cambridge
Scholarships founded by Lyon in 1571 were at Caius; a belief
strengthened by knowledge of a connection between Harrow
and Caius in 1563, when the old ecclesiastical school was
struggling on. Subjoined is a letter of the late Mr. C. E.
Long's, giving an account of his genealogical labours.

" The Parentage of John Lyon.
" SIR,
" Some time ago you requested me to endeavour to trace
the parentage of John Lyon, the Founder of Harrow School.
I have made the effort and have failed; but, while failing, I
have been enabled to place him in such close juxtaposition with
a family of the same name, and of some repute, in the same
vicinity, that there are the strongest probabilities in favour of
his having been of the blood of the parties whose history I
shall proceed to show. It may be well, in the first place, to
state in a few words all that we know of our Founder. He
resided at Preston, in the Parish of Harrow, in the condition,
as is said, of a ' wealthy yeoman,' had considerable landed
property, and left no issue. According to his monumental

brass (of late years so disgracefully mutilated—torn from its
original socket, the slab broken up, and the spot, hitherto
sacred as his place of sepulture, soon to be forgotten), he died
Oct. 3, 1592. No will nor administration of his effects has
been found either in the Prerogative Court of Canterbury or in
the Bishop of London's office. His widow, Joan, was buried,
according to the register, August 30, 1608, and her will or
administration are also wanting. Their only child, Zachary,
was buried May 25, 1583, and, judging by the size of the
respective brasses, he may have been about 13 years old.
The letters patent for the endowment of the School were
procured by Lyon 13 Eliz. (1571) ; we may, therefore, assume
that the date of his birth was about 1540. At nearly the same
period lived also a wealthy citizen of the same name, stated by
Stowe (vol. ii. p. 226) to have been the ' son to Thomas Lyon
of Pery-fare in Middx '—no doubt our well-remembered Perivale, of bathing renown, when ' Duck Puddle,' then a dirty
pond, was the only apology for ablution which a Harrow boy
had to show. It is far easier to understand a pedigree when
presented to the eye in a tabular form, but this is incompatible
with the columns of a public journal. I must, therefore,
endeavour, in a narrative form, to render my story as intelligible as may be. John Lyon, son, as is said, of Thomas Lyon
of Peryfare or Perivale, must have been ' a citizen of credit
and renown.' He belonged to the Grocers' Company, was
sheriff in 1550, and became Lord Mayor in 1554. During his
shrievalty he had a grant of arms, viz. Azure a fess or, charged
with a lion passant between two cinquefoils gules, between
three plates, each charged with a griffin's head erased sable.
By his first wife, Alice, he had a son of his own name, who
died before him, viz. in 1560, when his will was dated and
proved, leaving no issue by Mary his wife, whom he made his
executrix. The father, Sir John, who had been knighted during
his mayoralty, died in 1564, his will being dated and proved
in that year. He was a considerable landed proprietor in
Yorkshire, Lincolnshire, Berks, Essex, and Middlesex, and his
most remarkable bequest is seemingly connected with our
Founder, who predeceased him. Sir John appears to have had
a sister married to —— Randall, by whom she had a daughter
married to —— Adrian, of Kingston-upon-Thames. His

nephew and heir, Richard Lyon, is described in his will as of West Twyford in Middlesex, close to Perivale. He was buried at Twyford, and his will was dated and proved in 1579. His widow, Isabel, was his executrix. The *Inq. p. mortem* of this Richard is wanting to the volume where it should be found at the Rolls Office, but there is an excellent copy in the Court of Wards and Liveries Series. Henry Lyon was found to be his son and heir, and aged 27. Referring to his will, he had a second son, John, to whom he left his lands in Berkshire, near Abingdon; but, by a note from Norden, given in Lyson, *Environs of London* (vol. ii. part ii. p. 806), he seems to have resided at Longford, which he (Norden) calls 'the seat of John Lyon, Gent.' Besides George Lyon, the brother of Richard, and father of Dorothy before mentioned, there was a sister Alice, wife of —— Middleton. Richard Lyon had two daughters, one, Ethelred, married to William Gifford, the other, Dorothy, wife of Humphry Hyde. The Hydes were of Abingdon, in Berkshire, and their pedigree is entered in the Visitation (c. 18, f. 106, Lib. Coll. Arm.), where Richard Lyon is then described as of Willesden. The *Inq. p. mortem* of Henry Lyon, eldest son of Richard, was taken 33 Eliz., and relates to lands in Lincolnshire. George Lyon is described as his son and heir, and aged 7. John Lyon, the second son of Richard, died 8 C. I., when the Inquisition was taken for his property in Berkshire, and his heirs were found to be his nephew, William Gifford, aged 30, son of his sister Ethelred, and Humphry Hyde, his great-nephew, aged 15, grandson of his sister Dorothy. The issue, therefore, of his brother Henry must have been extinct, but the *Inq. p. m.* of Henry makes allusion to his will, dated October 8, 1590, wherein he leaves money ' for the advancement of his natural* son, John Lyon.' This will is, however, not forthcoming. We have now cleared away the immediate male relations of Sir John Lyon, and although it seems doubtful if our Founder could have been descended from Thomas Lyon of Perifare, the close connection with Harrow and the adjacent parishes conduct us to a very legitimate conclusion that he was nearly related, possibly first cousin, or first cousin once removed, to Sir John, viz. the son

---

* Up to about 1750, " natural " meant "legitimate." See N. & Q. 6th Series x., Sept. 20, 1884, p. 234; 2, " Filius Naturalis."

or grandson, perhaps, of a brother of Thomas of Peryfare.
Although my endeavours have ended in failure, I am not
without hope that some more fortunate and persevering genealogist may ultimately prove the point in question, and I shall
be happy if I have at all assisted in clearing a path for him
through the hitherto entangled jungle of the pedigree, or
perhaps I ought to say, in indicating a course across the wide
waste on which our Founder still stands so lonely and relation-
less, for I have never yet seen proof of his having had any
kindred at all.

"I am, Your Obedient Servant,
"L." (Mr. C. E. LONG.)

Harrow Gazette, March, 1861.

Much has happened since Mr. Long wrote this, and the
social status of the Harrow Founder was clearly higher than
experts believed in 1861. On the other hand, renewed search
through the Consistory Court Registers between 1500 and
1625, also through the Bishop of London's Registers of similar
date, together with those of Croydon,* has led to the following
negative results :—

1508.   William Lyon of Bassingbourne.   Very short will.
        This was undoubtedly the Founder's Uncle, who was
        buried at Royston, Cambridgeshire.   John Lyon
        himself was witness and executor.   It is disappoint-
        ing to find no mention of *Horsington Hill*, of which
        place William Lyon is generally described.

1559.   John Lyon, Junior, son of Sir John Lyon, who died
        early in life.

1562.   William Lyons of Brainsford (probably no relation).

1564.   Sir John Lyon of Twyford and Perivale (searched by
        Mr. C. E. Long).

1569.   Lady Elizabeth Lyon, wife of above (do.).

1579.   Richard Lyon (do.).

1591.   William Lyons, or Lions, of the New Inn.

1592.   John Lyon of Stepney.   Date coincident with the
        Founder's death.

160⅔.   George Lion.

* Conducted by Mr. Richard Sims, of the British Museum, at the author's
request.

1611. Agnes Lyon.
1615. Elizabeth Lyon.
1616. John Lyons of Mile End.
1617. Thomas Lyons.
1639. John Lyon of Twyford, whose will bears out Mr. Long's conclusions.

But by far the most important will discovered is the afore-named testament of John Lyon, of Twyford, *ob.* 1639, confirm-ing as it does the later portion of Mr. C. E. Long's researches.

Now it has been found that many of these wills have no interest for our readers, beyond identity of name, while Mr. C. E. Long has given the substance of Sir John Lyon's will, and that of his nephew and heir, Richard, whose second son, John, lived at Twyford, and left behind him a will, which was also utilised by Mr. Long, who has evidently been over most of the ground open for testamentary exploration.

We may add that such wills as Mr. Sims was enabled to peruse, viz. those of John Lions, 1559, William Lyons of Brainsford, 1562, and John Lyon of Mile End, 1616, yield no information regarding the Harrow Founder or his family ; and we state this without in any way desiring to close the door of an inquiry by no means concluded.*

It is no small thing to have rescued the earlier records from oblivion, and we do not doubt that more will yet be learned concerning the Lyons. One probable source of information has not yielded the fruit that we anticipated. The Court Rolls of Harrow Manor must necessarily have much to tell us of those who reorganised Harrow education in 1571, that is, of the Lyons, Gerards, and Pages, whose names are as household words, while this genealogical tangle surrounding the Founder would, through their agency, receive solution. But, with every

---

* When on the point of going to press, it has transpired that, when searching for the Founder's will, we have been engaged on a work of supererogation Deed No. 208 in the School list is headed, " A list of moneys expended in a prosecution of a complaint by the inhabitants of the hundred of Gore, co. Middlesex, against the Governors of John Lyon's School at Harrow." It is dated 20th January 1650, and contains the following:--" Item for search for John Lyon his will, both in the Pre-rogative, the Diocess, the Peculiar, and at Croydon, but without effect, £1 6s. 8d." If lost seventy-nine years after the school Foundation, there is little wonder that Mr. C. E. Long, going over the same ground some thirty years since, should fail to find the missing parchment, and that those acting for the writer meet with a similar fate in 1884-85.

desire to assist, Lord Northwick could only produce a copy of the orders and statutes, so that we are afraid valuable family papers have been lost during their removal from Middlesex to Warwickshire.*

" The following account of Eastbury, near Pinner, may not be uninteresting to some of our readers, as being formerly the residence, for many generations, of a family† who claimed relationship to the benevolent Founder of Harrow School, and lately (since the erection of a new mansion) of Baron Vaughan,‡ and now of Mrs. Marsh, the talented authoress. The original name of Eastbury was Easterburgh—Easterborough, afterwards corrupted into Eastbury. Easter was a Saxon goddess, and Frifth Wood, close to the place, signifies a Holy Wood. Frifth signifies Holy ; and it appears the name of the place is connected with some of the ancient Pagan rites. The Dingles,§ which in Saxon means ' burial-place,' lying just below the hill, tallies with this account. The ascent to Eastbury, from the Pinner side, is called Porridge Pot Hill. It was a beacon hill, and the name is evidently derived from the iron pot used for beacons. The drive to Watford, through Pinner, by Eastbury, is exceedingly beautiful."—*Harrow Gazette*, May 1st, 1856.

* In Brewer's *Beauties of England*, vol. x. part v. p. 601, is the following foot-note respecting Harrow Manor, written in 1816. " The rectory manor, with the advowson of the vicarage, are now the property of Lord Northwick. It may be observed that the Court Rolls of this manor, from a date as early as the first year of Richard II. to the present time, with very few chasms, are possessed by his Lordship, and are in a high state of preservation."

† The family of Smith.

‡ Uncle to Dr. Vaughan, Head-Master of Harrow School.

§ On the Pinner side, near Waxwell.

APPENDIX E.

RECTORS AND VICARS OF HARROW.

Rectors.		Vicars.	
1242	Derham, Edward de.		Wennington, John de.
1313	Bosco, William de.	1322	Tadelow, Richard de.
1330	Lytlington, Thomas de.		Pydele, Robert.
1351	Leech, John de.	1351	Northby, John.
1352	Raymond, Pelegrin.	1368	Riseburgh, John de.
	Buckingham, John de.	1401	Wendover, Henry.
1387	Mons, Guido de.	1433	Coterell, William.
1390	Baunton, William.		Weeke, George.
1401	Marchford, Simon.	1509	Jenyn, John.
	Kyrkham, Robert.	1538	Layton, Arthur.
1467	Byrkhed, John.*	1551	Dean, Richard.
1471	Winterborne, Thomas.		Crofts, Brian.
1478	Wilkinson, Thomas.	1601	Wildbloud, Humfrey.
1511	Tunstall, Cuthbert.	1625	Lance, William.
1522	Bolton, William.	1662	Wilcocks, Joseph.
1532	Warham, William.	1728	Saunders, Francis.
1537	Layton, Richard.	1776	Williams, Walter Lleward.
1544	Cocks, Richard.		
		1810	Cunningham, John Wm.
		1861	Joyce, Francis Hayward.

On a flat stone at the east end of Harrow Church is a fine brass of an Ecclesiastic, the crown of whose head, according to priestly custom, is represented as shaven. On either side of his rich cross are embroidered figures of ten saints, six male and four female, the name of each at their respective feet, with

* John Byrkhed by his will left to Harrow Parish his best gilt chalice and paten.—*Middlesex Archæological Journal,* 1860.

a brooch, whereon is the White Rose and Golden Sun known as the badge of the House of York from 1461 to 1485. John Byrkhed's arms appear on one corner of the brass and Archbishop Arundell's on the other.

A monkish rhyme on the Byrkhed tomb was thus translated by the late Mr. Niblett in 1844 :—

"Stay, traveller. Hark, the masses for the repose of John Byrkhed, lying here, bid you, he whom relentless death stayeth, reckoning by the year of our Lord 14$\frac{18}{68}$ (most likely 1468). The Rev^d. Father is of the number of the blessed at St. Cuthberga's shrine—Charity, Dignity, Fidelity. Careful conduct made him illustrious amongst the highest Prelates of the Realm. O God of Heaven, of Thy gracious goodness, grant a heavenly crown to him whom such honourable conduct adorned on earth."

"Byrkhed was probably indebted to Archbishop Arundell for his education; but after 1413, the date of that Primate's death, became Steward and friend of Archbishop Chicheley, who doubtless made him Rector of Harrow."—*Journal of the London and Middlesex Archæological Society*, 1860, " Sepulchral Brasses at Harrow," p. 11.

Mystery hangs over the hitherto assumed connection of Cardinal Wolsey with Harrow. He was not, as some have supposed, a Rector, and although a house in the town still bears his name, we are compelled to adopt the view of the Middlesex Archæological Society, and relegate to the region of mere legend both the rumour of Wolsey's sojourn at Headstone, and the accompanying story that an underground passage ran from Harrow to the moated farm-house known to antiquaries as the later residence of the Archbishops of Canterbury before the Reformation.

Possibly Henry VIII.'s great minister did enjoy some of the revenues of Harrow when Abbot of St. Albans during the time of pluralism. Otherwise it is difficult to explain the tradition that he was Rector. Without pretending to believe that Wolsey ever lived at Headstone, we nevertheless recommend a visit to that moated manorial dwelling, redolent in memories of the archiepiscopal past.

As regards the church at Harrow, knowledge of its former splendour is becoming clearer as time goes on. For instance,

we learn that in the year A.D. 1400 there were three altars in
the sacred fane, mention of such being made in the will of
Joan Bucberd of Preston found in the school archives.* It
is also satisfactory to be enabled to append the latest, and
presumably the most perfect, rendering of the inscription on
the Flambard brass.   Mr. Edward Scott, the latest exponent,
shall speak for himself.

To the Editor of the *Harrow Gazette.*

" Sir,—My attention has lately been drawn (in connection
with Mr. Percy Thornton's forthcoming book on 'Harrow
School and its Surroundings ') to the very curious inscription
on John Flambard's brass in the parish church.

" From time to time attempted solutions of this literary
puzzle have been sent to the pages of *Notes and Queries,* but
none have hitherto been deemed at all satisfactory. The reason
for such failure lies, I think, in the fact that the inscription
has been looked upon as conveying the exact wording intended
to be engraved by those who originally laid down the brass.
That this is not the case, I am convinced from a close examination during the past fortnight, both of the actual brass on the
floor of the chancel, and also of a rubbing kindly given me by
the Rev. W. Done Bushell. In the first place the engraver,
in working the upper line of the distich, made his words and
even letters so far apart from each other, that when he came
to the end of the line he had not room for all the words, and
so, making a hash of it, cut out a piece of the brass matrix and
supplied it by another, on which he placed the letters as close
as possible.   Then he roughly fitted it to the mutilated piece,
and left the traces of his bad workmanship only too glaring.
In the next place, this same engraver neither knew Latin, nor
the ordinary contractions of Latin words in mediæval times,
so that his copy of what was furnished him, when read as he
left it, becomes absolute nonsense. The inscription, before it
was versified, ran, I venture to think, thus :—' Johannes Flam-
bardus modo marmore tumulatur ordine Numinis. Numinis
quoque verbere hic tueatur de flumine Stygis.' Or in English
dress, thus :—' John Flambard is now buried in marble by the

* Appendix C.

ordinance of God. By God's stripes also may he be saved from the river of Hell.'

"This was now turned into a leonine distich, as follows :—

"(1.) John modo marmore Numinis ordine Flam tumulatur.

"(2.) Bard quoque verbere flumine de Stygis hic tueatur.

"This mode of dividing a person's name, whether Christian or surname, or indeed both, is common enough in epitaphs of the period, *temp.* Richard II., and need cause no difficulty. But the blunders that follow have made such nonsense of the whole inscription, that it is no wonder if those who looked upon the text as correct have abandoned the attempt to make sense of it.

"The brass now reads :—

"'Jon medo marmore Numinis ordine flam tumulat.

Bard q̊z verbere stigis E fune hic tueatur.'

"'Jon' now appears for 'John'; 'medo' for 'modo'; 'tu-mulat' for 'tumulatur'; 'quoue' for 'quoque'; 'E' for 'de'; and 'funere' for flumine.'

"With regard to this last palpable blunder the correction is easy enough, 'funere' and 'flumine,' when contracted, having exactly the same number of strokes, viz., 'fune' and 'flme,' and hence easily mistaken by an ignorant engraver, especially when, as in this case, he makes his 'u' come so far above the 'n' that the first stroke might be an 'l.'

"Those persons who are familiar with the common yet horrible expressions of that period, such as God's Life, God's Wounds, God's Blood, God's Death, will find no difficulty in the phrase, God's Stripes, or Numinis verbere.

"Tueo and Tueor are used as active and passive verbs in funeral inscriptions, as 'Rogo per Superos, qui estis, ossa mea tueatis,' &c.

"Hogarth Cottage,　　　　　　　"EDWARD J. L. SCOTT.
　　"11th November, 1884."

Harrow has a literary history of her own, as this volume shows; but in the church is buried a most notable collector of choice volumes in Mr. Edwards, the bookseller of Pall Mall. His searches for rare editions were carried out through all the European capitals, and fully deserve such prominence as can be given here.

Sir Samuel Garth, author of the *Dispensary*, and a celebrated physician, was also buried here in 1718. It has been said that he was at Harrow School ; but despite the attention drawn by the question being mooted in *Notes and Queries*, it has not been decided.

No lists or bills of Harrow School seem to have been preserved in the muniment chest until the end of the eighteenth century, an epoch which the Butler bills have since made familiar.

28

APPENDIX F.

EXTRACTS FROM DR. LONGLEY'S HARROW NOTE-BOOK.

WEEK'S BUSINESS IN DR. DRURY'S TIME.

Days.	Hours.	Forms (Mons Upper and Lower VI.).	Form V.	Shell, or Remove.	Form IV.—3 Removes.	Form III. 3 Removes.
Monday, whole school-day.	½ past VII.	Repetⁿˢ & Verses shown up.	Repⁿˢ Greek Testament		Repⁿˢ Selecta. ex Ovid	Repⁿˢ Ovid. &c.
	½ past VIII.	Virgil's Georgics. Gk. Testament	Do.	Do. the quantity rather less.	Gr. Test. construe and Parse.	
	L.	Virg. Æneid, ab⁴ 35 lines.	Do.		Turneine.	
	III.*	Dinner. Homer. ab⁴ 35 lines.	Do.		Verses given out.	
	v.†	Scriptores Romani, somewhat more yⁿ a page. Thesis (viπ·ⁿ rare) for a Latin Theme.	Do by Mr. Bromley.	by Mr. B.Evans		
Tuesday, whole holiday.	IV.	Bill, i.e. the Boys of all the Upper School called in the School; the Lower School separately by one of the Assistants.				The Monitor's Exercise given up on the Tuesday, was supposed to procure the Tuesday's Holiday. Upper Boys' Exercises looked over every morning in their presence, and at other spare times.
	XI.	Do.				
	L.	Dinner.				
	II.	Bill.				
	IV.	Do.				
	VI.	Do. The Master occasionally, and the Assistants in rotation, every night, call Bills at the several Boarding Houses.				

		Do.	Do.	Repⁿ Gᵏ Grammar. Ovid Metam. Particle or Gᵏ Repⁿ alterⁿ. Farnaby. Set Particles.	Private *Tutors.* Rev. Mr. Slade. Duke of Dorset. Rev. Mr. Birch. Lord Horbert Rev. Mr Blackall. Lord Plymouth.
whole school-day.			Repⁿ ... ... of Monday: the rest of the day the same as Monday. Set Translation & Essay alternately.		*Boarding Houses.* Miss Maxwell. Mrs. Leith. Mrs. Armstrong. Mrs. Griffiths. Rev. G. Evans. Mr Reeves. Mr. Bowen.
Thursday, ½ holiday.	½ past VII. XI. II. IV. VI.	Do.	Repⁿ Homer of Wednesday. Translation shown up Script. Græc., 40 lines. Set Lyrics of Greek Verses. Bill. Do. Do.	Do.. Repⁿ & show up Tranᵐ II Terence. Do.	
Friday, whole school-day.	½ past VII. XI. III. V.	Do. Repⁿ Map every fortnight. II. Cellarius. III. Repⁿ v. Horace Salt	Repⁿ Monday's Virgl Demosthenes, &c. Repⁿ of Wednesday's Virg. Horace's Satires Set Verses.	Repⁿ Show up Particles. Farnaby; Map: Guthries Gram. Gᵏ Gram. expl. Ovid construed. Verses set.	
Saturday, ½ holiday.	½ past VII. XI.	Do.	Repⁿ Verses shown up. Grahmede Ver: Xᵐᵃˢ Rel: Verses explained. Bills.	Do.. Repⁿ Gᵏ Grammar. vi. Monita Xtiana. Do.	
Sunday.	VIII. IX. VI. II. III. VI.		3rd Form. Script Hist. 4th Form. Gᵏ Test. Bill. Church. Sixth Form. Reading. Church. Bill	The boys are locked in during summer at ½ past eight; in winter at 6.	

28 *

WEEK'S BUSINESS UNDER DR. LONGLEY.

1829.

Sixth Form.

Monday.	½ past VII.	Repⁿ Friday's Horace. Look over Lyrics.
	XI.	Horace Odes 60 Lines.
	III.	Homer 50 Lines. Modern History.
	V.	Historia Romana 50 Lines. Set Theme.
Tuesday.		Bills at IX. XI. II. IV. and VI.
Wednesday.	½ past VII.	Repⁿ Monday's Homer. Look over Verses.
	XI.	Virgil's Æn. 50 Lines. Extracts f^m Roman Hist^y
	III.	Euclid and Vulgar Fractions.
	V.	Poessis Græca 50 Lines. 4 Pages of Melkin's Greece. Set Translation or Essay.
Thursday.	½ past VII.	Rep^{ns} Wednesday's Virgil. Look over Theme.
	XI.	Thucydides. Set Lyrics. Græcian Antiq^s and Chronology, &c.
	¼ past XII.	Modern History Lecture.
Friday.	½ past VII.	Repⁿ Monday's Horace. Look over Essay.
	XI.	Dem: de Coronâ, &c. 50 Lines. Græcian Antiq^s and Chronology, &c.
	III.	Greek Play.
	V.	Horace Sat. or Ep. 4 Pages of Melkin's Greece. Set Verses.
Saturday.	½ past VII.	Scholarship G^k Testament. Beausolre, &c.
	XI.	Thucydides and His^t Romana alternately.
Sunday.	VIII.	Epistles to Romans and Hebrews. Newton on Prophecies. Articles of Church of England.

Fifth Form. Classics and Exercises nearly the same as 6th *Form.* The Divinity. The Acts of the Apostles. Paley's Evidences, and Well's Geography of N. T.

Upper Shell.

	I.	II.	III.	IV.
Monday.	Rep[n]		Virgil or Horace.	Homer or P. Græc.	Hist. Romana
Wednesday.	Rep[n] & Verses		Do	Do	Corn. Nepos.
Thursday	Rep. & Theme	Xen. Anab.		
Friday.	Rep. & Tr[n]		Geography	Geography	Hor. Ep. or Satt.
Saturday.	Rep[n] & Lyrics	Gk. Test.		
Sunday (VIII.)	St. John's Gospel	Watt's		Some Treatise on Evi-
	St. Luke's do	Script. Hist.		dences.

Under Shell.

Rep[n] of Greek or Latin Verse every morning but Saturday and Sunday. On former Greek Grammar.

Monday	2nd 3rd & 4th School, Horace, P. Græc. & Hist. Rom.
Wednesday	Virgil. Homer. Corn. Nepos.
Thursday	Xen. Anabasis.
Friday	Geography. Retranslation of Anabasis & Horace Epp. &c.
Saturday	Greek Testament.
Sunday	St. Luke & St. John's Gospel. Watt's Scr. Hist. Evidences.

Fourth Form.

Monday	Rep[n] Short Ovid	G. Test.	Do.	Turseline
Wednesday	Do G. Gram.	Long Ovid.	Say G. Gram.	Farnaby
Thursday	Do G. Gram.	Virgil		
Friday	Do Virgil	Farnaby	Geography Maps looked over	Short Ovid
Saturday	Do Farnaby	Cæsar & Monita alternately		
Sunday	St. Matthew & St. Mark's Gospels. Wake's Catechism			

Third Form.

Monday	Evangelia Verses	Short Ovid	Exempla Minora Gk. Grammar Se-lectae Pr.
Wednesday	G. Grammar Verses b[t] up	Short Ovid	As on Monday
Thursday	G. Grammar	Short Ovid Exercise Ex. Min.	
Friday	G. Grammar Ex. b[t] up.	Short Ovid	Selecta G. Gram.
Saturday	Repeat Ovid	Monita Exercise Verses	Hartley's Geo-graphy.

1835. Theological pt. of Limon, instead of Monita on Saturdays. Historical Do. instead of Turseline, Miscellaneous inst[d] of Cæsar. *Anthologia Latina,* instead of Ovid's Metam. Electa, and Excerpta.

APPENDIX G.

A COMPLETE LIST OF HARROW SCHOOL, September 1839.
FOOTBALL QUARTER.

The Monitors.

G. C. Cherry.
— Platt.
— Bendyshe.
G. Morrier.
B. S. T. Mills.*
F. Howell.
R. Peel.†
A. C. Barclay.‡
C. Lloyd.
H. M. Wilkins.

VI. FORM.

F. Peel.§
— Frampton.
— Robertson.
H. H. Seymour.
Lord Henry Loftus.
T. Conolly.
— Keys.
— Ferrers.
T. Sanctuary.‖
F. Morewood.
— Hammond.
— Blackall.
— Faulder.

UPPER V. FORM.

T. B. Colenso.
— Kekewich.
J. G. Sheppard.
— D'Aeth.
— Newton.
E. H. Loring.
— Hamilton.
H. D. Des Voeux.¶
J. W. Perry.**
H. Scott.
A. Lawson.
— Young.
Boileau Pollen.
John Nicholson.
— Wilkinson.
— Smith.
— Cunningham.
E. C. Taylor.
E. M. Dewing.
— Colston, sen
— Colston, jun.
— Palmer.
— Alleyne.
— Royds.
— Atherley.

* Rector of Lawshall, near Bury St. Edmunds.
† Afterwards Sir Robert Peel.
‡ M.P. for Taunton.
§ Afterwards Sir F. Peel.
‖ Afterwards Archdeacon of Dorset, Canon Residentiary of Salisbury, and Vicar of Powerstock, Dorset.
¶ Afterwards Sir H. Des Voeux.
** Afterwards J. W. Perry-Wathington.

— Burdon.
Hon. G. T. O. Bridgeman.
V. K. Vade.
R. Gathorne.
— Larpent.
Hon. Douglas Gordon.

UNDER V. FORM.
— Wilbraham.
W. Ripley.
J. S. Bushby.
— Pownall.
H. Holland.*
Hon. H. Nelson.
— Mowbray.
— Skottowe.
W. A. Commerell.
Sir George Colthurst.
— Marillier.
— Wilkinson.
T. B. Sheriffe.
— Courtenay.
T. C. Taylor.
Lord FitzClarence.†
C. F. Surtees.
J. B. Parker.
— Carruthers.
— Honywood.

UPPER SHELL.
H. Scott.
T. Norcliffe.
— Filder.
A. Grant.
— Wilkins.
H. Gathorne.
— Cresswell.
G. C. Dickins.
F. Dawson.
— Phelips.

Hon. Frederick Fitz-Clarence.
H. Morgan.
— Drummond.
— Taylor.
— Keys.
— Boucher.
— Burroughes.
C. Rouse-Boughton.‡
— Coote.
Hon. William Henry Leigh.§
— Hinxman.
— Brisco.

UNDER SHELL.
— Dickinson.
C. Soames.‖
— Statham.
W. Nicholson.¶
J. Leach.
— Jefferson.
— Wilkinson.
R. H. Eustace.**
J. R. Cuthbert.
— Allen.
— Williams.
W. H. D'Oyly.
— Wanclyn.
— Palmer.
W. T. Hustler.
— Greenwood.

UPPER IV. FORM.
— Maycock.
Wentworth Bosville.
Tatton Sykes.††
Lord Robert Taylour.
— Dancer.
— Ferrers.
— Bird.

* Now Sir Henry Holland.
† Now Earl of Munster.
‡ Afterwards Sir C. R. Boughton.
§ Afterwards Lord Leigh.
‖ Rector of Mildenhall, in Wiltshire.
¶ M.P. for Petersfield.
** Now Rural Dean and Vicar of Great Sampford with Hempstead in Essex.
†† Now Sir Tatton Sykes.

Hon. Herbert W. E. Agar.
Hon. Charles Agar.*
— Sheppard.
R. B. Hesketh.
— Greenwood.
W. H. Woodhouse.
T. H. Whittaker.
E. Lewis.
R. P. Jenkins.
Arthur Haygarth.†
G. A. G. Calthorpe.

— Burge.
J. Marshall.

UNDER IV. FORM.

— Powell.
— Wilkins.
— Williams.
— Filder.
— Wilkinson.
— Statham.
— Marshall.

Total number of boys at Harrow during Football Quarter 1839 was 140, as above.

NAMES OF THOSE WHO CAME TO HARROW BEGINNING WITH RACQUET QUARTER, OR JANUARY 1840, UP TO CRICKET QUARTER, OR JULY (END OF) 1843.

NAMES OF THOSE WHO CAME TO HARROW BEGINNING RACQUET QUARTER, OR JANUARY 1840.

William Spottiswoode, sen.‡
Geo. A. Spottiswoode, jun.
— Allix.
A. H. Farmer.
— Hamilton.
C. O. Eaton.
— Strutt.
H. Tudway.
— Burdon.
R. Howell.
— Anderson.
R. Hustler.
— Saunders, sen.
— Saunders, jun.
T. Rawlinson.
H. Day.
— Ackerman.
— Deffell.

— Gurney, sen.
— Gurney, jun.
H. Jolliffe.
— Hewlett.
A. Mackenzie.
H. Mackenzie.
— Baker.
T. Chitty.
— Roualt.
Lord Kilworth.§
— Savage.
M. Grimston.
— Wilson.
— Sanctuary, maj.
— Sanctuary, mi.
— Sanctuary, min.
E. Dangerfield.
— Dangerfield.

* Killed at Sebastopol.
† Compiler of Cricket Scores and Biographies
‡ Buried in Westminster Abbey.
§ Afterwards Earl of Mount-Cashell.

T. D. Platt.*	— Skottowe, mi.
C. S. Currer.†	— Skottowe, min.
G. N. Boldero.	— Kindersley.
— De Salis, maj.	Montague Williams.
— De Salis, mi.	— Mivart.
— Skottowe, maj.	Hon. Percy Smythe.‡

The above all came to Harrow *between* Football Quarter 1839 and Football Quarter 1841, but are not arranged *exactly* in the order they came, as I did not begin to keep an exact account till Football Quarter 1842. However, I am almost sure that no names are *omitted*.

CAME TO HARROW DURING FOOTBALL QUARTER 1841.

R. P. Long.§	J. Cameron.
— Baxendale.	A. Cameron.
R. B. Willis.	Hon. Julian Fane.
— Grant.	— Walker.
— Young.	— Kindersley.
— Clarke.	— Hudson.
E. Blayds.‖	H. N. Oxenham.
D. Howell.	

CAME TO HARROW DURING RACQUET QUARTER 1842.

— Sperling.	— Daniell.
G. Hustler.¶	— Merivale.
— Goring.	— Tower.
— Everard.	— Rich.
— Palmer.	G. F. Dallas.
— Smith.	

CAME TO HARROW DURING CRICKET QUARTER 1842.

R. A. Darwin.	— Bromley.
— Dent.	P. L. Cloete.
— Wodehouse.	

CAME TO HARROW DURING FOOTBALL QUARTER 1842.

— Vaughan.	— Scott.
— Rennie.	— Maycock.
— Coney.	— Williams.
— Bosanquet.	— Sharpe.
— Baxter.	— McChlery.

* Perpetual Curate of Trinity, Portsea, Hampshire.
† Afterwards C. S. Roundell, M.P. for Grantham.
‡ Afterwards Viscount Strangford.
§ Afterwards M.P. for Chippenham.
‖ Afterwards E. Calverley.
¶ Rector of English Bicknor. Gloucestershire.

CAME TO HARROW DURING RACQUET QUARTER 1843.

— Dutton.
Henry Vernon.
Hon. G. F. Moore.

CAME DURING CRICKET QUARTER 1843.

— Harman.
— Bliss.
— Collier.

Mr. A. Haygarth, who sent us these lists, writes as follows :—
"During the four years I was at Harrow, from Sept. 1839 to
July 1843, only 236 boys were there altogether the whole time,
namely, 140 when I went there, and 96 new ones who came
during the four years.

"In the Cricket Quarter of 1842 only 5 new boys came, and
in the Racquet Quarter of 1843 only 3, and in the Cricket
Quarter of 1843 only 3 !!!

"I have put initials to those I knew."

A LIST OF HARROW SCHOOL DURING SUMMER OR CRICKET
QUARTER, JULY 1843.

The Monitors.

C. Soames.*
H. Gathorne.
A. Grant.
Hon. P. Smythe.†
J. Leach.
T. B. Sheriffe.
W. Nicholson.
J. S. Bushby.
G. A. Spottiswoode.
T. S. Chitty.

A. H. Farmer.
G. A. G. Calthorpe.
T. H. Whittaker.
R. Howell.
J. R. Cuthbert.
E. Lewis.
J. Marshall.
C. S. Currer.‡
E. Blayds.§
M. Williams.
R. P. Long.‖
Arthur Haygarth.¶

VI. FORM.

H. Day.
R. Hustler.

UPPER V. FORM.

F. W. T. Sperling.
T. Rawlinson.

* Afterwards Rector of Mildenhall, in Wiltshire.
† Afterwards Viscount Strangford.
‡ Afterwards C. S. Roundell, M.P. for Grantham
§ Afterwards E. Calverley.
‖ Afterwards M.P. for Chippenham.
¶ Compiler of Cricket Scores and Biographies.

E. Dangerfield.
— Strutt.
G. Hustler.
C. O. Eaton.
— De Salis.
W. McKenzie.
— Deffell.
M. Grimston.
W. H. Woodhouse.
W. Bosville.
Lord R. Taylour.
A. S. Hewlett.

UNDER V. FORM.

— Baxendale.
G. F. Dallas.
T. D. Platt.*
— Howell.
— Kindersley.
— Rich.
— Willis.
H. Tudway.
J. Cameron.
A. Cameron.
— Grant.
— Wilson.
Lord Kilworth.†

UPPER SHELL.

— Darwin.
— Maycock.
— Wodehouse.
— Goring.
— Coney.
— Rennie.
Hon. Julian Fane.

— Vaughan.
— De Salis, jun.
— Marshall, jun.
— Baxter.

UNDER SHELL.

— Sharp.
— Oxenham.
A. McKenzie.
H. McKenzie.
— Merivale.
— McChlery.
— Cloete.
— Smith.
J. C. Boldero.
— Tower.
— Walker.
Hon. G. F. Moore.
— Dutton.
— Bosanquet.
— Harman.
— Bliss.
— Collier.

UPPER IV.

— Gurney.
— Hudson.
— Williams.
Henry Vernon.

UNDER IV.

— Bromley.
— Everard.
— Sanctuary.
— Sanctuary.

* Now Perpetual Curate of Trinity, Portsea, Hampshire
† Now Earl of Mount-Cashell.

There were only 87 boys at Harrow, July 1843

APPENDIX H.

THE subjoined lists will show the gradual advancement of music at Harrow, as well as the high character of the compositions performed between July 1858 and July 1883. Mr. Farmer was first engaged at Michaelmas 1862.

1858	July 22	Dec. 4							
1859	April 9	July 23	Dec. 3						
1860	Mar. 31								
1861	Dec. 7								
1862	April 12	July 10	July 26	Nov. 22	Dec. 6				
1863	Mar. 28	July 9	July 25	Nov. 19					
1864	Mar. 19	July 23	Oct. 20	Dec. 10					
1865	Mar. 9	June 24	Dec. 9						
1866	Dec. 15	July 28							
1867	May 23	July 27	Dec. 7						
1868	Mar. 12	April 4	June 16	July 25	Nov. 10	Dec. 12			
1869	Mar. 20	June 9	July 24	F. D.	Nov. 2	Dec. 11			
1870	Mar. 31	April 9	July 23	F. D.	Matinee Xmas.	Dec. 10	Mar. 8		
1871	Feb. 25	April 1	June 15	June 23	July 29	Dec. 9			
1872	Mar. 23	July 27	F. D.	Dec. 14					
1873	April 5	July 14	July 21	July 26	Oct. 10	Dec 13			
1874	Mar. 28	July 25	F. D.	Dec. 12					
1875	Mar. 20	July 24	Oct. 14	Dec. 11					
1876	April 8	June 29	July 29	Oct. 12	Dec. 16				
1877	Mar. 24	July 5	July 20	July 28	Oct. 11	Oct. 26	Dec 15		
1878	Mar 27	June 11	July 4	Bach Lecture	July 27	Oct. 10	Oct. 17	Oct. 31	Dec. 14
1879	Feb. 25	April 5	May 21	July 3	Aug. 2	Oct. 3	Oct. 9	Oct. 31	Dec. 13
1880	Mar. 5	Mar. 20	June 11	July 1	July 24	Oct. 7	Oct. 27	Nov. 29	Dec. 11
1881	April 9	June 30	July 30	Oct. 6	Dec. 17				
1882	Mar.28-5	April 1	June 28	June 16	July 6	July 29	Oct. 12	Dec. 16	
1883	Mar. 19	May 25	July 5	July 28					

From July 22, 1858, to July 28, 1883, 127 Concerts.

Despite unexpected success, choral works with complete choir have not been found feasible on account of the advanced age at which boys now enter Harrow. Thus it is that, under the most favourable auspices, it would be difficult to find six trebles who could sing above G, and by the time *they* were trained, the breaking of voices which ensues at this period of life would have become imminent. (These notes we owe to a member of the Harrow Musical Society.)

A visit to the school services in the Chapel will impress the hearer with the fervour of the services, but lead him to contrast a moderate organ with the magnificent instrument in the new Speech-room.

COMPOSERS WHOSE WORKS HAVE BEEN PERFORMED BY THE
HARROW SCHOOL MUSICAL SOCIETY, 1858-1883.

—	No. of Works performed.	No. of times the Composer's name has occurred in the Programmes.	—	No. of Works performed.	No. of times the Composer's name has occurred in the Programmes.
Abt .	1	1	"Chorales"	9	22
Aptommas .	3	3	Clinton	2	4
Arne .	4	9	Cooke	4	5
Arnold	2	2	Coote	1	1
Auber	5	7	Corelli	3	6
Bach .	15	15	Costa .	2	3
Baildon	1	2	Czerny	1	1
Barnby	1	1	D'Albert	7	7
Bartholomew	1	1	Danby	2	2
Beale .	1	1	"Dances" (Na-		
Beethoven .	31	45	tional)	2	2
Bellini	4	4	Davy .	1	3
Bennett	1	1	De Beriot	1	1
Bishop	9	12	De Call	1	1
Blockley	2	4	Deffel	3	3
Blumenthal	1	1	De Lille	1	1
Boieldieu	1	1	Dibdin	2	6
Boyce	2	9	Dohler	2	2
Braham	2	6	Donizetti	4	4
Brahms	2	3	Douland	1	1
Callcott	4	12	Dressler	1	1
"Carols" .	2	8	Edwardes .	1	1
Chopin	4	4	Elliott	2	2

—	No. of Works per- formed.	No. of times the Composer's Name has occurred in the Programmes.	—	No. of Works per- formed.	No. of times the Composer's Name has occurred in the Programmes.
Farmer, H.	1	1	Lachner	1	1
Farmer, J.	108	380	Landemann	1	1
Festa	1	6	Lanner	2	2
Fitzgerald	1	1	Lindblad	1	1
Fleming	1	5	Lindpainter	1	2
Flotow	1	1	Loder	1	1
Ford	1	3	Luther	1	9
Ford and Saville	1	1	Macfarren	2	5
Forde	1	1	Macirone	1	1
"French Songs"	1	1	Mackenzie	1	1
Gastoldi	1	1	Marenzio	1	1
"German Airs"	7	8	Marriott	1	1
Glover	1	1	Martini	1	1
Gluck	2	3	Masson	2	2
Goss	3	4	Mazzinghi	1	2
Gounod	4	4	Mehul	1	2
Graun	1	1	Meinhardt	1	1
Hall	1	1	Mendelssohn	40	65
Handel	29	40	Meyerbeer	6	7
"Harrow Glee Book"	21	106	Moore	4	11
			Morley	3	10
"Harrow School Songs"	10	45	Mornington	2	2
			Mozart, L.	1	1
Hartmann	1	1	Mozart, W. A.	41	62
Hasse	2	2	Muller	1	1
Hatton	10	14	Musard	1	1
Hauff	1	1	"National Airs" (Selection)	1	2
Hauptmann	1	1			
Haydn	23	37	Neale	1	6
Herold	1	1	Nicolai	1	1
Himmel	1	3	Oesten	1	1
Hindle	1	1	"Old Songs"	18	35
Horn	1	1	Osborne	1	1
Horsley	4	11	Otto	1	1
Hortense, Queen	1	1	Ould	1	1
Hullah	1	1	Paer	1	1
Hummel	1	1	Paganini	1	1
"Hungarian Airs"	9	10	Paxton	2	2
"Irish Songs"	2	2	Pearsall	6	17
Jordan	1	3	Percy	1	1
Knyvett	1	2	Pinsuti	2	3

	No. of Works performed	No. of times the Composer's Name has occurred in the Programmes.			No of Works performed	No. of times the Composer's Name has occurred in the Programmes.
Purcell	4	12	Stuntz		1	8
Reay	1	1	Sullivan		3	8
Reese	1	2	Thalberg		1	1
Ridding	1	2	Thomas, A.		1	2
Rossini	15	22	Tinney		2	2
Salomon	1	1	Tolbecque		1	1
Scarlatti	1	1	Trühn		1	2
Schubert	19	26	Turner		1	1
Schumann	8	9	Vaccai		1	1
"Scotch Songs"	9	12	Verdi		3	3
Shield	1	3	Vieuxtemps		1	1
Silcher	1	2	Wagner		1	1
Singelée	4	4	Webbe		4	16
Smart	3	3	Weber		9	12
Smith, Stafford	2	2	Weelkes		1	1
Spohr	3	3	Weiss		1	2
Sterling	1	2	"Welsh Song"		1	5
Stevens	4	13	Wesley		1	1
Strauss	3	4	"Unidentified"		14	16
Strauss, jun.	2	2				

Mr. Farmer has composed music for *all* the popular School songs since 1862. Hence the frequency of his name in the above list. The Rev. J. A. Cruikshank, the Hon. Secretary of the Musical Society, has crowned services to Harrow extending over a quarter of a century by consolidating Mr. Farmer's efforts on behalf of harmony.

APPENDIX I.

ONE act of the above-mentioned Prime Minister's had such an important outcome at Harrow that it is impossible to avoid making some mention thereof. We allude to the anxious appeal which he made to Dr. Vaughan concerning the monitorial system, after the events connected with the Platt and Stewart case had rendered exercise of such authority extremely unpopular. The consequence was that the Harrow head-master gladly embraced the opportunity of making a clear explanation as to the origin of the monitorial system and its working at Harrow, together with a courageous defence of what the public seemed most disposed to condemn. Like Dr. Arnold, with whose example he stood fortified, Dr. Vaughan declared his preference for monitorial *discipline* as opposed to espionage, such as appeared to be the alternative necessary to check "certain minor offences against manners rather than morals—faults of turbulence, rudeness, offensive language, annoyance of others, petty oppression, and tyranny," prevalent as they are more or less in every school.

"This difficult task must be approached," said Dr. Vaughan, "by one of two ways—either by creating a body of ushers, masters of a lower order, to spy upon the boys, or allowing a chosen number of the ablest and more meritorious to exercise an authority emanating from the head-master, and responsible to him, but yet independent and free in its ordinary exercise."

"They are," said the writer, "charged with the enforcement of an internal discipline, the object of which is the good order, the honourable conduct, the gentleman-like tone, of the Houses and of the School. . . . .

"It is only on the discovery of grave and moral offences . . . that they are expected to communicate officially to the head-master faults of which they take notice.

"It follows as a matter of necessity that the monitors should possess some means of exercising and asserting their authority. Hence arises the old custom of *fagging*. It is a memento of monitorial authority. . . . .

"But there must also be some method of punishing diso-bedience, insubordination, turbulence, or other transgression."

By custom, varying, may be, in its rule, but still of some antiquity, a monitorial use of the cane had been allowed at Harrow.

In Dr. Wordsworth's time a substitute had been devised, such as setting lines to be written or learnt out of school, but scarcely likely to prove effective when power to enforce obedi-ence was absent. Therefore it is that Dr. Vaughan says—

"This custom, I repeat, I found established ; ignored, it may be, by previous masters, but not unknown. . . . ."

And, after allowing that every due check should be imposed to hinder undue exercise of monitorial power, an appeal to the master being a constitutional right on such occasions, Dr. Vaughan concludes his able paper with the following perora-tion :—

"However unpopular may be the avowal, I know that my duty is clear : to watch the operation of the system, to guard it from abuse, but, none the less, to adhere to it manfully, and to take my full share of its obloquy.

"It may be found impossible long to withstand such impres-sions as those to which your Lordship has adverted. To persons unacquainted with its practical operation the moni-torial system must always appear objectionable ; a cumbrous and uncertain substitute for zeal and vigilance on the part of the master. The time may come when public opinion will imperatively require the introduction of an opposite principle, of which it shall be the object to confine and preclude the expression of evil by the unceasing espionage of an increased staff of subordinate masters.

"The experiment may be tried ; I hope not at Harrow—certainly not by me. I see many difficulties, some evils in the present system ; some advantages, many plausibilities, in its

29

opposite; and yet I believe the one to be practically ennobling and elevating—the other essentially narrowing, enfeebling, and enervating. I well foresee the results of the change, come when it may—I know how pleasing, yet how brief, will be the lull consequent upon the establishment of a rule of equality and fraternity; how warm, perhaps, for the moment, the congratulations of some who have trembled for their sons' safety under the present (so-called) reign of terror; on the other hand, how gradual, yet how sure, the growth of those meaner and more cowardly vices which a monitorial system has coerced where it could not eradicate; and how impossible the return to that principle of graduated ranks and organised internal subordination, which, amidst some real and many imaginary defects, has been found by experience to be inferior to no other system in the formation of the character of an English Christian gentleman.

   " I have the honour to be, my Lord,
    " Your most obedient and faithful servant,
      " CHAS. J. VAUGHAN.
" Harrow, *December* 14, 1853."

We hope the pressure on our space has not precluded us from giving an intelligible *précis* of the eloquent Dean's argument. Dr. Vaughan has written, he tells us, on behalf of a system which he endeavoured to carry out at Harrow, and hopes will remain there long after his time, and therefore his letter should be studied by all who are interested in education on the hill, be they parents or scholars.

And, indeed, these reflections convinced Lord Palmerston, and calmed down a storm of half-informed discontent levelled against a system originated at Winchester by William of Wykeham, and adopted by Dr. Arnold as a result of his sojourn at the said College.[*]

We are not bent upon opening up an old controversy concerning the monitorial system, but on recording what the Dean of Llandaff still believes on the subject. It is, however, interesting to notice that at Eton, although a Sixth Form boy would be expected to notice and suppress breaches of manners, yet the delegation from master to scholar of powers and duties

  * See a letter to Viscount Palmerston, M.P., on the Monitorial System of Harrow School, by Charles John Vaughan. Murray, 1854.

prevalent at Harrow, Winchester, Westminster, Rugby, Shrewsbury, and elsewhere, has been, in King Henry VI.'s College, to a certain extent merged in the *Tutor*. It is the duty of this individual to exercise a moral superintendence over each of his pupils; and although such an institution exists in several schools, at Eton at least it has thrown the monitorial system into the shade.*

Nevertheless, the Fagging which Arnold and Vaughan associate with the last-mentioned means of school government flourishes without causing public scandal, or, indeed, inflicting hardship, while in theory the responsibility of senior boys as regards manners is as clear as when, in the year 1444, Waynflete brought William of Wykeham's mode of rule to Eton from Winchester.

* See *Report of Public School Commissioners on Eton*, p. 94.

APPENDIX J.

The Late Colonel F. Burnaby.

Between January 1855 and January 1857 the late Colonel Frederick Burnaby was an inmate of the late Mr. Middlemist's house at Harrow. He was a veritable giant amongst those around him in the Shell, and more famous for athletic propensities than devotion to the school duties.

Conspicuous for his courage at football, young Burnaby's high spirit and, we must add, combative nature, led him thus early in life to assert himself in the old-fashioned British fashion. His stubborn fight in the school milling-ground with one Atkinson, a Fifth Form boy, became an almost Homeric tradition amongst younger generations.

Fred Burnaby, according to Custos' recollection, was also very forward in the Squash that took place during the Election for Cricket Club Keepers (see page 369). As gentle as brave, he retained the friendship of many Harrow friends during life. Among those in the same form from time to time with this able and fearless officer were Mr. H. Chaplin, M.P., Mr. W. J. Courthope the Poet, and E. R. Wilberforce, the present Bishop of Newcastle.

Some day, when, in addition to the Crimean aisle of the School Chapel, another memorial is erected to Harrovians who died for their country, the name of Fred Burnaby will not be forgotten. Like Melvill, who fell protecting the colours after Isandlwana, and Viscount St. Vincent, slain in the Soudan, his memory will remain ever fresh on the Hill.

INDEX.

INDEX.

[Several interesting facts. discovered at the last moment. have been inserted in the Index in their alphabetical order. They are distinguished by being included in brackets.]

Harrow—*cont.*

and religious houses near, before the Conquest, 5; extent of manor of, 6*n*: St. Mary's Church, original building of, 5: church built at, by Lanfranc (cir. 1090), 5; Bishop of London claimed right of officiating there, 6*n*: dedication of, by Archbp. Anselm, 5; consecration oil stolen at dedication of, 6.

Thomas à Becket visits Archbp. Theobald at (1142), 7; Nigellus de Sackville, Rector of (1170), 8; Robert de Broc, Vicar of, 8; Rector and Vicar of, annoy Thomas à Becket, 8: they are excommunicated. 8: Thomas à Becket confers with Abbot of St. Alban's at, 9: and exercises hospitality at, 9: Vicarage endowed by St. Edmund (1240). 10: visitation held by Primate Boniface at (1250), 10; Archbp. Winchelsey there in 1300, 10; St. Mary's Church, probably rebuilt in reign of Edward III., 5: Manor of, occasional residence of archbishops till 1344, 6; extent of Archbp. of Canterbury's lands at (1344), 6*n*; Inquisition relating to (1344), 379; custom on reap-day at. *temp.* Richard II., 68*n*; John Byrkhed, Rector of (1418), 18; his legacy to the parish, 429*n*; Archbp. Chichele probably there in 1443, 13: early notices of, mostly ecclesiastical, 15; two battles fought near, in Wars of the Roses. 14: Bishop Tunstall, Rector of (1514), 17; flight to, from predicted swamping of London (1524), 16; Wolsey passed near in 1529, 18; he is said to have been Rector of, 17; his connection with, 430.

John Lyon holds property at (1584), 52; his lands at, attributed to gifts of pilgrims, 69; his lands at, held by those of his name from *temp.* Edward III., 69.

Early Rectors and Vicars of, 18; Archbp. Cranmer alienates his manorial rights at, to Henry VIII. (1543), 20; an ancient Cranmer Bible discovered near, 24; Richard Leyton, Rector of, 18; Dr. Richard Cox Rector of, 18; he is recalled by Queen Elizabeth, 304; Henry VIII. grants manors of, to Sir Edward North, 20; extent of vale of, 22; always distinguished for agriculture,

Harrow—*cont.*

22; probably early affected by urban influence, 22.

After the Reformation, 24; vagrancy at, after the Reformation, 24; John Lyon heads the rental list of, 69; Shakespeare's mention of a school at, 385: old school at, 382, xii.*n*; grammar taught at the Church house, 305: probably supported by voluntary contributions, 49; John Lyon Collector of Subsidies at, 53; John and Joan Lyon purchase land in (1571), 52; occupants of mansion at Osterley interested in education at, 353.

John Lyon founds school at (1571), 34; limits of the school-yard at, 414; description of country near, in Lyon's time, 32; situate in the Purevale, 33; view of, from Preston, 32; bathing-place at, called "Ducker," 32; owes its present consequence to the School, 34; John Lyon provides for repairing roads to, 35; Sir John Lyon, of Perivale, does the same, 56; John Lyon provides for teaching 30 poor children of, 44; thirty sermons yearly to be preached at parish church of, 46*n*; John Lyon is Bailiff and Parish Officer at (1580), 69; he and others lease lands at, 79; list of title-deeds of John Lyon of Preston in (1356–1580), 387–411; dates of burial of John Lyon, his wife, and son, 58: the ringing of John Lyon's knell at, 100.

Best corn near London procured at (cir. 1610), 67; Tudor sovereigns get wheat and flour at Heston, near Harrow, 68*n*; rents of School lands at, 416; old school-house at, mentioned, 67, 415; spoken of as a populous place (1610), 67; Rev. H. Wildblud, Vicar of, 82; Waldo family settle at (about 1625), 350; Charles I. visits (1646), 83; King Charles's Well at, 85; Thomas Pakeman, Nonconformist minister, ejected from (1662), 87; place of refuge during the Great Plague, 100; social barbarity at (1665), 88; parochial life at (1674–80), 96; Dr. Thomas Brian resigned Vicarage of (1699), 114*n*; buried there (1731), 114; Sir John Rushout owns Flambards, near, 354; returning prosperity at (1718), 108; old schoolhouse at, removed (1724), 385;

30 *

Y.

Z.

483

[This work goes forth to the public when Dr. H. M. Butler's career at Harrow has, to his own great regret and that of all who love Harrow and understand her needs, been nearly closed. Having accepted the Deanery of Gloucester, the coming summer will of necessity cause a change of ruler on the Hill. The writer has not trusted himself to do more than relate facts when dealing with the later portions of Harrow history, and any opinion of his regarding Dr. Butler's rule could scarcely fail to be tinged with such trace of partiality as warm friendship is somewhat apt to lead the wariest wielder of the pen to express. But there will scarcely be dissentient notes when this book concludes with acknowledging that not only has Dr. H. M. Butler given Harrow of his very best—and what that is his whole career tells—but he is about to leave the school crowded and in enjoyment of its full repute.]

LONDON :
PRINTED BY W. H. ALLEN AND CO., 13 WATERLOO PLACE, S.W.